CAREER OPPORTUNITIES IN EDUCATION

Susan Echaore-McDavid

Checkmark Books®
An imprint of Facts On File, Inc.

CAREER OPPORTUNITIES IN EDUCATION

Copyright © 2001 by Susan Echaore-McDavid

All rights reserved. No part of this book may be reproduced or utilized in any form or by any means, electronic or mechanical, including photocopying, recording, or by any information storage or retrieval systems, without permission in writing from the publisher. For information contact:

Checkmark Books
An imprint of Facts On File, Inc.
11 Penn Plaza
New York, NY 10001

Library of Congress Cataloging-in-Publication Data

Echaore-McDavid, Susan.
    Career opportunities in education / Susan Echaore-McDavid.
       p.   cm.—(Career oportunities series)
    ISBN 0-8160-4223-3 (hardcover : alk.paper)—ISBN 0-8160-4224-1 (pbk : alk.paper)
    1. Education—Vocational guidance—United States. 2. School employees—Job descriptions—United States. I. Title. II. Facts on File's career opportunities series.

LB1775.2.E33   2000
370'.23'73—dc21   00-037209

Checkmark Books are available at special discounts when purchased in bulk quantities for businesses, associations, institutions or sales promotions. Please call our Special Sales Department in New York at (212) 967-8800 or (800) 322-8755.

You can find Facts On File on the World Wide Web at http://www.factsonfile.com

Cover design by Nora Wertz

Printed in the United States of America

VB Hermitage 10 9 8 7 6 5 4 3 2 1
      (pbk) 10 9 8 7 6 5 4 3 2 1

This book is printed on acid-free paper.

*To two wonderful friends—Kathy Ferguson Siudzinski,
who planted the seed in my head (many years ago when we were teenagers)
that maybe I could write for a living, and Winifred Ho Roderman,
who took the chance and taught me how to make it come true!*

CONTENTS

Preface: How to Use This Book — vii
Acknowledgments — ix
Introduction — xi

PROFESSIONALS IN EARLY CHILDHOOD CARE AND EDUCATION

Child Care Aide — 2
Early Childhood Teacher — 4
Early Childhood Program Director — 7
Kindergarten Teacher — 10

TEACHERS IN ELEMENTARY SCHOOLS, MIDDLE-LEVEL SCHOOLS, AND HIGH SCHOOLS

Elementary School Teacher — 14
Middle School Teacher — 17
Junior High School Teacher — 20
High School Teacher — 23
Substitute Teacher — 26

K–12 TEACHING SPECIALISTS

Music Teacher — 30
Physical Education Teacher — 33
Reading Specialist — 36
Special Education Teacher — 39
Bilingual Teacher — 42
ESL (English as a Second Language) Teacher — 45

SPECIALISTS IN STUDENT SERVICES AND SPECIAL EDUCATION-RELATED SERVICES

School Nurse — 50
Educational Diagnostician — 52
School Psychologist — 54
School Social Worker — 57
Speech-Language Pathologist — 59
School Occupational Therapist — 62
Art Therapist — 65

SCHOOL SUPPORT STAFF

Teacher Aide (Instructional) — 68
Career Guidance Technician — 71
School Bus Driver — 73
Cafeteria Manager — 76
Campus Monitor — 78

COLLEGE AND UNIVERSITY FACULTY

Community College Instructor — 82
Professor — 85
Lecturer — 88

INSTRUCTORS IN ADULT EDUCATION AND CONTINUING EDUCATION

Vocational Instructor — 92
Adult Education Instructor — 95
Continuing Education Instructor — 98
Cooperative Extension Agent — 100
Correctional Instructor — 103

OVERSEAS TEACHING PROFESSIONS

Teacher, American Overseas School — 108
EFL (English as a Foreign Language) Teacher, Overseas — 110
Peace Corps Volunteer — 113

SCHOOL ADMINISTRATORS

Principal — 116
Assistant Principal — 119
Superintendent — 122
Assistant Superintendent — 125
Program Director — 128
Instructional Supervisor — 131

COLLEGE AND UNIVERSITY ADMINISTRATORS

Director of Admissions — 134
Registrar — 137

Director of Student Activities	139
Athletic Director	142
Director of Public Safety	145
Dean of Students	148
Director of Development	150
Dean (Academic)	153
Provost	155
President	158

COUNSELORS

School Counselor	162
College Career Counselor	165
Employment Counselor	168

HEALTH EDUCATORS

Health Educator	172
Nutritionist	175
Childbirth Educator	178
CPR/First Aid Instructor	181

LIBRARIANS

Public Librarian (City or County)	184
Children's Librarian	187
Library Media Specialist	190
Academic Librarian	193

EDUCATIONAL AND INSTRUCTIONAL TECHNOLOGY SPECIALISTS

Technology Director (District, or School-Wide, Level)	196
Instructional Technology Specialist (K–12 Schools)	199
Special Education Technology Specialist	202
Instructional Technology Specialist (Higher Education)	205
Language Technology Specialist (Higher Education)	207

CURRICULUM AND INSTRUCTION DEVELOPERS

Curriculum Specialist	210
Textbook Editor	212
Instructional Designer	215
Educational Software Developer	218

EMPLOYEE TRAINING SPECIALISTS

Trainer (In-House)	222
Training Developer	225
Training Manager	228

INDEPENDENT INSTRUCTORS

Music Teacher (Studio Owner)	232
Dance Teacher	235
Riding Instructor	237
Flight Instructor (Freelance)	239

FITNESS AND RECREATION PROFESSIONALS

Aerobics Instructor	242
Personal Trainer	245
Guide	248

ENVIRONMENTAL EDUCATORS AND ANIMAL TRAINERS

Environmental Educator	252
Park Naturalist	255
Humane Educator	258
Dog Trainer	260
Guide Dog Instructor	262
K-9 Trainer (Police Dogs)	264
Horse Trainer	267

APPENDIXES

I Educational Resources— Colleges and Universities	270
II Professional Unions and Associations	275
III State Education Licensure Agencies	287
IV Additional Resources for Information— Organizations and Internet Resources	290
V Bibliography	298

Index   303

PREFACE
How to Use This Book

In *Career Opportunities in Education,* you will learn about 91 different professions in the field of education. They include early childhood educators, school teachers, university lecturers, educational administrators, counselors, student service specialists, librarians, technology specialists, curriculum developers, school support staff, fitness professionals, corporate trainers, health educators, environmental educators, animal trainers, and others. Many of the professions described in this book are found in public and private schools and colleges. Many are also found in a wide variety of nonschool settings such as libraries, museums, music studios, businesses, publishing companies, corporations, government agencies, environmental centers, animal shelters, health clubs, recreational centers, hospitals, health care centers, community agencies, nonprofit organizations, and national parks.

For each profession, you'll learn what the job is like. You'll learn what basic requirements are needed to enter the profession. You'll also learn what the salary, job market, and advancement prospects are like for a profession. Perhaps after reading some, or all, of the professions in this book, you'll find one that is right for you.

Sources of Information

The information presented in *Career Opportunities in Education* comes from a variety of sources. They include:

- interviews with professionals and professional organizations
- questionnaires answered by professional individuals and organizations
- books about the different professions
- professional textbooks, handbooks, and manuals
- newspapers, magazines, and professional journals
- brochures, pamphlets, and other written materials from professional associations and firms, federal agencies, and other organizations

In addition, the Internet was a valuable resource. Hundreds of web sites were visited to learn about the many different professions that are described in this book—including web sites of public and private schools, colleges, universities, professional associations, federal agencies, libraries, personal pages of various professionals, on-line professional journals, and other related organizations and businesses.

How This Book is Organized

Career Opportunities in Education is designed to be easy to use and read. The 91 jobs are divided into 19 sections. A section may have three to 10 job profiles, and the profiles are between two and three pages long. Each profile follows the same format so that you can read the job profiles or sections in any order that you prefer.

Sections one through 10 discuss many familiar and not-so-familiar teacher, administrator, specialist, and support staff professions found in educational institutions, from preschools to universities. Sections 11 through 19 describe various types of educators and education-related professions that are found both in traditional school settings as well as in nontraditional settings such as companies, government agencies, libraries, parks, and outdoor settings.

The Job Profiles

The job profiles give you basic information about 94 education careers. Each job profile starts with *Career Profile,* a summary of a job's major duties, salary, job outlook, and promotion possibilities. It also sums up general requirements needed for a job, as well as special skills and personality traits that these professionals usually possess. The *Career Ladder* section is a visual presentation of a typical career path, showing what positions lead to and stem from the job being profiled.

The rest of the job profile is a narrative description that is divided into the following sections:

- The "Position Description" details a job's major responsibilities and duties and provides information about working conditions.
- "Salaries" presents a general idea of the wages that workers may earn. Most salary information comes from the U.S. Bureau of Labor Statistics or from salary surveys done by professional associations or other recognized organizations.
- "Employment Prospects" describes potential employers and the job outlook for today as well as for the future.
- "Advancement Prospects" discusses promotional career prospects and suggestions for alternative career paths.
- "Licensure/Certification" details any license, certification, or registration that may be required for a profession.

- "Education and Training" describes the type of diploma or degree that is needed to enter a profession. The section also discusses any training programs that may need to be completed.
- "Experience, Skills, and Personality Traits" discusses the minimum experience requirements that are needed for a job. It also describes some basic employability skills that employers want candidates to have. In addition, this section mentions some personality traits that successful professionals share with each other.
- "Unions/Associations" gives the names of some national professional organizations that professionals might join.
- "Tips for Entry" presents advice for finding jobs; suggestions for improving employability; and ways to find out more information on the Internet.

The Appendixes

At the end of the book are five appendixes that provide additional resources for the various professions described in *Career Opportunities in Education*. You can learn about colleges and universities that offer educational training for some professions. You can also find contact information for professional associations and other organizations that may provide you with general information about a profession. In addition, you can find titles of books, periodicals, and web sites that may give you further information and insight about the professions that interest you.

Changing Web Sites

Throughout *Career Opportunities in Education*, web site addresses for various professional organizations and other resources are provided so that you can learn more on your own. All the web sites were accessible as the book was being written. However, please keep in mind that web site owners may change URL addresses, remove web pages (to which you have been referred), or shut down their web sites completely. Should you come across a URL address that does not work, try this: enter the name of the organization or person in a search engine.

This Book Is Yours

Career Opportunities in Education is your reference book. Use it to read about jobs you have often wondered about. Use it to learn about educational professions that you never knew existed. Use it to start your search for the career of your dreams.

Good luck!

ACKNOWLEDGMENTS

I could not have written this book without the help of so many professionals and organizations concerned with the various education fields. In particular, I would like to thank the following: DiAnn K. Adams, Career Technician, Indian Trails Career Cooperative/Twin Lakes High School, Monticello, Indiana; Dory Adams; Joan Adams, St. James School, Montgomery, Alabama; Lori Arkin-Diem, Manager of Education and Community Programs, Animal Services, American Humane Association; Andrea Babbitt; Dana Barchak, Rapid City, South Dakota; Tim Bedley, Temecula Valley Unified School District; Laura Black, St. Mary Elementary School, Winchester, Massachusetts; Michelle Y. Blassengale, M.M.E.; L. Gaye Botts, Driver/Safety Trainer; Ursula Boyle, The Little Red Schoolhouse, Medford, Massachusetts; Tamora K. Brewer, Assistant Principal, Tzouanakis Intermediate School, Greencastle, Indiana; Janis Brock; Elyse Brown; Willeen W. Buchholz, Counseling Coordinator, West Irondequoit Central School District, Rochester, New York; Christina Burkart, Coquitlam District 43, Coquitlam, B.C., Canada; Gene Cain, Resource Teacher, Strategic Planning, The School Board of Broward County, Florida; David W. Carlson, President, DynoTech Software; Shelley Chambers.

Helen Chance, Statesboro, Georgia; Ken R. Churches, Director and Farm Advisor, Calaveras County, California; Stan Clark, President, Association of College Administration Professionals; Coalition of National Health Education Organizations; Sharon Conley, National Association of School Nurses; Valerie Cornelius, Ashtabula, Ohio; Tina Daberkow, Member Service Coordinator, American Association of School Administrators; James J. D'Anza; Jill Davis, Pre-K Teacher, Allen Bowden School, Tulsa, Oklahoma; Karen DeBord, Ph.D., Associate Professor and State Specialist, Child Development, North Carolina State University; Valerie Dehombreux, Cradleboard Elementary, Whiteriver, Arizona; Sheryl Dickstein, Ph.D., Director of Humane Education, ASPCA; Mrs. Sandra Di Ponio, Muir Middle School, Milford, Michigan; Laura Dowling; Peggy Drechsler, Area Specialized Dairy Agent, North Carolina Cooperative Extension Service; Tom Drummond, Child and Family Education Division, North Seattle Community College; Bess Emanuel, Director Credential Liaison, Center for Career Development in Early Care and Education, Wheelock College, Boston, Massachusetts; Lisa A. Estee; Maureen E. Farr, Snips and Snails Preschool, Port Jervis, New York; Paula Ferland, M.Ed., College of Education Faculty, East Tennessee State University; Zelandia Fero; Karen E. Finkel, Executive Director, National School Transportation Association.

Ken Fox; Charmiane Freeman; Susan Galletti, Associate Executive Director, National Association of Secondary School Principals; Linda Gallipoli; Natalie Gamboa; Bev Garcia, Educational Technology Specialist, Cornell College; Mrs. Mary J. Gasch, Nerinx Hall High School, Webster Groves, Missouri; Phoebe Gillespie, Ph.D., Recruitment/Retention Outreach Manager, National Clearinghouse for Professions in Special Education, Council for Exceptional Children; Terry Gilman, M.Ed., K–8 School Counselor, Lynden Christian School, Lynden, Washington; Teresa Glenn, Larinburg, North Carolina; Margaret W. Goldsborough, Director of Public Information and Resource Development, National Association of Independent Schools; Nancy Golubic, Market Street School, Boardman, Ohio; Jim Goske; Jodi Gullicksrud, Eleva-Strum School District, Wisconsin; Diane L. Harney, Administrative Assistant, National Office, American Art Therapy Association, Inc.; Wayne Hashiguchi, Principal, Denny Middle School, Seattle, Washington; Scott Hawbaker, Executive Assistant, National Association of County Agricultural Agents; Patricia Herbel, Elementary Principal, St. Leo's Elementary School, Minot, North Dakota.

Darrel Hess, Chairperson, Earth Sciences Department, City College of San Francisco, San Francisco, California; Stacey Hild, Elementary Music Teacher, North Carolina; Deanna Homer, Language Lab Supervisor, Oklahoma State University; Gen Hooper; Deborah House, Career Guidance Technician, Fayetteville Technical Community College, North Carolina; Carrie Howren; Teresa Ilgunas, Technology Coordinator, Jefferson School, Lennox School District; Alice Iverson; Jerry Jerman, Director of Marketing and Communication, College of Continuing Education, The University of Oklahoma; Denise Jessup; Jeff Johnson, District Technology Coordinator, Greendale School District, Greendale, Wisconsin; Karl Johnson, Technology Coordinator, Tipton Community Schools, Tipton, Iowa; Melanie Johnson, Recruitment and Career Development Representative, American Speech-Language-Hearing Association; Sandra Kangas, Director, Child & Adult Nutrition Services—DECA, Pierre, South Dakota; Nancy J. Keane, Rundlett Middle School; Terry L. Keeneth, ANR Educator (Gibson County), Purdue University; Rachel Kramer, Assistant Executive Director, Programs and Convention, Music Teachers National Association; Kirsten Lincoln; Amy Lindsay, Information

Services Assistant, MENC: The National Association for Music Education; Mary-Jo MacRae-Smith, Technology Mentor, New Brunswick Department of Education, New Brunswick, Canada.

Ina Lynn McClain, State 4-H Youth Development Specialist, Columbia, Missouri; Tharon McDavid; Linda M. McGuire, Technology Coordinator, Au Sable Valley Central School; Jonanne Haynes Manogue, M.S., Department of Kinesiology, University of Wisconsin-Madison; Ron Markley, Trainer/Director, Camelot K9 Academy, Loma, Colorado; Dianne Martinez; Eloisa Maria Martinez, Information Specialist and Administrative Assistant, Lamaze International; Brian Meegan, High School Principal and College Counselor, Bilkent University Prep School, Ankara, Turkey; Joseph Metzler, Assistant Contract Manager, Ryder Student Transportation Inc.; Carol Mezzacappa, Director, Young Dancers In Repertory and Dance Consort; Pam Michael, MBA, RD, Director, Networks Team, American Dietetic Association; Lori J. Moore, First-grade Teacher; Lawrence D. Newell, Ed.D., NREMT-P, Educational Consultant, National Safety Council; New York State Coalition for Health Education; Bonnie J. Nichols; Larry Olsen, Professor, Towson University, Towson, Maryland.

Colleen Pace, President, American Association of Riding Schools; Randy Palmer, North Mankato, Minnesota; Jim Pennington; Nancy Perry, Executive Director, American School Counselor Association; Dorothy Peselli; Beth Powell, Director, Public Policy and Legislation, American Mental Health Counselors Association; Doug Prouty, Contra Costa County Office of Education, California; Donna Ransdell, Ramona Unified School District, California; Sue Rarus, Manager, Information Services, MENC: The National Association for Music Education; Claudia Readwright; Becky Reed; Kathleen Remington, Masters of Education, Adjunct Faculty, Salt Lake Community College; Donna Richert, Our Lady Immaculate Catholic School; Winifred Ho Roderman; June Roman, Special Education Team Leader/Life Skills Teacher, Georgetown Middle School Georgetown, Kentucky; Bonnie Rubinstein; Allen Russell, Physical Educator, Columbine Elementary School, Grand Junction, Colorado.

Michele Schindler, M.Ed., N.C.C., Harborview Elementary Counselor, Juneau, Alaska; School Social Work Association of America; Viviane Scnhupbach; Bonni Schwiderson, Marquette, Michigan; Susan J. Scollay, Ph.D., Associate Professor and Director of Graduate Studies, Department of Administration and Supervision, University of Kentucky; Rhonda Shafer, 4-H Youth Specialist, University of Missouri Outreach and Extension; Elisa M. Simon, M.Ed., Secondary School Counselor, Lampeter-Strasburg High School, Lampeter, Pennsylvania; Kathy Ferguson Siudzinski; Sheryl Skufca, Library/Media Specialist; Julian A. Spain, Kubasaki High School, Department of Defense Dependents Schools—Pacific, Okinawa, Japan; Jenine Stanley, President, Guide Dog Users Inc.; Glenn Sterley; Laurie Thomas, Seventh Grade Teacher, Valley Jr. High, Carlsbad, California; Dana Topousis, Peace Corps Public Affairs Specialist; Ted Tull, Administrative Director, National Association for State Directors for Pupil Transportation Services.

Marilynn Vandor; Jennifer Vega, Secondary Technology Specialist/Curriculum Integrator, Malverne Union Free School District, Malverne, New York; Lawrence Vincent, Michigan Certified Teacher, Engadine, Michigan; Deborah Walsh; Elizabeth Warson, ATR-BC, LPC; Jim Watson, accredited NAPWDA Master Trainer and Mentor, Police K9 Unit-Retired (Ohio); Virginia Webb, Coordinator, On Site Services, National Food Services Management Institute, University of Mississippi; Mary Jo Weisenburger, Grade 8; Jennifer Johnson, Eighth-Grade Mathematics, Waluga Junior High School, Lake Oswego, Oregon; Fred Wesson, Director, American International School of Bucharest; Rosemary West, past president of the Educational Software Cooperative; Riley Whitsett, Teacher/Coordinator Marketing Education; Barbara A. Wilmer, Programs Division, National Association of Elementary School Principals; Nancy Wise; Tom Woods, Corrections Educator; Kimberlee Woodward, Substitute Teacher, Michigan; and Marc Zimmerman.

Most of all, I would especially like to thank Jim Chambers, my editor, for being so patient with me, and Richard McDavid, my husband, for reading over my manuscript and gently suggesting ways to improve awkward sentence structures and other grammar and word usage eccentricities of mine.

Thank you!

INTRODUCTION

Do you want a career in education? Are you puzzled about which profession to enter? Maybe you would like to be a teacher. Maybe not. Actually, the education industry offers a wide range of career opportunities—teaching as well as nonteaching professions. Most opportunities are found in public and private schools, two-year colleges, four-year colleges, and universities. Many opportunities are also found in businesses, corporations, government agencies, community agencies, nonprofit organizations, hospitals, museums, zoos, parks, fitness facilities, dance studios, resorts, recreational facilities, and many other settings outside of educational institutions.

Let's first look at some of the types of teaching professions that are available. In educational institutions, various instructors teach a wide variety of academic, vocational, and other subjects. They teach students of different ages and different grades from prekindergartners to doctoral candidates. Many teachers are specialists who provide instruction to students with special learning, reading, and language needs. Some of these teachers are special education teachers, reading specialists, bilingual teachers, ESL (English as a second language) teachers, and adult education teachers.

Teachers in nonschool settings provide a wide range of instructional services for their employers. In nonschool settings, teachers generally go by titles such as trainers, educators, instructors, or guides. They may work with employees, customers, clients, patients, or the general public on an individual basis or in groups. Some may work with animals and their handlers. Some teaching professionals in nonschool settings are corporate trainers, technical trainers, health educators, recreational leaders, personal trainers, environmental educators, dance instructors, tour guides, riding instructors, and guide dog trainers.

Now let's look at the different types of nonteaching professions. In both school and nonschool settings, educational administrators are needed to plan, coordinate, organize, manage, and oversee educational programs, departments, divisions, or institutions so that they run efficiently and effectively each day. Educational administrators may be supervisors, coordinators, directors, managers, or chief executive officers.

Educational specialists and support staff are other types of nonteaching professions. In both school and nonschool settings, they provide various types of services to assist educators, administrators, and students or clientele. They may assist with teaching, perform administrative support duties, provide counseling services, develop curriculum or instructional materials, maintain educational resources, develop technology resources, and so on. School psychologists, school nurses, educational technology specialists, instructional designers, academic librarians, educational diagnosticians, college career counselors, teacher aides, and bus drivers are some professions that you would find in educational institutions. Among those in nonschool settings are public librarians, employment counselors, textbook editors, educational software developers, nutritionists, and training developers.

Opportunities are also available for experienced educators, administrators, and specialists who wish to become self-employed or business owners. Teachers, for example, may become private tutors or teach private classes. Some other professionals who might choose to become self-employed are music teachers, flight instructors, personal trainers, dog trainers, textbook editors, educational software developers, childbirth educators, employment counselors, reading specialists, or art therapists. The success of freelancers and business owners depends on their ambition, business know-how, the local demand for their particular educational services, and other factors.

As you can see, there are many options in the education industry. The next step is to start learning about some of the various professions to find ones that interest you. In this book, you will learn about 91 different professions.

Job Outlook

The job prospect for many occupations in education is favorable at the present time. In public and private schools, teachers are currently in demand and the need is expected to grow, especially during the first part of 2000, due to the large number of retiring veteran teachers, an increase in the student enrollment rate, and state mandates to decrease class sizes. Teachers are particularly needed to provide instruction in math, science, and technology and in the areas of bilingual education and special education.

Many schools throughout the United States are also in need of qualified principals and superintendents. In addition, teaching assistants, school bus drivers, school psychologists, speech language pathologists, and technology specialists are currently in demand.

Other areas of education that show favorable employment prospects include professions in early childhood education, adult education, higher education, employee training, educational and instructional technology, fitness training, recreation, and animal training.

The Changing World of Education

You should know that the education industry is constantly creating new jobs to meet the needs of society. For example, in the 1970s, these professions were rare or did not exist at all in education: bilingual teacher, computer teacher, instructional technology specialist, special education technology specialist, school occupational therapist, art therapist, environmental educator, aerobics instructor, or childbirth educator. Today, all those professions are in demand.

Another thing to keep in mind about many professions is that roles may change with time. For example, school counselors today are found at all school levels and provide personal counseling as well as academic and vocational counseling. In decades past, school counselors mostly worked in high schools, providing academic and vocational counseling. Sometimes a role change is reflected by a profession's job title. An example of a relatively recent title change is that of the school librarian. In most schools, this position is called a school library media specialist because this profession manages both print and technology resources in a combination library and multimedia center.

A Note About Private Schools

In this book, you will learn that many of the teaching, administrative, specialist and support staff positions in public K–12 schools are also found in private K–12 schools. Private schools include day schools, boarding schools, and military academies, as well as parochial schools (those that are affiliated with a religious denomination, such as Roman Catholics, Lutherans, or Seventh-Day Adventists). Private schools may be coeducational, girls-only, or boys-only. They may be of any size or any configuration of grade levels.

Although the term *private school* is used throughout *Career Opportunities in Education,* you should be aware that some private schools are also known as independent schools. Independent schools are not part of or connected to any other organization. Independent schools have their own boards of trustees, and develop their own sources of funding.

Start Exploring Your Options

Career Opportunities in Education provides you with basic general information about 91 professions in education. When you come across occupations that interest you, take the time to learn more about them. You might read books that explore a profession in more depth. You might check out magazines and journals that professionals read for their work. If possible, talk with professionals about their jobs. Perhaps they might let you observe them at work.

In addition, use the Internet to continue your research. Check out personal web sites written by professionals. Many discuss their jobs and provide links to other web sites that have information about their professions. Also, visit web sites for the types of workplaces (schools, hospitals, libraries, parks, fitness centers, and so forth) in which you are interested. You can get an idea of what it may be like to work in such a setting.

Furthermore, get hands-on experience in different educational settings to help you decide what profession may be right for you. For example, you might volunteer to tutor younger children at your school. If you participate in recreational programs, scouting, or Sunday school, offer to help lead activities from time to time. You can also volunteer or obtain part-time or summer jobs with child care centers, schools, libraries, or educational programs in parks, zoos, museums, community agencies, health care centers, and other places that interest you. Along with discovering what you might like to become, you are gaining valuable experience upon which you are building your future career in education.

PROFESSIONALS IN EARLY CHILDHOOD CARE AND EDUCATION

CHILD CARE AIDE

CAREER PROFILE

Duties: Assist in the care, supervision, and education of infants, toddlers, and preschoolers; perform a variety of tasks as required

Alternate Titles: Child Care Worker, Teaching Assistant, Nursery School Aide

Salary Range: Minimum wage to $10 per hour

Employment Prospects: Excellent

Advancement Prospects: Good

Prerequisites:
  Licensure/Certification—Childhood Development Associate certificate preferred
  Education/Training—High school diploma; classroom or on-the-job training
  Experience—Some child care experience is preferred
  Special Skills and Personality Traits—Literacy and math skills; communication, teamwork, interpersonal, and self-management skills; mature, patient, open-minded, enthusiastic, energetic

CAREER LADDER

Early Childhood Teacher

Child Care Aide

Trainee

Position Description

Today, more and more parents must leave their babies and preschool children with child care providers so that they may go to work or school. The child care providers not only are entrusted with caring and protecting children but also with developing and stimulating their social, mental, emotional, and physical growth. Many of these providers are child care centers run by individuals, franchises, churches, community agencies, and public schools. Some child care centers are run on-site by companies and government agencies for their employees, clients, or customers. Child care centers may have programs for infants, toddlers, and preschoolers as well as after-school child care programs for children up to 12 years old.

Among the child care center employees are Child Care Aides. Under the supervision of child care teachers, Child Care Aides perform a variety of tasks. With infants, Child Care Aides feed them, change their diapers, bathe them, and dress them. Showing them love and warmth, Child Care Aides hold the babies regularly through the day. They play with the babies, sing songs, and talk to them to encourage laughter and smiles, as well as to help in their development and growth.

With toddlers and preschoolers, Child Care Aides participate in their games and activities. They read books to the children; listen to their imaginary stories; teach them songs; show them how to draw shapes; play make-believe games with them; play catch and other outside games with them; help them learn to count and say their ABCs; and so on. Furthermore, Child Care Aides help to build children's self-confidence and encourage them to discover, explore, create, and use their imagination.

Child Care Aides are also responsible for supervising children outdoors to make sure that they are playing safely and behaving appropriately. Under teachers' directions, aides help children learn good habits and social skills—for example, washing hands, waiting their turn, getting along with others, and saying "please" and "thank you."

In addition, Child Care Aides help prepare and serve snacks and meals to children. They help keep classrooms neat and tidy. They may wash dishes, wash toys, change bed or crib sheets, clean bathrooms, and so on.

Child Care Aides are constantly on the move—standing, bending, walking, stooping, and lifting—throughout the day. Each day is different from the other, yet Child Care Aides are ready to face any and all joyous, tearful, or chaotic situations.

Child Care Aides work full time or part time. Some work early morning and late evening hours to accommodate the work schedules of the child care center's clients.

Salaries

Most Child Care Aides earn hourly wages, often starting at minimum wage. Earnings are generally higher for those working in large child care centers and in public school programs such as Head Start. The 1998 estimated earnings for most Child Care Aides ranged between $5.50 and $9.65 per hour, according to the U.S. Bureau of Labor Statistics.

Employment Prospects

Child Care Aides work for child care centers, home care providers, nursery schools, preschools, Head Start programs, prekindergarten programs in public and private schools, and before-school and after-school care programs.

Jobs are readily available for Child Care Aides. The turnover rate is high due to the low wages. Also, job opportunities are expected to continually increase for the next few years because of the growing number of families who need high quality child care services.

Advancement Prospects

For many individuals, becoming a Child Care Aide is the first stepping stone to a career in early childhood care and education. With continuing education and experience, Child Care Aides can become preschool, kindergarten, or elementary school teachers, as well as early childhood program administrators. Another career option for Child Care Aides is to own child care businesses.

Licensure/Certification

Most employers prefer that Child Care Aides have a Child Development Associate (CDA) certificate, a nationally recognized professional credential for either a center-based, family child care, or home visitor setting. The CDA is a voluntary certification, which may be obtained through training programs sponsored by colleges, professional associations, or community agencies.

Many Child Care Aides obtain certification in first aid and cardiopulmonary resuscitation (CPR) skills.

Education and Training

Child Care Aides need a high school or general equivalency diploma. Many employers require that they also complete a minimum of early childhood education (ECE) units, which cover topics in child growth and development.

Generally, Child Care Aides receive on-the-job training.

Experience, Skills, and Personality Traits

No previous work experience is necessary; but applicants should have some experience taking care of infants, toddlers, and preschool children. They should be able to lift small children. They should have adequate reading, writing, and math skills. In addition, employers look for candidates who show they have good communication, teamwork, and interpersonal skills, as well as such self-management skills as: being able to follow instructions, getting to work on time, working independently, working under pressure, and so on. Some employers may require bilingual skills in Spanish, Russian, Chinese, or other languages.

Being mature, patient, open-minded, enthusiastic, and energetic are some personality traits that successful Child Care Aides share. They also find great joy being around infants and young children, and helping them grow and develop in positive ways.

Unions/Associations

Local, state, and national early childhood organizations, such as the National Association for the Education of Young Children, provide many professional services for Child Care Aides. These include networking opportunities, training workshops, continuing education programs, career counseling, and job listings.

Tips for Entry

1. As a middle school or high school student, you can find out if early childhood education is the field for you by volunteering at a nearby child care center or preschool. Call or visit the program and ask to speak to the director.
2. Talk with friends and relatives who have preschool children in early childhood programs. They may be able to tell you of job openings or persons to contact about work.
3. In most states, the minimum age for being a Child Care Aide is 18 years old. If you're less than 18, the requirement may be waived if you have a high school diploma or are enrolled in an occupational training program.
4. You can learn more about early childhood education on the Internet. To find pertinent web sites, enter either of these keywords in a search engine: "early childhood education" or "early childhood career."

EARLY CHILDHOOD TEACHER

CAREER PROFILE

Duties: Provide instruction that promotes social, physical, and intellectual growth in infants and young children; create age-appropriate activities; maintain a safe and healthy environment; perform other tasks as needed

Alternate Titles: Infant Teacher, Toddler Teacher, Preschool Teacher, Prekindergarten Teacher, School-Age Child Care Teacher

Salary Range: $12,000 to $30,000

Employment Prospects: Excellent

Advancement Prospects: Good

Prerequisites:
  Licensure/Certification—A teaching license, Childhood Development Associate certificate, or other certification
  Education/Training—Associate or Bachelor's degree
  Experience—One or more years working in a child care setting
  Special Skills and Personality Traits—Teaching, teamwork, interpersonal, communication, organizational, and management skills; patient, gentle, energetic, flexible, persevering, encouraging, firm, creative

CAREER LADDER

Early Childhood Program Director or Elementary School Teacher

Early Childhood Teacher

Assistant Teacher or Intern

Position Description

Early Childhood Teachers work in child care centers, home daycare programs, preschools, nursery schools, Head Start programs, and prekindergarten programs in public and private schools. Their primary responsibility is to nurture and educate infants and young children during the hours that the children's parents need to be at work or school. The number of hours that children are under the supervision of an Early Childhood Teacher varies according to the needs of their families. For example, one child might stay at a child care center for three hours twice a week while another child might stay for 10 hours five days a week.

Different Early Childhood Teachers work with different age groups from newborn infants to five-year-olds. State regulations limit the number of infants and children for which each teacher may be responsible. In most states, infant teachers may supervise six to eight babies while teachers of toddlers and preschoolers may supervise 10 to 20 children.

Many Early Childhood Teachers work with children who receive special instruction and related services for their physical, emotional, or learning disabilities. With these children, teachers must follow specific goals and objectives outlined on children's Individualized Education Programs (IEPs) that are developed by the teachers and specialists such as school psychologists, special education teachers, and school nurses. Early Childhood Teachers may consult special education teachers and other specialists for advice on implementing the IEPs.

Early Childhood Teachers establish a relationship with each child and help each child develop socially, physically, emotionally, intellectually, aesthetically, and morally. For infants, toddlers, and preschoolers, learning is done through play, questioning, observation, exploration, and discovery. Thus, teachers provide experiences and activities that help children use their powerful imagination and curiosity. Teachers develop a curriculum that introduces infants and young children to literacy, numbers, science, social studies, art, music, health, nutrition, technology, and other areas that affect their lives and the world around them. They try to work with all children every day in large groups, small groups, and on an individual basis.

Early Childhood Teachers make sure all activities, materials, and toys are developmentally age-appropriate for the children they work with. In addition, they plan activities that help children develop fine motor skills (such as holding crayons, drawing circles, and buttoning their jackets) and gross motor skills (such as running, hopping, jumping, walking, and skipping). Early Childhood Teachers also help children develop healthy and proper habits for eating, washing hands, putting toys away, and so on. In addition, they teach children social skills to get along with others.

Teachers create a daily routine so that children have an idea of what to expect. They plan different types of activities throughout the day—story time, outside play time, time in learning centers, large group activities (such as singing or performing finger puppet plays), small group activities, independent activities, quiet activities, meals, naps, and so on. Because very young children have short attention spans, activities are usually planned to last only 10 to 15 minutes.

Most Early Childhood Teachers create learning centers to develop different skills (for instance, fine motor skills, counting skills, and literacy skills), to explore different subject areas (such as science), and to develop imagination through creative arts. Simple, yet challenging, activities are developed for each learning center. Children can quickly get into the activities with few directions. Teachers change the activities daily or weekly, basing them on weekly themes, such as rain, autumn leaves, trains, or Chinese New Year.

With the help of assistant teachers and child care aides (or teaching assistants), Early Childhood Teachers monitor children's activities throughout the day. When necessary, they discipline children according to school policies. Early Childhood Teachers also are ready to respond to any emergency situation.

As one of their major duties, Early Childhood Teachers observe the children, assessing and evaluating each child's development. Whenever necessary, they adapt instruction or materials or space to accommodate their needs.

Because parents are children's primary teachers, Early Childhood Teachers keep in constant communication with parents. They consult with parents about their children's needs as well as discuss their children's growth and development in general. Teachers try to make contact with parents daily, by either talking with them or sending them notes, to let them know what happened with their children that day.

Other duties that Early Childhood Teachers have are:

- attend and participate in faculty meetings
- perform administrative tasks such as taking attendance and making reports
- train and supervise assistant teachers, child care aides, interns, and volunteers

Early Childhood Teachers work part time or full time. Those employed by child care centers usually work year-round while many employed by preschools and public school programs normally work a 10-month schedule.

Salaries

Salaries vary widely, depending on factors such as education, experience, credentials, type of program, and size of employer. Typically, Early Childhood Teachers in large child care centers and in public school programs earn higher wages. In 1998, the U.S. Bureau of Labor Statistics estimated that the mean annual wage was $19,530, and that most Early Childhood Teachers earned between $12,030 and $30,310 per year.

Some Early Childhood Teachers receive fringe benefits, such as sick leave, holiday pay, medical insurance, and retirement benefits.

Employment Prospects

Early Childhood Teachers work for public and private child care centers and preschools. Some early childhood care and education programs are sponsored by churches, hospitals, colleges and universities, as well as health centers, resorts, and other businesses that offer child care services for their customers. Some child care centers are sponsored by corporations and government agencies for their employees.

Jobs are readily available for Early Childhood Teachers. Most opportunities in private child care centers become available as teachers retire or advance to other positions with higher pay or more responsibilities.

Since the 1990s, more and more public schools are adding prekindergarten programs to their curriculum. This should open up a demand for Early Education Teachers with education degrees and state teaching licenses. Another growing area in early childhood education is the need for trained early childhood special educators.

Advancement Prospects

Within an organization, Early Childhood Teachers can advance to head teacher, teacher/assistant director, and program director. Generally, continuing education units are needed to advance further.

Many teachers pursue advancement by earning bachelor's or master's degrees and teaching credentials to obtain better paying positions in public schools or private schools with higher requirements. Some Early Childhood Teachers start their own early childhood programs.

Some other career options are: becoming university professors, researchers, or consultants in early childhood care and education.

Licensure/Certification

Requirements vary with different employers. Most private employers require Early Childhood Teachers to have a Child Development Associate (CDA) certificate, a voluntary professional credential that is recognized nationwide. The CDA certificate may be obtained through community colleges, community agencies, or professional associations. Some child care employers prefer their teachers to be certified as a Certified Childcare Professional (CCP) by the National Child Care Association.

Early Childhood Teachers employed by public schools must hold a state teaching credential in early childhood education. The type of credential and licensure requirements vary from state to state. Contact the state department of education for the state in which you wish to teach for specific information.

Education and Training

Requirements vary widely with the different employers. Early Childhood Teachers must have a high school or general equivalency diploma. In addition, most teachers need either an associate degree in early childhood education or a minimum number of units in early childhood education. To teach in prekindergarten programs in public schools, teachers need a bachelor's degree in either early childhood education or a liberal arts field. Some employers require teachers to have or to show they are pursuing a master's degree in early childhood education.

Early Childhood Teachers should have received basic instruction in child development, the learning process, teaching methods, and curriculum development.

Experience, Skills, and Personality Traits

Most employers require that applicants have at least one year of work experience as a child care aide or teaching assistant in a child care or preschool setting. They should also have a broad knowledge of the subjects—math, science, social studies, music, art, health, and so on—that they will be introducing to children.

Along with teaching skills, Early Childhood Teachers should have teamwork, interpersonal, and communication skills to interact with children, parents, and other staff members. They also need good organizational and management skills to complete all their duties and tasks each day.

Successful Early Childhood Teachers have unconditional love for each child and are open-minded in regard to each child's background and ability. Willing to be a child's advocate, Early Childhood Teachers are patient, gentle, energetic, flexible, and persevering. They are able to encourage children to explore and be creative, yet guide them with gentle firmness and discipline. Furthermore, they are creative, have a keen sense of humor, and are able to handle the stresses of many different or unexpected situations that naturally come with young children at play.

Unions/Associations

The National Association for the Education of Young Children, the National Head Start Association, and the Council for Exceptional Children are a few national organizations that Early Childhood Teachers might join along with local or state associations. These professional groups offer a wide variety of services such as teaching resources, continuing education programs, networking opportunities, and job listings. Early Childhood Teachers in public schools usually join a teacher's union such as the National Education Association or the American Federation of Teachers.

Tips for Entry

1. Get practical experience working with infants, toddlers, and preschoolers before entering the early childhood field.
2. Many early childhood programs advertise job openings in neighborhood newspapers. Look in the classified job ads under "teacher." You might also call or visit programs directly and talk with the program director about vacancies.
3. In some states, child care aides may be granted an emergency instructional permit during critical shortages of qualified Early Childhood Teachers in public schools. To find out more, contact your state department of education.
4. Some states, in collaboration with the U.S. Department of Labor, offer an apprenticeship program for early childhood practitioners. To find out what may be available in your area, contact your state employment office or the nearest U.S. Department of Labor office.
5. Many resources about early childhood education are available on the Internet. To start your search for relevant web sites, enter either of these keywords in a search engine: "early childhood teaching" or "preschool teacher."

EARLY CHILDHOOD PROGRAM DIRECTOR

CAREER PROFILE

Duties: Administer daily operations; develop policies and procedures; supervise staff; oversee curriculum development; perform other duties as required

Alternate Titles: Child Care Center Director, Preschool Director, Nursery School Director

Salary Range: $17,000 to $60,000

Employment Prospects: Good

Advancement Prospects: Good

Prerequisites:
  Licensure/Certification—Child Development Associate certificate or other certification is preferred
  Education/Training—Associate or bachelor's degree
  Experience—Previous experience as early childhood head teacher or assistant director; business experience desirable
  Special Skills and Personality Traits—Communication, listening, human relations, supervisory, office management, and conflict management skills; fair, honest, confident, organized, innovative, encouraging

CAREER LADDER

Director of a larger or more prestigious program, or Early Childhood Program Owner

↑

Early Childhood Program Director

↑

Assistant Director or Head Teacher

Position Description

Early Childhood Program Directors are responsible for administering private and public child care centers, preschools, nursery schools, and prekindergarten programs. The size and type of program differs for every Program Director. For example, a Program Director might run a large child care center that enrolls newborn babies to five-year-olds, which operates 12 hours a day. Another director might run a small preschool program that enrolls only three- and four-year-olds for half-day sessions.

The primary goal of all Early Childhood Program Directors is to ensure that their programs provide high quality early childhood care and education services to all children and their families. Program Directors must juggle many different responsibilities each day. They develop and implement policies and procedures that ensure a safe and healthy environment. For example, they might develop emergency evacuation plans or monitor procedures for dropping off and picking up children. They also make sure that programs are in compliance with government licensing regulations, as well as health and safety laws and regulations.

Early Childhood Program Directors coordinate all program activities—such as staff training workshops, new construction plans, or parent volunteer programs—and plan future events, such as parent open houses. Some Program Directors plan fund-raisers and write proposals for grants. Furthermore, they complete administrative tasks that include preparing budgets, contacting vendors and suppliers, making school purchases, and writing business correspondence.

Another major responsibility is putting together a high quality staff. Program Directors are in charge of recruiting, hiring, training, and firing teachers and child care workers. The directors check references of potential candidates, making sure they are knowledgeable in child development and have training in early childhood care and education. In addition, Program Directors develop regular in-service training so that staff may learn about new teaching skills and developments in early childhood care and education.

Early Childhood Program Directors also oversee a program's curriculum, which must reflect the educational philosophy that is established by the owners, board of trustees, or higher-level administrators. With the teaching staff, Program Directors design a curriculum that provides for the social, emotional, intellectual, physical, aesthetic, and moral development of children. Together, the director and staff plan a daily schedule that balances child-directed and teacher-directed activities; small, large, and individual activities; and outdoor and indoor activities. Daily lesson plans, however, are the responsibility of the teaching staff, with Program Directors providing guidance. In some programs, the Program Directors also perform teaching duties.

Program Directors maintain relationships with parents. Usually, the Program Directors are the first persons that parents meet when looking for a child care or preschool program. They give site tours, answer parents' questions, and discuss parents' needs and requirements for their children. Most Program Directors create and distribute school newsletters and bulletins to update parents with current activities, early childhood news, and so on.

Program Directors have other duties that are performed as required. For example, they may act as substitute teachers for absent staff members. They may give presentations at local conferences or professional development workshops. Or, they may handle program recruitment duties, such as placing advertisements and notices in newspapers.

Early Childhood Program Directors often work more than 40 hours each week. Many work on a year-round schedule while others work a 10- or 11-month schedule.

Salaries

Salaries vary widely, and are based on factors such as experience, education, credentials, location, and the type and size of a program. Program Director salaries may be as low as $17,000 for running a small (20–35 child) program in a rural area to as high as $50,000 to $60,000 for running a large, multisite program in an urban area, according to Bess Emanuel, Director Credential Liaison at the Center for Career Development in Early Care and Education at Wheelock College, in Boston, Massachusetts.

Some Early Childhood Program Directors receive a fringe benefits package that includes sick leave, vacation leave, health plans, and retirement benefits.

Employment Prospects

Early Childhood Program Directors are hired by child care centers, family day care programs, preschool programs, nursery schools, private schools, and public schools.

Labor market experts report that opportunities for early childhood educators, including Program Directors, are expected to increase in the next few years due to the number of families in which both parents work. Most opportunities become available as directors retire, resign, return to school, or advance to other positions.

Advancement Prospects

For many Early Childhood Program Directors, advancement is realized by higher wages or being hired by larger or more prestigious programs. Many also become owners of their own early childhood programs.

Program Directors might also further their careers as university professors, software developers, researchers, and consultants in early childhood care and education.

Licensure/Certification

Most employers prefer to hire candidates who have the Child Development Associate (CDA) certificate, a professional credential in the early childhood field. This is a voluntary certification, which may be obtained through community colleges, community agencies, or professional associations. Some child care centers require that their Program Directors have the Certified Childcare Professional (CCP) certificate or the National Administrator Credential (NAC) granted by the National Child Care Association.

New York and several other states offer an early childhood program administrative credential. Early childhood experts expect more and more states to introduce legislation for licensure of Early Childhood Program Directors. To find out about requirements in your state, contact the state department of education.

Education and Training

Requirements vary widely with the different employers. Many employers prefer to hire candidates with at least an associate or bachelor's degree in early childhood education (ECE). Some employers will hire candidates who have a minimum number of ECE units as long as they have several years of administrative experience overseeing early childhood care and education programs.

Experience, Skills, and Personality Traits

In general, employers choose candidates who have at least one year of experience as a teacher or assistant director in early childhood programs. Candidates should have some business experience or basic business skills, such as bookkeeping, operating office machines, and writing business correspondence.

Good candidates also show that they can be effective leaders, as well as show that they have adequate communication, listening, and human relations skills. They should also have supervisory, office management, and conflict management skills, which may be learned through previous experience or continuing education.

Successful Early Childhood Program Directors are fair, honest, confident, organized, and innovative leaders. They are able to foster a positive working environment in which staff members are willing to work together. Furthermore, they are problem solvers and can inspire and motivate staff to do their best for the children and families they serve.

Unions/Associations

Many Early Childhood Program Directors join local, state, and national professional associations for early childhood educators. Organizations such as the National Association for the Education of Young Children and the National Child Care Association provide professional resources and services such as current developments in their fields, job listings, networking opportunities, and continuing education programs.

Tips for Entry

1. To enhance your employability, enroll in business courses, such as bookkeeping and business writing. Also learn how to use word processing and spreadsheet software.
2. The Internet can be a valuable source for learning about opportunities nationwide. Employers often post job openings at web sites of professional associations, as well as at job bank web sites such as "America's Job Bank" or "Career Mosaic."
3. Join professional organizations to network with your peers. Also subscribe to professional magazines or on-line services so that you can keep up with current research, issues, and trends in early childhood education.
4. You can learn more about early childhood education on the Internet. To start searching for relevant web sites, enter either of these keywords in a search engine: "early childhood education" or "early childhood educator."

KINDERGARTEN TEACHER

CAREER PROFILE

Duties: Help five- and six-year-olds become accustomed to formal classroom settings; teach simple academic concepts and skills; create daily lesson plans; perform non-teaching tasks as required

Salary Range: $25,000 to $52,000

Employment Prospects: Good

Advancement Prospects: Good

Prerequisites:
   Licensure/Certification—Teaching credential or other certification
   Education/Training—Bachelor's degree; for licensed teachers, completion of an accredited teacher education program
   Experience—Student teaching, internship, or other teaching experience
   Special Skills and Personality Traits—Communication, teamwork, interpersonal, organizational, and management skills; patient, creative, flexible, enthusiastic, energetic

CAREER LADDER

Mentor Teacher or Administrative positions

Kindergarten Teacher

Student Teacher or Substitute Teacher

Position Description

In both public and private schools, kindergarten is part of the elementary school level. (Kindergarten is usually abbreviated as *K,* as in K through grade 3.) For many five- and six-year-olds, kindergarten is their first school experience. Thus, a Kindergarten Teacher's first teaching goal is to help children become comfortable and accustomed to a formal classroom setting.

Kindergarten Teachers may have anywhere from 15 to 30 students in their class. They are responsible for teaching all academic subjects, art, music, and physical education. (In some schools, specialists teach the latter three subjects.) If they have students with special language or learning needs, they modify teaching methods and materials for those students. Unlike in the other elementary grades, kindergartners learn mostly through concrete experiences, hands-on activities, and play.

Kindergarten Teachers develop their curriculum based on school guidelines. They create daily lesson plans that describe what concepts and skills would be taught on a particular day and how the teacher plans to instruct the students. Many Kindergarten Teachers set up several learning centers to involve students in activities that teach basic concepts and skills in math, reading, writing, science, and so on.

To help students feel secure, Kindergarten Teachers establish a daily routine so that students know what activities follow each other. Teachers designate blocks of time for different activities—reading, writing, math, science, art, physical education, health and so on. Each activity usually lasts 10 to 15 minutes because of children's short attention spans. Teachers will also alternate activities to accommodate children's need to move about from time to time. In addition, teachers plan activities for the whole class, for small groups, and for the individual student.

Recent changes in federal legislation of special education programs have allowed for more special education students—children with learning, emotional, and physical disabilities—to receive their instruction in general education classrooms. (In some schools, general education and special education teachers work together on creating lesson plans and providing instruction.) For their special education students, Kindergarten Teachers follow certain instructional goals and objectives that are outlined on students' Individualized Education Programs (IEPs). Kindergarten

Teachers may be also involved in providing assessments of special education students, as well as helping develop IEPs.

Kindergarten Teachers also complete other duties. They assess each student's development and keep parents informed of their child's progress. They take attendance and do other administrative tasks. They may supervise hallways, lunchrooms, and other school areas during recess and lunch times. They may also supervise and direct teacher aides, student teachers, and parent volunteers. Furthermore, they participate in faculty meetings and school committees.

Kindergarten Teachers teach half-day sessions (between 2.5 and 3.5 hours) or full-day sessions (6 hours). However, they put in many more hours to complete all their tasks—making lesson plans, contacting parents, attending meetings, and so on. Most Kindergarten Teachers have a 10-month work schedule, from September to June; some have a year-round work schedule.

In most public school systems, teachers receive tenure after completing three to five years of continuous teaching service. With tenure, teachers cannot be fired without just cause.

Salaries

Salaries vary from state to state as well as from school to school. Factors such as experience, education, credentials, and school budgets determine what a teacher may earn. Typically, salaries are higher in public schools than in private schools. According to the 1997–98 teacher salary survey by the American Federation of Teachers, the average annual salaries for public school teachers, including Kindergarten Teachers, ranged between $27,839 and $51,727. The national average annual salary for beginning teachers was $25,735.

Kindergarten Teachers may receive fringe benefits, such as sick leave, holiday pay, health plans, and retirement benefits.

Employment Prospects

Teaching opportunities in both public and private schools are expected to be favorable for the next few years. This is due to the large number of teachers reaching retirement age; the increasing rate of student enrollment; and the lowering of the teacher-to-student ratio in many states.

Opportunities, however, vary widely by regions and school funding. Prospects are best in private schools located everywhere but the east and west coasts. In public schools, jobs are more readily available in urban inner cities, rural areas, and areas with a high rate of population growth.

Advancement Prospects

Kindergarten Teachers have several ways to advance their careers. Experienced teachers can become mentor teachers, providing guidance to beginning teachers. With additional education and endorsements, Elementary School Teachers in public schools can teach special subjects (such as art and physical education) or teach in special areas (such as bilingual education and special education). They can also become counselors, educational technologists, or other school-related professionals.

School administration is also another career path. In private schools, teachers can become school heads, deans of students, or other administrators. In public schools, teachers can become school principals and central office administrators with additional education and credentials.

Kindergarten Teachers might also enter other areas of education. For example, they may become adult education instructors, corporate trainers, or educational software developers.

Licensure/Certification

In public schools, Kindergarten Teachers must hold an early childhood education or elementary education teaching credential. The type of license and licensing requirements vary from state to state. (For specific information, contact the state board of education for the state in which you wish to teach.) In addition, Kindergarten Teachers may need to complete continuing education units and, eventually, a master's degree, for licensure renewal.

All private schools have their own requirements for teacher certification. Some schools require that Kindergarten Teachers have a state teaching license. Some private schools, such as Montessori schools, require internal teaching certifications. Other schools may require certification from certain school accreditation groups, professional associations, or other recognized organizations.

Education and Training

Kindergarten Teachers usually have a bachelor's degree in a liberal arts field. To become licensed teachers, they must complete an accredited teacher education program that includes courses in child development, teaching pedagogy, and instruction of subject matter, as well as a supervised field practicum.

In many schools, beginning teachers are assigned to "mentor teachers," who advise them on lesson plans, class management, and so on. Many schools require teachers to attend in-service workshops throughout the year.

Experience, Skills, and Personality Traits

Both public and private schools hire candidates who have experience teaching young children. They may have been student teachers, interns, substitute teachers, teacher aides, and so on.

Along with teaching skills, Kindergarten Teachers need good communication, teamwork, and interpersonal skills to work with students, school staff, and parents. To juggle their many responsibilities, Kindergarten Teachers also need adequate organizational and management skills.

Being patient, creative, flexible, enthusiastic, and energetic are some personality traits that successful Kindergarten Teachers share. They also have a good sense of humor and can think quickly on their feet. Above all, they are committed to teaching kindergartners, and thoroughly enjoy being with this age group.

Unions/Associations

Many Kindergarten Teachers join local, state, and national professional associations that provide teaching resources, continuing education programs, opportunities for networking, and so on. The National Association for the Education of Young Children, for example, specifically serves early childhood educators. Most public school teachers belong to either of these teacher unions: the National Education Association or the American Federation of Teachers.

Tips for Entry

1. Find out if you would like working with large groups of five- and six-year-olds for several hours each day. Gain experience by volunteering or working in kindergarten classes, Sunday school, after-school programs, recreational programs, and so on.
2. Be sure to use the placement center at your school or university when you're job hunting. There, you can learn about job postings and educator job fairs, as well as get help writing resumes and interviewing for jobs.
3. To find private and independent schools with kindergarten programs, look in city telephone books. Many books have a listing such as this in the yellow pages: "Schools—Academic—Pre-School and Kindergarten."
4. The Internet is a valuable resource for learning more about teaching kindergartners. To start searching for pertinent web sites, use the keyword "kindergarten" in a search engine.

TEACHERS IN ELEMENTARY SCHOOLS, MIDDLE-LEVEL SCHOOLS, AND HIGH SCHOOLS

ELEMENTARY SCHOOL TEACHER

CAREER PROFILE

Duties: Provide instruction of academic and most nonacademic subjects to all students; create daily lesson plans; perform nonteaching duties as assigned

Alternate Titles: Elementary Teacher, Primary School Teacher

Salary Range: $25,000 to $52,000

Employment Prospects: Very Good

Advancement Prospects: Good

Prerequisites:
 Licensure/Certification—A teaching credential or other certification
 Education/Training—Bachelor's degree; for licensed teachers, completion of an accredited teacher education program
 Experience—Student teaching, internship, or other teaching experience
 Special Skills and Traits—Communication, teamwork, interpersonal, organizational, and management skills; flexible, creative, enthusiastic, energetic, patient

CAREER LADDER

Mentor Teacher or Administrative positions

Elementary School Teacher

Student Teacher or Substitute Teacher

Position Description

Elementary school is where the academic careers of most students begin. They learn to read, write, and do basic math operations, and begin to learn basic facts and concepts about the world around them. The typical age range of elementary school students is six to 12 years old.

Most public and private elementary schools are made up of first through fifth grades. Some schools go up to sixth grade, and others go up to eighth grade. (Kindergarten is usually part of elementary schools too.)

Starting at first grade, Elementary School Teachers are responsible for providing instruction of the academic subjects—math, language arts, science, and social studies—to 20 to 30 students. (In private schools, teachers generally have smaller classes.) They may also teach art, music, physical education, and computer skills, but in some schools, many of those subjects are taught by teaching specialists. Elementary School Teachers also help students develop learning skills—such as study skills and problem-solving skills—as well as social skills—how to behave, how to get along with each other, and so on.

As part of planning for their classes, Elementary School Teachers also make schedules. They decide when each subject is to be taught during the week, as well as the order of subjects during the school day. They confer with music teachers, physical education teachers, and other teaching specialists to schedule when the specialists should teach the class during the week. Elementary School Teachers also decide when students with special reading, language, or learning needs should be scheduled to receive individual tutoring, therapy, or other special services.

Elementary School Teachers are knowledgeable in the different subjects they teach. They follow school curriculum guidelines to develop the units of study for each subject. Some Elementary School Teachers have multi-age classes, in which students from two grades are combined. Teachers then must follow the curriculum guidelines for both grades.

Elementary School Teachers are responsible for creating daily lesson plans, which are usually filed with the school principal's office. The lesson for each subject is outlined—the lesson's content, purpose, and learning objectives; how the lesson is taught; and what exercises and activities are used to reinforce learning.

Because students have different abilities, skill levels, learning styles, and maturity levels, Elementary School Teachers use a variety of teaching methods and strategies. They also use films, tapes, computers, and other audiovisual aids to help with their instruction. In addition, they decorate their classrooms and create bulletin board displays to reflect the seasons, holidays, and unit themes to reinforce and motivate learning.

Elementary School Teachers are also responsible for monitoring their students' academic progress. They review students' assignments and give students feedback on their work. They also administer quizzes and tests to check students' comprehension of new learning. At the end of each quarter or semester, they evaluate each student's academic performance and assign a grade as well as comment on the development of his or her learning skills and social skills.

From time to time, Elementary School Teachers may have special education students—children with learning, emotional, and physical disabilities—as members of their classes. (Federal laws mandate that special education students receive their instruction in general education classrooms whenever possible.) For each special education student, Elementary School Teachers follow instructional goals and objectives that are outlined in a student's Individualized Education Program (IEP). If help is needed to implement IEPs, they consult special education teachers. In some schools, general education and special education teachers work together to provide instruction to all students in class. Furthermore, Elementary School Teachers may be involved in providing assessments of special education students and helping to develop IEPs.

Elementary School Teachers perform many other tasks; for example, they:

- gather teaching and student materials
- create student exercises and activities
- confer with parents about their children's development and academic progress
- take daily attendance
- perform monitoring duties during class breaks
- sponsor extracurricular activities such as clubs, sports, and after-school tutoring sessions
- attend school functions and events
- participate in faculty meetings and on school committees
- may supervise teacher aides, interns, or school volunteers

Typically, Elementary School Teachers work long hours each day, sometimes as many as 10 to 12 hours, to complete all their tasks—planning lessons, contacting parents, grading papers, attending school functions, and so on. Most Elementary School Teachers have a 10-month work schedule, usually from September to June.

Before the beginning of a school term, Elementary School Teachers may be reassigned to teach another grade level or teach in another school. In most public school systems, teachers receive tenure after completing three to five years of continuous teaching service. With tenure, teachers cannot be fired without just cause.

Salaries

Salaries vary, and depend on factors such as education, experience, credentials, and school budgets. Typically, salaries are higher in public schools than in private schools. According to the 1997–98 teacher salary survey by the American Federation of Teachers, the national average annual salary for public school teachers—including Elementary School Teachers—was $39,437. Average annual salaries ranged from $27,839 to $51,727. The national average annual salary for beginning teachers was $25,735. In some schools, Elementary School Teachers may earn additional pay for coaching, being club advisers, and sponsoring other extracurricular activities.

In addition to a salary, most Elementary School Teachers receive a fringe benefits package that includes sick leave, vacation leave, health benefits, life insurance, retirement benefits, and so on.

Employment Prospects

Teaching opportunities in both public and private schools are expected to be favorable for the next few years. This is partly due to the increasing rate of student enrollment, the large force of veteran teachers reaching retirement age, and the lowering of the student-to-teacher ratio in many states.

Opportunities, however, vary widely by regions and school funding. In public schools, jobs are more readily available in urban inner cities, rural areas, and areas with a high rate of population growth.

Advancement Prospects

Several different career paths are available for Elementary School Teachers. Experienced teachers can become mentor teachers who provide guidance to beginning teachers. With additional education and endorsements, Elementary School Teachers can teach special subjects (such as art and physical education) or teach in special areas (such as bilingual education and special education). They can also become counselors, librarians, or other school-related professionals.

School administration is another career path open to Elementary School Teachers. In private schools, teachers can work their way up to become department heads, school heads, or other administrators. In public schools, teachers need additional education and credentials to become school principals and district administrators (such as curriculum specialists, program directors, and superintendents).

Elementary School Teachers can pursue careers in other areas of education. For example, they can become community college instructors, university professors, corporate trainers, textbook editors, or educational software developers.

Licensure/Certification

To teach in public schools, Elementary School Teachers must hold a valid elementary education credential. The type of license and licensure requirements vary from state to state. (For specific information, contact the state board of education for the state in which you wish to teach.) In addition, they may need to complete continuing education units and, eventually, attain a master's degree for licensure renewal.

Many private schools require certification from state boards of education, school accreditation groups, professional associations, or other recognized organizations. Some schools, such as Waldorf schools, require internal teaching certifications, which are obtained after completing their training programs.

Education and Training

Elementary School Teachers must have at least a bachelor's degree, usually in liberal arts, to teach in public and private schools. Many Elementary School Teachers have master's degrees. To become licensed teachers, Elementary School Teachers complete an accredited teacher education program that includes course work in pedagogy and instruction of subject matter, as well as a supervised field practicum.

In many schools, beginning teachers are assigned to mentor teachers who advise them with lesson plans, class management, and so on. Many schools require teachers to attend in-service workshops throughout the year.

Experience, Skills, and Personality Traits

Employers look for candidates who have previous teaching experience with young children as a student teacher, intern, substitute teacher, and so on. Additionally, most private schools look for candidates who have a strong background in extracurricular activities, such as sports or drama.

Elementary School Teachers need strong communication, interpersonal, and teamwork skills as they must work well with students, staff, and parents. In addition, teachers need adequate organizational and management skills to handle the many tasks that they must complete each day.

Being flexible, creative, enthusiastic, energetic, and patient are some of the personality traits that successful Elementary School Teachers share. In addition, they have a deep compassion for young children, as well as a strong desire to help them succeed in the learning process.

Unions/Associations

Most public school teachers belong to either of these teacher unions: the National Education Association or the American Federation of Teachers. Many teachers also join local, state, and national professional associations that provide teaching resources, continuing education programs, opportunities for networking, and so on. Some organizations they might join are the Council for Exceptional Children and the National Association for the Education of Young Children.

Tips for Entry

1. Get lots of (volunteer or paid) experience working with groups of young children. As a middle school or high school student, you might baby-sit, tutor, read stories in library read-aloud programs, be a classroom aide, assist in after-school child care programs, coach children's sports, or work in recreational programs.
2. Be sure the elementary school level is the right level for you before enrolling in a teacher education program. Talk with Elementary School Teachers in different grades. Also visit several classes while they are in session.
3. As a student teacher or intern, develop a teaching portfolio to bring to job fairs and interviews. In it, keep copies of your resume, professional letters of reference, samples of your lesson plans, and photographs of your classes that show bulletin boards, learning centers, student work, and so on.
4. To learn more about private and independent schools, contact the National Association of Independent Schools or the Council for American Private Education. (Their addresses are listed in Appendix IV.)
5. You can learn more about elementary schools on the Internet. Use the keyword "elementary school" to get a list of web sites to read.

MIDDLE SCHOOL TEACHER

CAREER PROFILE

Duties: Provide instruction for core subjects and create lesson plans, usually in collaboration with other teachers; perform nonteaching duties as assigned

Salary Range: $25,000 to $52,000

Employment Prospects: Excellent

Advancement Prospects: Good

Prerequisites:
    Licensure/Certification—A teaching credential or other certification
    Education/Training—Bachelor's degree; for licensed teachers, completion of an accredited teacher education program
    Experience—Student teaching, internship, or other teaching experience
    Special Skills and Personality Traits—Communication, teamwork, interpersonal, management, and organizational skills; creative, flexible, fair, patient, tolerant

CAREER LADDER

Mentor Teacher or Administrative positions

↑

Middle School Teacher

↑

Student Teacher or Substitute Teacher

Position Description

Middle school is one of two middle-level models in public and private school settings; it is the school level between elementary school and high school. (The other middle-level model is the junior high school.) Most middle schools are made up of sixth through eighth grades; some middle schools also include fifth grade. Middle school students are normally between the ages of 11 and 14.

Since the 1970s, more school systems have been building new middle schools, as well as changing many junior high schools to the middle-school model. According to many middle-grades experts, the structure, curriculum, and instructional strategies in middle schools better fulfill the social, emotional, physical, and developmental needs of young adolescents as they grow into adulthood.

Typically, teams of two to four Middle School Teachers are assigned to teach a group of students (for example, 80 students) at the same grade level. The team is responsible for the instruction of the core academic subjects—math, science, social studies, and language arts. Each teacher is responsible for teaching one or more subjects. For example, in a three-member team, one Middle School Teacher might teach math and science, another, Language Arts, and the other, social studies.

The exploratory classes—art, music, physical education, foreign language, health, and so on—are taught by specialists. Students might receive instruction in these subjects once or twice a week or daily within a grading period.

Following curriculum guidelines, the core subject teachers usually work together to plan the units of study for the academic subjects. Middle School Teachers may organize the units in themes, such as the environment or myths and legends, to help students understand the connection between core subjects. Teachers then create lesson plans for their particular subjects incorporating the current unit theme.

Class periods for the core subjects are typically combined in blocks of two to four hours. With longer class periods, Middle School Teachers can teach lessons, as well as reinforce—and enrich—learning with hands-on activities, project-based learning, group work, and independent work. Teachers can also take advantage of using computers, the Internet, the library or media center, and other resources to help facilitate learning.

Many Middle School Teachers have special education students—children with learning, emotional, and physical disabilities—as part of their classes. Changes in federal legislation of special education programs have mandated that special education students receive their instruction in general education classrooms whenever possible. For their special education students, Middle School Teachers must follow instructional goals and objectives that are outlined in students' Individualized Education Programs (IEPs). Middle School Teachers may also be involved in providing assessments of special education students, as well as helping develop IEPs. (In some schools, special education teachers are assigned to work collaboratively with general education teachers to create lesson plans and teach lessons to all students—special education and general education students—in class.)

All Middle School Teachers are responsible for monitoring their students' academic progress. Along with reviewing students' classwork, homework, and projects, they give quizzes and tests to check students' comprehension. At the end of each grading period, Middle School Teachers evaluate each student's work and assign a grade for his or her academic performance.

Middle School Teachers perform many nonteaching duties. They contact parents to discuss their children's academic performance and behavior. They do daily administrative tasks such as taking roll, marking students late or absent, collecting absence slips, and making school announcements. Middle School Teachers may be assigned teacher aides, school volunteers, or student teachers, whom they train, supervise, and assign specific tasks to complete. In addition, Middle School Teachers participate in faculty meetings and on school committees.

Most Middle School Teachers also sponsor extracurricular activities: for example, they may coach sports, advise class councils, supervise student clubs, sponsor community service activities, or provide after-school tutoring sessions. In some schools, Middle School Teachers may have lunchroom, bus, or other monitoring duties. Teachers may be assigned to help supervise attendance at school games, dances, and other school functions. Furthermore, Middle School Teachers act as counselors and mentors—directly and indirectly—to their students.

Middle School Teachers put in long hours each school day to complete all their duties. They often bring work home to complete at night and on weekends. Most Middle School Teachers have a 10-month work schedule, from September to June.

Before the beginning of a school term, teachers may be reassigned to teach another grade level or teach in another school. In most public school systems, teachers receive tenure after completing three to five years of continuous teaching service. With tenure, teachers cannot be fired from their jobs without just cause.

Salaries

Salaries vary, and depend on factors such as education, credentials, experience, and school budgets. Typically, salaries are higher in public schools than in private schools.

According to the 1997–98 teacher salary survey by the American Federation of Teachers, the national average annual salary for public school teachers, including Middle School Teachers, was $39,437. Average annual salaries ranged from $27,839 to $51,727. The national average annual salary for beginning teachers was $25,735. In some schools, Middle School Teachers may earn additional pay for coaching, being class advisers, and sponsoring other extracurricular activities.

In addition to a salary, most Middle School Teachers receive fringe benefits, such as sick leave, holiday pay, health benefits, and retirement benefits.

Employment Prospects

Teaching opportunities in public and private schools are currently favorable and are expected to continue for the next several years due to the large force of veteran teachers who are reaching retirement age. Opportunities should also grow due to the increasing rate of student enrollment nationwide and the increasing number of states that are passing laws that lower the student-to-teacher ratio. Jobs in public schools are more readily available in urban inner cities, rural areas, and areas with a high rate of population growth.

Middle School Teachers with endorsements in special education, computer education, bilingual education, or English as a Second Language (ESL) are currently in demand by schools nationwide.

Advancement Prospects

Middle School Teachers can pursue several career paths. Experienced teachers can become mentor teachers who advise beginning teachers. Licensed teachers can obtain additional endorsements to coach, teach in special areas such as bilingual education, or teach special subjects such as music and technology. With further education and licensure, Middle School Teachers can become counselors, librarians, school psychologists, or other school-related professionals.

School administration is also a path open to Middle School Teachers. In private schools, teachers can work their way up to positions such as school heads, division heads, or dean of students. With additional education and licensure, public school teachers can become school principals and district administrators.

Furthermore, Middle School Teachers can pursue careers in other areas of education. For example, they can become college professors, technical trainers, or educational software developers.

Licensure/Certification

To teach in public schools, Middle School Teachers must hold a valid teaching credential. The type of credential differs from state to state. In some states, Middle School Teachers hold an elementary education credential; while in other states, they hold a secondary education credential. In a few states, they hold a middle-grades credential. Licensure requirements vary from state to state. (For specific information, contact the state board of education for the state in which you wish to teach.) In addition, Middle School Teachers may need to complete continuing education units and, eventually, attain a master's degree for licensure renewal.

Many private schools require certification from state boards of education, school accreditation groups, professional associations, or other recognized organizations. Some schools, such as Montessori schools, require internal teaching certifications, which are obtained after completing their training programs.

Education and Training

Middle School Teachers must have at least a bachelor's degree in liberal studies or in any field with the required course work to teach one or more core subjects—math, language arts, science, and social studies. All licensed teachers should have completed an accredited teacher education program, with course work in pedagogy and instruction of subject matter, as well as a supervised field practicum.

In many schools, beginning teachers are assigned to mentor teachers who advise them with curriculum development, classroom management, and so on. Many schools require teachers to attend in-service workshops throughout the year, which cover topics such as new teaching methods and cultural diversity.

Experience, Skills, and Personality Traits

Entry-level Middle School Teachers usually have previous experience teaching young adolescents as student teachers, interns, substitute teachers, teacher's aides and so on. In addition, teachers in private schools generally have a strong background in sports, drama, community service, or other extracurricular activities.

To work with students, staff, and parents, Middle School Teachers need adequate communication, teamwork, and interpersonal skills. Additionally, they need strong organizational and management skills to complete their many different tasks each day.

Successful Middle School Teachers have several personality traits in common, such as being creative, flexible, fair, patient, and tolerant. They also have a fine sense of humor. Additionally, they are passionate about teaching young adolescents and are in tune with the physical, emotional, and social changes that their students are going through.

Unions/Associations

Most public school teachers belong to either of these teacher unions: the American Federation of Teachers or the National Education Association. Many Middle School Teachers join local, state, and national professional associations that provide teaching resources, continuing education programs, opportunities for networking, and so on. Some national organizations that they might join are the National Middle School Association and the International Reading Association.

Tips for Entry

1. Get lots of (volunteer or paid) experience working with groups of young adolescents in recreational programs, youth organizations, church youth groups, scouting, and so on.
2. Contact public and private schools where you wish to teach to learn about job vacancies. Submit an application even if jobs are not currently available. Call back from time to time to learn the status of your application.
3. An alternative path for teacher licensure is available for those who would prefer to obtain their credential by teaching full-time in a classroom under the supervision of certified educators. To learn more, contact your state board of education or a school district office.
4. Many private and independent schools offer internship programs. For more information, contact schools in your area or the National Association of Independent Schools, 1620 L Street NW, Washington, D.C. 20036-5605. The phone number is (202) 973-9700. Its web site is *http//www.nais.org*.
5. Learn more about middle schools on the Internet. To start searching for relevant web sites, use either of these keywords in a search engine: "middle school" or "middle level schools."

JUNIOR HIGH TEACHER

CAREER PROFILE

Duties: Provide instruction for several courses in one or more subject areas; create lesson plans; perform non-teaching duties as requested

Alternate Titles: Junior High School Instructor

Salary Range: $25,000 to $52,000

Employment Prospects: Fair

Advancement Prospects: Good

Prerequisites:
  Licensure/Certification—A teaching credential or other certification
  Education/Training—Bachelor's degree; for licensed teachers, completion of an accredited teacher education program
  Experience—Student teaching, internship, or other teaching experience
  Special Skills and Personality Traits—Communication, interpersonal, teamwork, management, and organizational skills; fair, patient, tolerant, flexible, creative

CAREER LADDER

Mentor Teacher or Department Head

↑

Junior High Teacher

↑

Student Teacher or Substitute Teacher

Position Description

The junior high school, one of two middle-level models in public and private school systems, was established to instruct young adolescents who are adjusting to physical, emotional, and social changes as they grow into adulthood. The other middle-level model is the middle school. Unlike middle schools, junior high schools are modeled after the high school structure and curriculum and instructional design in order to prepare young adolescents academically for high school.

Most junior high schools are made up of either seventh and eighth grades or seventh through ninth grades. Junior high students may range from ages 12 to 15.

In junior high school, the school day is divided into several class periods and students move from class to class. They receive daily instruction in the core subjects—language arts, social studies, math, and science. Other subjects such as music, art, physical education, health, foreign languages, technology, and industrial arts are taught daily or once or twice a week within a grading period.

Like high school teachers, Junior High Teachers are specialists in their subject matter—English, social studies, mathematics, science, art, music, physical education, foreign language, and so on. They are assigned courses to teach at different grade levels. For example, a junior high social studies teacher might teach world history to ninth graders, government to eighth graders, and history and geography to seventh graders.

Junior High Teachers generally have between 20 and 35 students in a class. (Teachers in private schools normally have smaller classes.) Along with teaching subject matter, Junior High Teachers teach students learning skills—such as problem solving, critical thinking, and using resources to find answers. Directly or indirectly, Junior High Teachers also act as mentors and counselors to their students.

Following curriculum guidelines, Junior High Teachers develop a course syllabus that outlines the topics and sequence of topics to be taught for each course. They also create a daily lesson plan for each class, as well as prepare for each lesson by studying the topic, gathering materials, creating exercises and activities, setting up experiments or demonstrations, and so on.

Class periods are usually 50 to 55 minutes long, and within that time, Junior High Teachers take attendance, collect assignments, review the previous day's work, present the day's lesson, and make class assignments. Most instruction is done through lecture, group discussion, demonstration, and modeling. Teachers might use films, videotapes, and other audiovisual equipment to help reinforce instruction. Some teachers also supplement learning by having students work with computer programs or access the Internet during class time.

Many junior high schools have flexible block schedules in which periods are two to four hours long. Classes are then scheduled for alternate days. With flexible block schedules, teachers can provide additional reinforcement and enrichment activities to help students learn new concepts and skills. They can also use a variety of teaching methods (such as small group instruction, individual coaching, and independent work) to reach the different learning styles and skill levels of their students.

In many junior high schools, special education students—children with learning, emotional, and physical disabilities—are assigned to general education classrooms, which are often identified as inclusive classrooms. (Changes in federal law have mandated that special education students receive their instruction in general education classrooms whenever possible.) With special education students, Junior High Teachers must follow instructional goals and objectives that are outlined in students' Individualized Education Programs (IEPs). When needed, they consult with special education teachers for assistance in implementing IEPs. In some schools, general education and special education teachers collaborate in creating lesson plans for inclusive classrooms and teaching the classes together. Furthermore, Junior High Teachers may be involved in providing assessments of special education students, as well as helping develop IEPs.

Junior High Teachers are also responsible for monitoring students' academic progress. They maintain a record book of students' test scores, grades for class assignments, and so on. At the end of each grading period, teachers evaluate each student's work and assign a grade for their performance.

Junior High Teachers have many other duties, among them:

- developing, teaching, and enforcing class rules and procedures
- correcting homework and assignments and providing students feedback about their work
- conferring with students and their parents about students' work and behavior
- performing administrative tasks such as taking attendance and making school announcements
- coaching after-school sports or sponsoring extracurricular activities, such as clubs, debate teams, and tutoring sessions
- supervising attendance at games, concerts, and other school functions
- participating in department and faculty meetings and school committees
- supervising teacher aides, interns, or school volunteers

Junior High Teachers work long hours, often completing their many tasks at home in the evenings and the weekends. Most Junior High Teachers have a 10-month work schedule, usually September to June.

Before the beginning of a school term, Junior High Teachers may be reassigned to teach another grade level or teach in another school. In most public school systems, teachers receive tenure after completing three to five years of continuous teaching service. With tenure, teachers cannot be fired from their jobs without just cause.

Salaries

Experience, education, credentials, and school budgets are some factors that determine what teachers may earn in their schools. Typically, salaries are higher in public schools than in private schools. According to the 1997–98 teacher salary survey by the American Federation of Teachers, the national average annual salary for public school teachers—including Junior High Teachers—was $39,437. Average annual salaries ranged from $27,839 to $51,727. The national average annual salary for beginning teachers was $25,735. In some schools, Junior High Teachers may earn additional pay for coaching, being class advisers, and sponsoring other extracurricular activities.

In addition to a salary, most Junior High Teachers receive fringe benefits such as sick leave, health insurance, life insurance, and retirement benefits.

Employment Prospects

Junior High Teachers are employed by public schools and private schools. Job opportunities in both settings are expected to be favorable for the next few years due to the increasing rate of student enrollment, the large force of teachers reaching retirement age, and the growing number of school reform laws lowering the student-to-teacher ratio in the classroom.

Junior High Teachers with additional licensure in math, science, special education, computer education, bilingual education, or English as a Second Language (ESL) should find available opportunities because of shortages in those subject areas.

(Note: When school administration changes a junior high school to a middle school, Junior High Teachers' jobs are generally not affected. They may continue teaching in the new middle school, or be reassigned to teach high school, adult education, or other grade level.)

Advancement Prospects

Several career paths are open for Junior High Teachers to pursue. Experienced teachers can become mentor teachers or department heads. Licensed teachers can obtain additional endorsements to coach, teach other subjects, or teach in special areas such as bilingual education or special education. With advanced education and credentials, Junior High Teachers can become counselors, school psychologists, music therapists, educational diagnosticians, or other school-related professionals.

Junior High Teachers can also pursue a career in school administration. In public schools, teachers can become school principals and district administrators with additional education and licensure. In private schools, teachers can work their way up to become school heads, admissions directors, and other administrative positions.

Furthermore, teachers may pursue careers in other areas of education. For example, they may become college professors, technical trainers, librarians, or museum educators.

Licensure/Certification

Public schools require Junior High Teachers to hold a secondary education credential with an endorsement in each subject area that they teach. Licensure requirements vary from state to state. (For specific information, contact the state board of education for the state in which you wish to teach.) In addition, Junior High Teachers may need to complete continuing education units and, eventually, obtain a master's degree for licensure renewal.

Many private schools require certification from state boards of education, school accreditation groups, professional associations, or other recognized organizations. Some schools, such as Waldorf schools, require internal teaching certifications, which are obtained after completing their training programs.

Education and Training

To teach in public and private junior high schools, teachers must have a bachelor's degree in the primary subject area that they teach. Many Junior High Teachers in public and private schools have master's degrees in their disciplines. All licensed teachers must complete an accredited teacher education program, which includes course work in pedagogy and instruction of subject matter, as well as a supervised field practicum.

In many schools, beginning teachers are assigned to mentor teachers who advise them with lesson plans, class management, and so on. Throughout the year, Junior High Teachers attend in-service workshops, which cover new teaching methods, conflict resolution strategies, and other professional topics.

Experience, Skills, and Personality Traits

Schools generally hire Junior High Teachers who have previous teaching experience with young adolescents. They may have been student teachers, substitute teachers, teacher's aides, museum educators, church teachers, and so on. In addition, private schools look for candidates with a strong background in sports, drama, community service, and other extracurricular activities.

Like all teachers, Junior High Teachers must have strong communication, teamwork, and interpersonal skills as well as organizational and management skills in order to complete their many different duties each day.

Being fair, patient, tolerant, flexible, and creative are some personality traits that successful Junior High Teachers share, along with having a fine sense of humor. They also have a passion for teaching young adolescents and are sympathetic to the physical, emotional, and social changes that adolescents are going through.

Unions/Associations

Many Junior High Teachers join local, state, and national professional associations that provide teacher resources, continuing education programs, networking opportunities, and other services. Some organizations serve specific disciplines, such as the National Science Teachers Association, the National Council of Teachers of English, or the National Council of Teachers of Mathematics. Most Junior High teachers in public schools belong to either of these two unions: the American Federation of Teachers or the National Education Association.

Tips for Entry

1. Get lots of experience working with young adolescents in volunteer or paid positions. For example, you might coach youth teams, counsel youth in community programs, tutor in after-school programs, or become a teacher's aide in middle-level schools.
2. If you wish to teach in a certain state, contact that state's board of education to learn about their licensure requirements. Then choose an approved teacher education program that would prepare you to fulfill the requirements.
3. Many states offer alternative ways for obtaining a teaching credential. For information, contact your state board of education or a school district office.
4. Most private schools begin recruiting teachers for their fall term between February and May.
5. Learn more about junior high schools and middle level schools, in general, on the Internet. To start finding pertinent web sites, use any of these keywords in a search engine: "junior high school," "middle school," or "middle level schools."

HIGH SCHOOL TEACHER

CAREER PROFILE

Duties: Provide instruction for several courses in one or more subject areas; create lesson plans; perform non-teaching duties as requested

Alternate Title: Secondary School Teacher

Salary Range: $25,000 to $52,000

Employment Prospects: Excellent

Advancement Prospects: Good

Prerequisites:
  Licensure/Certification—A teaching credential or other certification
  Education/Training—Bachelor's degree; completion of an accredited teacher education program
  Experience—Student teaching, internship, or other teaching experience
  Special Skills and Personality Traits—Communication, interpersonal, teamwork, organizational, and management skills; patient, tolerant, flexible, creative, fair

CAREER LADDER

Mentor Teacher or Department Head

High School Teacher

Student Teacher or Substitute Teacher

Position Description

High school is the last level of compulsory education in the United States. Most public and private high schools are made up of ninth through 12th grades; some high schools include only 10th to 12th grade. In high school, teachers and other staff prepare adolescent students (most between the ages of 14 and 18) to become responsible, participating adults in society, as well as provide students with essential knowledge and skills to become lifelong learners.

High School Teachers are specialists in their subject matter, and may be part of one or more high school departments, such as social studies, physical education, or industrial arts. They teach courses in different grades. For example, a high school science teacher might teach general science to ninth graders, biology to 10th graders, and anatomy to 11th and 12th graders.

Most High School Teachers provide instruction for classes in English, social studies, mathematics, science, fine arts, foreign language, physical education, and other subjects that are required for high school graduation and for future enrollment in colleges and universities. Many High School Teachers also teach courses in business, culinary arts, building and construction, auto services, agriculture, or other vocational areas that can prepare students for enrollment in apprenticeship programs and technical and vocational schools as well as for obtaining employment after high school graduation.

Typically, High School Teachers have six or seven classes with as few as 15 or as many as 35 students in a class. (The class load for teachers is usually smaller in private schools.) Most High School Teachers instruct between 120 and 180 students each school day.

For each course, High School Teachers develop a course syllabus that outlines the topics to be taught within a quarter, semester, or year. In addition, they create daily lesson plans for each course, and prepare the lessons for each class. Lesson preparation may involve studying a topic, gathering teaching materials, creating student materials, setting up demonstrations or experiments, and so on. (In most public high schools, teachers get a free period for preparing lessons.)

Within a class period, High School Teachers complete attendance tasks; collect homework; review the previous day's lesson; present the new lesson through lecture, demonstration, and modeling; check students' understanding of concepts and skills with written and oral exercises, quizzes, or tests; and assign classwork, homework, and projects. To help reinforce instruction, High School Teachers may use films, slides, videotapes, and other audiovisual equipment. Many teachers also supplement instruction by having students work with computer programs as well as access the Internet during class time.

In many high schools, flexible block schedules are used in which periods are two to four hours long. Classes are then scheduled for alternate days. With flexible block schedules, High School Teachers can plan more complex lessons with hands-on activities and independent research work. In addition, teachers have the chance to work with students who may need more individual attention.

High School Teachers are responsible for monitoring students' academic progress. They maintain a record book of students' test scores, grades for class assignments, and so on. At the end of each grading period, teachers evaluate each student's work and assign a grade for his or her academic performance.

Some High School Teachers are assigned to teach inclusive classrooms that include special education students, or children with behavioral disorders, learning disabilities, or visual, hearing, or physical impairments. (Changes in federal law have mandated that special education students receive their instruction in general education classrooms whenever possible.) With special education students, High School Teachers follow instructional goals and objectives that are outlined in students' Individualized Education Programs (IEPs). High School Teachers may also be involved in providing assessments of special education students, as well as helping develop IEPs. In some schools, general education and special education teachers collaborate in creating lesson plans and providing instruction to all students in inclusive classrooms.

High School Teachers have many other duties. They might:

- confer with students and their parents about students' work and behavior
- be assigned to a group of students to meet with and advise each day
- sponsor extracurricular activities (such as clubs, student government, or school publications) or coach athletic teams
- supervise school dances, games, concerts, plays, or other school functions
- participate in department and faculty meetings and on school committees
- supervise teacher aides, interns, or school volunteers

Most High School Teachers work beyond the regular school day, and often complete their tasks (making lesson plans, calling parents, grading papers, etc.) at home during evenings and on weekends. Most High School teachers have a 10-month work schedule, from September to June.

High School Teachers in most public schools receive tenure after completing three to five years of continuous teaching service. With tenure, teachers cannot be fired without just cause.

Salaries

Salaries vary, and depend on factors such as education, credentials, experience, and school budgets. Typically, the pay is higher in public schools than in private schools. In the 1997–98 school year, the national average annual salary for public school teachers, including High School Teachers, was $39,437, according to the American Federation of Teachers. Average annual salaries ranged from $27,839 to $51,727. The national average annual salary for beginning high school teachers was $25,735.

Along with their salary, High School Teachers receive fringe benefits, such as health plans and retirement plans. In addition, High School Teachers may earn additional pay for each extracurricular activity they sponsor and each sport they coach.

Employment Prospects

Due to the increasing rate of student enrollment and the large force of teachers reaching retirement age, teaching opportunities in both public and private schools are expected to be favorable for the next few years. In public schools, jobs are more readily available in urban inner cities and rural areas, as well as in areas with a high rate of population growth.

Math, science, and computer education teachers are in particular demand by both private and public schools.

Advancement Prospects

High School Teachers can pursue a number of career paths. Experienced teachers can become mentor teachers and department heads. With additional education and credentials, licensed High School Teachers can teach in special areas such as bilingual education and special education. They can also become guidance counselors, school librarians, educational technologists, or other school-related professionals.

High School Teachers can also advance to administrative positions. In private schools, teachers can work their way up to be school heads, deans of students, or other administrators. With advanced education and licensure, public school teachers can become principals and district administrators.

High School Teachers can also pursue careers in other areas of education. For example, they can become correction instructors, corporate trainers, textbook editors, or educational consultants.

Licensure/Certification

High School Teachers in public schools are required to hold a secondary education credential with an endorsement in each subject area that they teach. Licensure requirements vary from state to state. (For specific information, contact the state board of education for the state in which you wish to teach.) In addition, High School Teachers may need to complete continuing education units and, eventually, a master's degree for licensure renewal.

Many private schools require certification from state boards of education, school accreditation groups, professional associations, or other recognized organizations. Some schools, such as Waldorf schools, require internal teaching certifications, which are obtained after completing their training programs.

Education and Training

Requirements vary from school to school; but in general, High School Teachers need at least a bachelor's degree in the primary subject that they are teaching. Many High School Teachers in both public and private schools have master's degrees in their subjects. All state-licensed teachers must complete an accredited teacher education program that includes pedagogy, instruction of subject matter, and a supervised field practicum.

In many schools, beginning teachers are assigned to mentor teachers who advise them with lesson plans, classroom management, and so on. In addition, many High School Teachers are required to attend mandatory in-service workshops throughout the year.

Experience, Skills, and Personality Traits

Employers typically choose candidates who have previous teaching experience with adolescents as student teachers, interns, substitute teachers, and so on. Along with teaching experience, private schools desire candidates with a strong background in sports, drama, community service, or other extracurricular activities.

Candidates should have strong communication, teamwork, and interpersonal skills to work well with students, parents, and school staff. In addition, they should have adequate organizational and management skills to complete the various duties that are required of High School Teachers each day.

Successful High School Teachers generally have a fine sense of humor and share several personality traits, such as being patient, tolerant, flexible, creative, and fair. Additionally, they have a talent and passion for teaching adolescents, willing to reach out and listen to their students' questions and concerns.

Unions/Associations

High School Teachers join local, state, and national professional organizations that provide teaching resources, continuing education programs, network opportunities, and so on. Some organizations serve specific disciplines, such as the National Science Teachers Association, the National Art Education Association, or the National Council of Teachers of English. In addition, most public school High School Teachers belong to either of these two unions: the American Federation of Teachers or the National Education Association.

Tips for Entry

1. Volunteer or obtain jobs in settings that provide you with experiences to work with groups of teenagers.
2. Subscribe to professional teaching magazines, such as *Education Week,* to learn about nationwide job opportunities and to keep up with current educational events and issues.
3. Develop a teaching philosophy—your teaching mission, goals, objectives, and so on. Being clear in your mind about your purpose for teaching can give you more confidence in job interviews as well as in the classroom.
4. To find out what it would be like to work at a particular private school, you might work first as a substitute teacher.
5. You can get an idea of what different high schools are like on the Internet. Use the keyword "high school" in any search engine to get a list of web sites to read.

SUBSTITUTE TEACHER

CAREER PROFILE

Duties: To fill in for an absent teacher and teach his or her daily lesson plans and perform his or her nonteaching duties; perform other duties as assigned

Salary Range: $40 to $100 or more per day

Employment Prospects: Excellent

Advancement Prospects: Limited, if not planning to obtain permanent teaching jobs

Prerequisites:
    Licensure/Certification—A teaching credential or substitute teacher's certificate
    Education/Training—A bachelor's degree; for licensed teachers, completion of an accredited teacher education program
    Experience—Student teaching, internship, or other teaching experience
    Special Skills and Personality Traits—Communication, interpersonal, self-management, and class management skills; firm, decisive, flexible, creative, resourceful

CAREER LADDER

Teacher

↑

Substitute Teacher

↑

Student Teacher or Former Teacher

Position Description

Occasionally, teachers are absent from their classes for various reasons—illness, personal business, mandatory attendance at professional development workshops, and so on. Substitute Teachers are then contacted to fill in for the absent teachers to teach their daily lesson plans, as well as complete their nonteaching duties, such as monitoring students during recesses and supervising club meetings.

When teachers know they will be absent, they put in a request at the school office for a Substitute Teacher. Schools may call Substitute Teachers either in the evening (usually after 5:00 P.M.) or early morning (usually between 6:00 A.M. and 7:00 A.M.) with an assignment. Substitute Teachers often accept assignments in subjects in which they are not formally trained. An assignment may be short-term—for several hours or one or more days—or long-term—for several weeks or months.

Most Substitute Teachers receive short-term assignments, working the absent teachers' schedule—for example, 7:30 A.M. to 3:30 P.M. Typically, they are requested to report to school 15 to 30 minutes earlier so that they can become familiar with the school as well as the absent teacher's routine. Upon reporting to the school office, Substitute Teachers receive classroom keys. They check the absent teachers' mailbox for daily lesson plans, notes from the absent teacher, and any school announcements that are to be made in class. Substitute Teachers also familiarize themselves with the school's rules, the day's schedule, procedures for fire drills, and so on.

Substitute Teachers go over the absent teacher's lesson plans before students arrive in class. Most teachers provide Substitute Teachers with the materials needed to teach the day's lessons or give instructions for preparing instructional materials. If a teacher has not left any lesson plans, or if a Substitute Teacher wants to alter the lesson plans, the Substitute Teacher must first talk with the principal or the appropriate school official. (Some Substitute Teachers carry emergency lesson plans with them so that they are ready for any class should a teacher forget to leave lesson plans.)

From time to time, a teacher's lesson plan does not fill out the class period. Substitute Teachers might then assign exercises or activities to supplement a lesson; for example, a Substitute Teacher might pick out vocabulary words from the day's lesson and have students use the words in sentences. Many Substitute Teachers bring in crossword puzzles, word games, and other activities for students to do if they finish their work early.

Substitute Teachers are responsible for maintaining class order and have the authority to discipline students according to school policies and procedures. If misbehaving students become uncontrollable, Substitute Teachers may send them to the principal's office or request help from the principal or other administrator.

At the end of the school day, Substitute Teachers usually leave the absent teachers a brief summary of the day's activities, including lesson results and student behavior.

Work days for Substitute Teachers are flexible. They can choose how many days and which days of the week they wish to work.

Salaries

Substitute Teachers are paid a per diem, or daily rate, that ranges from $45 to $100 or more per day, depending on the school or school district. Those with teaching credentials usually receive a higher per diem rate. Substitute Teachers may receive an increase in the daily rate after working the same assignment for a maximum number of days. In some school districts, long-term Substitute Teachers may receive a regular teacher's per diem rate.

Employment Prospects

Substitute Teachers are hired by private and public schools for all grade levels—prekindergarten to high school. Many Substitute Teachers work for one or more private schools and/or public school districts.

Job opportunities are readily available nationwide. In the late 1990s, many schools reported a shortage of qualified Substitute Teachers. This trend should continue for the next few years as an increasing number of Substitute Teachers find permanent positions due to the need for replacing a large force of retiring teachers and the creation of additional positions to handle increasing student enrollment.

Advancement Prospects

Many individuals make substitute teaching their career because of the freedom and flexibility of choosing when and where to work, as well as the opportunity to teach different classes and different grade levels. For many Substitute Teachers, receiving choice assignments is an advancement. For many educators, substitute teaching was the stepping stone for starting their careers.

Licensure/Certification

Licensure requirements for Substitute Teachers differ among the states, public school districts, and private schools. Generally, Substitute Teachers are required to hold a valid teaching credential or a local Substitute Teacher Certificate. Some employers require only proof that Substitute Teachers have completed an accredited teacher preparation program. (For more information, contact the public and private schools where you wish to work.)

Education and Training

Most private and public schools require that Substitute Teachers have a bachelor's degree in any field. Some schools accept applicants with a high school or general equivalency diploma if they also have a minimum number of college units.

More and more school districts provide an orientation session for Substitute Teachers, covering topics such as school policies, procedures, and rules; substitute teacher responsibilities; and classroom management strategies.

Experience, Skills, and Personality Traits

Substitute Teachers should have previous teaching experience, particularly with the age groups in the grade levels to which they will be assigned. Many public school districts require that Substitute Teachers have one or more years of classroom teaching experience.

Along with teaching skills, Substitute Teachers need strong communication skills, interpersonal skills, self-management skills (getting to class on time, self-motivation, etc.), and class management skills. Successful Substitute Teachers share several personality traits, such as being firm, decisive, flexible, creative, and resourceful.

Unions/Associations

Many Substitute Teachers join professional associations that provide teaching resources, continuing education programs, opportunities for networking, and other services. Some organizations—such as the International Reading Association, the Council for Exceptional Children, and the National Council for the Social Studies—serve teachers with particular interests.

Tips for Entry

1. When you first start as a Substitute Teacher, accept most, if not all, assignments that are offered you. If you turn down too many assignments, you may not be called as often as you want.
2. Many schools have a priority substitute list. If you like substituting at a specific school, ask the principal if there is such a list and to be placed on it.
3. Many resources are available on the Internet for Substitute Teachers, including message boards that allow networking with Substitute Teachers throughout the United States. To start a search of pertinent web sites, use either of these keywords in a search engine: "substitute teacher" or "substitute teaching."

K–12 TEACHING SPECIALISTS

MUSIC TEACHER

CAREER PROFILE

Duties: Provide general music, choral, or instrumental instruction; create lesson plans; perform nonteaching duties as requested

Alternate Titles: Music Specialist, Band Teacher, Orchestra Teacher, Choral Teacher, Band Director, Choral Director, Orchestra Director

Salary Range: $25,000 to $52,000

Employment Prospects: Good

Advancement Prospects: Good

Prerequisites:
　Licensure/Certification—A teaching credential or other certification
　Education/Training—Bachelor's or master's degree; for licensed teachers, completion of an accredited teacher education program
　Experience—Student teaching, internship, or other teaching experience
　Special Skills and Personality Traits—Performance skills; interpersonal, teamwork, communication, organizational, and management skills; patient, creative, flexible, enthusiastic, energetic

CAREER LADDER

Mentor Teacher or Department Head

↑

Music Teacher

↑

Student Teacher or Substitute Teacher

Position Description

Most public and private schools have a music program as part of their school curriculum for all grade levels, prekindergarten to 12th grade. As specialists in their discipline, Music Teachers introduce schoolchildren to the joy and beauty of music, and teach them basic vocal and instrumental skills.

In elementary and middle-level schools, students usually receive music instruction once or twice a week. Music Teachers at these school levels have the challenge of teaching classes in different schools. It is common, for example, for a Music Teacher to teach five classes at three different schools in one day. At the high school level, music classes are electives and are taught daily by Music Teachers.

Music Teachers provide different instruction at the different grade levels. In prekindergarten, kindergarten, and elementary grades, Music Teachers guide children in activities such as singing, clapping, moving, dancing and playing percussion instruments. They also begin teaching music history and music patterns (such as beat, rhythm, and tempo). In some schools, Music Teachers begin teaching fifth and sixth graders how to play individual instruments.

In the middle-level grades, Music Teachers provide instruction in general music (basic music theory and music appreciation), choral singing, and instruments for band or orchestra. The choir and instrumental classes usually participate in annual school music concerts performed before their communities.

In high school, Music Teachers teach band, choir, and orchestra classes, which are elective classes. As part of their instruction, Music Teachers direct the student bands, orchestras, and choral groups in public performances throughout the year. For example, a band might play at school football games or an orchestra might perform the musical score for a high school play. In many communities, the high school music department is the only source for performance art.

In some high schools, music departments participate in regional, state, or national musical competitions. Music Teachers are responsible for preparing students for the competitions, as well as for supervising and managing students while traveling to and from competitions and during the competitions. In addition, Music Teachers organize the trips—obtaining permission slips; making arrangements for transportation; finding chaperones; and so on. Music Teachers may also be involved in raising funds for transportation, uniforms, meals, and other needs for the music competitions and other music activities.

Like all schoolteachers, Music Teachers carry out their school policies, goals, and objectives. Depending on the school, Music Teachers may be responsible for creating their own curriculum based on school guidelines or other standards. Additionally, they create and prepare daily lesson plans; assess and evaluate students' work; and confer with students and their parents about students' work and behavior. If special education students are part of their classes, Music Teachers modify lessons to fit the students' abilities. A special education teacher is usually available to help Music Teachers with instructional strategies.

Music Teachers—at all school levels—have other duties that may include:

- performing administrative tasks such as taking attendance
- supervising detention or study hall
- acting as a corridor, lunch room, or playground monitor during class breaks
- sponsoring extracurricular activities
- supervising and directing teacher aides, student teachers, and volunteers
- supervising attendance at school functions
- participating in faculty meetings and on school committees

Their work hours often extend into the evenings and on weekends to complete their tasks—grading papers, attending meetings, conferring with parents, fund-raising, and so on. Most Music Teachers have a 10-month work schedule, usually from September to June.

Most public schools give teachers tenure after completing three to five years of continuous teaching service. With tenure, teachers cannot be fired without just cause.

Salaries

Salaries vary and depend on factors such as education, credentials, experience, job responsibilities, and school budgets. Typically, salaries are higher in public schools than in private schools. According to the 1997–98 teacher salary survey by the American Federation of Teachers, the average annual salary for public school teachers, including Music Teachers, ranged between $27,839 and $51,727. The average annual salary for beginning teachers was $25,735.

In addition to a salary, most Music Teachers receive a fringe benefits package that includes holiday pay, sick leave, health benefits, and retirement benefits.

Employment Prospects

Music Teachers are employed in both private and public school settings. Job opportunities are expected to be good for the next few years as many schools will need to find replacements for veteran Music Teachers who are reaching retirement age. In general, teaching jobs are more available in rural areas, urban inner cities, and areas that are experiencing rapid growth.

Advancement Prospects

Music Teachers have several advancement opportunities in schools. Along with becoming mentor teachers, they can become music directors and department heads. They can also pursue administrative positions. Private school teachers can work their way up to positions such as school heads and development directors. With additional education and licensure, public school teachers can become principals, instructional supervisors of music, program directors, and so on.

In addition, Music Teachers can pursue other areas or interests in music. For example, they can become conservatory educators, music librarians, church choir directors, music therapists, music arrangers, or private music teachers.

Licensure/Certification

To teach in public schools, Music Teachers must hold a valid teaching credential in music education. Some states require an endorsement for each music specialty (such as choral or band) that a Music Teacher plans to teach. Licensure requirements vary from state to state. (For specific information, contact the state board of education for the state in which you wish to teach.) Music Teachers may need to complete continuing education units for licensure renewal.

Many private schools require certification from state boards of education, school accreditation groups, professional associations, or other recognized organizations. Some schools, such as Montessori schools, require internal teaching certifications, which are obtained after completing their training programs.

Education and Training

A bachelor's or master's degree in music education is needed to teach in public or private schools. Those applying for teaching licensure must complete an accredited teacher education program that includes course work in pedagogy and instruction of subject matter, as well as a supervised field practicum.

In many schools, beginning teachers are assigned to mentor teachers who advise them with lesson plans, classroom management, and so on. Music Teachers may be required to attend in-service training throughout the year.

Experience, Skills, and Personality Traits

Employers typically hire Music Teachers who have student teaching or other teaching experience with the age groups whom they would be teaching. Employers look for candidates who have musical talent and skills, as well as performance skills. Candidates must be able to work well with people—students, school staff, parents, and the public—thus they need teamwork, communication, and interpersonal skills. In addition, they need organizational and management skills to accomplish the many different tasks that must be done each day.

Some personality traits that successful Music Teachers share are being patient, creative, flexible, enthusiastic, and energetic. They also have a fine sense of humor. In addition, they have a deep passion for inspiring children to learn about music and to perform it.

Unions/Associations

Music Teachers join local, state, and national professional associations that provide teaching resources, continuing education programs, networking opportunities, and so on. Some organizations are specifically for music teachers, such as MENC: The National Association for Music Education and the American String Teachers Association. Most Music Teachers in public schools belong to either of these unions: the National Education Association or the American Federation of Teachers.

Tips for Entry

1. Get experience performing music with a group, such as church choirs or a community band. Also get lots of experience working with the age groups that you wish to teach.
2. Many music educators recommend that high school students prepare themselves for the hard work of being a college music major. They suggest that students regularly practice their music reading, music notation, aural skills, and other basic music skills. In addition to being skilled in voice or an instrument, students should possess fundamental piano keyboard skills.
3. On the Internet, you can learn more about teaching music in schools. You might start by visiting the web site for MENC: The National Association for Music Education (*http://www.menc.org/*).

PHYSICAL EDUCATION TEACHER

CAREER PROFILE

Duties: Provide physical fitness and physical activity instruction; create daily lesson plans; may coach competitive sports; perform nonteaching duties as requested

Alternate Titles: Physical Education Specialist

Salary Range: $25,000 to $52,000

Employment Prospects: Good

Advancement Prospects: Good

Prerequisites:
  Licensure/Certification—A teaching credential or other certification
  Education/Training—Bachelor's degree; for licensed teachers, completion of an accredited teacher education program
  Experience—Student teaching, internship, or other teaching experience
  Special Skills and Personality Traits—Interpersonal, teamwork, communication, organizational, and management skills; self-disciplined, firm, fair, observant, flexible, creative

CAREER LADDER

Mentor Teacher or Department Head

Physical Education Teacher

Student Teacher or Substitute Teacher

Position Description

Most private and public schools have a physical education program for all grade levels—kindergarten to high school—that promotes not only good health and physical competence, but also boosts self-esteem and encourages enjoyment of physical activity. As specialists in their discipline, Physical Education Teachers help students develop lifetime habits of including physical activity into their daily lives.

Physical education instruction is different at each school level. In elementary school, Physical Education Teachers instruct students once or twice a week, usually for 30 minutes. (Many Physical Education Teachers in public schools travel from school to school to teach classes.) In the primary grades, they develop students' gross motor skills—running, jumping, skipping, and so on—and abilities to play cooperative games. Beginning ball activities and working with apparatus, such as jump ropes, are introduced. Beginning sports skills are introduced in the upper elementary grades.

In most middle-level schools, physical education classes are taught every day. Physical Education Teachers teach six or seven periods each day. Instruction includes physical fitness, dance, formal sports skills, and recreational games. In some middle schools and junior high schools, Physical Education Teachers are responsible for teaching health classes.

In high school, Physical Education Teachers also teach six or seven periods of physical education. Some of the activities they teach are physical fitness, dance, weight training, swimming, gymnastics, individual sports, dual sports, and team sports.

At all grade levels, Physical Education Teachers are responsible for planning safe physical activities. They make sure instruction is developmentally appropriate for all students within their classes. If special education students are part of their classes, Physical Education Teachers modify instruction to fit their abilities. (A special education teacher is usually available to help Physical Education Teachers with instructional strategies.) Furthermore, Physical Education Teachers help students develop sports skills such as communication, responsibility, teamwork, and sportsmanship.

As part of their teaching duties, Physical Education Teachers create and prepare daily lesson plans. They assign students class projects, and give quizzes or tests to check students' understanding of new concepts and skills. Physical Education Teachers monitor students' progress, and evaluate their performance at the end of each grading period. Teachers also meet with students and parents to discuss students' work and behavior.

Physical Education Teachers also perform nonteaching duties. They do administrative tasks, such as taking attendance and reading aloud school announcements. They may monitor hallways, lunchrooms, and other parts of the campus during recesses and lunchtimes. Most teachers attend school games, dances, and other functions to help supervise attendance. They may sponsor extracurricular activities, such as clubs, student government, and school publications. They may also supervise and direct teacher aides, student teachers, and volunteer aides. In addition, they participate in faculty meetings and serve on school committees.

Some Physical Education Teachers coach girls' and boys' teams that participate in school athletic leagues. Football, basketball, baseball, volleyball, tennis, soccer, swimming, golf, wrestling, field hockey, and track and field are some of the sports that different Physical Education Teachers coach.

As part of their coaching duties, Physical Education Teachers guide and supervise teams in practice and prepare students for competitions. The coaches are responsible for managing and supervising teams as they travel to and from games and during games. Coaches may also organize competitions that take place in their schools—contacting league officials, referees, and scorekeepers; writing press releases; making sure the grounds, such as baseball diamonds and football fields, are maintained and ready for play; and so on. In addition, Physical Education Teachers, in the role of coaches, may be involved in fund-raising for uniforms, equipment, travel expenses, and other needs for the teams.

Physical Education Teachers work long hours, often into the evenings and on weekends to complete all their tasks. Most Physical Education Teachers have a 10-month work schedule, usually from September to June.

Most public schools give teachers tenure after completing three to five years of continuous teaching service. With tenure, teachers cannot be fired without just cause.

Salaries

A Physical Education Teacher's salary varies from school to school, with salaries typically higher in public schools than in private schools. The American Federation of Teachers reports that in the 1997–98 school year, the national average annual salary for public school teachers, including Physical Education Teachers, was $39,437. Beginning teacher salaries averaged $25,735 per year while the average annual salaries ranged from $27,839 to $51,727. In many schools, Physical Education Teachers receive extra compensation for each sport they coach. They may also receive additional pay for other extracurricular activities they sponsor.

Most Physical Education Teachers receive fringe benefits such as sick leave, vacation leave, medical insurance, and retirement benefits.

Employment Prospects

Physical Education Teachers are employed in both private and public school settings. Job opportunities are expected to be good for the next few years as many schools will need to find replacements for veteran Physical Education Teachers who are reaching retirement age. In general, teaching jobs are more available in rural areas, urban inner cities, and areas that are experiencing rapid growth.

Advancement Prospects

Physical Education Teachers can pursue several career paths. Experienced teachers can become mentor teachers and department heads, as well as head coaches and athletic directors. With additional education and endorsement, Physical Education Teachers can become Adapted Physical Education Teachers, specialists who instruct special education students with physical, emotional, or mental disabilities. They can also become school counselors, educational technologists, or other school-related professionals.

Additionally, they can pursue administrative positions. Private school teachers can work their way up to become school heads and other administrators. With additional education and licensure, public school teachers can become principals, instructional supervisors, program directors, or other school administrators.

Physical Education Teachers can also pursue other areas in their field. For example, they may become university professors, recreation center directors, professional coaches, athletic trainers, or educational consultants.

Licensure/Certification

Physical Education Teachers in public schools must hold a valid teaching credential. The type of license and licensure requirements vary from state to state. Those wishing to coach may need to obtain a coaching endorsement for each sport they plan to coach. (For specific information, contact the state board of education for the state in which you wish to teach.) Physical Education Teachers may need to complete continuing education units and, eventually, obtain a master's degree for licensure renewal.

Many private schools require certification from state boards of education, school accreditation groups, professional associations, or other recognized organizations. Some schools, such as Waldorf schools, require internal teaching certifications, which are obtained after completing their training programs.

Education and Training

Most Physical Education Teachers hold either a bachelor's or master's degree in physical education. Those applying for teaching licensure must complete an accredited teacher education program that includes pedagogy, instruction of subject matter, and a supervised field practicum.

In many schools, beginning teachers are assigned to mentor teachers who advise them with lesson plans, classroom management, and so on. Many schools require teachers to attend in-service workshops throughout the year.

Experience, Skills, and Personality Traits

Most employers choose candidates who have previous experience teaching physical fitness and sports to children, such as student teachers, coaches, and recreational leaders. Many employers prefer Physical Education Teachers who have coaching experiences in competitive sports.

Physical Education Teachers should have strong interpersonal, teamwork, and communication skills as they must be able to work well with students, school staff, and parents. In addition, teachers need organizational and management skills to complete the various tasks they must handle each day.

Successful Physical Education Teachers have several personality traits in common, such as being self-disciplined, firm, fair, observant, flexible, and creative. In addition, they are passionate about teaching children to appreciate lifelong physical fitness, sportsmanship, and the many different physical activities.

Unions/Associations

Physical Education Teachers join local, state, and national teaching associations that provide teaching resources, continuing education programs, network opportunities, and so on. Some organizations, such as the National Association for Sport and Physical Education, specifically serve Physical Education Teachers. Typically, Physical Education Teachers in public schools belong to either of these unions: the American Federation of Teachers or the National Education Association.

Tips for Entry

1. As a middle school, junior high, or high school student, you can begin getting valuable experience working with children. Volunteer (or apply for part-time jobs) in summer camps, community recreation programs, or children's sports leagues, such as baseball or soccer.
2. As an adult, find work in private gyms as aerobics instructors, trainers, and so on.
3. On the Internet you can learn more about teaching physical education in schools. To find relevant web sites, use the keyword "physical education" in any search engine.

READING SPECIALIST

CAREER PROFILE

Duties: Develop, implement, and evaluate school-wide reading programs; perform assessments; provide resources and consulting services to teachers and other school staff; promote reading; perform other duties as needed

Alternate Titles: Reading Supervisor

Salary Range: $27,000 to $52,000

Employment Prospects: Fair

Advancement Prospects: Limited

Prerequisites:
  Licensure/Certification—Teaching credential with a reading specialist endorsement
  Education/Training—Master's degree; for licensed teachers, completion of an accredited reading specialist credential program
  Experience—Two or more years of classroom teaching; some administrative experience
  Special Skills and Personality Traits—Interpersonal, teamwork, communication, supervisory, and program management skills; patient, flexible, creative, hardworking

CAREER LADDER

Lead Reading Specialist or Reading Coordinator

↑

Reading Specialist

↑

Teacher

Position Description

To succeed in school, work, and everyday life, people need adequate reading skills—understanding vocabulary, reading comprehension, critical reading skills, reading and following instructions, interpreting information, understanding graphics, finding information, and so on. Thus, public and private schools provide developmental, remedial, early intervention, and other reading programs for all grade levels, kindergarten through 12th grade.

In many schools, the reading programs are coordinated by Reading Specialists, who are trained in providing effective reading instruction. They may provide guidance to teachers in specific grade levels or in certain schools in a school system. In small schools or school systems, Reading Specialists provide guidance to teachers at all grade levels.

Responsibilities for Reading Specialists vary from school to school. Most Reading Specialists assist administrators in the development of reading programs that follow state educational guidelines or frameworks and align with national and other professional standards. Many Reading Specialists perform reading assessments to determine students' reading abilities when requested by parents, teachers, administrators, or other school personnel. Some Reading Specialists are responsible for coordinating the administration of all formal standardized testing in a school.

Most Reading Specialists act as resources for teachers, parents, and administrators. They distribute useful information, materials, and current research that may help teachers with their instruction. They may provide parents with reading lists and tips about how to get their children to read more at home. Many Reading Specialists plan and conduct in-service training, presenting new reading methods and techniques for improving students' reading skills in academic and nonacademic subjects.

Reading Specialists also provide consulting services to individual teachers. Reading Specialists might discuss various reading and classroom teaching strategies that may help students with reading problems in a teacher's classroom. In addition, specialists might model instructional techniques for teachers. Some Reading Specialists also provide intervention services, working with students individually or in small groups.

In addition, Reading Specialists promote reading in the schools and the community. For example, they may encourage teachers to allow for time in class to read; or they motivate students by providing them with nonfiction and fiction books that match their individual interests. Many Reading Specialists organize school-wide reading contests, reading book clubs, author days, book fairs, and other programs and events to encourage students to read.

Reading Specialists sometimes work into the evenings and on weekends to attend meetings, confer with parents, complete paperwork, and so on. Most Reading Specialists have a 10-month work schedule, usually from September to June.

Salaries

Reading Specialists normally receive a salary based on their school's teacher salary schedule. According to the 1997–98 teacher salary survey by the American Federation of Teachers, the average annual salaries for teachers in public schools ranged from $27,839 to $51,727. In addition to a salary, Reading Specialists receive fringe benefits such as health plans, vacation leave, and retirement benefits.

Employment Prospects

Reading Specialists are hired by public and private schools. Most job opportunities become available as Reading Specialists retire, resign, or advance to other positions. Schools may create additional positions when school funding is available.

Advancement Prospects

Promotions are limited to a few supervisory and administrative positions. With additional education and licensure, Reading Specialists can pursue other school administrative positions such as principals, curriculum specialists, school program directors, or assistant superintendents. Additionally, they can pursue careers in other areas of education; for example, they might become university professors, reading consultants, educational software developers, or private reading program directors.

Licensure/Certification

In public schools, Reading Specialists must hold a valid teaching credential in addition to a reading specialist endorsement. Licensure requirements for a reading specialist credential vary from state to state. (For specific information, contact the state board of education for the state in which you wish to work.) Completion of continuing education units may be required for licensure renewal.

All private schools have their own requirements for teacher certification. In some schools, Reading Specialists must have state licensure. Other schools may require certification from a specific school accreditation group, professional association, or other recognized organization. Some private schools, such as Waldorf schools, require internal teaching certifications.

Education and Training

Reading Specialists have a master's degree in education or reading education. To obtain a reading specialist credential, teachers must complete a reading specialist program from an accredited reading education program. The program includes courses on the reading process, instructional strategies, diagnosis in reading, reading in the content areas, and so on. It also includes a supervised field practicum.

Experience, Skills, and Personality Traits

Reading Specialists should have previous classroom teaching experience. To obtain licensure, Reading Specialists need two or more years of classroom teaching, depending on the state where they live. In addition, they should have some administrative experience. Reading Specialists also need interpersonal, teamwork, communication, supervisory, and program management skills in order to perform their responsibilities effectively each day.

Successful Reading Specialists share several personality traits, such as being patient, flexible, creative, and hardworking. They have a passion for reading and the desire to help children find the joy, and competency, in reading for themselves.

Unions/Associations

Most Reading Specialists join local and state professional reading councils and reading teacher associations. Many also join the International Reading Association, a national organization. These organizations provide services such as current research, professional resources, continuing education programs, and networking opportunities. In addition, most Reading Specialists in public schools belong to either of these unions: the American Federation of Teachers or the National Education Association.

Tips for Entry

1. To learn more about the profession, talk with Reading Specialists. If possible, help out on book fairs and other promotional programs that the Reading Specialist in your school may organize.
2. Some college and university education departments offer a graduate program that combines the reading education and Reading Specialist credential

programs. The credential program is finished first thus allowing students the opportunity to obtain employment while completing their master's program.

3. You can learn more about reading issues on the Internet. One place to start is at the International Reading Association's web site (*http://www.reading.org*).

SPECIAL EDUCATION TEACHER

CAREER PROFILE

Duties: Provide instruction to students with disabilities; prepare lesson plans, provide consulting services to general education teachers; participate in Individualized Education Program (IEP) meetings; complete paperwork; perform other duties as needed

Alternate Titles: Special Education Resource Teacher; Visually Impaired Teacher, Learning Disabled Teacher, and other titles that reflect the area of specialization

Salary Range: $25,000 to $52,000

Employment Prospects: Excellent

Advancement Prospects: Good

Prerequisites:
  Licensure/Certification—A teacher's credential with a special education endorsement
  Education/Training—Bachelor's or master's degree; for state licensure, completion of an accredited special education teacher education program
  Experience—Student teaching, internship, or other teaching experience with children with disabilities
  Special Skills and Personality Traits—Interpersonal, teamwork, communication, organizational, behavior management, report-writing skills; patient, honest, creative, flexible, firm

CAREER LADDER

Mentor Teacher or Department Head

Special Education Teacher

Teacher, Substitute Teacher, or Student Teacher

Position Description

Public and private schools are mandated by the Individuals with Disabilities Education Act (IDEA), a federal law, to provide special education programs and related services to children with disabilities from newborn to age 21. The law ensures that all special education students receive the same instruction and assessment that regular students receive in general education classrooms. Special education programs serve children with autism, traumatic brain injury, mental retardation, specific learning disabilities, visual impairment, hearing impairment, speech or language impairment, orthopedic impairment, serious emotional disturbance, and multiple disabilities. Gifted and talented children are also served by special education programs.

Special Education Teachers, who are trained in one or more specialties, provide instruction in academic subjects as well as other skills that students need to succeed in school and in life. They help students develop behavioral management skills—getting along with others, being comfortable in social situations, practicing socially acceptable behavior, and so on. Many also help students learn study skills. Some Special Education Teachers help students develop life skills for an independent life. For example, they might teach students how to read bus schedules or balance checkbooks. Some teachers help students prepare for life after high school by teaching them job search skills and providing career counseling.

When planning instruction, Special Education Teachers follow instructional goals and objectives and evaluation procedures that are outlined on students' Individualized Education Programs (IEPs). Special Education Teachers may be involved in providing assessments and evaluations of special education students, as well as developing IEPs.

Special Education Teachers teach in a variety of settings. Some teach in self-contained classrooms, providing instruction for all subjects to a small group of special education students. The students usually have different abilities, skill levels, and learning styles, so teachers must modify instruction to fit each student's needs. To help with instruction, teachers may use specialized equipment such as audiotapes, educational software programs, and computers with synthesized speech.

Many special education students are mainstreamed into general education classrooms to receive instruction alongside regular students for one or more subjects. Some special education students receive instruction for all subjects in general education classrooms. These classrooms are often referred to as inclusive classrooms. In some inclusive classrooms, general education teachers and Special Education Teachers work collaboratively to prepare lesson plans and provide instruction to all the students. Special Education Teachers use their expertise to adapt the lessons and materials to the skill levels and abilities of the special education students.

Many Special Education Teachers work in resource rooms, providing support services to special education students in general education classrooms. They work with special education students in resource rooms for a few hours each day on specific subjects, such as math or reading. The teachers individualize instruction to fit the students' abilities and learning styles so that they can best learn their lessons. For example, a learning disabled student learns best aurally, so the Special Education Resource Teacher helps the student read his math assignments aloud.

Some Special Education Teachers travel from school to school providing instructional support to special education students in the different schools. Most traveling, or itinerant, Special Education Teachers work with visually, hearing, and physically impaired students.

As part of their duties, resource and itinerant Special Education Teachers also provide consulting services to general education teachers. They help general education teachers modify their teaching methods and instructional materials to fit the needs of their special education students.

Some Special Education Teachers are also case managers, overseeing the IEP for each student on their caseload. As case managers, they make sure IEPs are being implemented and followed by general education teachers, special education teachers, and specialists such as school social workers and speech-language pathologists. Case managers also schedule and coordinate meetings; maintain individual IEP files; and act as liaison between schools and parents.

Some Special Education Teachers supervise teacher aides and volunteer aides who help them with instruction and clerical work. Some Special Education Teachers also supervise and advise student teachers.

Depending on the school, Special Education Teachers may perform other tasks, such as monitoring duties, study hall supervision, and extracurricular activity supervision. They also participate in faculty meetings and on school committees.

Special Education Teachers work long hours each day, often completing tasks at home in the evenings and on weekends. Most work 10-month schedules, from September to June.

Most public schools offer tenure to teachers after they have completed three to five years of continuous service. With tenure, teachers cannot be fired from their jobs without due cause.

Salaries

Along with a salary, Special Education Teachers usually receive fringe benefits, such as sick leave, medical insurance, and retirement benefits. Their pay depends on factors such as licensure, education, experience, and school budgets. Salaries are typically higher in public schools than in private schools. According to the American Federation of Teachers 1997–98 teacher salary survey, the national average annual salary for public school teachers, including Special Education Teachers, was $39,437. The national average salary for beginning teachers was $25,735 and the average annual salaries ranged between $27,839 and $51,727.

Employment Prospects

Special Education Teachers work for public and private schools. Job opportunities are readily available at all school levels—preschools, elementary schools, middle level schools, and high schools. According to the Council for Exceptional Children, special education is an area of critical need in most states. The greatest demand is for teachers of students with emotional disturbance and other low-incidence disabilities such as autism, visual impairment, hearing impairment, and orthopedic problems. A new and growing demand is for bilingual Special Education Teachers, especially in Texas, California, and Florida.

Advancement Prospects

With additional education and licensure, Special Education Teachers can advance to any number of professions. They may become special education work study coordinators, program supervisors, or directors. They may also become educational diagnosticians, adapted physical education teachers, or special education technology specialists. In addition, they may become school psychologists, social workers, speech pathologists, creative arts therapists, and other professionals who provide related services to special education students.

Special Education Teachers also can pursue school administrative positions. In private schools, teachers can become school heads, deans of students, and other administrators.

With additional education and licensure, teachers in public schools can become principals and district administrators such as curriculum specialists and assistant superintendents.

Additionally, Special Education Teachers can pursue careers in other areas of education. For example, they may become corporate trainers, textbook editors, university professors, or educational consultants.

Licensure/Certification

In public schools, Special Education Teachers must hold a valid teaching credential in elementary, middle-level, or secondary education with a special education endorsement in each specialty—learning disabled, severely handicapped, visually impaired, and so on—that they wish to teach. The type of special education licensure and requirements vary from state to state. (For specific information, contact the state board of education for the state in which you wish to teach.) Special Education Teachers may be required to complete continuing education units and, eventually, obtain a master's degree for licensure renewal.

All private schools have their own requirements about teacher certification. Some schools require that Special Education Teachers have a state teaching license. Some private schools, such as Montessori schools, require internal teaching certifications. Other schools may require certification from certain school accreditation groups, professional associations, or other recognized organizations.

Education and Training

Special Education Teachers must have a bachelor's or master's degree in the discipline for which they receive their teaching credential. Many Special Education Teachers also have a master's degree in special education.

Licensed teachers have completed a teacher education program leading to special education licensure in addition to the general teacher education training program for the teaching credential. The special education teacher program includes a supervised field practicum and course work in the different disabilities, pedagogy, assessment and testing strategies, behavior management techniques, and laws regarding special education.

Beginning teachers may be assigned to mentor teachers who advise them with lesson plans, classroom management, and so on. Many Special Education Teachers enroll in continuing education programs to keep up with new teaching methods, changes in laws, and so on.

Experience, Skills, and Personality Traits

Schools typically hire entry-level Special Education Teachers who have previous experience working with children with disabilities. For example, they may have been student teachers, teacher aides, peer tutors, counselors, or volunteers in special education settings.

Interpersonal, teamwork, and communication skills are necessary for Special Education Teachers. They must be able to work well with their students as well as with teachers, administrators, school-related professionals, and parents. Furthermore, Special Education Teachers should develop strong organizational, behavior management, and report-writing skills.

Being patient, honest, creative, and flexible are some of the personality traits that successful Special Education Teachers share. They also have a good sense of humor. In addition, they are firm, being able to set limits to students' behavior. Above all, they love special-needs children unconditionally and are open to the challenges of teaching them.

Unions/Associations

Special Education Teachers join local, state, and national professional organizations that provide teaching resources, continuing education programs, network opportunities, and so on. Some organizations specifically serve special needs teachers, such as the Council for Exceptional Children and the Learning Disabilities Association of America. In addition, Special Education Teachers in public schools belong to either of these unions: the American Federation of Teachers or the National Education Association.

Tips for Entry

1. Gain experience working with children with different disabilities, as well as with the different ages (infants to age 21) in a variety settings—schools, residential facilities, juvenile detention centers, psychiatric settings, and so on. You might also volunteer with community programs that serve children with disabilities, such as Special Olympics, United Cerebral Palsy Association, or The Arc (formerly known as the Association for Retarded Citizens).
2. Many school districts offer alternative credentials for Special Education Teachers. Contact a district central school office to find out what may be available.
3. Use the job interview to get more specific information about a position. After the interviewers have asked their questions, ask yours. Have them clarify what your responsibilities would be. Find out what the class load is like, what the school's philosophy on special education is, what kind of support special education teachers receive, and so on.
4. To learn about special education on the Internet, you might start by visiting the web site for the Council for Exceptional Children (*http://www.cec.sped.org/*).

BILINGUAL TEACHER

CAREER PROFILE

Duties: Provide instruction of academic subjects in English and a second language; create daily lesson plans; perform other duties as requested

Alternative Title: Bilingual Education Teacher

Salary Range: $25,000 to $52,000

Employment Prospects: Excellent

Advancement Prospects: Good

Prerequisites:
  Licensure/Certification—Teaching credential with a bilingual education teaching endorsement
  Education/Training—Bachelor's or master's degree; for licensed teachers, completion of an accredited teacher education program
  Experience—Student teaching, internship, or other teaching experience in bilingual or ESL settings
  Special Skills and Personality Traits—Literate in a second language; communication, interpersonal, teamwork, organizational, and management skills; patient, flexible, creative, sensitive

CAREER LADDER

Mentor Teacher or Department Head

Bilingual Teacher

Teacher or Student Teacher

Position Description

Thousands of children in public and private schools are only minimally able to speak, read, write, or understand English. Some schoolchildren have no English language skills at all. Thus, these limited-English-proficient (LEP) students have two goals in school—to learn English and to learn the subjects that are being taught at their grade level. (Research shows that it generally takes between five to seven years to develop enough English language skills to understand academic instruction.)

Many schools use bilingual programs and/or ESL (English as a Second Language) programs to help LEP students. Each program has a different focus. ESL programs teach LEP students only English language skills, providing instruction only in English. In bilingual programs, Bilingual Teachers provide instruction of academic subjects in two languages—English and the native language of the LEP students in the class, which may be Spanish, Russian, Korean, Chinese, Vietnamese, Tagalog, and so on.

Bilingual programs are mostly used in kindergarten, elementary grades, and middle-level grades. There are different types of bilingual programs, but almost all bilingual programs have an ESL component in which LEP students are "pulled out" from their bilingual classes for a few hours a day to learn English language skills. One type of bilingual program is the transitional bilingual program in which Bilingual Teachers teach subjects in English, and use the native language only to help students understand instruction. Another type is the developmental bilingual program. In this program, Bilingual Teachers provide instruction in both languages so that children can become literate in both English and their native language. Classes in transitional and developmental bilingual programs are usually made up of LEP students who all speak the same native language. Still another type of program is the two-way immersion bilingual program, in which Bilingual Teachers use both English and a second language to teach the academic subjects. Classes in this program are made up of LEP students and native English-speaking students. (Successful two-way immersion programs are popular with many English-speaking parents who want their children to learn valuable second language skills and fluency as well as be exposed to a cross-cultural learning environment.)

Bilingual Teachers are responsible for preparing lesson plans in two languages. They often create their own student materials because of the lack of published materials. In addition, Bilingual Teachers continually assess and monitor their students' performance and behavior. In some schools, Bilingual Teachers work collaboratively in preparing lesson plans and providing instruction to students.

Bilingual Teachers also perform many nonteaching duties. They complete administrative tasks, such as taking attendance and reading school announcements. Many may have monitoring duties during class breaks; they may also help supervise attendance at school functions. Some Bilingual Teachers supervise and direct bilingual aides, tutors, and school volunteers who may be assigned to help them in class. In addition, Bilingual Teachers participate in faculty meetings and on school committees. Some teachers also coach after-school sports or sponsor extracurricular activities, such as school clubs, computer labs, or tutoring programs.

Some Bilingual Teachers are resource teachers for one or more schools or school districts, working with LEP students who are "pulled out" from their general education classrooms. Many Bilingual Teachers also provide consulting services to general education teachers who have LEP students in their classrooms. In addition, some Bilingual Teachers are in charge of administering and coordinating language assessment tests.

Bilingual Teachers work long hours, often into the evenings and on weekends to complete all their tasks. Most have a 10-month work schedule, usually from September to June.

Most public schools give teachers tenure after completing three to five years of continuous teaching service. With tenure, teachers cannot be fired without just cause and due process.

Salaries

Salaries are typically higher in public schools than in private schools. The American Federation of Teachers reports that the national average annual salary for beginning teachers in public schools, including Bilingual Teachers, was $25,735 for the 1997–98 school year. The average annual salaries for teachers ranged from $27,839 to $51,727. Some schools pay additional compensation to Bilingual Teachers who coach or sponsor extracurricular activities.

In addition to a salary, Bilingual Teachers receive fringe benefits such as sick leave, holiday pay, health plans, and retirement benefits.

Employment Prospects

Bilingual Teachers are employed by public and private schools. Many schools throughout the United States, particularly in Florida, Texas, and California, report a shortage of qualified, licensed Bilingual Teachers who are literate in Spanish. Depending on the region, teachers literate in Russian, eastern European languages, Chinese, Korean, Vietnamese, or Southeastern Asian languages are also in demand.

Advancement Prospects

Bilingual Teachers have several advancement opportunities. They may become mentor teachers, department heads, or program coordinators. They can pursue administrative positions, becoming assistant principals, principals, and administrators in the central school office. Furthermore, they can pursue their careers in other settings. For instance, they might become educational researchers, university professors, textbook editors, or bilingual education consultants.

Licensure/Certification

Bilingual Teachers in public schools must hold a teaching credential in elementary, middle level, or secondary education along with a bilingual education endorsement. (For information about requirements, contact the state board of education for the state in which you wish to teach.) Bilingual Teachers may need to complete continuing education units and, eventually, a master's degree for licensure renewal.

Many private schools require certification from state boards of education, school accreditation groups, professional associations, or other recognized organizations. Some schools require internal teaching certifications, which are obtained after completing their training programs.

Education and Training

Because Bilingual Teachers teach academic subjects, they should have at least a bachelor's degree in their discipline. For example, to teach bilingual classes in elementary grades, a Bilingual Teacher might have a bachelor's degree in liberal studies. In some schools, a master's degree in education or other related field is required.

Licensed Bilingual Teachers have completed an accredited teacher education program for elementary, middle, or secondary education licensure, as well as a bilingual education program leading to bilingual education licensure. The bilingual education program includes a supervised field practicum and courses in second language acquisition theory and pedagogy that focuses on integration of language.

In some schools, new Bilingual Teachers may be assigned to mentor teachers who advise them on teaching strategies, classroom management, and so on. Many schools require Bilingual Teachers to attend in-service workshops throughout the year.

Experience, Skills, and Personality Traits

In general, Bilingual Teachers should have previous teaching experience in bilingual or ESL settings. They should be sufficiently proficient in a second language in order to assess a student's language proficiency in both the native language and English.

Because Bilingual Teachers must work well with students, parents, and school staff, they should have adequate communication, interpersonal, and teamwork skills. In addition, organizational and management skills are also needed to complete the many, different tasks that must be done each day.

Successful Bilingual Teachers share several personality traits, among them patience, flexibility, and creativity. They are sensitive to the needs and changes that take place in children as they learn a second language in a new culture. In addition, Bilingual Teachers are passionate about helping all students succeed in their school careers.

Unions/Associations

Bilingual Teachers join local, state, and national professional organizations that provide teaching resources, continuing education programs, networking opportunities, and so on. Some organizations specifically serve bilingual educators, such as the National Association for Bilingual Education and TESOL, Inc. (Teachers of English to Speakers of Other Languages, Inc.). In addition, most public school Bilingual Teachers belong to either of these two unions: the American Federation of Teachers or the National Education Association.

Tips for Entry

1. Keep up your second language proficiency, taking classes, if necessary. You should be literate in reading, writing, and speaking skills in your second language.
2. Many school districts offer alternative certification programs to encourage bilingual aides and individuals literate in Spanish or other languages in demand to become Bilingual Teachers. To learn what may be available in your area, contact the state board of education or a school office.
3. For more information about bilingual education on the Internet, visit these web sites: the National Clearinghouse for Bilingual Education (*http://www.ncbe.gwu.edu*) and the National Association for Bilingual Education (*http://www.nabe.org*).

ESL (ENGLISH AS A SECOND LANGUAGE) TEACHER

CAREER PROFILE

Duties: Teach English as a second language to limited-English-proficient (LEP) students; provide consulting services to mainstream ESL teachers; perform other duties as required

Salary Range: $25,000 to $52,000

Employment Prospects: Excellent

Advancement Prospects: Good

Prerequisites:
  Licensure/Certification—Teaching credential with an ESL teaching endorsement
  Education/Training—Bachelor's or master's degree; for licensed teachers, completion of an accredited teacher education program
  Experience—Student teaching or other teaching experience in ESL settings; knowledge of other cultures is desirable
  Special Skills and Personality Traits—Communication, interpersonal, teamwork, organizational, and management skills; patient, flexible, creative, respectful

CAREER LADDER

Mentor Teacher or Department Head

ESL Teacher

Teacher or Student Teacher

Position Description

Every year, thousands of children who have little or no English language skills enroll in public and private schools in the U.S. Their primary language may be Spanish, Japanese, Korean, Chinese, Khmer, Lao, Tagalog, German, Polish, Russian, Ukrainian, Arabic, and so on. Linguistic research shows that most LEP children are able to learn social English language skills within one to three years. But it takes longer for LEP students to learn sufficient academic English language skills in order to be successful in school.

To help LEP students, many schools have English as a Second Language (ESL) programs that provide English language acquisition services. ESL programs are found at all school levels—elementary schools, middle-level schools, and high schools. They are run by ESL Teachers and other staff members who are specialists in English language acquisition.

In most ESL programs, LEP students are pulled out from their general education or bilingual classrooms for a few hours each day to receive instruction in English language skills—listening, speaking, reading, and writing skills. ESL Teachers provide all instruction in English although classes are typically made up of students who have different native languages. ESL Teachers may or may not know a second language; however, they are aware of the transitions that immigrants and refugees experience as they learn a new language and culture. Many ESL Teachers have teacher aides who are fluent in native languages to help LEP students.

Different teaching methods are used to instruct ESL students. For example, many ESL teachers use the language arts approach in which reading, spelling, grammar, writing, literature, and speech are taught and developed at the same time. Students learn these English language skills in the context of learning content such as the water cycle, American symbols, or a current event.

Like all other schoolteachers, ESL Teachers create and prepare daily lesson plans. Many ESL Teachers create their own student materials—worksheets, word games, and so on—because of the lack of published materials. In addition, ESL Teachers continually assess students' skill levels and monitor their progress.

In many schools, advanced ESL students are placed in ESL mainstream content area classes, such as U.S. history, general science, and math, which are taught by general education teachers. Some ESL Teachers are responsible for conducting in-service workshops and providing consulting services to mainstream ESL teachers. They may teach mainstream ESL Teachers about ESL teaching methods and second-language acquisition theories. ESL Teachers may also advise mainstream ESL teachers on how to alter their teaching strategies and modify instructional materials, as well as discuss the cultural differences among their ESL students.

Most ESL Teachers have nonteaching duties, such as taking daily attendance, performing monitoring duties during class breaks, conferring with parents, participating in faculty and school committee meetings, and supervising at school functions. Many ESL Teachers also sponsor extracurricular activities, such as clubs and after-school tutoring programs.

ESL Teachers work long hours, often completing tasks (calling parents, grading papers, preparing lesson plans, and so on) from their homes in the evenings and on weekends. Most ESL Teachers have 10-month work schedules, usually working from September to June.

Most public schools give teachers tenure after they have completed three to five years of continuous teaching service. With tenure, teachers cannot be fired without just cause and due process.

Salaries

Salaries vary, and depend on factors such as licensure, degrees, experience, and school budgets. Salaries are typically higher in public schools than in private schools. In the 1997–98 school year, the national average annual salary for beginning teachers in public schools was $25,735, according to the American Federation of Teachers. Average annual salaries for all public school teachers, including ESL teachers, ranged from $27,839 to $51,727. In some schools, ESL Teachers may receive extra compensation for coaching after-school sports or sponsoring extracurricular activities.

In addition to a salary, ESL Teachers receive fringe benefits such as vacation leave, medical insurance, dental insurance, and retirement benefits.

Employment Prospects

ESL Teachers work in both public and private schools where jobs are readily available at all grade levels. According to TESOL, Inc. (Teachers of English to Speakers of Other Languages, Inc.), trained, qualified ESL Teachers are in great demand, particularly in California, Florida, Illinois, New York, Texas, as well as in most urban areas in any state.

Advancement Prospects

ESL Teachers can advance their careers in any number of ways. They may become mentor teachers, department heads, and program coordinators. They may also pursue administrative positions, becoming principals or central office administrators. Additionally, they can pursue careers in other areas of education; for instance, they can become university professors, English language development researchers, textbook editors, or private ESL program administrators.

Licensure/Certification

To teach in public schools, ESL Teachers must hold a teaching license in elementary, middle level, or secondary education along with an ESL teaching endorsement. (For information about current requirements, contact the state board of education for the state in which you wish to teach.) ESL Teachers may also need to complete minimum continuing education units and, eventually, obtain a master's degree for licensure renewal.

Private schools may require certification from state boards of education, school accreditation groups, professional associations, or other recognized organizations. Some schools require internal teaching certifications. Other schools require no certification at all.

Education and Training

ESL Teachers need either a bachelor's or master's degree, depending on state licensure or school requirements.

Licensed ESL Teachers have completed an accredited teacher education program in elementary, middle, or secondary education, as well as an ESL education program leading to licensure. The ESL education program includes a supervised field practicum and course work in second language acquisition, teaching methods in ESL, testing and evaluation of ESL students, and ESL materials development.

In some schools, beginning ESL Teachers are assigned to mentor teachers who advise them about teaching strategies, behavior management, and so on. Many ESL Teachers are required to attend in-service workshops throughout the year.

Experience, Skills, and Personality Traits

In general, employers choose candidates who have practical experience teaching LEP students as student teachers, volunteer tutors, and so on. Employers prefer candidates who have knowledge of other cultures and have learned a second language, regardless of proficiency. Furthermore, they look for candidates who have strong communication, interpersonal, teamwork, organizational, and management skills, which teachers need to complete their many different duties each day.

Successful ESL Teachers share several personality traits, such as being patient, flexible, creative, and respectful. They are also passionate about teaching, and enjoy and appreciate working with people from different cultures.

Unions/Associations

Many ESL Teachers belong to TESOL, Inc. (Teachers of English to Speakers of Other Languages, Inc.), a professional organization that offers networking opportunities, teacher resources, continuing education programs, and other services. In addition, ESL teachers belong to other local, state, and national teacher organizations. Most ESL Teachers in public schools belong to one of these unions: the American Federation of Teachers or the National Education Association.

Tips for Entry

1. Gain experience working with people of other cultures. For example, you might volunteer as a tutor in ESL programs in schools, community centers, churches, and other settings.

2. Broaden your experience of other cultures. You might learn another language, read books or watch films and videotapes about different cultures, attend ethnic festivals, eat at ethnic restaurants, or learn to cook ethnic dishes. You might visit other countries as a tourist or a volunteer with a group such as the Peace Corps. Or, you might teach English abroad for private and public schools, language institutes, and private corporations.

3. You can learn more about teaching ESL in schools on the Internet. You might start by visiting TESOL's web site (*http://www.tesol.org*).

SPECIALISTS
IN STUDENT SERVICES
AND SPECIAL EDUCATION-
RELATED SERVICES

SCHOOL NURSE

CAREER PROFILE

Duties: Provide first aid treatment; monitor students' health; provide health assessments and evaluations; provide health education and health counseling; perform other duties as required

Salary Range: $20,000 to $45,000

Employment Prospects: Good

Advancement Prospects: Limited

Prerequisites:
  Licensure/Certification—Registered nurse license; school nurse certification
  Education/Training—Bachelor's degree; for school licensure, completion of an accredited school nurse program
  Experience—One year of work experience as a registered nurse
  Special Skills and Personality Traits—Communication, listening, interpersonal, teamwork, problem-solving, organizational, and recordkeeping skills; calm, patient, sympathetic, caring, trustworthy, respectful

CAREER LADDER

Lead School Nurse

School Nurse

Student

Position Description

Almost all public and private schools (preschools to high schools) have a School Nurse available for their students on campus. As a registered nurse with special training, the School Nurse's main purpose is to provide quality health care to students.

School Nurses have many different responsibilities. One area of responsibility is providing first aid treatment to students when they become ill or injured during the school day.

Another area of responsibility is monitoring students' health and maintaining their health records. School Nurses make sure that all students have received necessary immunizations, and notify parents to have their children get shots if they have not. Each year, School Nurses conduct or arrange for vision, hearing, scoliosis, growth, and other mandated screenings. When needed, School Nurses provide parents with referrals to medical doctors, opthalmologists, and other health care professionals.

If School Nurses suspect that students have disabilities that may be causing learning problems, they can refer students to a school assessment team. The team determines if students have any disabilities that may qualify them for the school's special education program.

In many schools, School Nurses may be part of a student assessment team to provide student health assessments and evaluations. School Nurses may also participate in developing Individualized Education Programs (IEPs) for special education students. An IEP outlines the goals and objectives for instruction and related services that School Nurses or other school specialists might provide.

Most School Nurses provide health education services to students, parents, and school staff. They are resource persons for teachers in health instruction. They may plan and conduct in-service training for teachers and other school staff. Some School Nurses are responsible for planning and teaching health classes to students. Many School Nurses also participate in developing health curriculum for their schools or districts. In addition, many School Nurses help school administrators develop procedures for school safety, accident prevention, and other health policies.

Many School Nurses provide health counseling to students, individually or in small groups. They cover issues such as mental health problems, substance abuse, eating disorders, and pregnancy so that students can make responsible decisions about their health and lifestyles.

In addition, School Nurses may be responsible for any of these duties:

- help plan in the control and prevention of colds, flu, and other communicable diseases
- administer prescribed medications to students
- maintain health education resource files
- act as liaison between school, home, and community
- participate in investigating cases of suspected child abuse and neglect

School Nurses may be assigned to one or more schools. They may be full-time or part-time employees.

Salaries

Salaries vary, and depend on factors such as education, experience, job duties, and school budgets. In a 1997 salary survey by *School Nurse News,* most School Nurses earned an annual salary between $20,000 and $45,000. In some schools, School Nurses receive additional pay for teaching health classes.

In addition to a salary, School Nurses receive fringe benefits such as medical insurance and retirement benefits.

Employment Prospects

Along with private and public schools, School Nurses are employed by county and state health departments. Most positions become available as School Nurses retire, resign, or advance to other positions. With the increasing number of students with special needs, the demand for School Nurses should be steady. However, the creation of new opportunities depends on the availability of school funding.

Advancement Prospects

Promotions within the school setting are limited to few supervisory and administrative positions; and those are mostly found in large schools and school districts. With additional education and licensure, School Nurses can become school nurse practitioners, which leads to higher pay and complex responsibilities.

Another career option is to work in other settings—hospitals, rehabilitation facilities, nursing homes, and so on. School nurses can also pursue other nursing specialties, such as clinical nurse specialists, certified nurse-midwives, or nurse practitioners. Still other options include becoming community college instructors or university professors.

Licensure/Certification

School Nurses must be state licensed registered nurses. In addition, many states require that School Nurses in public schools and some private schools be licensed by the state board of education. Requirements for registered nurse and School Nurse licensure vary from state to state. For specific information, contact the nursing and education licensing boards for the state in which you wish to work.

Education and Training

School Nurses must have graduated from an accredited nursing program in which they earned a diploma, associate degree, or bachelor's degree in nursing, depending on their state's requirement for registered nurses. In most states, a bachelor's degree is needed to obtain school nurse licensure.

To obtain school nurse licensure, registered nurses must complete an accredited school nurse program, which includes course work in education, health education, prevention of illness, health promotion, and health maintenance. In addition, students complete a supervised field practicum in one or more school settings.

Experience, Skills, and Personality Traits

Many schools require at least one year of work experience as a registered nurse, preferably in a school or other public health setting. Also, many schools prefer hiring School Nurses with some teaching experience.

To complete their many different duties each day, School Nurses need communication and listening skills, interpersonal and teamwork skills, as well as problem-solving, organizational, and recordkeeping skills.

Successful School Nurses share many personality traits, such as being calm, patient, sympathetic, caring, trustworthy, and respectful. They also genuinely enjoy being around schoolchildren and care for their well-being.

Unions/Associations

School Nurses might join the National Association of School Nurses, the American Nurses Association, or the American School Health Association in addition to other state and local healthcare provider organizations. These professional associations provide School Nurses with services such as networking opportunities, information resources, continuing education programs, and job listings. School Nurses in public schools may be represented by these unions: the National Education Association or the American Federation of Teachers.

Tips for Entry

1. In high school, you can begin preparing for a nursing career by taking classes in science, biology, chemistry, mathematics, psychology, and English.
2. Get experience working with children in health care settings. For example, you might volunteer in hospitals, health clinics, or community health programs.
3. To learn more about the School Nurse profession on the Internet, visit the web site for the National Association of School Nurses (*http://www.nasn.org*).

EDUCATIONAL DIAGNOSTICIAN

CAREER PROFILE

Duties: Provide student assessments; help develop education plans for individual students; provide consultation services to parents and school staff; perform other duties as required

Alternate Title: Learning Disabilities Teacher-Consultant

Salary Range: $27,000 to $52,000

Employment Prospects: Good

Advancement Prospects: Limited

Prerequisites
  Licensure/Certification—Teaching credential with an Educational Diagnostician (or Learning Disabilities Teacher-Consultant) endorsement
  Education/Training—Master's degree; completion of an approved certification program
  Experience—Three years as a classroom teacher
  Special Skills and Personality Traits—Leadership, teamwork, interpersonal, and communication skills; careful, logical, thorough, sympathetic

CAREER LADDER

Student Services Coordinator

Educational Diagnostician

Teacher

Position Description

Educational Diagnosticians are specialists who determine if students' academic failures are due to learning problems, and if the basis of their learning problems is a learning disorder, or disability. A learning disability is caused by a condition, such as dyslexia, brain dysfunction, brain injury, or developmental aphasia, which affects the way the brain is able to process information. Thus a student with a learning disability would have trouble performing one or more of these skills: listening, speaking, reading, writing, spelling, and doing math. Learning disabled students may also have problems with paying attention, coordination, and self-control.

The job duties of Educational Diagnosticians vary from school to school; but, in general, their primary function is to perform student assessments as part of school assessment teams, which may be composed of teachers, administrators, school psychologists, school social workers, school nurses, and other school specialists. Different assessment teams determine whether students are eligible for special education, bilingual education, or other programs that may help students succeed academically in school. Team members work together to obtain an in-depth assessment of students referred by teachers, parents, administrators, or other school specialists. Each team member performs a student assessment according to his or her expertise.

When performing student assessments, Educational Diagnosticians administer several standardized tests to determine students' achievement levels in reading, writing, and math, as well as general information in science, social studies, and other subjects. They assess students' cognitive and sensory abilities in areas such as reasoning, comprehension, visual processing, and short-term memory. Upon completion of their assessments, Educational Diagnosticians write reports of their findings with recommendations to help the students succeed in school.

Many student assessments are performed for placement in special education programs. When a student is placed in a special education program, then the assessment team develops an Individualized Education Program (IEP) for the student. In general, the IEP describes the annual goals and learning objectives for the student, the types and amounts of special education instruction and related services (such as occupational therapy) that are needed, and the evaluation procedures for measuring the student's progress.

Educational Diagnosticians also provide consultation services to parents, teachers, and other school staff. For example, they might help individual teachers modify teaching methods and techniques for more effective instruction. Or, Educational Diagnosticians might help instructional supervisors develop in-service workshops that cover topics such as dyslexia, teaching strategies, and current laws such as the Individuals with Disabilities Act (IDEA).

As part of their job, Educational Diagnosticians write required correspondence, reports, and proposals. They also complete forms and other paperwork in compliance with federal and state laws as well as local education agency policies and procedures. In addition, they keep up with current legislation and research on testing methods, learning disabilities, and other topics and issues relevant to their field through individual study or continuing education.

Educational Diagnosticians may be assigned to one or more schools in a school system. They work 40 hours a week, and on occasion may work longer to attend meetings, complete paperwork, confer with parents, and so on.

Salaries

Most Educational Diagnosticians earn a salary based on their school's teacher salary schedule. According to the American Federation of Teachers, the average annual salaries for public school teachers ranged from $27,839 to $51,727 for the 1997–98 school year. In addition to a salary, Educational Diagnosticians receive fringe benefits such as medical insurance, vacation leave, sick leave, and retirement benefits.

Employment Prospects

In addition to public and private schools, Educational Diagnosticians are employed by hospitals, corporate settings, private practices, and state and federal agencies.

The National Clearinghouse for Professions in Special Education reports that the job outlook for Educational Diagnosticians in schools looks favorable. Most positions become available as Educational Diagnosticians retire, resign, or advance to other positions. The growing number of students with special learning problems each year may create a need for more experienced Educational Diagnosticians. However, the creation of new positions in schools is dependent on available funding.

Advancement Prospects

For many Educational Diagnosticians, advancement is realized by earning higher wages and receiving higher-level responsibilities such as supervisory or administrative tasks. With advanced training and licensure, Educational Diagnosticians can become principals and school district administrators. Other career options include becoming professors, researchers, and consultants.

Licensure/Certification

In public schools, Educational Diagnosticians must hold a valid teaching license, as well as hold an Educational Diagnostician, or Learning Disabilities Teacher-Consultant, endorsement. (For specific information, contact the board of education for the state in which you wish to teach.) Educational Diagnosticians may need to complete continuing education units for licensure renewal.

Education and Training

Most schools require that Educational Diagnosticians have a master's degree in education. To be licensed, Educational Diagnosticians must complete an accredited certification program, which includes a supervised internship and courses such as educational assessment, psychology of learning, and teaching strategies in special education.

Experience, Skills, and Personality Traits

Most schools require that Educational Diagnosticians have three or more years of classroom teaching experience. To complete their many different duties, Educational Diagnosticians need leadership, teamwork, interpersonal, and communication skills. Successful Educational Diagnosticians share several personality traits such as being careful, logical, thorough, and sympathetic.

Unions/Associations

The Council for Exceptional Children and the Learning Disabilities Association of America are two national organizations that Educational Diagnosticians might join in addition to other local, and state associations. These organizations offer the opportunity to network with colleagues, as well as to obtain services such as professional resources and continuing education programs.

Tips for Entry

1. Talk with Educational Diagnosticians to learn more about their jobs.
2. As graduate students, attend professional conferences for Educational Diagnosticians to network with professionals in the field. Some of your contacts may be able to help you find a position when you begin your job search.
3. You can learn more about learning disabilities on the Internet. You might start by visiting the Learning Disabilities Association of America's web site (*http://www.ldanatl.org*). Or use the keyword "learning disabilities" in any search engine to find pertinent web sites to read.

SCHOOL PSYCHOLOGIST

CAREER PROFILE

Duties: Provide psycho-educational assessments, counseling, crisis intervention, and consultation services; perform other duties as required

Salary Range: $40,000 to $85,000

Employment Prospects: Good

Advancement Prospects: Limited

Prerequisites:
  Licensure/Certification—School Psychologist credential; may need state occupational license
  Education/Training—Master's, education specialist's, or doctoral degree; for school licensure, completion of an accredited credential program
  Experience—Internship for one school year
  Special Skills and Personality Traits—Interpersonal, teamwork, leadership, social, communication, organizational, time management, and report-writing skills; tactful, flexible, dependable, patient, compassionate

CAREER LADDER

Lead School Psychologist

School Psychologist

Intern

Position Description

School Psychologists are specialists in child development and psycho-educational assessment. While working in public and private schools, they collaborate with parents, teachers, and other school staff to resolve learning and behavioral problems of preschoolers, children, and teenagers. Their responsibilities vary according to the needs of the schools for which they work. For example, one School Psychologist might provide services only for special education programs while another School Psychologist might perform only assessment services.

Performing student assessments is the primary responsibility of most School Psychologists. In most schools, School Psychologists are part of assessment teams with teachers, administrators, and other specialists, such as School Social Workers, Speech-Language Pathologists, and School Nurses. Each team member performs an assessment on a referred student according to his or her expertise. With the completed assessments, the team develops an intervention plan that may include placement of a student in bilingual education, special education, or other program.

When performing assessments, School Psychologists use a combination of methods that include observing students in classrooms and playgrounds and reviewing students' school records. They also interview students and their parents and teachers, as well as have them complete questionnaires. In addition, School Psychologists administer a battery of tests to assess different areas such as intelligence, academic achievement, motor functioning, visual-motor perception, sensory impairments, emotional functioning, and personal adjustment.

When students are placed in special education programs, School Psychologists—along with parents, teachers, and other school specialists who will be providing related services—develop Individualized Education Programs (IEPs) that outline the goals and learning objectives for the students. The IEPs also describe what related services, such as counseling, are to be provided.

Another area of responsibility for School Psychologists is providing direct services to students and their families. They might provide individual or group counseling to students to help them with personal, social, or emotional problems. They might do interventions with students and their families to help solve conflicts that are related to learning and personal adjustment. School Psychologists also provide crisis intervention for all students and school staff after critical events, such as the sudden death of a student or in the aftermath of an act of violence in the school or community.

School Psychologists also provide consultation services to parents, teachers, and other school staff. For example, School Psychologists might work with parents to develop a behavior management plan for their children, or they might advise classroom teachers on strategies for motivating students in their classes.

School Psychologists might also:

- develop and conduct in-service training, covering topics such as child development and classroom management strategies
- develop and conduct workshops for parents on parenting skills, substance abuse, self-esteem, and other related topics
- evaluate academic programs, behavior management procedures, and other school services
- assist in the development of school programs that meet the psychological, educational, and sociological needs of students
- work with the school and community to plan community services for children and families
- supervise School Psychologist interns

As part of their job, School Psychologists write required correspondence, reports, and proposals. They also fill out forms and other paperwork in compliance with federal and state laws as well as local education agency policies and procedures. In addition, through independent reading, continuing education, and professional networking, they keep up with current issues, changes in state and federal laws, and developments in areas such as intervention strategies and working with parents.

School Psychologists may be assigned to work in one or more schools. They are employed part time or full time and often create their own work schedule. Usually, School Psychologists work more than a 40-hour week to complete paperwork, meet with parents, attend meetings, do research, and so on.

Salaries

In public schools, most School Psychologists receive a salary based on the teacher schedule or the administrative salary schedule. In addition to a salary, School Psychologists receive fringe benefits such as medical insurance, sick leave, holiday pay, and retirement benefits.

According to a 1997 salary survey by the American Psychological Association, the median annual salary for its School Psychologist members ranged from $40,000 to $85,000. The median annual salaries for those with master's degrees was between $40,000 and $72,000, and for those holding a doctorate, between $51,000 and $85,000.

Employment Prospects

Besides public and private schools, School Psychologists work for universities, private practices, community agencies, mental health centers, hospitals, and clinics.

Since the late 1990s, a shortage of qualified School Psychologists has been reported nationwide. In most states, schools require School Psychologists on staff in order to comply with state and federal laws regarding special education and other government-funded programs. In particular, the growing number of special education students in the last few years is creating a demand for more School Psychologists.

Advancement Prospects

Advancement opportunities are limited to few supervisory and administrative positions with student services or special education services. For many School Psychologists, advancement is realized by earning higher wages or taking on greater responsibilities, whether by assignment or their own initiative.

An alternative career option for School Psychologists is to work in different settings, such as residential treatment facilities or community mental health centers. Some other options are: to work for private practices, start their own practices, or become researchers or university professors.

Licensure/Certification

In public schools, School Psychologists must hold a School Psychologist credential. To work in private schools, School Psychologists may need to be licensed from the state board of psychology. (For more information about requirements, contact the education and psychology licensing boards for the state in which you wish to work.) School Psychologists may need to complete continuing education units for licensure renewal.

Education and Training

School Psychologists must have at least a master's degree, preferably in school, counseling, or clinical psychology. Many schools require an Education Specialist's degree while some require a doctoral degree.

To obtain school licensure, graduate or doctorate students must also complete an accredited program for school psychologists that includes course work in areas such as evaluation techniques, learning theories, exceptional children, individual and group counseling skills. They must also complete an internship for one school year under a certified school psychologist.

Experience, Skills, and Personality Traits

Entry-level School Psychologists must have completed an internship in a school setting. Many also have previous experience working with children and teenagers as tutors, counselors, teachers, coaches, and so on.

Because they must work well with students, parents, school staff, and others, School Psychologists need strong interpersonal, teamwork skills, leadership, social, and communication skills. They also need organizational, time management, and report-writing skills to complete their various duties each day.

Some personality traits that successful School Psychologists share are being flexible, tactful, dependable, patient, and compassionate. They are willing to be advocates for their students and enjoy working with children. They also have a strong commitment to help children grow and develop.

Unions/Associations

In addition to state and local professional organizations, School Psychologists might join the National Association of School Psychologists and the American Psychological Association. These organizations provide a variety of services, such as networking opportunities, professional resources, continuing education programs, and job listings.

Tips for Entry

1. Get experience working with children with disabilities. For example, you might volunteer in special education classrooms and with groups such as the Special Olympics.
2. Before committing yourself to a graduate or doctorate program in school psychology, be sure you know what the field is about. Talk with School Psychologists to learn what their workday is like, what challenges they face, what they like about their work, and so on.
3. Many states accept the Nationally Certified School Psychologist (NCSP) certificate from out-of-state applicants as an initial substitute for the School Psychologist credential. To learn more about this voluntary, professional certificate, contact the National Association of School Psychologists at (301) 657-0270, or write to the association at 4340 East West Highway, Suite 402, Bethesda, Md. 20814. Or visit its web site at *http://www.naspweb.org*.
4. To find relevant web sites about School Psychologists on the Internet, use the keyword "school psychologist" in any search engine.

SCHOOL SOCIAL WORKER

CAREER PROFILE

Duties: Provide counseling, referrals, and other social work services to students and their families; provide student assessments; perform other duties as required

Salary Range: $20,000 to $80,000

Employment Prospects: Good

Advancement Prospects: Limited

Prerequisites:
   Licensure/Certification—School Social Worker certification; may need a state license or be state certified or registered
   Education/Training—Bachelor's or master's degree; for school licensure, completion of an accredited credential program
   Experience—Previous social work experience with children, adolescents, and their families
   Special Skills and Personality Traits—Communication, listening, interpersonal, teamwork, organizational, and report-writing skills; independent, responsible, committed, sympathetic, sensitive, objective, respectful

CAREER LADDER

Lead School Social Worker

School Social Worker

Graduate Student or Social Worker

Position Description

In many public and private schools, School Social Workers are available to provide social work services to students and their families. They provide a variety of services, including individual, group, and family counseling. They help students with a wide variety of difficulties—emotional problems, behavioral problems, health problems, and developmental disabilities. They also help students who are dealing with homelessness, child abuse, neglect, family conflicts, pregnancy, substance abuse, alcoholism, and other issues. Furthermore, School Social Workers help all students and staff during critical times, such as after an act of violence, natural disaster, or other crisis in the school or community.

School Social Workers generally manage between 40 and 80 cases that may include both general education students and special education students. Each case begins with an assessment to determine a student's needs and what resources would best meet those needs.

Typically, School Social Workers act as school liaisons between schools and families. They contact parents to discuss students' problems and to get their support for students' needs. School Social Workers may identify community resources that can help students and their families with their problems, providing referrals as well.

In most schools, School Social Workers are part of assessment teams that determine if students have disabilities and are eligible for special education programs or other programs. Social Workers are responsible for providing social history assessments that cover areas such as students' family life, school history, and emotional behavior.

School Social Workers perform other duties, which vary from school to school. They might:

- assist in developing Individualized Education Programs (IEPs) for special education students
- plan and facilitate in-service workshops, covering topics such as violence prevention, parenting issues, and compulsory attendance
- help develop school programs, such as peer counseling
- provide consultations with individual teachers
- give classroom presentations on topics such as substance abuse
- monitor student attendance records
- network with social agencies, employment offices, health care providers, community agencies, and so on

In addition, School Social Workers are responsible for completing various reports, forms, and other paperwork in compliance with state and government laws and local education agencies' policies and procedures. Through independent study, continuing education, and professional networking, they stay current with school issues, changes in legislation, and new research in their field.

School Social Workers may be assigned to one or more schools, providing services on scheduled days, as well as being available for emergency situations. Some School Social Workers work exclusively with special education students. Most School Social Workers work beyond their 40-hour week to meet with parents, attend meetings, handle emergencies, and so on.

Salaries

Annual salaries for School Social Workers range between $20,000 and $80,000 per year with most School Social Workers earning salaries in the $40,000 range, according to the School Social Work Association of America. Salaries depend on factors such as education, experience, geographical location, and school budgets.

In addition to a salary, School Social Workers receive fringe benefits such as holiday pay, vacation leave, health plans, and retirement benefits.

Employment Prospects

School Social Workers are employed by public and private schools, as well as by Head Start centers, special education placement offices, and early intervention programs.

The field of school social work is currently growing in many states, partly due to the increasing enrollment in special education programs. However, the creation of new positions in schools is dependent on the availability of school funding.

Advancement Prospects

For many School Social Workers, advancement is realized by earning higher wages and receiving higher-level responsibilities such as supervisory or administrative tasks. In some states, School Social Workers can become school administrators with advanced education and licensure.

School Social Workers might choose to work in other settings, such as health care, family services, and corrections. Some other career paths they might pursue are becoming university professors or researchers, or going into private practice.

Licensure/Certification

Some states require School Social Workers to be licensed, certified, or registered with the state social work licensing board. Other states require social work certification from the state board of education. Many states require both a state license and school social work certification. (Contact the social work and teacher licensing boards for the state in which you wish to practice for specific information.) School Social Workers may need to complete continuing education units for licensure renewal.

Education and Training

Educational requirements vary from state to state. Most states require School Social Workers to have a master's degree in social work (MSW) earned from a graduate program accredited by a nationally recognized agency such as the Council on Social Work Education. MSW graduates are trained to perform assessments and case management; individual, family, and group counseling; and supervisory and administrative duties. In some states, School Social Workers must complete an accredited education program that leads to school licensure.

Experience, Skills, and Personality Traits

Typically, employers choose candidates who have previous social work experience providing services to children, adolescents, and their families. Many schools hire MSW graduates who completed their field placement in school, child welfare, or similar settings.

Because they must work well with students, parents, school staff, and others, School Social Workers need excellent communication, listening, interpersonal, and teamwork skills. They also need strong organizational and report-writing skills in order to complete their various duties.

Successful School Social Workers have several personality traits in common, such as being independent, responsible, committed, sympathetic, sensitive, and objective.

Unions/Associations

Most School Social Workers join local, state, and national professional associations to take advantage of professional services such as continuing education programs, training programs, networking opportunities, job listings, and professional resources. Two national groups that many School Social Workers join are the School Social Work Association of America and the National Association of Social Workers.

Tips for Entry

1. Get experience working with children and adolescents in school, community, and other settings.
2. To enhance your employability, you may want to obtain the School Social Work Specialist certification granted by the National Association of Social Workers (NASW). To learn more, contact NASW at (800) 638-8799, or visit its web site (*http://www.naswdc.org*).
3. Learn more about social work and school social work on the Internet. You might start by using these keywords in a search engine to find relevant web sites: "social work" or "school social work."

SPEECH-LANGUAGE PATHOLOGIST

CAREER PROFILE

Duties: Provide assessments and treatments for speech and language disorders; perform other duties as required

Salary Range: $32,000 to $50,000

Employment Prospects: Excellent

Advancement Prospects: Limited

Prerequisites:

    Licensure/Certification—A state license or other requirement; school credential; Certificate of Clinical Competence in Speech-Language Pathology (CCC-SLP) certification

    Education/Training—Master's degree; for school licensure, completion of an accredited certification program

    Experience—Clinical field placement

    Special Skills and Personality Traits—Interpersonal, teamwork, communication, report-writing, organizational, and management skills; warm, patient, tolerant, persistent, resourceful, creative

CAREER LADDER

Lead Speech-Language Pathologist

↑

Speech-Language Pathologist

↑

Graduate Student

Position Description

Learning takes place through the process of communication. So students who have speech and language disorders may not be able to succeed academically without help. In public and private schools, Speech-Language Pathologists diagnose students for speech and language disorders and provide intervention whenever needed.

Most Speech-Language Pathologists work in two or more schools. Their caseloads may range from 20 to 70 children, preschool to high school age. They help students who:

- cannot make speech sounds clearly or at all
- have speech rhythm and fluency problems such as stuttering
- have voice quality problems—for example, too high or too harsh
- have trouble understanding and producing language
- have attention, memory, problem solving, or other cognitive communication disorders
- have swallowing difficulties or other related problems

Students' speech and language problems may be congenital, developmental, or acquired, and may have resulted from a cleft palate, stroke, brain injury, cerebral palsy, voice pathology, emotional problems, or mental retardation.

Speech-Language Pathologists develop treatment plans that fit each student's particular needs. They work with students individually or in small groups, one or more times a week. Speech-Language Pathologists also work with teachers to develop teaching strategies that may help students improve their communication development and participation in class.

Speech-Language Pathologists also collaborate with students' families to provide treatment plans, as well as give them progress reports. They may also provide families with counseling related to speech and language issues. And, when needed, they refer students and families with other complicated issues to licensed and certified professionals.

Another major responsibility for Speech-Language Pathologists is conducting thorough and balanced assessments. Usually, they are part of assessment teams, which vary and differ from school to school. Some teams provide assessments to develop intervention strategies for teachers to address the learning needs and interests of certain students. Other teams do evaluations to determine if students have disabilities that qualify them for special education programs or other programs. Some teams develop Individualized Education Programs (IEPs) for special education students. The IEPs outline the goals and objectives for instruction and related services, such as those offered by the Speech-Language Pathologist.

Speech-Language Pathologists use a variety of tools when doing an assessment. That includes reviewing pertinent school records, collecting and reviewing samples of students' work, observing students, and sometimes interviewing students. Speech-Language Pathologists may have parents and teachers complete checklists, surveys, and questionnaires about the students along with interviewing the teachers and parents.

Speech-Language Pathologists also administer standardized tests to measure skills such as language comprehension; following directions; use of syntax, semantics, and morphology; and auditory processing of language. In addition, they diagnose functions such as articulation, fluency, and swallowing.

Other duties vary for Speech-Language Pathologists. They might:

- provide consultation services to school staff—for example, a Speech-Language Pathologist might explain to a teacher the linguistic rules of a student's dialect so that he or she may modify her teaching methods
- conduct in-service training workshops on topics such as classroom strategies that may enhance communication for all students
- provide prevention services—for example, teach high school students about lifestyle choices that may affect their communication skills, as well as their future children
- help design literacy and language arts programs that incorporate the instruction of reading, writing, speaking, and listening skills
- act as case manager for individual IEPs—be responsible for scheduling and coordinating assessments, monitoring progress of IEP, completing documentation, keeping contact with parents, and so on

Speech-Language Pathologists must complete a lot of paperwork in compliance with federal and state laws as well as local education agency policies and procedures. For example, they write assessment reports, IEPs, lesson plans, treatment notes, and progress reports, and fill out various forms. Speech-Language Pathologists also are responsible for keeping up with current legislation and developments in their field.

Speech-Language Pathologists may be employed part time or full time by schools. Some are in private practices and work for schools on a contractual basis.

Salaries

Salaries vary, depending on factors such as education, experience, geographical location, and school budgets. In 1997, the annual median salaries for Speech-Language Pathologists ranged from $32,500 to $50,000, according to a survey by the American Speech-Language-Hearing Association (ASHA). The annual median salary for school-based Speech-Language Pathologists was $40,000.

In addition to a salary, Speech-Language Pathologists receive fringe benefits such as health plans, vacation leave, and retirement benefits.

Employment Prospects

Besides private and public schools, Speech-Language Pathologists work for hospitals, home care health agencies, adult day care centers, rehabilitation centers, health care facilities, industry, research laboratories, and private practices.

Job opportunities for Speech-Language Pathologists in schools have been growing for the last few years and are expected to continue for some time. This is partly due to the growing number of special education students who need related services, which must be provided to all eligible schoolchildren between the ages of three and 21.

Shortages of Speech-Language Pathologists have been reported by schools in inner cities and rural areas. There is also a demand for qualified professionals to work with limited-English-proficient students.

Advancement Prospects

Advancement opportunities in schools are limited to lead and supervisor positions. With additional education and credentials, Speech-Language Pathologists can become school administrators.

Another career option is to work in other settings, such as hospitals, rehabilitation centers, and so on. Some other career paths are: becoming university professors, academic researchers, or laboratory researchers.

Licensure/Certification

In most states, Speech-Language Pathologists must either register with the state or hold a state license. Many states also require school-based Speech-Language Pathologists to hold a pupil services or clinical rehabilitative services credential. Some states require them to hold a teaching license as well. (To learn about requirements for the state in which you wish to practice, contact the state's education and speech-language pathologist licensing boards.) Continuing education units may need to be completed for licensure renewal.

Furthermore, in most states, Speech-Language Pathologists must hold a Certificate of Clinical Competence in Speech-Language Pathology (CCC-SLP) granted by the American Speech-Language-Hearing Association (ASHA). This voluntary certification is recognized by every state; it allows Speech-Language Pathologists to provide independent clinical services and supervise support personnel.

Education and Training

Speech-Language Pathologists need at least a master's degree in speech-language pathology to obtain both a state license and the CCC-SLP certification. In many states, Speech-Language Pathologists must complete an approved teacher education program leading up to school licensure. The program generally includes a supervised field practicum and course work in areas such as education, psychology, and classroom instruction and management.

Experience, Skills, and Personality Traits

Entry-level Speech-Language Pathologists must have completed clinical field placement in school settings. In some states, they must also have previous teaching experience.

Some skills that Speech-Language Pathologists need for their work are interpersonal, teamwork, communication, report-writing, organizational, and management skills.

Successful Speech-Language Pathologists share several personality traits, such as being warm, patient, tolerant, persistent, creative, and resourceful. In addition, they enjoy working with children.

Unions/Associations

The American Speech-Language-Hearing Association (ASHA) and the Council for Exceptional Children are two national organizations that Speech-Language Pathologists might join in addition to local and state professional groups. These organizations provide services such as professional resources, continuing education programs, and networking opportunities.

Tips for Entry

1. In high school, you can begin preparing for a career in speech-language pathology by taking science, English, and public speaking classes.
2. Most employers prefer to hire candidates whose degrees are from ASHA-accredited graduate programs. For more information, call ASHA at (800) 498-2071 or visit its web site (*http://www.asha.org*).
3. When you begin your job search, network with colleagues, professors, alumni, friends, and others who may know about job openings.
4. You can learn more about speech-language pathology on the Internet. To start, use the keyword "speech-language pathology" in any search engine to find relevant web sites.

SCHOOL OCCUPATIONAL THERAPIST

CAREER PROFILE

Duties: Provide student assessments, intervention, and treatment plans; perform other duties as required

Salary Range: $30,000 to $87,000

Employment Prospects: Very Good

Advancement Prospects: Limited

Prerequisites:
  Licensure/Certification—State license; school credential, Occupational Therapist Registered (OTR) certification
  Education/Training—Bachelor's or master's degree; for school licensure, completion of an accredited certification program
  Experience—Clinical internship in school settings
  Special Skills and Personality Traits—Interpersonal, teamwork, problem solving, communication, organizational, and management skills; patient, respectful, tactful, creative, energetic

CAREER LADDER

Lead School Occupational Therapist

School Occupational Therapist

Intern

Position Description

Many public and private schools have occupational therapy services available to help students who may not have sufficient motor and self-help skills to function in the school environment. For example, some students may have difficulty processing sensory information; some students may be unable to manipulate learning materials such as pencils, books, and paper; or some students may be physically unable to move without someone's help. Working with students in their classrooms or in resource rooms, Occupational Therapists help children develop needed skills to succeed academically, personally, and socially.

School Occupational Therapists are specialists in the analysis and adaptation of daily activities in the school environment. Their responsibilities include screening and evaluating fine motor, gross motor, visual perception, self-help, and other skills that can affect school performance. They also identify students' weak and strong areas, as well as develop intervention plans and monitor students' progress.

School Occupational Therapists work with students at all school levels, preschool to high school. Some School Occupational Therapists work with infants and toddlers either in their homes or in child care settings. Many School Occupational Therapists work exclusively with special education students—children who have learning disabilities, mental retardation, physical impairments, emotional impairments, cerebral palsy, or other disabilities. With special education students, School Occupational Therapists often collaborate with general education and special education teachers as well as with speech-language pathologists, physical therapists, school social workers, and other school specialists.

School Occupational Therapists work with students individually or in small groups. For each student on their caseloads, School Occupational Therapists create purposeful and age-appropriate activities that help children develop and practice the skills they lack or in which they are limited—fine motor skills, gross motor skills, visual perception skills, handwriting skills, organization skills, concentration skills, problem-solving skills, self-help skills, daily living skills, and so on. Activities are also developed to improve students' balance, coordination, and muscle strength. Therapy includes paper and pencil exercises, physical exercises, and using computer software programs; therapy is often incorporated into play activities and daily lessons.

School Occupational Therapists might also help students by:

- modifying their environment in the classroom, such as rearranging their desks and other work spaces
- teaching them how to organize themselves in the classroom so that they can pay attention to their tasks
- teaching them specific tasks, such as opening, closing, and organizing their desks, using a computer, or using eating utensils
- providing them with adaptive equipment, such as special seats, splints, and wheelchairs, and instructing them and their teachers and parents on their use

School Occupational Therapists usually are part of student assessment teams that may be composed of general education teachers, special education teachers, parents, school psychologists, school nurses, and other school specialists. Some teams use student assessments to develop intervention strategies for general education teachers. Other teams do evaluations to determine if students have disabilities that qualify them for special education programs. Some teams develop Individualized Education Programs (IEPs) for special education students. The IEPs outline the goals and objectives for instruction and related services, such as those offered by the Occupational Therapist.

As part of their duties, School Occupational Therapists communicate with parents. They inform parents of their children's progress. They also suggest activities that parents can do with their children at home to develop and improve their skills.

School Occupational Therapists also provide consultation services to teachers and other school staff. For example, they might suggest strategies for teachers to use with students who have short attention spans. Or, they might help school administrators make schools more accessible to children in wheelchairs and walkers.

Their job requires completing assessment reports, IEPs, treatment notes, progress reports, forms, and other paperwork in compliance with federal and state laws as well as local education agency policies and procedures. School Occupational Therapists also are responsible for keeping up with current legislation and developments in their field.

School Occupational Therapists may be assigned to work at one or more schools. They may be part-time or full-time employees. Some School Occupational Therapists work for private practices and so provide their services on a contractual basis.

Salaries

According to the U.S. Bureau of Labor Statistics, the estimated annual salaries in 1998 for most Occupational Therapists (in all settings) ranged between $30,850 and $86,540. In addition to a salary, School Occupational Therapists receive fringe benefits such as vacation leave, medical insurance, and retirement benefits.

Employment Prospects

Besides private and public schools, School Occupational Therapists work in child care centers, community agencies, and private practices.

According to the National Clearinghouse for Professions in Special Education, employment opportunities for Occupational Therapists in schools are expected to grow rapidly in the next few years.

Advancement Prospects

Promotions in schools are limited to lead and supervisory positions. With continuing education and additional licensure, School Occupational Therapists can become school administrators such as special education directors. They can also become university professors and researchers, or start their own private practice. Another option is to work in another setting, such as a hospital, home health care service, nursing home, community mental health center, adult day care program, job training service, or residential care facility.

Licensure/Certification

School Occupational Therapists must hold a state license for occupational therapists. To work in public schools, they must also be licensed by the state board of education. Requirements vary for both licenses from state to state. (For more information, contact the occupational therapist and education licensing agencies for the state in which you wish to practice.) School Occupational Therapists may need to complete continuing education units for licensure renewal.

In addition, many schools require School Occupational Therapists to have the Occupational Therapist Registered (OTR) certification, granted by the National Board for Certification in Occupational Therapy, Inc.

Education and Training

School Occupational Therapists need either a bachelor's or master's degree in occupational therapy. Occupational therapy majors study subjects such as anatomy, kinesiology, neurology, psychology, occupational therapy theory and techniques, and the impact of disability on daily life and work skills. In addition, they complete supervised clinical internships.

In many states, School Occupational Therapists must complete an approved teacher education program leading up to school licensure, which includes a supervised field practicum and course work in education, classroom instruction and management, and other areas.

Experience, Skills, and Personality Traits

Entry-level School Occupational Therapists must have completed a clinical internship, preferably in a school setting. In addition, they need adequate interpersonal, teamwork, problem solving, communication, organizational, and management skills to complete their various duties each day.

Being patient, respectful, tactful, creative, and energetic are a few of the personality traits that successful School Occupational Therapists share. They also enjoy working with children and share a commitment to helping children succeed in their school careers.

Unions/Associations

Occupational Therapists might join the American Occupational Therapy Association and the Council for Exceptional Children as well as other local and state professional associations. These groups provide opportunities for networking with colleagues and taking advantage of continuing education programs and other professional services.

Tips for Entry

1. You can prepare for a career in occupational therapy while in high school by taking any or all of these courses: biology, chemistry, physics, health, art, and social studies.
2. Talk with School Occupational Therapists to learn more about their profession. Call local school district offices to find out how to contact professionals in your area.
3. You can learn about occupational therapy on the Internet. To find relevant web sites, use these keywords in a search engine: "occupational therapy" or "school occupational therapist."

ART THERAPIST

CAREER PROFILE

Duties: Use the combination of art and therapy to provide intervention and treatment plans; provide student assessments; perform other duties as requested

Salary Range: $25,000 to $38,000

Employment Prospects: Limited, but the field is expected to grow

Advancement Prospects: Limited

Prerequisites:
    Licensure/Certification—A state art therapist or counseling license; school credential in some states; Registered Art Therapist (ATR) or Registered Art Therapist, Board Certified (ATR-BC) certification
    Education—Master's degree in art therapy, art, or related field
    Experience—Internship in school settings or other settings with children
    Special Skills and Personality Traits—Interpersonal, teamwork, organizational, communication, and report-writing skills; calm, patient, attentive, trustworthy, compassionate

CAREER LADDER

Owner of private practice

Art Therapist

Graduate Student

Position Description

Art has proven to be a useful tool in the assessment of children's mental health as well as in intervention. Many children often are unable or unwilling to express themselves verbally. Art, as a form of communication, may be one way that children can express their thoughts and emotions. Through their artwork and the artistic process, children may be able to express feelings that are too difficult to talk about while gaining insight into what may be troubling them.

In many public and private schools, Art Therapists are available to work with children—preschoolers to high schoolers—whose behavioral problems, emotional problems, or developmental disabilities are interfering with their ability to learn successfully. As mental health professionals, Art Therapists incorporate art and its creative process with traditional therapy.

Art Therapists work with individual students or with small groups of students. They give crayons, paints, chalk, clay, and other art materials to students, and encourage the students to express themselves in any art form. They might direct students in the type of project to do or have them decide on their own. Therapists also nurture students' creativity, letting them discover positive self-expression through personal artwork. In so doing, the students' confidence and self-esteem increase.

When an artwork (drawing, painting, sculpture, collage, etc.) is completed, the Art Therapist studies the piece and determines what symbolic images or themes may be present. Depression, aggression, fear, frustration, or other emotions, for example, may be expressed through color, form, and other art elements. The Art Therapist also discusses the artwork with the child.

Art Therapists also use the art process to help children develop, improve, and maintain abstract thinking skills, social skills, communication skills, and coping skills along with discovering personal feelings and self-awareness.

Most Art Therapists in schools work exclusively with special education students. Their duties may include being part of assessment teams that determine if students are eligible for special education programs. Art Therapists may also help in developing Individualized Education Programs (IEPs) for special education students with whom they will work. The IEPs outline the goals and learning objectives for instruction as well as for treatment plans by art therapists and other specialists.

Many Art Therapists also provide consultation services to parents, teachers, and other school staff. Some may plan and conduct in-service workshops for teachers and administrators.

As part of their job, Art Therapists complete reports and fill out forms and other paperwork in compliance with federal and state laws as well as local education agency policies and procedures. They also provide oral or written progress reports for parents. In addition, Art Therapists make sure they have a sufficient supply of art media and materials for sessions and maintain safe and usable art tools and equipment.

Art Therapists are employed part time or full time by schools. Some Art Therapists have private practices and provide services on a contractual basis. In addition, many Art Therapists continue with their art careers as painters, sculptors, and so on.

Salaries

The American Art Therapy Association reports that beginning Art Therapists earn about $25,000. The median annual income ranges between $28,000 and $38,000.

Employment Prospects

Besides schools, Art Therapists work in residential facilities, adult day care centers, hospitals, mental health facilities, rehabilitation centers, and correctional institutions. Some Art Therapists have their own private practices.

Art therapy is a young, but growing field. Schools are reporting increased use of Art Therapists as part of the related services that schools offer with special education programs.

Advancement Prospects

Art Therapists who work for schools have few opportunities to advance to supervisory and administrative positions. Promotions, however may mean leaving clinical practice. Those with advanced degrees have the option to teach and do research at the college and university level. With state licensure, Art Therapists can go into private practice.

Licensure/Certification

In most states, Art Therapists must have appropriate state licensure to practice; however, few states have an actual art therapy licensing standard. Many states award individual Art Therapists counseling licenses upon proving that their degrees and course work are equivalent to those of other professional counselors. In addition, schools may require Art Therapists to obtain a school specialist credential. (To find out what may be required for the state in which you wish to practice, contact both the state counseling and education licensing boards.) Art Therapists may need to complete continuing education units for licensure renewal.

Most Art Therapists obtain professional certification through the Art Therapy Credentials Board, Inc. The Registered Art Therapist (ATR) and Registered Art Therapist, Board Certified (ATR-BC) credentials are recognized standards for the profession.

Education and Training

Art Therapists must have a master's degree in art therapy, in art with an emphasis in art therapy, or in a related field with at least 21 semester units in art therapy. Most art therapy graduate programs are two years long and include course work in art therapy, psychology, and studio art, as well as a supervised field practicum.

Experience, Skills, and Personality Traits

Entry-level Art Therapists in schools must have completed an internship, preferably in a school setting or other settings that involved working with children. In addition, Art Therapists need interpersonal, teamwork, organizational, communication, and report-writing skills to complete the many different tasks they must perform each day.

Successful Art Therapists share several personality traits such as being calm, patient, attentive, trustworthy, and compassionate. They are also sensitive to people's needs and their ways of expressing themselves.

Unions/Associations

Art Therapists might join the American Art Therapy Association or the National Coalition of Arts Therapies Associations. Both organizations provide professional services such as continuing education programs, professional resources, and opportunities for networking with colleagues.

Tips for Entry

1. Get experience working in a special education program, hospital, rehabilitation center, or other setting to find out if art therapy is the right field for you.
2. Many professionals recommend that aspiring Art Therapists enroll in a graduate program approved by the American Art Therapy Association (AATA). To learn more, write to: AATA, 1202 Allanson Road, Mundelein, Ill. 60060, or call them at (847) 949-6064. Or visit the association's web site at *http://www.arttherapy.org*.
3. Use the Internet as a tool when you do a job search. For example, you might create your own home page to post your resume.
4. You can learn more about Art Therapists on the Internet. To find relevant web sites, use the keyword "art therapy" in any search engine.

SCHOOL SUPPORT STAFF

TEACHER AIDE (INSTRUCTIONAL)

CAREER PROFILE

Duties: Provide teachers with instructional and clerical support; perform duties as required

Alternate Titles: Paraeducator, Instructional Aide, Teacher Assistant, Paraprofessional, Bilingual Assistant, Special Education Paraeducator

Salary Range: Minimum wage to $20 per hour

Employment Prospects: Excellent

Advancement Prospects: Limited prospects without additional education

Prerequisites:
  Licensure/Certification—Some states or schools require a license, certification, or permit
  Education/Training—A high school or general equivalency diploma; on-the-job training
  Experience—One or more years working with children
  Special Skills and Personality Traits—Communication, reading, writing, math, teamwork, interpersonal, and self-management skills; patient, fair, flexible, creative

CAREER LADDER

Teacher

Teacher Aide

Trainee

Position Description

Teacher Aides work in public and private schools, providing teachers with much needed instructional and clerical support. Responsibilities and tasks for Teacher Aides vary and differ from school to school, and also vary among Teacher Aides within a school. Some Teacher Aides work extensively with students with limited English proficiency while others work exclusively with special education students (children with disabilities). Other Teacher Aides perform only noninstructional tasks such as supervising children during recess.

In general, instructional Teacher Aides assist teachers with classroom instruction under the teachers' supervision and direction. Teacher Aides might assist teachers with class demonstrations such as science experiments, or operate audiovisual equipment such as film projectors and cassette players for teachers. Teacher Aides might circulate around the classroom to check students' work to make sure they understand the day's lesson and to help students when needed. For limited-English-proficient students, bilingual Teacher Aides may explain or clarify instructions and lessons in students' native languages.

Teachers sometimes have their aides tutor students individually or in small groups by reviewing past lessons or providing extra practice for math, reading, or other skills. Teacher Aides may also be directed to coordinate discussion groups with the task of encouraging all students to participate. In addition, Teacher Aides help monitor student behavior as well as maintain class order and discipline. Teacher Aides give teachers feedback on students with whom they have worked, either orally or in notes.

Many Teacher Aides help teachers with lesson preparations. For example, teachers might have aides type activity sheets, photocopy student records, or collate tests. Teacher Aides may be asked to obtain textbooks, audiovisual equipment, and other materials from the appropriate school offices. Many teachers also ask their assistants to help create and put up classroom decorations, bulletin boards, and learning centers.

In addition, many Teacher Aides maintain student files and perform other clerical duties. For example, many take care of daily attendance tasks, such as taking roll, collecting absence and tardy notes, recording attendance, and so on. They also collect permission slips for student activities (such as field trips), as well as collect fees for lunch programs and other school programs and activities. Many Teacher Aides score tests, assignments, and homework in accordance with the teachers' answer keys. Some Teacher Aides record assignment grades and test scores in the teacher's grade book or computer files. Some Teacher Aides are also responsible for keeping inventory of classroom supplies and informing teachers when new supplies are needed.

Teacher Aides perform many other duties as requested, such as:

- supervising students during recesses and lunch breaks
- performing housekeeping tasks to maintain a safe and clean classroom
- arranging field trips
- contacting parents about participating in class activities

Teacher Aides work part time or full time during the school year. Most Teacher Aides work between three and eight hours each school day.

Salaries

Teacher Aides usually are paid an hourly wage. According to the U.S. Bureau of Labor Statistics, the estimated hourly wage in 1998 for most Teacher Aides was between $5.63 and $11.52 per hour. The mean hourly wage was about $8.22 per hour.

The American Federation of Teachers reports that the average wage is $8 per hour for the Teacher Aides they represent; and that wages range from minimum wage to $20 per hour.

Many Teacher Aides also receive fringe benefits, such as sick leave, medical insurance, tuition reimbursement, and retirement benefits.

Employment Prospects

Teacher Aides work for private and public elementary schools, middle-level schools, and high schools.

Job opportunities are readily available and expected to grow throughout most of the nation partly due to the increasing rise of student enrollment. In addition to new openings, Teacher Aides are needed to replace those who retire, resign, and return to school to become teachers. Teacher Aides are especially in demand for special education, bilingual education, and English as a Second Language (ESL) programs. However, the number of jobs available in a school is tied to its particular needs as well as the limitations of its budget.

Advancement Prospects

Opportunities for Teacher Aides are generally limited to pay raises and receiving additional—as well as more complex—responsibilities. For many educators, the Teacher Aide position had been the first stepping stone in their careers.

During teacher shortages, many schools encourage Teacher Aides to pursue their bachelor's degrees and teaching credentials. Many public schools offer tuition reimbursement plans and other incentives in return for a teaching commitment for a certain length of time.

Licensure/Certification

In some states, Teacher Aides in public schools hold either state or local licensure or certification, which is renewed every few years. For example, Teacher Aides in Illinois, Texas, and New York must be state certified while in Kansas only special education Teacher Aides are required to obtain licensure. More and more states are expected to introduce legislation that requires Teacher Aides in public schools to be licensed or certified, or to complete a minimum of college training, as well as in-service training and continuing education units each year. Private schools may have their own licensure or certification requirements for Teacher Aides.

Some schools require that Teacher Aides hold a valid driver's license.

Education and Training

To qualify for most positions, Teacher Aide applicants must have a high school or general equivalency diploma. Some schools also require a minimum number of college units, depending on the duties that are to be performed. An increasing number of employers prefer Teacher Aides who have completed one or more years of college.

Teacher Aides typically learn their duties on the job. More schools are providing Teacher Aides with preservice training in addition to their on-the-job training. Some schools provide Teacher Aides with in-service training throughout the school year to enhance and improve their skills.

Experience, Skills, and Personality Traits

Many employers require Teacher Aides to have one or more years of experience working with children. In addition, Teacher Aides should have knowledge of the subject matter in which they would be helping students, be familiar with how schools are organized and run, as well as have an understanding of teaching methods and materials. In addition, they have—or show they are able to learn—various skills, such as simple recordkeeping, operating audiovisual equipment, and using office equipment.

Teacher Aides must have adequate communication, reading, writing, and math skills, as well as teamwork and interpersonal skills. They should also have good self-management skills—getting to work on time, taking initiative, understanding and following directions, and so on. For those working with bilingual or ESL students, Teacher Aides must be proficient in a second language such as Spanish, Russian, Vietnamese, or Korean. (Most schools require that bilingual aides pass an oral and written language competency test.)

Some personality traits that successful Teacher Aides share are patience, fairness, flexibility, and creativity. Additionally, they are able to motivate and inspire children to learn.

Unions/Associations

Many Teacher Aides in public schools belong to a local union, such as the American Federation of Teachers, the National Education Association, or the Service Employees International Union, which negotiates wages and working conditions with school administrations.

Teacher Aides are eligible to join local, state, and national educator associations in the areas of their interests, such as the Council for Exceptional Children, the National Association for the Education of Young Children, or the National Association for Bilingual Education. These organizations provide professional services, such as continuing education programs, networking opportunities, and job listings.

Tips for Entry

1. You can start obtaining work experience while in the middle grades and high school. For example, you might volunteer as a student aide, tutor, or peer counselor with the lower grades. Or, you might volunteer or work part time for libraries, recreational centers, Sunday schools, scout troops, and so on.
2. Continue your education, whether formally through college and continuing education courses or informally through independent study. Having knowledge of various subjects, topics, and current events is helpful for understanding students' lessons in addition to enhancing your employability. (Note: Many community colleges offer associate programs that prepare graduates to become Teacher Aides.)
3. Contact public and private schools directly to learn about job openings and requirements.
4. Learn how to use computers as more and more teachers are incorporating computers with their instruction.
5. You can learn more about education on the Internet. One place to start is at *Education World,* an on-line resource for educators. Its web site address is *http://www.education-world.com/.* If you wish to learn more about specific educational areas, such as special education, bilingual education, or early childhood education, then use those terms as keywords in any search engine. For better results, enter a keyword between quotation marks.

CAREER GUIDANCE TECHNICIAN

CAREER PROFILE

Duties: Collect, organize, and distribute resources about careers and education; help students, teachers, counselors, and other school staff use the available resources; provide clerical support; perform duties as required

Alternate Title: Career Guidance Specialist

Salary Range: Minimum wage to $15 per hour

Employment Prospects: Limited

Advancement Prospects: Limited prospects without further education

Prerequisites:
   Licensure/Certification—None required
   Education/Training—A high school or general equivalency diploma
   Experience—Two years of office clerk experience, or equivalent education and experience
   Special Skills and Personality Traits—Reading, research, problem solving, communication, listening, interpersonal, and teamwork skills; enthusiastic, patient, tactful, courteous, flexible, organized, resourceful

CAREER LADDER

Lead Career Guidance Technician

Career Guidance Technician

Trainee

Position Description

Many public and private middle-level schools and high schools have career centers where students can learn about possible options for themselves after high school graduation. These centers are usually part of school counseling departments and are run by Career Guidance Technicians under and direction of the school counselors.

Career centers provide a variety of resources for students, teachers, and other school staff that may include:

- encyclopedias, dictionaries, handbooks, books, videos, and other reference materials about occupations, careers, labor market information, job search skills, and so on
- catalogs, directories, pamphlets, brochures, and applications for two-year colleges, four-year colleges, universities, technical schools, and vocational programs
- announcements, flyers, brochures, and pamphlets about scholarships, financial aid, college admission tests, apprenticeships, military information, and so on
- computer programs on careers, colleges, and so on
- access to relevant web sites on the Internet

Career Guidance Technicians are responsible for displaying information (catalogs, brochures) about scholarships, schools, tests, etc. as they are received in the mail. Technicians also make sure resources are current and remove old items. Many technicians contact schools, test services, community organizations, employment centers, and other sources to request current information. In addition, many technicians browse through catalogs and advertisements and suggest to counselors any books, software, and other materials that may be useful to the career center.

Most Career Guidance Technicians are also responsible for training students, school staff, and others on using the career center. They may give tours of the center. They may also teach individuals how to run the different computer programs and how to access the Internet to obtain career information.

Career Guidance Technicians also help students with specific questions about occupations, colleges, vocational schools, and so on. They might suggest to students which resources (books, computer programs, Internet, and so on) to research; they might help students with the research; they might do the research themselves.

Career Guidance Technicians are also responsible for providing clerical support to the career center. They answer phones—taking messages, routing calls, and responding to informational requests about services and programs—as well as receive and route mail. They type and proofread letters, memos, reports, and related materials; they may also compose routine correspondence. Some Career Guidance Technicians also maintain student files.

Career Guidance Technicians' other duties may include scheduling appointments for students, counselors, and outside visitors and making arrangements for guest speakers and field trips. Career Guidance Technicians also keep inventory of all items in the career center, and make sure all equipment is maintained and in working order. In addition, they keep the center clean, neat, and tidy. They do other tasks as required by counselors.

Career Guidance Technicians work part time or full time, throughout the school year.

Salaries

Career Guidance Technicians generally receive hourly wages, often beginning at minimum wage. According to the U. S. Bureau of Labor Statistics, the 1998 estimated wages for most general office clerks—which include Career Guidance Technicians—ranged from $6.05 to $14.78 per hour. In addition to a salary, Career Guidance Technicians may be eligible for fringe benefits such as medical insurance, sick leave, and retirement benefits.

Employment Prospects

Career Guidance Technicians are employed by private and public schools, colleges, and universities.

The number of job opportunities are limited as Career Guidance Technician is a relatively new occupation. More and more schools are creating career centers to meet the growing interest for helping middle school, junior high, and high school students evaluate career goals. However, the creation of new positions depends on the availability of school funding.

Advancement Prospects

Most Career Guidance Technicians realize advancement by receiving pay increases and higher-level responsibilities, such as supervisory duties. Experienced Career Guidance Technicians can obtain positions in community college, four-year college, university, and private career guidance centers, where salaries are higher and responsibilities more complex. Another career option is to pursue further education and obtain a master's degree in counseling and become vocational or school counselors in schools, colleges, and private practice.

Licensure/Certification

As of 1999, none of the states required any special licensure for Career Guidance Technicians.

Education and Training

Applicants need at least a high school or general equivalency diploma. Most employers prefer applicants with an associate degree or some college training. Career Guidance Technicians receive on-the-job training.

Experience, Skills, and Personality Traits

Many employers require that Career Guidance Technicians have two years of office work experience or equivalent education and experience. They should also have a general understanding of how a career center works.

To complete their duties effectively, Career Guidance Technicians must have competent reading and research skills, as well as adequate problem-solving, communication, listening, interpersonal, and teamwork skills.

Successful Career Guidance Technicians share several personality traits such as being enthusiastic, patient, tactful, courteous, flexible, organized, and resourceful.

Unions/Associations

Many Career Guidance Technicians in public schools belong to a local union, such as the American Federation of Teachers, the National Education Association, or the Service Employees International Union, which negotiates wages and working conditions with school administrations.

In addition, Career Guidance Technicians might join local, state, and national organizations, such as the National Career Development Association. By joining professional organizations, they can take advantage of career resources, continuing education programs, networking opportunities, and other services.

Tips for Entry

1. In middle school or high school, visit your career center or one at a local community college. Talk with the Career Guidance Technician and learn more about his or her job. If possible, volunteer to work in the career center to obtain hands-on experience.
2. Contact schools directly to learn about job openings and requirements.
3. On the Internet, you can learn more about career guidance. To find relevant web sites, use either of these keywords in a search engine: "career guidance" or "career guidance center."

SCHOOL BUS DRIVER

CAREER PROFILE

Duties: Safely transport children to and from school and their homes; perform pre-trip inspections; enforce school regulations; perform other duties as required

Salary Range: Minimum wage to $14 per hour

Employment Prospects: Excellent

Advancement Prospects: Limited

Prerequisites:
 Licensure/Certification—State driver's license; commercial driver's license (CDL) with a passenger or school bus endorsement; School Bus Driver certification; first aid and cardiopulmonary resuscitation (CPR) certificates
 Education/Training—High school or general equivalency diploma
 Experience—Six months or more driving experience
 Special Skills and Personality Traits—Leadership, communication, interpersonal, and self-management skills; independent, flexible, calm, patient, tolerant, pleasant, courteous, stable

CAREER LADDER

Lead School Bus Driver

School Bus Driver

Trainee

Position Description

Every school day in the United States, School Bus Drivers transport millions of students in the familiar yellow school buses to public and private schools (preschools to high schools), as well as bring them back home. They also transport students, teachers, and chaperones to and from field trips, games, and other school events.

School Bus Drivers' primary responsibility is the safety of all children and adults riding on their buses. They have been trained to drive in any kind of traffic, observing all traffic laws, as well as to operate the school buses in a safe and efficient manner in sun, fog, wind, rain, snow, or any other weather condition. They are also trained to handle emergency evacuations and provide first aid treatment in emergency situations.

Most School Bus Drivers are assigned two or more routes, or runs, to complete in the morning and afternoon. One route may be for a high school or middle-level school while the other route is for an elementary school. On some routes, School Bus Drivers pick up students for two different schools. The drivers follow a time schedule for each route, which is usually about one hour long.

Some School Bus Drivers are assigned routes for picking up and delivering special education students—children with disabilities. They drive specially-designed school buses that have seat belts, harnesses, or other passive restraint systems, and which have the ability to accommodate wheelchairs. Some School Bus Drivers also do mid-morning routes, picking up and delivering kindergarten or preschool children. (Bus aides may be assigned on routes for preschool children to help School Bus Drivers buckle children in and escort children on and off the buses.)

Following standard procedures for loading and unloading passengers, School Bus Drivers pick up and drop off students at designated stops on their routes as well as at the designated passenger loading zones at schools. School Bus Drivers make sure everyone is seated and all doors are closed before starting the bus off. They also make sure students stay seated until the bus has come to a complete stop and they have been told it is safe to exit the bus.

Sometimes, School Bus Drivers escort students across the street. They make sure that students cross at least 10 feet in front of the bus. (The 10 feet directly in front of the bus is a danger zone as drivers behind the bus have trouble seeing children in that zone.) When the drivers see that a street is safe to cross, they escort the students to the other side of the street.

On preschool and kindergarten routes, School Bus Drivers make sure that parents, or other designated persons, are at the stops to pick up their children. If no one is at the stop or home to pick up a child, the School Bus Driver notifies the bus dispatcher or school office. The School Bus Driver may try to deliver the child again after completing his or her route, or bring the child back to the school office to be picked up by the parents.

School Bus Drivers are responsible for enforcing school rules and regulations on their buses. Following standard procedures, they maintain discipline and control student behavior as they see fit. For example, they may assign seats in order to separate students who are causing trouble or refer misbehaving students to school administrators. If needed, schools may assign a bus monitor to help School Bus Drivers manage student behavior.

In addition, School Bus Drivers are responsible for the safe operating condition of their buses. They are required by law to perform a pre-trip inspection before beginning their first route. They make sure their buses have gasoline, oil, brake fluids, and so on, that tires are full of air, windshields and windshield wipers are clean, and lights and horns are in working order. They check fuses, wheels, engine compartments, tailpipes, and exhaust systems, as well as make sure that mirrors, side windows, stop arms, crossing gates, service doors, and rear emergency doors are working fine. Furthermore, they make sure that emergency equipment is in working order, fire extinguishers are charged, and first aid kits are equipped. If anything needs maintenance or repair, School Bus Drivers get it fixed immediately.

School Bus Drivers also inspect the condition of their buses after each run. They sweep out the interiors of the buses, if necessary. In addition, they check for belongings that children may have left behind, and bring them to the school office. Some School Bus Drivers are also responsible for washing their buses on a regular basis.

As part of their job, they complete a daily record of their hours, bus mileage, number of runs, number of students per busload, and so on. School Bus Drivers are also responsible for keeping driving licenses and professional certifications up-to-date. In most schools, School Bus Drivers participate in emergency exit drills for school bus riders once or twice a year. Some schools also require School Bus Drivers to attend school bus orientation meetings for parents at the beginning of the school year.

School Bus Drivers work full time or part time while school is in session. Most begin their workdays at 6:00 A.M. Part-time drivers have several hours free between their morning and afternoon routes. Many full-time employees have other duties in addition to driving a bus; for example, some train new School Bus Drivers while others work on the maintenance crew. Some School Bus Drivers hold down other part-time positions, such as playground supervisors, food service workers, and custodians.

Salaries

School Bus Drivers earn hourly wages, which vary with the different employers. New bus drivers often start at minimum wage. According to the U.S. Bureau of Labor, the estimated hourly wage in 1998 for most School Bus Drivers ranged between $5.59 and $14.00.

In addition to a salary, some School Bus Drivers receive fringe benefits such as medical insurance, sick leave, and retirement benefits.

Employment Prospects

School Bus Drivers work for public and private schools (preschools to high schools), as well as for local or national school transportation contractors.

Job opportunities are readily available, especially for part-time positions. Schools and student transportation contractors nationwide are experiencing a current shortage of qualified School Bus Drivers. In addition, opportunities are expected to increase through 2008, and possibly beyond, due to the growing rate of student enrollment in public and private schools.

Advancement Prospects

School Bus Drivers can become dispatchers and trainers as well as advance to lead and supervisor positions. Those interested in administrative roles can work their way up to branch, district, and regional managers with school transportation contractors, or transportation directors in public school districts. Another career option is to apply for positions with public or private bus transit systems.

Licensure/Certification

School Bus Drivers must hold a valid state driver's license in addition to a CDL with a passenger or school bus endorsement. In most states, School Bus Drivers need a School Bus Driver certification, which is granted upon completion of a preservice training program. Furthermore, School Bus Drivers must have valid first aid and cardiopulmonary resuscitation (CPR) certificates.

Education and Training

School Bus Drivers need at least a high school or general equivalency diploma. In most states, they must complete a preservice school bus safety and training program that includes classroom training and behind-the-wheel training. Many School Bus Drivers are required to complete in-service training each year.

Experience, Skills, and Personality Traits

In general, School Bus Drivers should have six months or more driving experience. They are also able to handle the stress of driving groups of children in any traffic condition or any emergency situation.

To complete their daily duties effectively, School Bus Drivers need adequate leadership skills, communication skills, interpersonal skills, and self-management skills—they should be able to follow instructions, work under stressful conditions, and so on.

Successful School Bus Drivers share several personality traits such as being independent, flexible, calm, patient, tolerant, pleasant, courteous, and stable. Furthermore, they enjoy driving and have a genuine respect and love for children.

Unions/Associations

Many School Bus Drivers in public schools join a local union such as the American Federation of Teachers, the National Education Association, or the Service Employees International Union, which negotiates wages and working conditions with school administrations. School Bus Drivers are also eligible to join the National Association for Pupil Transportation, which provides opportunities for networking, training programs, and other professional services.

Tips for Entry

1. During School Bus Driver shortages, many employers provide free training for CDL exams. Some employers offer incentives such as sign-up bonuses and part-time positions in other areas to encourage qualified individuals to apply.
2. Employers have their own set of requirements for School Bus Drivers. For example, you'll need to meet a minimum age requirement; pass physical examinations, background checks, and drug tests; and so on. Contact the employers for whom you would like to work for their job requirements.
3. On the Internet, you can learn more about School Bus Drivers and school bus safety. To start, use the keyword "school bus" in any search engine to find relevant web sites.

CAFETERIA MANAGER

CAREER PROFILE

Duties: Oversee the daily operations of a school's food service program; supervise and train staff; set up and enforce safe and sanitary standards; perform other duties as required

Alternate Titles: Food Service Manager, School Nutrition Manager, Cafeteria Director

Salary Range: $14,000 to $46,000

Employment Prospects: Fair, in school settings

Advancement Prospects: Limited, in school settings

Prerequisites:
  Licensure/Certification—None is required
  Education/Training—High school or general equivalency diploma; college or technical school training in food service preferred
  Experience—Three years work experience; supervisory experience preferred
  Special Skills and Personality Traits—Leadership, program management, interpersonal, teamwork, math, communication and report-writing skills; independent, self-disciplined, organized, fair, flexible, hardworking

CAREER LADDER

Food Service Director

Food Service Manager

Lead Food Service Worker or Assistant Manager

Position Description

School cafeterias are run by Cafeteria Managers who oversee—as well as assist—their staff in food preparation, serving meals, storing food and supplies, and keeping the equipment and facilities safe and clean. Depending on the size of their school, Cafeteria Managers may supervise a staff as few as two or as many as 15 or more. They make sure that their staff follows standard procedures for safety and quality control at all times.

Cafeteria Managers complete many different duties each day, including:

- estimating the amount of foods to be prepared
- making sure that equipment and supplies needed for the day are available
- supervising the preparation, cooking, and serving of foods
- assigning tasks to different staff members
- completing required paperwork for nutritional and fiscal accountability

Cafeteria Managers also maintain inventories of foodstuff and supplies; estimate the quantities of food and supplies to be ordered; order food and supplies; receive deliveries; and evaluate the quality of fresh foods, baked goods, and other foodstuff. In addition, they arrange for equipment maintenance and repairs, as well as for outside maintenance services, such as waste removal and pest control. Furthermore, Cafeteria Managers make sure that their food service programs are in compliance with federal, state, and local laws, regulations, and health codes.

Their responsibilities also include staff training and development along with providing daily guidance to their staff. In addition, they plan work schedules, complete time sheets, and perform staff evaluations. As leaders, Cafeteria Managers try to create a relaxed environment so that their staff can work together efficiently.

Many Cafeteria Managers help in the planning of school menus, which are the responsibility of nutrition specialists, food service directors, or other school personnel who are registered dietitians. Nutritional analyses are performed on each dish and food to make sure that menus are well-balanced and follow dietary guidelines established by the U.S. Department of Agriculture. Additionally, menus are developed to offer several selections, including vegetarian, low fat, and ethnic—such as Italian, Chinese, or Mexican—dishes. In some schools, Cafeteria Managers encourage students to participate in the development of the school menus.

In many schools, Cafeteria Managers run food service programs that participate in the federal government's school meals programs which provide low-cost or free meals to children who meet eligibility guidelines. Participating schools receive reimbursements for each meal they serve that meets federal guidelines, as well as free commodities from the U.S. Department of Agriculture. Cafeteria Managers are responsible for keeping accurate records of the meals sold in order to receive proper reimbursements. They may also be responsible for reviewing and approving family applications for free meals.

Cafeteria Managers may be under the supervision of their school principal or an administrator, such as a food service director, who manages several school cafeterias. Most Cafeteria Managers work full time during the school year.

Salaries

Salaries vary from school to school, and depend on factors such as experience, education, and school budgets. According to the U. S. Bureau of Labor Statistics, the estimated annual salary for most Food Service Managers, in school and nonschool settings, ranged from $14,430 to $45,520 in 1998.

In addition to a salary, most Cafeteria Managers receive fringe benefits such as sick leave, vacation leave, health plans, and retirement benefits.

Employment Prospects

Food service manager jobs are expected to increase in the next few years in nonschool settings, especially in the restaurant and hospitality industries. Most opportunities in school settings become available as Cafeteria Managers retire, resign, or advance to other positions.

Advancement Prospects

Many school Cafeteria Managers achieve advancement by receiving higher salaries and obtaining positions with increasingly complex responsibilities. With additional education and experience, Cafeteria Managers can advance to higher positions—field managers, nutrition specialists, and food service directors. Another option is to pursue careers in other food service settings.

Licensure/Certification

As of 1999, none of the states required any special licensure for school-based Cafeteria Managers. Schools may require Cafeteria Managers to hold a valid state driver's license.

Education and Training

Cafeteria Managers must have at least a high school or general equivalency diploma. Many Cafeteria Managers have an associate degree in food service management or have completed college training in food management, dietetics, and supervision.

Most schools require Cafeteria Managers to complete annual in-service training or other training provided by professional organizations.

Experience, Skills, and Personality Traits

Most employers require that Cafeteria Managers have at least three years of previous experience preparing and serving food in large quantities, preferably in an institutional setting. Many employers also prefer that entry-level managers have previous supervisory experience or training in methods and techniques used in supervision.

Along with leadership and program management skills, Cafeteria Managers need interpersonal and teamwork skills in order to work with people of various personality types. In addition, they need strong math, communication, and report-writing skills.

Being independent, self-disciplined, organized, fair, flexible, and hardworking are some personality traits that successful Cafeteria Managers share. Additionally, they are committed to contributing to children's academic success by providing them with healthy and tasty meals.

Unions/Associations

Many Cafeteria Managers join the American School Food Service Association, a national organization, along with other local and state food service associations. These organizations provide continuing education programs, job listings, and networking opportunities, and other professional services.

Many Cafeteria Managers in public schools are eligible to join a local union, such as the National Education Association, the American Federation of Teachers, or the Service Employees International Union.

Tips for Entry

1. Contact schools and school districts directly to learn about job vacancies and requirements.
2. Learn how to use a computer, because many school cafeterias now use computers for meal planning, gathering statistics, completing paperwork, and so on.
3. You can learn more about school nutrition programs on the Internet. To find pertinent web sites, use either of these keywords in a search engine: "school nutrition program" or "child nutrition."

CAMPUS MONITOR

CAREER PROFILE

Duties: Supervise students in assigned school areas during recess, lunch period, and other class breaks; enforce school regulations and rules; perform other duties as required

Alternate Titles: School Monitor, Playground Supervisor, Paraprofessional

Salary Range: Minimum wage to $11 per hour

Employment Prospects: Fair

Advancement Prospects: Limited

Prerequisites:
  Licensure/Certifications—First aid and CPR certification; may need a state driver's license
  Education/Training—High school or general equivalency diploma
  Experience—One or more years working with children
  Special Skills and Personality Traits—Leadership, interpersonal, teamwork, oral communication, writing, and self-management skills; may need computer skills and basic office skills; fair, calm, patient, flexible, tactful, observant, levelheaded, trustworthy

CAREER LADDER

Lead Campus Monitor

Campus Monitor

Trainee

Position Description

In many public and private schools, Campus Monitors help teachers and administrators oversee the safety and welfare of the students. They assist in monitoring students' behavior and enforcing school rules and regulations. These staff members are found in elementary schools, middle-level schools, and in high schools. (In elementary schools, Campus Monitors are usually known as playground supervisors, lunchroom monitors, and bus monitors.)

Under the supervision of a principal, dean of students, or other administrator, Campus Monitors work directly with students. They maintain high visibility on campus and become familiar with the students, gaining their trust as adult figures to whom students can come for help. Campus Monitors are trained to handle many different situations, including student misbehavior, unsafe play or activity, injuries, accidents, arguments, fights, and so on.

Campus Monitors are authorized to give students warnings about their behavior, as well as refer them to appropriate school personnel for counseling and discipline. Depending on the situation, Campus Monitors may intervene alone or assist other school personnel. Many Campus Monitors have the authority to contact law enforcement personnel for immediate assistance in very critical situations.

In most elementary schools and some middle-level schools, Campus Monitors normally work during recesses, lunch periods, and other class breaks; they are assigned to watch over students on playgrounds, in cafeterias or lunch areas, and in bus lines. On occasion, Campus Monitors may be asked to enforce disciplinary plans for individual students during recesses and lunch periods; for example, a student who has misbehaved in class is required to sit alone quietly on a bench during recess.

In most high schools and some middle-level schools, Campus Monitors are assigned to patrol specific areas of a school campus that may include common areas, hallways, bathrooms, parking lots, and the campus perimeter. In addition to lunch periods and class breaks, Campus Monitors patrol their assigned areas while classes are in session. They stop students who are out of class to check for authorized hallway passes. They also make sure that visitors are permitted to be on campus. Additionally, they watch for nonstudents loitering on campus or cruising in vehicles around or near the school, and keep an eye out for vandalism, illegally parked vehicles, use of illegal substances (drugs, alcohol, cigarettes), and other inappropriate activity. If necessary, Campus Monitors contact school administrators, school security, or local law enforcement about any trespassers or suspected illegal activities.

At all school levels, Campus Monitors are required to file oral or written reports with school administrators regarding accidents, fights, harassment, use of illegal substances, and other incidents. They also report student truancies and give an account of student disciplinary actions that they may be overseeing. In addition, Campus Monitors let administrators know about unsafe equipment, damaged property, campus areas that need maintenance, and so on.

Campus Monitors work between two and eight hours a day, depending on the needs of their schools. They may also work after school, evenings, and weekends to assist with supervision at school functions.

Salaries

Campus Monitors generally earn hourly wages. Entry-level monitors may start at minimum wage. According to the U.S. Bureau of Labor Statistics, the estimated wage for most educational assistants, including Campus Monitors, in 1998 was between $5.59 and $10.89 per hour.

Many Campus Monitors receive fringe benefits such as sick leave and medical insurance.

Employment Prospects

Campus Monitors are employed by public and private schools. Most opportunities become available as Campus Monitors resign, return to school, or advance to other positions. Additional jobs are created from time to time when funding is available.

Advancement Prospects

Advancement opportunities are limited to lead and supervisor positions.

The Campus Monitor position can be a stepping stone for any number of career paths. With advanced education and licensure, Campus Monitors might pursue careers in teaching, counseling, social work, or education administration. Or, Campus Monitors might obtain training and education in protective services, and become school resource officers, school security officers, and, eventually, school security consultants.

Licensure/Certifications

As of 1999, none of the states required any special licensure for Campus Monitors. However, many schools require that Campus Monitors hold a valid state driver's license as well as have first aid and cardiopulmonary resuscitation (CPR) certification.

Education and Training

Most schools require that Campus Monitors have at least a high school or general equivalency diploma. Many middle-level schools and high schools prefer candidates with one or more years of college training in social work or law enforcement.

Campus Monitors typically receive on-the-job training.

Experience, Skills, and Personality Traits

In general, employers prefer Campus Monitors who have one or more years of experience working with children of all ages. They also have some knowledge of student behavior and nonphysical disciplinary practices for maintaining student discipline and order. In addition, they are physically fit and able to move continuously during their work shifts.

To complete their responsibilities effectively, Campus Monitors need leadership, interpersonal, teamwork, communication, and writing skills. They also have excellent self-management skills—they can understand and follow directions, are able to work independently, handle stress on the job, make mature decisions, and so on. Campus Monitors may need computer skills and basic office skills for high school positions.

Successful Campus Monitors share several personality traits such as being fair, calm, patient, flexible, tactful, observant, levelheaded, and trustworthy.

Unions/Associations

Many Campus Monitors in public schools are eligible to join school unions such as the National Education Association, the American Federation of Teachers, or the Service Employees International Union. Those unions provide contract negotiations, continuing education programs, networking opportunities, and other benefits.

Tips for Entry

1. Talk with Campus Monitors at schools in your area to learn what their specific job duties are.
2. Contact schools directly to learn about job vacancies and job requirements.
3. You can learn more about school security and safety on the Internet. For pertinent web sites, use these keywords in a search engine: "school security" or "safe schools."

COLLEGE AND UNIVERSITY FACULTY

COMMUNITY COLLEGE INSTRUCTOR

CAREER PROFILE

Duties: Teach general education, developmental, or vocational courses in a two-year college; perform other duties as required

Alternate Titles: Professor; also known by the subject taught (such as History Instructor or Cosmetology Instructor)

Salary Range: $34,000 to $55,000

Employment Prospects: Good for part-time positions

Advancement Prospects: Limited

Prerequisites:
　Licensure/Certification—Teaching credential, occupational license, and/or professional certification may be required
　Education/Training—A master's degree or equivalent
　Experience—Previous teaching experience in community college settings preferred
　Special Skills and Personality Traits—Communication, interpersonal, teamwork, organizational, and management skills; independent, analytical, intellectual, versatile, adaptable, curious, creative

CAREER LADDER

Tenured Instructor or Professor

↑

Instructor or Assistant Professor

↑

Part-time Instructor

Position Description

Community College Instructors work at two-year colleges that serve the educational needs of the local communities as well as provide training for the local professions, businesses, industry, and government agencies. In some community colleges, the faculty are given the title *professor;* and are ranked academically from instructor, assistant professor, associate professor, and full professor. Some public and private two-year colleges are known as junior colleges or technical colleges.

Students at community colleges can be any age and often come from different ethnic and socioeconomic backgrounds. They may go to school part time or full time to fulfill different educational goals—for example, to learn a specific vocation, earn credits to transfer to four-year college, pass a high school equivalency diploma examination, improve work skills, or learn about a subject for fun.

Most Community College Instructors teach in programs that lead to associate degrees or occupational certificates. Many Instructors teach general education courses in liberal arts and sciences programs, which prepare students to transfer to four-year institutions. (General education courses in community colleges usually fulfill lower undergraduate requirements in four-year institutions.) Some Instructors also teach developmental courses in reading, writing, or math to help students improve their skills to succeed at college-level work.

Many Community College Instructors teach courses for vocational (or occupational) and technical programs such as dental hygiene, nursing, police science, business services, telecommunications, culinary arts, cosmetology, automotive services, and hospitality services.

Some institutions offer community service programs in which Instructors integrate academic instruction with volunteer service in the community. For example, an English Instructor might require students in an American literature class to tutor participants in an adult literacy program. Community College Instructors might also teach in continuing education programs that offer noncredit courses to members of the general public who wish to gain new knowledge or improve skills.

Community College Instructors are part of a department or division that corresponds to their subject or field (such as computer science, geography, horticulture, or early childhood education). For each term, they are assigned courses, as part of a prescribed curriculum, by the department chair or division dean. For example, a math Instructor might teach basic arithmetic, finite mathematics, geometry, and applied mathematics for the spring semester. Instructors have flexible hours that may include teaching courses every day or every other day as well as teaching classes at night or on weekends. Depending on the course, an Instructor's class load may range from 25 to 75 or more students.

For each of their courses, Instructors are responsible for developing a syllabus that outlines the topics and sequence of topics to be taught. Although they may be given predetermined textbooks, Instructors can decide which parts of the texts to assign to students. Instructors develop and use multiple teaching methods to motivate students to engage in their own learning as well as to help them develop critical thinking skills. Instructors may use lectures, laboratory work, self-paced formats, computer-assisted instruction, multimedia demonstrations, individualized instruction, and so on. Some Community College Instructors teach on-line courses or courses on cable or closed-circuit television.

As in any teaching profession, Community College Instructors perform administrative tasks such as keeping attendance records. They grade students' papers, lab work, and exams, and give students critical feedback about their work. At the end of a term, Instructors evaluate students' overall performance and assign letter grades. In addition, Instructors maintain scheduled office hours to advise students on academic matters.

As part of their duties, Instructors participate in faculty meetings and work with colleagues to develop and evaluate courses, programs, and services. Many Instructors also serve on school committees that handle academic or administrative issues for the institution. Some Instructors become student club advisers or work with community organizations.

Community College Instructors are also responsible for keeping up with developments in their disciplines as well as in teaching methodologies, multicultural issues in learning, the use of computer technology for instruction, and so on. Their professional development may be pursued through independent study, networking with colleagues, and participating in professional workshops and conferences. Though teaching is the main emphasis at two-year colleges, Instructors are encouraged to conduct scholarly research projects and have their results published in scholarly journals, books, and electronic media.

Instructors may also propose new courses to teach in their department or the community college extension program. A proposal for a new course would include a rationale for teaching the course, the purpose of the course, the scope and sequence of topics to be taught, the number of days to be taught, and so on.

Full-time faculty generally teach five courses, which is equivalent to 15 teaching hours; however, most Instructors typically work between 40 to 50 hours a week—teaching courses, holding office hours, preparing for classes, grading papers and exams, participating in staff and committee meetings, and so on. Most two-year institutions have a tenure track for full-time Instructors. (With tenure, Instructors cannot be fired without just cause and due process.)

In recent years, due to tight budgets in many two-year colleges, 50 percent or more of the faculty are part-time Instructors. (Those who have primary jobs in government, private industry, nonprofit research, or other educational institutions, are known as adjunct instructors.) Part-time Instructors teach between one to three courses, usually in the evenings and on weekends. They have limited administrative and student advising duties. Many are not given office space, so they spend little time on campus.

Many part-time Instructors teach at more than one community college in different parts of a city, county, or region. Some also teach courses for extension programs in community colleges, colleges, or universities.

Salaries

Salaries vary, and depend on factors such as an Instructor's experience and education as well as the type, size, and location of the two-year college. According to a 1998–99 survey by the American Association of University Professors, full-time faculty in two-year colleges receive average salaries that range from $34,316 to $54,875. Faculty at public institutions receive higher average salaries than private, independent, or church-related institutions.

In addition to salaries, full-time Instructors receive fringe benefits such as health plans and retirement benefits. Part-time Instructors rarely receive fringe benefits.

Part-time Instructors are usually paid a fee for each of the courses that they teach. In a 1998 study by the National Education Association, most part-time Instructors in California, Washington, Minnesota, and Michigan earned between $1,500 and $5,000 per course. The study reports that half of the respondents earned less than $2,500 per course.

Employment Prospects

Private and public two-year colleges, technical colleges, junior colleges, and community colleges hire Instructors for part-time or full-time positions.

Competition is keen, particularly for full-time tenure track positions. Most opportunities are for part-time positions or for nontenured full-time positions.

In general, the best prospects are in fields that meet the immediate needs of the business world. Current demands are for Instructors in technical areas such as computer science and applied technology as well as in the fields of chemistry and biology.

Advancement Prospects

Many Community College Instructors, or professors, realize advancement through full-time positions, tenure, and pay raises. Instructors interested in administrative and management careers may become department chairs, program coordinators, assistant deans, and deans. (Having a doctoral degree enhances, but does not guarantee, an individual's chances for obtaining top administrative positions.)

Community College Instructors have the option to move to other careers in education, becoming corporate trainers, adult education teachers, university lecturers, or researchers. They can also pursue careers in their chosen fields, working for the government, private industries, community organizations, or other institutions.

Licensure/Certification

Community College Instructors who teach in vocational and technical programs must hold valid professional licenses and certifications. In some states, Instructors may require additional teaching licensure or certification by their professional licensing board or board of education. (Contact the occupational licensing board or board of education in the state where you would like to teach for more information.)

Education and Training

For academic subjects, Community College Instructors need master's degrees in their subjects, or in related fields with a minimum number of units in each of the subjects they would teach. Employers sometimes hire Instructors who have a bachelor's degree, if they have qualified professional work experience.

Educational requirements for Instructors in vocational or occupational certificate programs vary from college to college. Vocational Instructors have master's degrees in their subject, or associate or bachelor's degrees along with qualified professional work experience.

Some colleges or individual departments assign mentors to new Instructors to advise them with instruction.

Experience, Skills, and Personality Traits

Community colleges prefer Instructors who have previous teaching experience, particularly at the community college level. Additionally, employers look for candidates who have an excellent background in their discipline and are willing to teach a wide variety of courses. Good candidates also demonstrate that they are sensitive and respectful of the diversity of the student body that is often found in community colleges.

Community College Instructors should have strong communication, interpersonal, and teamwork skills to work well with students, colleagues, and administrators. In addition, Instructors should have effective organizational and management skills to complete their duties each day.

Successful Community College Instructors share several personality traits such as being independent, analytical, intellectual, versatile, adaptable, curious, and creative. They have a strong desire to pursue knowledge in their field as well as to teach and share the knowledge with their students.

Unions/Associations

Community College Instructors join different professional associations to take advantage of networking opportunities, professional development, professional resources, and other services. Along with belonging to local, state, and national organizations that serve their specific fields, they join groups such as the American Association for Higher Education, American Association for Adult and Continuing Education, and the National Association of Scholars. They may also join the American Association of University Professors, in which some chapters in public institutions negotiate contracts with administrators. Community College Instructors in public institutions are also eligible to join these two teacher unions: the National Education Association and the American Federation of Teachers.

Tips for Entry

1. Get teaching experience in community college settings by applying for part-time or temporary lecturer positions.
2. As a student, join professional associations and network with professionals. Contact them when you are ready to do a job search for leads to current or upcoming vacancies on their campuses.
3. Send your resume to department chairs at all the two-year colleges where you would like to work. (Be sure to emphasize your teaching experience.) Call each department chair a few days after sending your resume and introduce yourself. If no jobs are currently available, keep calling back from time to time. It is common for colleges to hire new Instructors at the last minute for part-time Instructors who have suddenly left for full-time positions.
4. The Internet is a valuable tool for doing a job search. Many two-year colleges have web sites which include job listings for current vacancies so check the sites of colleges where you would like to work. You can usually find job listings for community college positions at these web sites: the American Association of Community Colleges (*http://www.aacc.nche.edu*) or the *Chronicle of Higher Education* Career Network (*http://chronicle.com/jobs*).

PROFESSOR

CAREER PROFILE

Duties: Teach undergraduate or graduate courses within an academic unit; conduct scholarly research; perform other duties as required

Alternate Titles: Instructor, Assistant Professor, Associate Professor, Full Professor, Visiting Professor, Adjunct Professor

Salary Range: $31,000 to $83,000

Employment Prospects: Good for part-time positions

Advancement Prospects: Limited

Prerequisites:
  Licensure/Certification—Occupational licensure and professional certification may be required
  Education/Training—A doctoral degree
  Experience—Previous teaching experience
  Special Skills and Personality Traits—Communication, presentation, interpersonal, teamwork, social, organizational, and management skills; independent, intelligent, analytical, inquiring, self-motivated, confident

CAREER LADDER

(Full) Professor

↑

Associate Professor

↑

Assistant Professor

Position Description

College and university faculty prepare students for careers that require bachelor's, master's, or doctoral degrees—for example, lawyers, architects, teachers, accountants, FBI agents, business managers, medical doctors, veterinarians, engineers, and journalists. Also, many college and university Professors conduct research projects that can lead to important discoveries in technology, medicine, astronomy, genetics, agriculture, psychology, sociology, archaeology, and so on, that benefit society.

Professors belong to specific academic units which comprise departments or divisions. For example, a college might have a department of social science with history, geography, economics, anthropology, and political science as some of its academic units. Each term, Professors are assigned to teach several undergraduate or graduate courses within a prescribed curriculum.

For each of their courses, they develop a course syllabus that outlines the topics and sequence of topics to be taught as well as bibliographies for outside reading assignments. They are also responsible for preparing lectures and laboratory experiments. Depending on the course, Professors may lecture to hundreds of students in large halls, instruct small groups in classrooms or laboratories, or lead discussions in seminars made up of 10 or fewer students. Some Professors teach on-line courses or courses on cable or closed-circuit television.

Their teaching responsibilities include assigning papers and administering exams. They grade papers and exams and return them to their students with positive and critical comments. At the end of each term, Professors evaluate their students' academic performances with a letter grade. At large universities teaching assistants and graders are usually available to help Professors with administering exams, grading papers and exams, leading discussion sections, and supervising laboratory experiments.

Professors are required to hold regularly scheduled office hours, usually three to six hours a week, for meeting with students and advising them in course and career matters. Many Professors are responsible for supervising students with their research projects. For example, they may provide guidance to undergraduate students with independent study projects, graduate students with their theses, or doctorate candidates with their dissertations. Some Professors also supervise postdoctoral students who are managing their own research projects.

At universities and many colleges, Professors are expected to conduct academic research and to write up the results of their research for publication in scholarly journals, books, and electronic media. For many Professors, their research is usually a continuation of the work begun during their doctoral program. Some research projects are conducted in collaboration with colleagues or students.

Part of the research process includes the writing of grant proposals to obtain funds from private corporations, government agencies, and other funding sources. The money pays for equipment and supplies, travel to research sites, overhead costs, financial support for themselves and research assistants, and so on. Some Professors support their own research projects during unpaid summer terms.

Along with teaching and research, Professors are required to participate in faculty meetings where they discuss and handle departmental matters, curriculum, equipment purchases, hiring, and so on. Professors are also expected to serve on academic and administrative advisory committees which deal with institutional policies. Additionally, many Professors perform community service, such as providing consultation services to community agencies, nonprofit organizations, corporations, government agencies, and other institutions. Many Professors also serve on committees, panels, or commissions established by government agencies.

Due to the flexible nature of their profession, Professors can participate in various nonacademic activities. For example, they might:

- conduct seminars or workshops for professional associations
- go on lecture tours
- contribute articles to professional publications; act in an editorial capacity to a professional journal; or review manuscripts or proposals on an ad hoc basis
- participate in a musical, dramatic, or other artistic performance
- practice a profession, such as law, on a part-time basis
- testify as an expert witness in a court of law

Professors are responsible for keeping up with developments in their field through independent study, networking with colleagues, and participating in professional conferences and workshops.

The number of hours that Professors divide among teaching, research, and other duties varies according to their situation and the type of institution where they work. Generally, undergraduate faculty teach 12 to 15 hours per week while graduate faculty usually teach 10 hours or less. University Professors typically spend more time conducting research than Professors in baccalaureate institutes (four-year colleges). Also, senior Professors usually spend a large portion of their time conducting research rather than teaching.

On most campuses, there are four academic ranks for Professors—instructor, assistant professor, associate professor, and (full) professor. Professors may be appointed to part-time or full-time positions. Many full-time Professors are tenured—that is, they are assured of a job at an institution until they retire or resign. With tenure, they cannot be fired without just cause and due process.

Salaries

Salaries vary, and depend on factors such as a professor's rank, his or her field, the type of institution, and the geographical location. Full Professors typically earn the highest salaries. Earnings are also higher for teachers in law, medicine, engineering, and business. Salaries tend to be highest in the western Pacific and New England regions and lowest in the southern region.

According to a 1998–99 survey by the American Association of University Professors, the average salaries for instructor, assistant, associate, and full Professor ranged from $31,411 to $83,207.

Many Professors make additional earnings from research projects, publications, consulting work, lecture tours, teaching courses for college extension programs or professional associations, and so on.

Full-time Professors receive benefits such as health plans and retirement benefits; some Professors receive housing and transportation allowances. Many schools also provide funds for faculty research and professional development.

Part-time faculty receive few fringe benefits.

Employment Prospects

Professors are hired by private and public four-year colleges and universities for either tenure track or non–tenure track positions.

Most opportunities become available as Professors retire, resign, or advance to higher positions. An increase in student enrollment and faculty retirement is expected to continue through 2008, thus creating a demand for additional opportunities.

In recent years, fewer tenure-track positions become available each year. Due to tight budgets, colleges and universities have been hiring more part-time faculty or offering prospective full-time faculty limited contracts of one to five years which may be renewed. The competition is high for both tenure and non–tenure track positions at any college.

Job prospects are generally better in fields where there is a demand for experts in the private sector, such as in business, engineering, health science, computer science, physical science, and mathematics.

Advancement Prospects

Professors advance through the ranks as instructor, assistant professor, associate professor, and full professor. Full Professors can advance administratively up the ladder to department chair, faculty dean, provost, and eventually college or university president.

Appointments and promotions are based on Professors' records of teaching, research, publication, and community service. Receiving promotions is separate from being given tenure.

Tenure-track positions start at either the Instructor or Assistant Professor level with tenure attained at the Associate Professor rank. Usually after six years, an Assistant Professor's record is reviewed by the tenured faculty in his or her academic unit and then voted on (to decide whether to recommend the candidate for tenure). The school's board of trustees makes the final decision to grant tenure to a Professor. With tenure, Professors have prestige, professional freedom, and job security for the rest of their academic career. Job satisfaction is extremely high, and few tenured Professors leave the profession.

Tenured or nontenured Professors who wish to leave the academic world can pursue employment in government agencies, businesses, companies, nonprofit institutions, and professional organizations. They can also become consultants in their fields.

Licensure/Certification

Professors in disciplines such as law, medicine, psychology, or engineering need appropriate occupational licenses and professional certifications.

Education and Training

Professors must hold doctoral degrees in their field of specialization. In general, their academic career includes at least four years of undergraduate work for a bachelor's degree, then one to two years of graduate study for a master's degree. This is followed by four to six years in a doctoral program which includes a dissertation on original research that they complete in their major field of study. Upon completion of their doctorate, some students complete an additional two or more years in postdoctoral research and study.

Experience, Skills, and Personality Traits

Depending on the institution's mission, candidates may need to demonstrate that they have a strong teaching or research background. For example, smaller liberal arts colleges emphasize teaching over research.

Additionally, candidates should have excellent communication and presentation skills as well as interpersonal and teamwork skills to establish rapport with students and colleagues. They should also have adequate social skills as Professors commonly attend various college functions. Furthermore, candidates should have strong organizational and management skills.

Successful Professors share several personality traits such as being independent, intelligent, analytical, inquiring, self-motivated, and confident. They enjoy being part of the academic world as teachers and researchers.

Unions/Associations

Professors join different professional associations to take advantage of networking opportunities, professional development, resources, and other services. Along with belonging to local, state, and national organizations that serve their disciplines, Professors join the American Association for Higher Education and the National Association of Scholars.

Many also join the American Association of University Professors, in which some chapters in public institutions negotiate salaries and benefits for their members. Professors in public institutions are also eligible to join the higher education divisions of the National Education Association and the American Federation of Teachers.

Tips for Entry

1. Experts recommend that doctoral candidates gain teaching experience before they earn their doctoral degrees. For example, they might teach courses at their institution, community colleges, or college extension programs.
2. When applying for a position, read the job announcement carefully. Also learn something about the school—whether it is more research-oriented or more teaching-oriented, and so on. Then tailor your resume and cover letter to fit the position. For example, if you know the school is more interested in teaching, then you would want to emphasize your teaching strengths and experiences.
3. The Internet is a valuable tool for keeping up-to-date with issues and trends in higher education, networking with colleagues around the world, doing a job search, and so on. For example, visit the following web sites to learn more about higher education: the Department of Education/Office of Postsecondary Education (*http://www.ed.gov/offices/OPE*), ERIC Clearinghouse On Higher Education (*http://www.eriche.org*), the American Association for Higher Education (*http://www.aahe.org*), and the American Association of University Professors (*http://www.aaup.org*).

LECTURER

CAREER PROFILE

Duties: Teach undergraduate or graduate courses on a temporary basis in four-year colleges and universities; advise students; perform other duties as required

Alternate Titles: Visiting Lecturer, Adjunct Lecturer, Senior Lecturer

Salary Range: $33,000 to $39,000

Employment Prospects: Good

Advancement Prospects: Limited

Prerequisites:
　Licensure/Certification—Occupational licensure and professional certification may be required
　Education/Training—A master's or doctoral degree
　Experience—Previous teaching experience
　Special Skills and Personality Traits—Communication, interpersonal, teamwork, organizational, and management skills; independent, analytical, intellectual, flexible, creative

CAREER LADDER

Senior Lecturer

Lecturer

Doctoral Candidate

Position Description

College and university Lecturers are temporary faculty members who have been appointed to teach courses for one or more departments (such as history, physical science, elementary education, or theater arts). They usually are not required to conduct research or publish creative work because of their heavy teaching loads. Lecturers who hold another staff or academic position may be appointed as Adjunct Lecturers.

Lecturers teach one to four undergraduate or graduate classes per term. The courses are usually basic requirement classes and can be for any academic unit in a department. For example, a Lecturer in a Classics Department might teach beginning Latin, classical Greek, and Roman religion. Their teaching load may be reduced if they are performing extensive program development for a department, or are helping students in a production such as a play or concert.

For each course they teach, Lecturers develop a syllabus that outlines the topics to be taught. Lecturers also prepare for their classes—studying the topic, writing lecture notes, gathering materials for lab demonstrations, choosing appropriate assignments within assigned texts, compiling bibliographies for outside reading assignments, and so on.

Their instruction may involve presentations to small groups of students in classrooms or to hundreds of students in large lecture halls. Lecturers may also supervise students in laboratory or field experiments. Many Lecturers use computer technology as teaching aids in their instruction.

Lecturers are also responsible for administering and grading student papers and examinations. They evaluate students' work in a timely manner, giving students critical feedback. At the end of each school term, Lecturers evaluate students' overall performance with a letter grade and report the grades to the appropriate office.

As part of their duties, Lecturers keep regular office hours each week to advise students on academic and career matters. Lecturers may be responsible for directing students in independent studies or supervising students, such as teacher education majors in practicum field experiences. Some Lecturers act as advisers to student organizations.

Some Lecturers are given the additional duty of assisting program coordinators within their departments. For example, they might help in the development and evaluation of courses; collect program data; help with student recruitment; prepare student advisement materials; or design professional development activities for teaching assistants or part-time faculty.

Lecturers are responsible for keeping up with developments in their discipline as well as in teaching methodologies, multicultural issues in learning, the use of technology in instruction, and so on. Professional development may be acquired by independent study, networking with colleagues, and participating in professional workshops and conferences.

Lecturers may be appointed to part-time or full-time positions, which are non–tenure track. They normally receive limited term contracts for one to three years or longer, which may be renewed.

Many part-time Lecturers also hold down other jobs. They might teach courses in community colleges or college extension programs as well as teach classes, seminars, or workshops for professional associations. Some Lecturers find part-time employment in government, business, private industry, nonprofit, and community organizations as consultants, researchers, program developers, writers, and so on.

Salaries

According to a 1998–99 survey by the American Association of University Professors, the average annual salary for Lecturers in four-year colleges and universities ranged from $33,833 in baccalaureate institutions to $39,161 in doctoral institutions. Lecturers in private and independent colleges earned higher average salaries than Lecturers in public or church-related institutions.

Depending on an institution's policy, College Lecturers might receive fringe benefits such as medical insurance and retirement benefits.

Employment Prospects

Along with teaching in four-year colleges and universities, Lecturers are also hired by community colleges as well as by college and university extension programs.

Job prospects are currently good for part-time Lecturer positions as well as for limited term contracts for full-time positions. However, the competition is high for most faculty positions.

Advancement Prospects

Generally, the position of Lecturer is a stepping stone to academic positions as Instructor, assistant professor, associate professor, and so on up to college president.

With experience and advanced degrees, Lecturers may be appointed to the rank of Senior Lecturer, which confers a status of superior performance as well as higher pay.

Licensure/Certification

Lecturers who are in professions such as nursing and occupational therapy must hold appropriate licensure and professional certification.

Education and Training

Lecturers in universities and four-year colleges should have doctoral degrees. Many institutions hire Lecturers with master's degrees if they have qualifying professional work experience.

Experience, Skills, and Personality Traits

Lecturers should have previous teaching experience, for example, as a teaching assistant, at the four-year college or university level. Employers look for candidates who are able to teach introductory courses within their discipline.

To work effectively with students, colleagues, and others, Lecturers should have adequate communication, interpersonal, and teamwork skills. In addition, they should have effective organizational and management skills to complete their duties each day. Successful Lecturers share several personality traits such as being independent, analytical, intellectual, flexible, and creative.

Unions/Associations

Lecturers join different professional associations to take advantage of networking opportunities, professional development, professional resources, and other services. Along with belonging to local, state, and national organizations that serve their specific disciplines, Lecturers might join any of the following: the American Association for Higher Education, the National Association of Scholars, or the American Association of University Professors.

Tips for Entry

1. Many colleges and universities have a pool of qualified lecturers whom they contact at any time to fill temporary positions. Contact the colleges and universities where you would like to work and find out if they have such a pool for which you can apply.
2. College and university extension programs are constantly looking for new courses to offer. If you have an idea for a course, talk with the appropriate staff member at an extension program.
3. The Internet can provide you with sources to keep up with developing issues and trends in higher education. On the Internet, you can also find community bulletin boards and mailing lists (also known as *listservs*) that can be used to network with colleagues across the nation. To begin a search of relevant web sites, enter the keyword "higher education" in a search engine.

INSTRUCTORS IN ADULT EDUCATION AND CONTINUING EDUCATION

VOCATIONAL INSTRUCTOR

CAREER PROFILE

Duties: Provide instruction for courses in a vocation or trade; create lesson plans; perform other duties as required

Alternate Title: A title, such as Paralegal Instructor or Welding Instructor, that reflects the vocation or trade being taught

Salary Range: $18,000 to $64,000

Employment Prospects: Good

Advancement Prospects: Limited

Prerequisites:
  Licensure/Certification—A teaching credential and occupational license or professional certification may be required
  Education and Training—Associate, bachelor's, or master's degree; for licensed teachers, completion of an accredited teacher education program
  Experience—Generally three to six years of work experience; some teaching experience
  Special Skills and Personality Traits—Communication, interpersonal, teamwork, organizational, and management skills; patient, inspiring, flexible, creative, resourceful

CAREER LADDER

Department Chair or Program Coordinator

↑

Vocational Instructor

↑

Professional in one's field

Position Description

Vocational education prepares individuals for entry-level positions in business, skilled trades, health, agriculture, marketing, technology, protective services, education, and other fields. (Vocational education is also known as *career and technical education*.) Professions include: automotive technician, avionics maintenance technician, carpenter, chef, computer repair technician, cosmetologist, court reporter, dental hygienist, electrician, emergency medical technician, firefighter, graphic artist, home health care aide, landscape designer, occupational therapist assistant, office assistant, paralegal, preschool teacher, veterinary technician, vocational nurse, and so on.

Most occupational programs are between six months to two years long, and generally lead to an associate degree and/or professional certification. Courses in the different vocational programs are taught by Vocational Instructors who are experienced professionals in their fields.

Vocational Instructors are responsible for developing a course outline, or syllabus, and lesson plans for each class they teach. Instruction usually includes lectures and demonstrations. Many instructors create a classroom environment that simulates an actual work site so that students can get hands-on experience. Students use professional equipment and tools as well as perform exercises and activities that are similar to the real-life work tasks. For example, students in automotive technology classes might do car tune-ups using electronic equipment like those found in professional auto shops.

As students must meet basic levels of proficiency for entry-level positions, Instructors monitor students' progress and give them critical feedback. They assign additional practice exercises for students who need extra help. Vocational Instructors also administer quizzes and exams to students to check their comprehension of knowledge and skills. In addition, they maintain records of students' progress throughout the course. Vocational Instructors may be required to evaluate the overall performance of their students with letter grades at the end of school terms.

Many Vocational Instructors teach job search skills—how to find a job, complete a job application, and so on. They also teach employability skills that help students keep jobs, such as critical thinking, problem solving, leadership, safety, and self-management skills. Some Vocational Instructors are responsible for supervising student interns at actual work sites.

Vocational Instructors are also responsible for keeping up with developments in their profession as well as in vocational education. For example, they might enroll in continuing education courses sponsored by professional associations or college extension programs, read professional journals and books, or network with colleagues. Some instructors return to the field and work for a short period of time.

In addition, Vocational Instructors participate in faculty meetings to discuss curriculum, vocational education trends, professional development, and other relevant matters. Many instructors also participate on school committees.

Vocational Instructors work part time or full time. Instructors in public institutions usually have a nine- or 10-month work schedule while instructors in private vocational and technical schools teach year-round. Full-time instructors in public institutions may be eligible for tenure; with tenure, they cannot be fired without just cause.

Salaries

Salaries vary, and depend on factors such as education, experience, and type of school. According to the U.S. Bureau of Labor Statistics, the estimated annual salary in 1998 for most Vocational Instructors ranged from $18,010 to $63,850.

Full-time Vocational Instructors receive fringe benefits such as sick leave, holiday pay, health plan, and retirement benefits. Depending on their employer, part-time instructors may receive some fringe benefits.

Employment Prospects

Vocational Teachers are employed by public and private school systems, community colleges, college and university extension programs, private vocational and technical schools, job training centers, community agencies, labor unions, correctional facilities, and professional associations.

Opportunities are expected to grow through the year 2006 to meet the increasing enrollment in vocational programs. Businesses and companies continue to need new employees who are trained for entry-level positions. Also, many individuals enroll in vocational and technical classes to learn new job skills or a new trade.

Most opportunities are expected to be available for part-time positions or nontenured full-time positions. The best job prospects are in fields such as computer technology, automotive mechanics, and medical technology that meet the immediate needs of the business world.

Advancement Prospects

Many Vocational Instructors realize advancement through pay raises and full-time positions. Instructors interested in administrative positions can become department chairs, program coordinators, assistant deans, and deans. Advanced degrees may be required to obtain top administrative positions.

Licensure/Certification

Vocational Instructors in public institutions may be required to hold a vocational education credential with an endorsement in each subject that they teach. Type of licensure and licensing requirements vary from state to state. (To learn about the requirements for the state where you wish to teach, contact the state board of education.) Continuing education units and, eventually, a master's degree may be required for licensure renewal.

Private schools may require instructor certification from state boards of education, professional associations, or other recognized organizations.

Furthermore, Vocational Instructors may be required to have current occupational licenses and professional certification. Some professions require instructor certification from their state occupational license board. (For more information, contact your state occupational license board.)

Education and Training

Education requirements vary from school to school. Both public and private postsecondary institutions prefer that Vocational Instructors have master's degrees in their fields. If a master's degree is not offered or required in a field, schools accept a bachelor's or associate degree with a minimum number of years of professional experience.

To become licensed teachers, Vocational Instructors complete an accredited teacher education program that includes course work in pedagogy and instruction, as well as a supervised field practicum.

Experience, Skills, and Personality Traits

In general, Vocational Instructors should have three to six years of work experience with at least one year of journey-level experience or its equivalent. Additionally, they should have previous teaching experience or knowledge of vocational instruction.

Vocational Instructors need communication, interpersonal, and teamwork skills to work well with students, colleagues, and others. Organizational and management skills are also needed to handle a variety of duties each day.

Successful Vocational Instructors are patient, inspiring, flexible, creative, and resourceful. They enjoy teaching others about their trade or vocation.

Unions/Associations

Vocational Instructors join different professional associations to take advantage of networking opportunities, professional development, professional resources, and other services. Along with belonging to organizations that serve their specific professions, they join groups for vocational educators, such as the Association for Career and Technical Education, the National Association of Industrial and Technical Teacher Educators, SkillsUSA-VICA, and the American Society for Training and Development.

Vocational Instructors in community colleges are eligible to join either of these teachers unions: the National Educational Association or the American Federation of Teachers.

Tips for Entry

1. Talk with Vocational Instructors in different settings to get an idea if this profession might be for you. If possible, observe their classes. Or get hands-on experience by volunteering as a classroom aide.
2. Apply directly to public and private schools where you would like to work. Contact them on a regular basis to let them know you are still interested in a position.
3. You can learn more about vocational education on the Internet. To start, you might visit these web sites: Association for Career and Technical Education (*http://www.acteonline.org*), or Vocational Education Resources (*http://pegasus.cc.ucf.edu/~sorg/vocation.html*).

ADULT EDUCATION INSTRUCTOR

CAREER PROFILE

Duties: Provide instruction for literacy, English literacy, or other adult education program; develop curriculum, lessons, and instructional materials; perform other duties as required

Alternate Titles: Adult Basic Education Teacher, GED Instructor, ESL Instructor

Salary Range: $13,000 to $47,000

Employment Prospects: Good

Advancement Prospects: Limited

Prerequisites:
  Licensure/Certification—Teaching credential or other certification may be required
  Education/Training—A bachelor's or master's degree
  Experience—Previous teaching experience in adult education settings
  Special Skills and Personality Traits—Communication, interpersonal, teamwork, organizational, and management skills; patient, understanding, trustworthy, supportive, flexible, creative, resourceful

CAREER LADDER

Lead Teacher or Program Coordinator

Adult Education Teacher

Student Teacher

Position Description

Almost every community in the United States has an adult education program run by a school, community college, community center, church, or other organization. Men and women enroll in adult education classes to achieve specific educational goals—for example, to learn English for the U.S. naturalization test, earn a high school diploma, be able to understand materials (e.g. blueprints) at their job site, or learn to write personal letters.

Several types of adult education programs are available. One is the adult basic education (ABE) program which provides instruction in basic reading, writing, and math skills to adults with low-level skills or no skills at all. ABE Instructors teach the skills in the context of work and life situations that are relevant to their students. For example, an ABE instructor might introduce a lesson on multiplying mixed numbers by asking students how they would double measurements in recipes.

Some Adult Education Instructors work in adult secondary education programs which prepare students to take an examination for a high school equivalency diploma. The most common program is the General Education Development (GED) program for the GED certificate. GED Instructors provide instruction in the five academic areas that are tested—mathematics, literature, science, social studies, and writing skills.

The English as a Second Language (ESL) program is another type of adult education program. ESL Instructors teach English language skills—speaking, listening, reading, and writing—to adults who have limited English language proficiency. Adult Education Instructors also teach classes in family literacy, workplace literacy, employability, U.S. citizenship, and older adult literacy programs.

Depending on the program, Adult Education Instructors might follow a prescribed curriculum, work with colleagues to develop a curriculum, or be responsible for creating the curriculum for their courses. All instructors, however, are responsible for planning and preparing lesson plans for their classes. Many instructors create original instructional materials because of lack of program funds to buy materials. (Some instructors write brief grant proposals, ask publishers for donations, or organize students in fund-raising activities to obtain materials for their classes.)

Instructors use various teaching methods, including class work, small group work, and one-on-one coaching. They modify instruction to fit students' interests as well as their skill levels and learning styles so that they can succeed in achieving their educational goals. Instructors assign exercises and activities that reinforce and enhance students' knowledge and skills. They review students' work, giving them positive reinforcement on their performance as well as ways to improve their work. Instructors also check students' comprehension with quizzes and tests. Many Adult Education Instructors use computers and audiovisual equipment to augment their instruction.

In addition to their instructional duties, Adult Education Instructors participate in faculty meetings to discuss program development, budgets, fund-raising, teaching methods, and so on. Instructors also stay current with developments in their profession through independent study, continuing education courses, and networking with colleagues.

Adult Education Instructors work part time or full time. Their schedules vary, and may include teaching classes at night and on weekends.

Salaries

Salaries vary, and depend on factors such as education, experience, and type of employer. According to the U.S. Bureau of Statistics, the estimated annual salary for most Adult Education Instructors in 1998 was between $13,070 and $47,430.

Most full-time Instructors receive fringe benefits such as sick pay, health plans, and retirement benefits. Part-time instructors rarely receive fringe benefits.

Employment Prospects

Adult Education Instructors are employed by public schools, community colleges, extension programs in colleges and universities, community centers, senior centers, libraries, community-based agencies, labor unions, religious organizations, correctional facilities, and senior centers.

During the 1990s, adult education programs saw a growth in enrollment due to more employers requiring higher levels of reading, writing, and math skills from job applicants and employees. This growth is also due to the U.S. Immigration and Naturalization Service requiring basic competency in civics and the English language for U.S. naturalization. The demand for adult education programs is expected to continue through the year 2006. Most opportunities become available as Adult Education Instructors resign or advance to other positions. Organizations may create new positions when funding is available.

Advancement Prospects

Advancement is limited to the positions of lead Adult Education Instructors and program coordinators. In educational institutions, instructors can advance to higher administrative positions, which may require advanced degrees and experience. Many Adult Education Instructors realize advancement through higher wages and additional teaching assignments, or full-time positions.

Being an Adult Education Instructor has been a stepping stone for many teachers, principals, university professors, counselors, textbook editors, educational technologists, and other educators in the field.

Licensure/Certification

Adult Education Instructors who teach academic subjects in schools and state-supported postsecondary institutions may be required to hold an adult education teaching credential. The type of licensure and licensing requirements vary from state to state. (To find out the requirements for the state where you wish to teach, contact the state board of education.) Licensed teachers may need to complete continuing education units and, eventually, a master's degree, for licensure renewal.

Noneducational institutions may require English literacy instructors to hold appropriate teaching credentials or professional certification such as the Teaching English as a Foreign Language (TEFL) certificate.

Education and Training

Requirements vary with the different employers but, in general, Adult Education Instructors should have bachelor's degrees in any field as long as they have qualifying work experience. Many employers prefer instructors with master's degrees in adult education.

Licensed instructors would have completed an accredited teacher education program, which includes course work in pedagogy, instruction for adult learners, as well as a supervised field practicum.

Experience, Skills, and Personality Traits

Employers choose candidates who have previous teaching experience in the type of adult education programs for which they are applying. In addition, candidates must be knowledgeable in the subject matter they would be teaching. Furthermore, candidates must show that they are sensitive and respectful of the particular needs of adult learners.

To perform their work effectively, Adult Education Instructors should have strong communication, interpersonal, and teamwork skills as well as adequate organizational and management skills.

Being patient, understanding, trustworthy, supportive, flexible, creative, and resourceful are some of the personality traits that successful Adult Education Instructors share.

They enjoy working with adult education students and have a strong desire to help them achieve their educational goals.

Unions/Associations

Many Adult Education Instructors join professional organizations to take advantage of teacher resources, continuing education programs, networking with colleagues, and other professional services. Along with local and state organizations, they might join national organizations such as the American Association for Adult and Continuing Education and TESOL (Teaching English to Speakers of Other Languages, Inc.).

Tips for Entry

1. Get experience working in different adult education programs and settings. For example, you might volunteer as a tutor in a community center ESL program, public library adult literacy program, community college ABE class, or workplace literacy program at a job site.
2. To find out about job vacancies and requirements, contact public schools, community colleges, community-based agencies, and state employment offices.
3. You can learn more about adult education issues, trends, and programs on the Internet. Here are some web sites you might visit: the U.S. Department of Education Office of Vocational and Adult Education (*http://www.ed.gov/offices/OVAE/adusite.html*), the American Association for Adult and Continuing Education (*http://www.albany.edu/aaace/*), or the National Institute for Literacy (*http://novel.nifl.gov*).

CONTINUING EDUCATION INSTRUCTOR

CAREER PROFILE

Duties: Teach noncredit courses in a wide variety of subjects, such as computer programming, cooking, physical fitness, history, humanities, crafts, gardening, and so on; develop course outline and lesson plans; perform other duties as required

Alternate Title: A title, such as Quilting Teacher, that reflects the subject being taught

Salary Range: $13,000 to $47,000

Employment Prospects: Good

Advancement Prospects: Limited

Prerequisites:
  Licensure/Certification—Occupational license and professional certification as required by profession
  Education/Training—Bachelor's degree or equivalent
  Experience—Professional experience; previous teaching experience desired
  Special Skills and Personality Traits—Communication, interpersonal, teamwork, organizational, and management skills; patient, inspiring, flexible, creative, resourceful

CAREER LADDER

Program Coordinator

↑

Continuing Education Instructor

↑

Professional in one's field

Position Description

Many schools, colleges, community centers, private learning centers, professional associations, museums, and other institutions offer continuing education programs that are available to adults who wish to learn about a particular topic, learn new skills for their career, or just enjoy learning. Continuing programs offer a variety of classes which vary from one institution to the next. For example, an adult school might offer classes about local history, amateur astronomy, the Internet, computer applications for carpenters, planning a wedding, line dancing, yoga, landscape design, organic pest control, sign language, or Italian, to mention only a few!

Some continuing education programs offer certificate programs for vocations (such as a paralegal or a technical trainer specialist) or for particular skills (such as driving a forklift or performing cardiopulmonary resuscitation). Some programs specialize in courses for a specific profession, such as rescue technician or EFL (English as a Foreign Language) Teacher.

Continuing education classes are taught by instructors who are experts in the subject matter, which may be related to their profession or personal interest. For example, a Continuing Education Instructor teaches a class on writing children's picture books and a beginning knitting class. Professionally, she is an author of children's books, and knitting is one of her longtime hobbies. In college and university extension programs, many credit courses are taught by professors and instructors who are part of the regular faculty on the campuses.

Continuing Education Instructors are responsible for developing the content of their courses. For each course, they define the objectives—what students will learn from the class—and what type of assessment they will use to determine that students are meeting the course objectives. Instructors also outline the topics that will be covered at class meetings. In addition, Instructors decide what supplies and instructional materials they will need for the class.

Instructors are also responsible for creating lesson plans, which involves developing class exercises and activities that provide students with hands-on experience. Preparation also includes studying the topic to be taught, developing student handouts, gathering instructional materials and equipment needed for the class, and so on.

Continuing Education Instructors use instructional methods appropriate to the subject matter, such as lectures, demonstrations, modeling, group work, and individual instruction. Many instructors use computers and audiovisual equipment to augment their instruction.

Depending on the nature of the course, Instructors might hold classes once or twice a week throughout a term. Classes generally run from one to four hours. Some classes are short-term; for example, an instructor might teach a one-day class for making holiday centerpieces. Most Instructors teach in the evenings or on Saturdays.

Most Continuing Education Instructors teach one or two classes each term. Many instructors write proposals for courses they would like to teach, and send them to continuing education programs. A program accepts new courses that fit the needs of the community the program serves.

Many Continuing Education Instructors have other full-time or part-time jobs. Some instructors teach classes for other continuing education programs.

Salaries

Salaries vary, and depend on factors such as education, experience, type of employer, and location. According to the U.S. Bureau of Statistics, the estimated annual salary for most Continuing Education Instructors in 1998 was between $13,070 and $47,430.

Continuing Education Instructors work on a contractual basis, and are usually paid a flat fee for each course they teach.

Employment Prospects

Job opportunities are constantly available for Continuing Education Instructors as an increasing number of adults are enrolling in courses for personal enrichment. In addition, continuing education programs are constantly in need of instructors for new course offerings. Most opportunities, however, are for part-time positions.

Advancement Prospects

Continuing Education Instructors realize advancement through higher pay, and teaching additional classes due to popular demand. Instructors interested in administrative positions can advance to full-time positions, such as program coordinators and directors.

Most Continuing Education Instructors have a career in other fields. For many instructors, teaching continuing education classes is part of their overall career development.

Licensure/Certification

Continuing Education Instructors do not need teaching licenses. However, they may need professional licenses or certification to teach vocational subjects or particular skills. For example, an instructor who teaches standard first-aid courses must be certified to teach first aid and cardiopulmonary resuscitation.

Education and Training

Educational requirements vary, and depend on the type of course being taught. Employers generally require that Continuing Education Instructors have a bachelor's degree. However, years of experience in the subject matter may be substituted for educational training.

Experience, Skills, and Personality Traits

Continuing Education Instructors should have extensive experience with the subject matter they are teaching. Employers prefer that instructors have some teaching experience.

To work well with students, Continuing Education Instructors should have adequate communication, interpersonal, and teamwork skills. Organizational and management skills are also needed to handle teaching duties effectively.

Being patient, inspiring, flexible, creative, and resourceful are some personality traits that successful Continuing Education Instructors share.

Unions/Associations

Continuing Education Instructors join different professional associations to take advantage of networking opportunities, professional development, professional resources, and other services. Along with belonging to organizations that serve their specific professions, they might join the American Association for Adult and Continuing Education, a national organization that serves adult and continuing education instructors.

Tips for Entry

1. Get teaching experience by volunteering to teach workshops or classes at senior centers, community centers, recreation centers, museums, and so on.
2. Look through catalogues of the different continuing education programs in your city or area to find out what classes are available. Contact the continuing education programs directly to learn about job vacancies as well as requirements for instructors and submitting course proposals.
3. You can learn more about different continuing education programs on the Internet. To get a list of relevant web sites, enter "continuing education" in any search engine.

COOPERATIVE EXTENSION AGENT

CAREER PROFILE

Duties: Develop, implement, and evaluate educational programs in agriculture, natural resource management, community and economic development, family concerns, and 4-H and youth development; perform other duties as required

Alternate Titles: County Agent, Extension Educator, or a title such as Agriculture Agent that reflects an education area

Salary Range: $25,000 to $75,000

Employment Prospects: Good

Advancement Prospects: Good

Prerequisites:
  Licensure/Certification—A state driver's license
  Education/Training—Bachelor's or master's degree
  Experience—Previous work experience with the Cooperative Extension Service
  Special Skills and Personality Traits—Teaching, public relations, program management, computer, communication, writing, leadership, interpersonal, and teamwork skills; calm, independent, responsible, hardworking, creative, resourceful

CAREER LADDER

Lead Cooperative Extension Agent

Cooperative Extension Agent

Assistant or Associate Cooperative Extension Agent

Position Description

The Cooperative Extension Service (CES) is a federal nonformal education system in partnership with the United States Department of Agriculture (USDA) and state land-grant universities. Created in 1914, CES provides free educational programs in agriculture, natural resource management, community and economic development, family and consumer science, and 4-H and youth development to rural, suburban, and urban communities throughout the country. The programs are based on research that has been conducted by the USDA and state land-grant university scientists.

The responsibility of developing, implementing, and evaluating educational programs belongs to Cooperative Extension Agents in county CES offices. Usually in charge of one program area, Cooperative Extension Agents oversee various educational programs that meet the needs of the communities they serve. For example, an agriculture Cooperative Extension Agent might manage programs such as sustainable agriculture, water quality, waste management, forestry, consumer horticulture, and use of computers in agriculture. Or, a Cooperative Extension Agent in the area of family and consumer education might direct programs in child development, parent education, nutrition and wellness, and family resource management. In smaller offices, Cooperative Extension Agents may handle more than one program area.

Cooperative Extension Agents develop educational programs alone, with other staff members, and as part of a team of agents from several county offices. They also obtain input from individuals, agencies, and organizations within the community. Extension specialists and educators at the state land-grant universities act as resources for the county agents.

Most Cooperative Extension Agents oversee several different educational programs at the same time. They complete various tasks for each program, such as:

- coordinating program activities
- writing brochures, pamphlets, information sheets, and other materials on topics (such as food safety, pest control, and child development) for consumers
- writing press releases and other announcements about upcoming educational programs and distributing them to local newspapers, TV stations, and radio stations as well as to public places such as libraries and community centers
- writing grant proposals and developing other resources to raise funds for educational programs
- conducting workshops, classes, or demonstrations
- planning meetings or conferences
- supervising participants, such as 4-H members, as they prepare for special events
- providing consultation services to individuals, businesses, or organizations
- recruiting, training, and supervising volunteers as leaders, office support staff, and program assistants
- networking with farm bureaus, social services agencies, and community organizations
- answering consumer questions in person, over the phone, by E-mail, and by letters
- completing paperwork

Cooperative Extension Agents typically work more than 40 hours a week. Their work involves traveling to meetings and activities within the counties they serve.

Salaries

Salaries vary from state to state. Cooperative Extension Agents with advanced degrees, extensive experience, or supervisory and administrative duties can expect to earn higher wages. According to the National Association of County Agricultural Agents, most agents earn an annual salary between $25,000 and $75,000.

In addition to a salary, Cooperative Extension Agents receive fringe benefits such as health plans, sick leave, and retirement benefits.

Employment Prospects

Cooperative Extension Agents are employed in every state, the District of Columbia, and the United States territories; however, not all counties may have a county extension office.

Most job opportunities become available to replace agents who retire, resign, or advance to higher positions. Additional opportunities are created according to an extension office's needs as well as available funding.

The National Association of County Agricultural Agents reports that the southern states, such as Georgia, Florida, Texas, and Tennessee, have strong county extension programs which continue to grow.

Advancement Prospects

Cooperative Extension Agents can advance to supervisory and administrative positions, eventually becoming unit leaders or county extension directors. Many Cooperative Extension Agents prefer to pursue advancement by earning higher wages and receiving complex assignments of their choice. Some Cooperative Extension Agents realize advancement by obtaining positions in larger county offices. Cooperative Extension Agents can also become specialists and administrators at the state and federal levels.

Licensure/Certification

Cooperative Extension Agents may be required to hold valid state driver's licenses.

Education and Training

Depending on the state, Cooperative Extension Agents need either a bachelor's or master's degree related to the program area in which they are working. For example, a Cooperative Extension Agent in agriculture might have a degree in agriculture, agriculture education, or a related field. Or, a Cooperative Extension Agent in family and consumer education might have a degree in family and consumer sciences, home economics education, child development and family relations, or a related field.

In some states, candidates with bachelor's degrees are hired for assistant agent positions, and upon acquiring their master's degrees may be promoted to Cooperative Extension Agent.

Experience, Skills, and Personality Traits

Employers hire Cooperative Extension Agents who have previous experience working with the Cooperative Extension Service. This may include work as volunteers and college internships in addition to participating in the 4-H program as children. Along with strong academic skills, candidates should have practical experience in agriculture, nutrition, and other subjects that are part of the program area for which they are applying.

To complete their work effectively each day, Cooperative Extension Agents need skills in teaching, public relations, program management, computer use, communication, and writing. They also need leadership, interpersonal, and teamwork skills.

Successful Cooperative Extension Agents share several personality traits such as being calm, independent, responsible, hardworking, creative, and resourceful. They enjoy teaching as well as working with people and animals.

Unions/Associations

Cooperative Extension Agents join professional organizations to take advantage of networking opportunities, continuing educational programs, professional resources, and other services. Some organizations for the different Cooperative Extension Agents are: the National Association of County Agricultural Agents, the National Association of Extension 4-H Agents, and the National Extension Association of Family and Consumer Sciences.

Many Cooperative Extension Agents join professional organizations that are related to their discipline, such as the American Farm Bureau, the American Dairy Science Association, or the American Association of Family and Consumer Sciences. Many also join Epsilon Sigma Phi, a fraternal organization for all cooperative extension professionals.

They are also eligible to join the American Association for Adult and Continuing Education.

Tips for Entry
1. While still in school, you can begin gaining valuable experience working with CES. As a middle school or high school student, you might join a 4-H club if one is available in your community. In college, become a CES intern. You might also become a volunteer at a county extension office.
2. Talk with Cooperative Extension Agents to learn more about their profession. To find a county extension office, look under the county government listings in the white pages of any telephone book. Look for either "County Extension Office" or "Cooperative Extension Service."
3. To learn about job openings, contact county extension offices directly. To find out about opportunities nationwide, visit the web page for the Cooperative State Research, Education, and Extension Service Job Bank Bulletin (*http://www.reeusda.gov/1700/job/jobc.htm*).
4. On the Internet, you can learn more about the Cooperative Extension Service. To start, you might visit the web site for the Cooperative State Research, Education, and Extension Service (*http://www.reeusda.gov*). Or enter these keywords in a search engine to get a list of web sites: "cooperative extension service" or "county extension office."

CORRECTIONAL INSTRUCTOR

CAREER PROFILE

Duties: Provide instruction to incarcerated inmates as part of a specific educational program; perform other duties as required

Alternate Title: A title, such as Vocational Instructor, that reflects an educational program

Salary Range: $13,000 to $64,000

Employment Prospects: Good

Advancement Prospects: Limited

Prerequisites:
  Licensure/Certification—A teaching credential
  Education/Training—Bachelor's degree; for licensed teachers, completion of an accredited teacher education program
  Experience—Previous experience teaching in an adult education program; vocational instructors must have professional work experience
  Special Skills and Personality Traits—Communication, interpersonal, teamwork, organizational, and management skills; caring, calm, honest, patient, tolerant, creative, resourceful

CAREER LADDER

Lead Instructor

Correctional Instructor

Student Teacher, School Teacher, Adult Education Instructor, or Vocational Instructor

Position Description

Many jails, prisons, and other correctional facilities provide educational programs for juvenile and adult inmates as part of their rehabilitative treatment plans. Studies show that effective educational programs can help inmates obtain adequate academic, vocational, and life skills as well as gain self-esteem to become successful members of society.

Correctional facilities provide different types of educational programs which are taught by different Correctional Instructors. Some Correctional Instructors teach basic reading, writing, and math skills to inmates. Some instructors help inmates prepare for examinations which lead to a high school equivalency diploma. Other Correctional Instructors teach academic subjects as part of an associate or bachelor's degree program.

Many Correctional Instructors are known as vocational instructors. They teach inmates basic knowledge and skills for trades or vocations, such as printing, welding, baking, or automotive repair.

Some Correctional Instructors teach English as a Second Language (ESL) classes to inmates who have limited English language proficiency. Others are special education teachers, providing direct instruction or consultation services to general education instructors. (Federal law mandates that persons under 22 years old who have disabilities—physical impairments, learning disabilities, or behavioral disorders—are eligible for special education programs and related services.)

As separate classes or as part of another course, many Correctional Instructors teach inmates employability skills that can help them find and keep jobs upon release. Some Correctional Instructors teach classes in life skills—critical thinking and problem-solving skills as well as everyday skills such as balancing a checkbook, comparison shopping, and reading and following directions.

Correctional Instructors develop curriculum and instruction that meets the particular abilities and interests of each student. Their teaching responsibilities include:

- preparing a course outline for each subject they teach
- performing an assessment of each student's abilities and interests, which may include administering diagnostic and standardized tests
- preparing lesson plans and student exercises and activities
- choosing appropriate teaching materials to use with individual inmates
- providing instruction on an individual basis or in small groups
- monitoring each student's academic progress and behavior, and keeping attendance and performance records
- correcting papers and tests, and returning them to students with positive remarks about their performance and ways to improve their work
- completing a final evaluation report on each student at the end of a course
- providing guidance counseling as needed

Correctional Instructors are responsible for supervising inmates at all times. They monitor students' activities in their classroom, shop, or other assigned area. Instructors may be asked to track students as they move from an assigned area and to notify correctional officers of student movement. When students break any rules of conduct, instructors write disciplinary reports and direct them to the appropriate staff member. Instructors also maintain an inventory of equipment, tools, and supplies and report any thefts or misuse.

Correctional Instructors work with counselors, therapists, and other educational staff members to develop, monitor, and evaluate effective treatment plans for their students. For example, a Correctional Instructor might develop reading lessons that incorporate anger management skills.

Furthermore, Correctional Instructors are responsible for understanding and following all administrative rules, policies, and procedures at the correctional facilities where they work.

Correctional Instructors work part time or full time on a year-round schedule.

Salaries

According to the U.S. Bureau of Labor Statistics, the estimated 1998 annual salary earned by most adult education instructors, including Correctional Instructors who taught nonvocational courses, was between $11,960 and $50,439. Those who taught vocational courses generally earned between $18,010 and $63,850.

In addition to a salary, Correctional Instructors receive fringe benefits such as sick leave, vacation pay, health plan, and retirement benefits.

Employment Prospects

Correctional Instructors work in juvenile and adult correctional facilities at the local, state, and federal levels. Some Instructors are employed by private prisons.

Qualified Correctional Instructors are always in demand, especially for temporary part-time positions. Most opportunities become available as individuals retire, resign, or advance to other positions. Additional jobs are created from time to time when funding is available.

Advancement Prospects

Advancement opportunities are typically limited to lead teachers and program coordinators. Instructors in correctional education systems that are organized like school districts can advance to administrative positions such as principals and central office administrators.

Correctional Instructors might follow other career paths in correctional education. For example, they can become researchers, curriculum developers, program developers, or program administrators in correctional education departments, correctional education advocacy groups, and other organizations.

Licensure/Certification

Licensure requirements differ from state to state. In most states, Correctional Instructors who teach literacy, life skills, and academic subjects must hold appropriate teaching credentials in elementary education, secondary education, adult education, or special education. Correctional Instructors who teach vocational courses must hold a vocational credential with endorsements in the subjects being taught. (For specific information, contact the state board of education for the state in which you wish to teach.) In addition, Correctional Instructors may need to complete continuing education units and, eventually, a master's degree for licensure renewal.

Education and Training

Employers require that Correctional Instructors hold a bachelor's degree. Most Correctional Instructors have bachelor's degrees in disciplines that relate to the subject matter they teach. Correctional Instructors who teach vocational subjects may not be required to have a bachelor's degree if they fulfill the experience requirement.

Most licensed Correctional Instructors complete an accredited teacher education program leading to licensure. The program includes course work in pedagogy, instruction of subject matter, as well as a supervised field practicum.

Experience, Skills, and Personality Traits

Experience requirements vary from employer to employer. In general, they hire teachers for literacy and academic subjects who have previous experience teaching adults in remedial or special education programs, alternative high schools, adult schools, or job skills training programs. Correctional Instructors who teach vocational subjects must have professional work experience.

Because their job involves working with inmates and other correctional staff members, Correctional Instructors need excellent communication, interpersonal, and teamwork skills. Additionally, they need strong organizational and management skills.

Successful Correctional Instructors share several personality traits such as being caring, calm, honest, patient, tolerant, creative, and resourceful. They also have a good sense of humor. Furthermore, they are passionate about helping incarcerated inmates succeed in their educational goals.

Unions/Associations

Correctional Instructors join local, state, and national professional organizations to take advantage of services such as continuing education programs, training programs, networking opportunities, job listings, and teacher resources. Many join the Correctional Education Association, an organization specifically for correctional educators. Some instructors also join education organizations, such as the American Association for Adult and Continuing Education, the Council for Exceptional Children, or the International Reading Association. In addition, Correctional Instructors might join an organization that serves all correctional professionals, such as the American Jail Association and the American Correctional Association.

Tips for Entry

1. Get experience working with inmates in juvenile and adult correctional facilities by volunteering as a teacher or tutor.
2. Many Correctional Teachers recommend learning about emotional and behavioral disabilities as well as special education methodologies.
3. To learn about vacancies and qualifications, contact the correctional facilities where you would like to work.
4. To learn more about correctional education on the Internet, you might visit the web site for the Office of Correctional Education with the U.S. Department of Education (*http://www.ed.gov/offices/OVAE/OCE/index.html*). To get a list of relevant web sites to read, enter the keyword "correctional education" in any search engine.

OVERSEAS TEACHING PROFESSIONS

TEACHER, AMERICAN OVERSEAS SCHOOL

CAREER PROFILE

Duties: Provide instruction for assigned subjects at a designated grade level (K–12); create daily lesson plans; perform other duties as required

Salary Range: $11,000 to $72,000

Employment Prospects: Good

Advancement Prospects: Good

Prerequisites:
　Licensure/Certification—A teaching credential; U.S. citizenship
　Education/Training—Bachelor's degree
　Experience—One to three years of classroom teaching experience
　Special Skills and Personality Traits—Communication, teamwork, interpersonal, organizational, and management skills; flexible, creative, enthusiastic, energetic, patient

CAREER LADDER

Department Chair, or a teaching position in an overseas school of choice

↑

Teacher, American Overseas School

↑

Classroom Teacher

Position Description

Overseas Teachers generally work for private and independent schools that are run by individuals, private companies, and churches, and can be found in or near every major foreign city. These overseas schools are specifically for children or dependents of Americans who live and work for U.S. government agencies, the U.S. military, private companies, churches, and so on.

Many overseas schools, sometimes known as American or international schools, receive assistance from the U.S. Department of State in the form of grants or other resources. However each of the schools is governed by its own board of directors. Along with American teachers and administrators, a school's staff also includes citizens from the local areas and other countries. The school staff develops its own American-based curriculum according to the school's educational philosophy as well as host-country laws and regulations. Most schools are academically based and prepare students for entry into American colleges and universities.

American Schools may be any combination of grade levels, from kindergarten to 12th grade. The student bodies are usually composed of American children as well as children from other nations.

Many Overseas Teachers work in Department of Defense Dependent (DoDD) schools which are operated by the U.S. Department of Defense. They instruct the dependents of military and civilian personnel in the Department of Defense who are based overseas.

The DoDD schools make up a worldwide school system with school levels from prekindergarten to community college. The DoDD school system follows the same structure and curriculum as the U.S. public school systems. The schools provide college preparatory programs as well as vocational career programs. They also provide special needs programs such as special education programs and ESL (English as a Second Language) programs.

Overseas Teachers are assigned to provide instruction for one or more subjects, and may be assigned to teach one or more grade levels. English is the primary language for instruction in all American overseas schools. In some private American schools, the local language is also used for instruction. Class loads are typically smaller in American overseas schools than in U.S. public schools.

Overseas Teachers develop a course outline for each subject they teach; they also are responsible for creating and preparing daily lesson plans. (In many private and independent schools, teachers help develop the school curriculum.)

Overseas Teachers monitor and evaluate students' progress as well as confer with students and parents about students' work and behavior. They also perform administrative tasks, such as taking attendance and making school announcements. Most teachers sponsor extracurricular activities—coaching sports, advising clubs, directing school plays, and so on. In addition, Overseas Teachers participate in faculty meetings and serve on school committees. Furthermore, they perform other duties as requested, such as supervising children during class breaks.

Overseas Teachers usually receive a renewable one-year or two-year contract.

Salaries

A teacher's salary varies and depends on factors such as education, credentials, experience, and size and type of school. For the 1998–99 school year, teachers with DoDD schools earned an annual salary between $27,945 and $56,065. According to the International Schools Services, annual salaries for Overseas Teachers in American-sponsored schools ranged from $11,000 to $72,000.

Overseas Teachers usually receive a benefits package that may include health insurance, retirement benefits, free housing or housing allowance, round-trip transportation from the United States to the host city, and so on.

Employment Prospects

Opportunities vary from school to school. Most positions become available as teachers resign or advance to other positions. Job prospects are usually good for experienced classroom teachers as well as for those who are willing to work in more than one geographical location.

Advancement Prospects

Teaching in American overseas schools is part of an educator's overall career development. Many Overseas Teachers return to the United States and pursue teaching and administrative positions in private and public schools, colleges, and universities. For teachers who make a lifelong career in overseas teaching, advancement is usually realized through higher earnings and assignments in preferred overseas schools. Overseas Teachers can also pursue department chairs, principals, director of development, and other administrative positions. Additional education and school administrative licensure may be required.

Licensure/Certification

DoDD schools and most American overseas private and independent schools require Overseas Teachers to have a valid teaching credential in elementary, middle, or secondary education with the proper endorsement for each subject they shall be teaching.

DoDD teachers are required to be U.S. citizens.

Education and Training

Employers require that Overseas Teachers have bachelor's degrees in their disciplines. Many licensed teachers have master's degrees in their subjects or in education.

Experience, Skills, and Personality Traits

Most employers require Overseas Teachers to have two to three years of classroom teaching experience. Many prefer candidates who can teach several subjects as well as several grade levels. DoDD schools require at least one year of teaching experience which may be fulfilled by the student teacher requirement for credential programs.

Like all classroom teachers, Overseas Teachers need adequate communication, interpersonal, teamwork, organizational, and management skills to fulfill their duties effectively each day.

Successful Overseas Teachers share several personality traits, such as being flexible, creative, enthusiastic, energetic, and patient. They have a fine sense of humor as well as a sense of adventure. Additionally, they have a respect for different cultures and a desire to learn about them.

Unions/Associations

Many Overseas Teachers join professional organizations to take advantage of networking opportunities, training workshops, and other professional resources. One organization specifically for Overseas Teachers is the Association for the Advancement of International Education. Overseas Teachers might also join professional organizations that serve their particular disciplines, such as the International Reading Association and the National Council of Teachers of Mathematics.

Tips for Entry

1. Many recruiters recommend that if you are interested in working for specific schools, you should write each school directly in September and October.
2. Many schools send representatives to recruitment fairs throughout the United States. To find out about recruitment fairs, inquire at college and university placement centers. Or contact the Office of Overseas Schools, U.S. Department of State, Room H328, SA-1, Washington, D.C. 20522-0132. Phone: (202) 261-8200. E-mail: *OverseasSchools@state.gov*.
3. Use the Internet to learn more about teaching in American overseas schools. Here are some web sites you might visit: Department of Defense Dependents Schools (*http://www.odedodea.edu*); Office of Overseas Schools, U.S. Department of State (*http://www.state.gov/www/about_state/schools*); and National Association of Independent Schools (*http://www.nais.org*)—click on the link to "Careers in Independent Schools."

EFL (ENGLISH AS A FOREIGN LANGUAGE) TEACHER, OVERSEAS

CAREER PROFILE

Duties: Teach English to nonnative speakers in foreign countries; prepare lesson plans; perform other duties as required

Salary Range: Salaries are competitive with local teaching salaries

Employment Prospects: Excellent

Advancement Prospects: Limited

Prerequisites:
  Licensure/Certification—TEFL or CELTA certification may be required if an individual does not have a master's degree
  Education/Training—Bachelor's degree in any field, or a master's degree in TESOL (Teaching English to Speakers of Other Languages), or related field
  Experience—One to two years teaching experience
  Special Skills and Personality Traits—Teaching, technology, communication, interpersonal, organizational, and management skills; outgoing, flexible, open-minded, creative, resourceful, hardworking, dedicated

CAREER LADDER

Lead EFL Teacher

EFL Teacher

TEFL (Teaching English as a Foreign Language) Student

Position Description

Throughout the world, English is taught as a foreign language in many elementary schools, high schools, colleges, and universities as well as commercial language schools and other private language programs. Local citizens wish to learn English for specific reasons. For example, businesspeople might learn English because they wish to do business with American companies. Or, high school students might learn English in order to pass English language requirements on local university entrance examinations.

In most schools overseas, English is taught by EFL (English as a Foreign Language) Teachers who are native speakers. They are trained in the particular methodologies for foreign language teaching. Depending on the school, EFL Teachers may teach all or some English language skills—speaking, listening, reading, and writing skills. Some EFL Teachers only provide conversational English instruction so that students may have intensive speaking and listening practice.

Most EFL Teachers teach several classes each day to preschool children, elementary students, high school students, university students, business professionals, company employees, or private citizens. Each class may have 15 to 45 students.

EFL Teachers are responsible for assessing students' abilities, and providing instruction that matches their skill levels. In addition, EFL Teachers develop lessons that are age-appropriate and fit students' purposes for studying English. They use a variety of teaching methods, including group and individual instruction. Some EFL Teachers are able to supplement their instruction with tape cassette players, audiovisual equipment, and computers.

Like all teachers, EFL Teachers monitor their students' progress, and develop additional exercises and activities for students who need extra help. They also administer quizzes and tests to check their progress.

Their other duties include performing daily administrative tasks, such as taking roll, that their employers may require. They also participate in faculty meetings and attend school functions, such as school parties and graduation ceremonies.

Instructional support for EFL Teachers varies from program to program. For example, some programs provide instructors with a course syllabus and all necessary teaching materials so that teachers can focus on providing instruction. Some programs require that teachers develop the curriculum, course syllabus, and instructional materials.

Work schedules vary from teacher to teacher, and, depending on their contract, may be obligated to teach 15 to 40 hours a week. They might work early morning, late afternoon, and evening hours. Many teachers also work on Saturdays.

EFL Teachers typically sign a renewable one- or two-year employment contract.

Salaries

Salaries vary, depending on an individual's education and experience as well as the type of employer and the stability of a country's economy. EFL Teachers generally earn lower salaries overseas than in the United States; however, their salaries are competitive with the local salaries—and sometimes higher than the local standards—so most teachers are able to live a comfortable lifestyle overseas. Some teachers earn additional money by offering private tutoring services.

Many employers provide EFL Teachers with fringe benefits such as health care insurance, free housing, and paid transportation to and from their assignments and the United States.

Employment Prospects

Overseas, EFL Teachers work for commercial language schools, colleges and universities, elementary and secondary schools, and private companies who have language programs for their employees.

Because English is recognized as the common language for world trade and international relations, opportunities are readily available in most foreign countries. EFL Teachers are especially in demand in China, Japan, Korea, Taiwan, and Russia as well as many countries in Southeast Asia, Eastern Europe, Middle East, South America, and Central America.

Advancement Prospects

Being an EFL Teacher overseas is usually part of an educator's overall career development. After a few years of teaching overseas, most EFL Teachers return home and continue careers in education or other fields.

Some EFL Teachers make a full career out of teaching overseas, and realize advancement through better employment contracts as well as by working in different parts of the world. Some EFL Teachers start their own private language schools overseas.

In a commercial language school, EFL Teachers can become recruiters, trainers, and administrators in the United States or abroad.

Licensure/Certification

More employers are requiring that applicants have professional certification if they do not have a master's degree in an acceptable field. The two voluntary certificates that are recognized by most employers worldwide are the Certificate in English Language Teaching to Adults (CELTA) or the Teaching English as a Foreign Language (TEFL) certificate. (To find TEFL or CELTA programs in your area, contact college and universities as well as private language schools.)

Education and Training

Most employers require that applicants have a bachelor's degree in any field. In many countries, a bachelor's degree is required to obtain a work permit. Colleges, universities, and other employers require a master's in TESOL (Teaching English to Speakers of Other Languages), applied linguistics, English with an emphasis in TESOL, or other related field.

Many employers require applicants to have completed training in second language acquisition, pedagogy, materials development, curriculum design, and so on, which is fulfilled by completing an appropriate graduate or professional certification program.

Experience, Skills, and Personality Traits

Many employers require applicants to have one to two years of teaching experience, preferably teaching English language skills to nonnative speakers. Fluency or proficiency in the native language of the foreign country is not necessary. However many EFL Teachers learn the native language to gain a fuller experience.

Along with teaching skills, applicants should be able to use audiovisual equipment and computers. In addition, EFL Teachers need communication, interpersonal, organizational, and management skills to perform their duties effectively.

Successful EFL Teachers share several personality traits such as being outgoing, flexible, open-minded, creative, resourceful, hardworking, and dedicated. They also have a respect for other cultures and have a sense of adventure.

Unions/Associations

TESOL, Inc. (Teaching English to Speakers of Other Languages, Inc.) and the International Association of Teachers of English as a Foreign Language are two organizations that many EFL Teachers join. These organizations provide teacher resources, networking opportunities, training workshops, and other professional services.

Tips for Entry

1. Gain practical experience teaching English to nonnative speakers. For example, you might tutor students in an ESL (English as a Second Language) program in a school, community college, or community agency.
2. Take time to do thorough research on living and working abroad. Learn about the country where you

wish to work—its history, political situation, culture, climate, work permits, and so on. One valuable source for general information is a country's embassy or consulate office.
3. To work in a foreign country, you must have a U.S. passport, visa, and work permit. Some employers do all the necessary paperwork for obtaining the proper visas and work permits.
4. Get references on a prospective employer from current and previous employees before signing a contract. Also review an employment contract carefully before signing it. Make sure the terms—salary, benefits, work conditions, living conditions, and so on—clearly state what you agree to.
5. You can learn about current and future job openings overseas without leaving the United States. Many employers advertise openings in major city newspapers.
6. The Internet can help you learn more becoming an EFL Teacher overseas. For a list of relevant web sites to read, enter the keyword "teaching English overseas" in any search engine. Or start by visiting these web sites: the TESOL Placement Bulletin (*http://www.tesol.edu*), TEFL Professional Network (*http://tefl.com/index.html*), "Dave Sperling's ESL Cafe's Job Center" (*http://wwwcificnet.net/%7esperling/jobcenter.html*), and The Digital Education Network's EFL Job Centre (*http://www.jobs.edunet.com*).

PEACE CORPS VOLUNTEER

CAREER PROFILE

Duties: Provide volunteer service in a foreign country; perform duties as required by assignment; help with other community projects as needed

Salary Range: A monthly stipend for living expenses; a readjustment allowance upon completion of service

Employment Prospects: Excellent

Advancement Prospects: None

Prerequisites:
  Licensure/Certification—Professional licensure or certification is not necessary, but may improve chances of being chosen
  Education/Training—Bachelor's degree; three months' preservice training
  Experience—Varies, and depends on the assignment
  Special Skills and Personality Traits—Skills vary, depending on the assignment; mature, patient, flexible, adaptable, creative, resourceful, dedicated

CAREER LADDER

Career of Choice

Peace Corps Volunteer

Trainee

Position Description

The Peace Corps is a United States federal agency that sends American volunteers to undeveloped and underdeveloped nations in Africa, Europe, the Mediterranean, Asia, the Pacific Islands, Central America, and South America. Peace Corps Volunteers commit to a two-year term of service to help communities in one of six areas—education, community development, health and nutrition, agriculture, business, or environment.

Education Volunteers teach English in university settings, or teach English, math, or science to students in middle and secondary schools. Some Peace Corps Volunteers train teachers in university teacher-training programs or in-service training programs in local schools. Volunteers might instruct teachers in special education methodologies; secondary education teachers in English language acquisition; or primary education teachers in health, language arts, environment, childhood development, or other relevant subjects.

Community Development Volunteers assist communities in developing health, job training, youth development, and other programs that may benefit the local people. Volunteers with construction and skilled trade experience are assigned to teach vocational education in local schools, technical institutes, and training centers; or they might be assigned to local community or government agencies to help plan and build construction projects.

Peace Corps Volunteers in the area of health and nutrition might teach community classes and workshops. Some Volunteers might train local teachers, community leaders, and community groups in public health topics such as maternal and child health, basic nutrition, AIDS education, and hygiene related to water and sanitation conditions. Some Volunteers assist local health clinics and other local organizations to identify health education needs, develop health programs, raise money for health care materials, and so on. Other Volunteers assist in planning and building new water and sanitation facilities, or improving old facilities.

Many Agriculture Volunteers are assigned to work with local farmers to help them increase food production and their income, as well as promote environmental conservation. Volunteers with a background in agricultural production, farm management, or agribusiness teach farmers and extension agents in formal training institutions, or work with small farmers, cooperatives, nongovernmental organizations, and agribusinesses.

Business Volunteers are assigned to a wide variety of projects in schools, universities, technical institutes, government agencies, cooperatives, business centers, environmental organizations, social service agencies, and so on. Many advise private and public businesses, cooperatives, and nongovernmental organizations. Some assist cities and regional governments with planning and implementing economic development strategies. Some conduct community workshops or teach classes in business planning, finance management, business courses, English, and so on.

Environment Volunteers are assigned to help communities promote environmental education and awareness in natural conservation, such as sustainable use of forest resources or sanitation management in urban areas. Some Environment Volunteers work on forestry projects to conserve natural resources, such as soil conservation, watershed management, or flood control. Some Volunteers provide technical assistance and training on natural resource conservation to personnel in natural parks and reserves.

Salaries

Peace Corps Volunteers do not receive a salary, but they do receive a monthly stipend for food, housing, transportation, and incidentals. They also receive medical and dental benefits as well as two vacation days for every month of service. Additionally, their transportation to and from their host countries is paid by the agency.

Upon completion of their service, Peace Corps Volunteers receive a readjustment allowance of $225 for each month of their two-year term as well as for their three months of preservice training.

Employment Prospects

Opportunities for Peace Corps Volunteers should be excellent in the first decade of the 21st century, as federal legislation was enacted in 1999 to expand the Peace Corps from 7,000 volunteers to 10,000 volunteers by 2003.

To become Peace Corps Volunteers, applicants must be U.S. citizens at least 18 years old. They must also pass every step of the selection process that includes an application, oral interview, medical and dental clearance, legal clearance, and FBI background check. The selection process usually takes six to 12 months.

Advancement Prospects

Upon completion of their service, Peace Corps Volunteers have valuable work—and life—experience to build upon as they pursue their chosen careers in education, business, law, social work, technology, or other field.

Returned Volunteers may apply for domestic and overseas positions within the Peace Corps as trainers, recruiters, program administrators, and so on. But the length of employment for any position is limited to a total of five years.

Licensure/Certification

Having job-related licensure or professional certification in teaching, construction trades, business, and other areas may not be required; however, it does improve candidates' chances of being accepted.

Education and Training

The Peace Corps prefers that Volunteers have bachelor's degrees. But the education requirement may be waived if candidates have qualifying work experience.

All Peace Corps Volunteers receive three months of intensive training in their host countries before beginning their tour of duty. Training consists of instruction in the local language and culture as well as any technical skills Volunteers may need for their assignments.

Experience, Skills, and Personality Traits

Requirements vary and depend on the type of assignments for which applicants apply. For example, Volunteers who work with at-risk children should have at least six months' work experience while Volunteers who provide technical assistance to park rangers should have three years' work experience in park administration, wildlife management, or other related field.

Successful Peace Corps Volunteers share several personality traits such as being mature, patient, flexible, adaptable, creative, resourceful, and dedicated. They have a good sense of humor and enjoy adventure. In addition, they are sensitive to and respectful of different peoples and their culture and traditions.

Unions/Associations

Peace Corps Volunteers may join local, regional, and international professional associations in their field that provide networking opportunities, professional resources, and other valuable services.

Tips for Entry

1. If you are a college junior or senior, you may be able to apply early and receive an assignment upon your graduation. For information, contact a regional Peace Corps recruiting office. Call (800) 424-8580 to find the number of your regional office.
2. You can learn more about the Peace Corps on the Internet. To start, visit the web site for the Peace Corps (*http://www.peacecorps.gov/home.html*).

SCHOOL ADMINISTRATORS

PRINCIPAL

CAREER PROFILE

Duties: Provide educational leadership and site management for an elementary, middle, junior high, or high school; oversee curriculum and instruction, staff supervision and evaluation, support services, staff development, student discipline, business services, and community relations; perform duties as required

Alternate Title: Headmaster, in private schools

Salary Range: $64,653 to $74,380 (average salaries for principals at different school levels)

Employment Prospects: Excellent

Advancement Prospects: Fair

Prerequisites:
   Licensure/Certification—School administrator credential with a principal endorsement
   Education/Training—Master's degree; for licensed principals, completion of an educational administration program
   Experience—Several years of classroom teaching experience; supervisory and administrative experience preferred
   Special Skills and Personality Traits—Communication, public speaking, interpersonal, team building, conflict management, time management skills; self-motivated, energetic, organized, creative, flexible, patient, honest, trustworthy, courageous

CAREER LADDER

Assistant Superintendent or other higher-level school administrator

↑

Principal

↑

Assistant Principal or School Teacher

Position Description

Principals are the head administrators of elementary, middle, junior high, and high schools. Their job is to ensure that schools provide the best education to students of all backgrounds and abilities. They are responsible for several administrative areas, including curriculum and instruction, staff supervision and evaluation, support services, staff development, student discipline, business services, and community relations. In public schools, Principals are under the supervision of superintendents, who administer school districts. In private schools, Principals (who are usually called *Headmasters*) are directed by higher-level administrators or boards of trustees.

As instructional leaders, Principals coordinate the curriculum programs for the different grade levels at their schools. They also oversee special programs (such as special education, bilingual education, and reading programs) that help students who have special learning, reading, and language needs. Working collaboratively with teachers, Principals develop and implement new instructional programs and activities that may help students succeed in their learning. In addition, Principals review textbooks, supplementary materials, and supplies to determine whether they are appropriate for the subject matter and for students. In small rural schools, Principals might teach one or more grades.

A major responsibility of Principals is providing support and guidance to all staff members. As the educational leader, Principals model behavior that they expect from their staff. Their staff includes certificated personnel—such as teachers, counselors, coaches, librarians, and assistant principals. It also includes classified staff—teacher aides, secretaries, clerks, custodians, food service workers, campus monitors, and so on. Principals might also supervise school nurses, speech language pathologists, school psychiatrists, and other pupil services personnel.

Principals are responsible for providing in-service training for all staff members. In addition, they resolve conflicts among the staff when necessary. Performing staff evaluations is also another duty that they perform. Furthermore, Principals make recommendations to their superintendents (or boards of trustees) regarding staff promotions, demotions, transfers, contract renewals, and terminations.

Another duty is coordinating the various extracurricular activity programs that are available for students—such as interscholastic sports, student government councils, service clubs, and school publications. Many Principals also create student reward programs such as a student of the month program to recognize positive behavior and growth.

Principals are also responsible for maintaining student discipline. During breaks, lunch periods, and between class periods, many Principals get out to the hallways, cafeteria, and grounds where they can be visible and accessible to the students. Along with monitoring student behavior, Principals take the opportunity to get to know as many students as possible. When students misbehave, Principals are responsible for disciplining them. They might also meet with parents to discuss their children's behavior. With serious misconduct, Principals may recommend that a student be suspended from school.

As building, or school, managers, Principals are responsible for administering the different student services (such as food service and transportation) and administrative programs (such as security and information systems) that are essential to the daily operation of their schools. Usually, they delegate responsibilities to other staff members who work under their direction. For example, a Principal would authorize the cafeteria manager to take charge of the school's breakfast and lunch programs, or the assistant principal to oversee the security program.

Their jobs require completing many different tasks each day. Their duties include, but are not limited to:

- handling problems and crises as they arise
- monitoring all programs to make sure they follow school policies and regulations as well as local, state, and federal laws and guidelines
- coordinating the schedules for classes, in-service workshops, extracurricular activities, student assemblies, school functions, and so on
- conducting assessments of the different instructional, business services, and noninstructional programs
- administering and preparing school budgets
- preparing reports, writing correspondence, and completing paperwork
- maintaining accurate records and files of students, staff, instructional programs, support services, school activities, and so forth
- planning emergency preparedness programs and conducting fire, safety, and other emergency drills
- recruiting and selecting school staff members
- investigating complaints and concerns brought forth by parents, students, staff, and the general public
- coordinating or participating in school fund-raising activities
- attending student games, assemblies, dances, and other school functions

In public schools, Principals are required to attend school district meetings and functions. They serve on district committees and work collaboratively with district personnel and staff from other schools.

As representatives of their schools, Principals maintain positive community relations. Using the local media, Principals keep parents and the general public up-to-date with the schedules of school events and student performances. They also inform the community of pertinent issues such as school discipline policies, new instructional programs, and teacher salary negotiations. Most Principals are active members of school parent groups. They also network with community leaders, business leaders, social service agencies, and community groups, as well as serve on community committees, task forces, or boards.

Principals work very long hours each day. They often work evenings and weekends to complete reports, attend school functions, appear at community events, conduct professional workshops, and so on.

In public schools, many principals have tenure, which means they cannot be fired without just cause. The current trend, however, in many states is to do away with tenure for principals. In recent years, more and more school districts are offering Principals higher salaries and/or renewable limited-term contracts in place of tenure.

Salaries

Salaries vary, and depend on factors such as education, experience, school budget, and location. Typically, salaries are higher in public schools than in private schools. A 1997–98 salary survey by the Educational Research Service reports the following average annual salaries for principals in public schools:

- $64,653 in elementary schools
- $68,740 in middle schools
- $74,380 in high schools

Some school districts award Principals with bonuses for achieving certain goals, serving on special committees, or other accomplishments.

In addition to a salary, Principals receive fringe benefits such as sick leave, vacation leave, health insurance, and retirement benefits.

Employment Prospects

Most job vacancies become available as Principals retire or advance to other positions. The number of opportunities is expected to increase by 10 to 20 percent through 2008, according to the Bureau of Labor Statistics, due to a large number of retirements.

In the late 1990s, school districts nationwide reported a shortage of qualified candidates for principal positions at all school levels in any setting—rural, suburban, and urban. Many experts believe this trend is likely to continue for the next few years.

Advancement Prospects

Principals can become assistant superintendents or other higher-level school administrators, and, eventually, school superintendents. Many Principals prefer being building administrators; they realize advancement through pay increases, professional recognition, and/or obtaining positions in larger school systems.

Principals can also pursue other paths in education. For example, they can become educational administrators or consultants with state and federal educational agencies, nonprofit organizations, or educational consulting firms.

Licensure/Certification

In public schools, Principals must hold a school administration credential with a Principal endorsement. Licensure requirements vary from state to state. (For specific information, contact the state board of education for the state where you wish to work.)

Private schools may require Principals, or Headmasters, to hold state licensure or professional certification from school accreditation organizations, professional associations, or other recognized organizations.

Education and Training

Principals in public schools need a master's degree in educational administration or related field. Private schools require that Principals have at least a bachelor's degree; however, many have either a master's or doctoral degree.

Licensed Principals have completed an educational administrator program from an accredited university. They have completed courses such as educational leadership, school law, school finances, curriculum and instruction, as well as a supervised internship.

Some school districts have mentor programs for new principals in which they receive formal or informal training for a certain period of time. Furthermore, Principals pursue their own professional development; for example, they attend professional workshops and seminars on topics such as conflict resolution, team building, instructional leadership, and curriculum planning and development.

Experience, Skills, and Personality Traits

In general, Principals must have previous classroom teaching experience and some supervisory and administrative experience. In public schools, candidates are usually required to have three to five years of full-time classroom teaching experience. Schools may waive this requirement if candidates have teaching experience along with administrative or supervisory experience.

Along with leadership, supervisory, and administrative skills, Principals need strong communication, public speaking, interpersonal, team building, conflict management, and time management skills to do their work effectively.

Successful Principals share several personality traits, such as being self-motivated, energetic, organized, creative, flexible, patient, honest, trustworthy, and courageous. In addition, they have a strong commitment to education and are able to inspire staff, parents, and others to participate in the development of quality educational programs.

Unions/Associations

Principals join different local, state, and national associations to take advantage of professional services such as continuing education programs, professional resources, and networking opportunities. Some organizations are:

- National Association of Elementary School Principals
- National Association of Secondary School Principals
- National Middle School Association
- Association for Supervision and Curriculum Development
- Phi Delta Kappa
- American Federation of School Administrators

Tips for Entry

1. Take advantage of workshops and seminars for aspiring Principals. The National Association for Elementary School Principals and the National Association for Secondary School Principals are two organizations that offer these types of programs from time to time.
2. Contact schools or district central offices directly to learn about job vacancies and requirements.
3. On the Internet, you can learn more about the Principal profession. You might start by visiting these web sites: the National Association of Elementary School Principals (*http://www.naesp.org*) or the National Association of Secondary School Principals (*http://www.nassp.org*).

ASSISTANT PRINCIPAL

CAREER PROFILE

Duties: Assist the school principal in the daily management of an elementary, middle, junior high, or high school; be responsible for designated administrative programs; provide instructional leadership; perform duties as required

Alternate Titles: Vice Principal, Assistant Administrator, Assistant Headmaster

Salary Range: $53,206 to $60,999 (average salaries for assistant principals at different school levels)

Employment Prospects: Good

Advancement Prospects: Fair

Prerequisites:
  Licensure/Certification—School administrator credential with a principal endorsement
  Education/Training—Master's degree; for licensed Assistant Principals, completion of an educational administration program
  Experience—Classroom teaching; supervisory or administrative experience preferred
  Special Skills and Personality Traits—Communication, interpersonal, teamwork, organizational and self-management skills; self-motivated, energetic, creative, patient, flexible, honest, calm

CAREER LADDER

Principal

↑

Assistant Principal

↑

School Teacher

Position Description

Assistant Principals provide support to principals in elementary, middle, junior high, and high schools, by assisting with site management and instructional leadership. They assist with enforcing school policies and standards as well as local, state, and federal laws and guidelines. When principals are absent, Assistant Principals carry out the leadership duties and make administrative decisions accordingly. (In private schools, Assistant Principals are known as *Assistant Headmasters*.)

Their responsibilities and duties vary from school to school. They assist principals with:

- developing, implementing, and evaluating instructional programs and activities
- recruiting, selecting, supervising, and evaluating school staff—teachers, teacher aides, counselors, librarians, secretaries, clerks, food service workers, bus drivers, and so on
- managing student discipline
- reporting and monitoring student attendance
- planning staff development programs
- developing master schedules of classes, school activities, and so forth
- creating emergency preparedness plans
- writing student and faculty handbooks
- preparing school budgets
- performing hall and lunchroom monitor duty
- performing public relations tasks—for example, contacting local media about school events, honor roll lists, student recognition awards, and so forth

Usually, Assistant Principals are assigned to coordinate one or more administrative areas, such as student discipline, student attendance, instructional supervision for certain grades, school security, or training for new teachers. Large schools often have two or more Assistant Principals, each of whom is responsible for certain administrative areas. For example, a high school might have two Assistant Principals, one in charge of school attendance and student discipline and the other responsible for student activities.

Like Principals, Assistant Principals try to be visible and accessible to students. Before school, after school, during class breaks and lunch periods, and even during the time between class periods, many Assistant Principals are out in the hallways, cafeterias, playgrounds, and other areas, interacting with students as well as monitoring their behavior. They become familiar with as many students as possible, learning their names and listening to how they are doing. From time to time, Assistant Principals counsel students on personal, educational, and vocational matters. Assistant Principals also aid principals with school discipline, which typically involves meeting with students and their parents and administering appropriate discipline, such as detention.

Assistant Principals also contribute to the development of student extracurricular activities. They assist in scheduling activities, finding sponsors, fund-raising, coordinating field trips, and so on. Many Assistant Principals supervise student government councils, coordinate peer mediation activities, and coach sports. Assistant Principals also attend and supervise school games, dances, concerts, and other activities.

Assistant Principals participate in faculty meetings and on school committees. On occasion, they attend district meetings or conferences sponsored by professional associations, educational agencies, or other organizations as their schools' representatives.

In addition, Assistant Principals contribute to maintaining positive community relations. They become active members of school parent groups as well as network with community leaders, business leaders, social service agencies, and community groups.

Furthermore, Assistant Principals pursue their own professional development, attending professional workshops and seminars on topics such as conflict resolution, instructional leadership, and curriculum planning and development.

Most Assistant Principals work more than 40 hours a week, including many nights and weekends.

Salaries

Salaries vary, and depend on factors such as education, experience, level of responsibility, and school budget. Typically, salaries are higher in public schools than in private schools. A 1997–98 salary survey by the Educational Research Service reports the following average annual salaries for assistant principals in public schools:

- $53,206 in elementary schools
- $57,768 in middle schools
- $60,999 in high schools

Assistant Principals typically receive fringe benefits, such as sick leave, vacation leave, health insurance, and retirement benefits.

Employment Prospects

Most opportunities for Assistant Principals become available as individuals retire, resign, or advance to higher administrative positions. In the next few years, opportunities are expected to grow due to the increase in school enrollment and administrative workload. Because of tight budgets, many school districts are expected to hire additional assistant principals rather than open new schools.

Advancement Prospects

With additional experience and training, Assistant Principals can become principals as well as program coordinators and directors in the school district central office, assistant superintendents, and, eventually, superintendents.

Assistant Principals can also pursue other careers in education. For example, they might become educational software developers, counselors, librarians, corporate trainers, or educational researchers.

Licensure/Certification

In public schools, Assistant Principals must hold a valid school administration credential with a principal endorsement. Licensure requirements vary from state to state. For specific information, contact the state board of education in the state where you wish to work.

Many private schools require state licensure or professional certification from school accreditation organizations, professional associations, or other recognized organizations.

Education and Training

Assistant Principals in public schools need a master's degree in educational administration or a related field. In most private schools, Assistant Principals need a bachelor's degree in any field; however, many have master's degrees.

To obtain state licensure, Assistant Principals must have completed an educational administration program from an accredited university. They have completed courses such as educational leadership, school law, school finances, curriculum and instruction, as well as completed a supervised internship.

Experience, Skills, and Personality Traits

Employers generally choose candidates who have previous classroom teaching experience. Most prefer that candidates have some school administrative or supervisory experience. In addition, candidates are able to demonstrate that they have successful instructional and leadership experience at the appropriate school level.

Assistant Principals need strong communication, interpersonal, and teamwork skills in order to work effectively with teachers, students, parents, and others. In addition, Assistant Principals need strong organizational and self-management skills—the ability to handle stress, prioritize tasks, meet deadlines, understand and follow directions, and so on.

Being self-motivated, energetic, creative, patient, flexible, honest, and calm are a few personality traits that successful Assistant Principals share. They have a strong commitment to providing quality education to students of all backgrounds and abilities.

Unions/Associations

In addition to local and state professional educator associations, Assistant Principals join groups specifically for school administrators, such as the National Association of Elementary School Principals, the National Association of Secondary School Principals, and the American Association of School Administrators. These organizations provide professional services such as current research findings, continuing education programs, job listings, and networking opportunities. Many Assistant Principals also belong to the American Federation of School Administrators, a union for school administrators.

Tips for Entry

1. As a teenager, you can begin gaining supervisory and administrative experience. Participate in school clubs, student government, and other extracurricular activities, and take advantage of opportunities to lead, plan, organize, and coordinate activities.
2. Talk with Assistant Principals as well as principals. Learn from them what experiences and skills you should obtain.
3. To learn more about school administration on the Internet, visit the web site of the ERIC Clearinghouse on Educational Management (*http://eric.uoregon.edu*).

SUPERINTENDENT

CAREER PROFILE

Duties: Provide leadership to all schools within a school system; implement policies and standards established by the school board; oversee the administration of all instructional programs, support services, and business services; maintain community relations; perform duties as required

Alternate Title: President, in private schools

Salary Range: $88,000 to $200,000

Employment Prospects: Good

Advancement Prospects: Limited

Prerequisites:
   Licensure/Certification—School administrator credential with superintendent endorsement
   Education/Training—An advanced degree; completion of an educational administration program
   Experience—Classroom teacher, principal, and central office administrator experience
   Special Skills and Personality Traits—Management, supervisory, executive, communication, interpersonal, team building, and social skills; patient, flexible, honest, trustworthy, compassionate, analytical, creative, courageous, energetic

CAREER LADDER

Superintendent of a larger school system

↑

School Superintendent

↑

Assistant, Associate, or Deputy Superintendent

Position Description

In the United States, public schools are organized into school districts that are administered by Superintendents. They are responsible for providing instructional leadership and management of all schools within their districts. (In private schools consisting of several school levels, the top position is termed the *President*.)

School districts differ in size and composition. Thus, a Superintendent might manage a suburban K–8 school district that is made up of three elementary schools and one middle school; another Superintendent might manage a metropolitan K–12 school district that has over 25 elementary, middle, junior high, and high schools.

Superintendents are selected by school boards that are composed of elected citizens of the communities that the school districts serve. The school boards establish the missions and goals for the schools. Working within the parameters of state laws and regulations and community values, the school boards establish policies and standards regarding curriculum, transportation, building maintenance, staff development, student services, labor relations, and so forth. Superintendents ensure that the policies and standards are realized and followed by every school in their districts. They are held accountable for all successes and failures of schools under their jurisdiction.

As Superintendents are the experts in education, they advise school boards on the best ways to handle matters regarding the school district and school administration. Additionally, Superintendents keep school boards informed on what is happening in the schools.

Working from the school district central office, Superintendents oversee four major areas:

- curriculum and instruction—for example, core curriculum, reading, special education, bilingual education, and vocational education

- support services—such as pupil services, curriculum development, and instructional supervision
- noninstructional services—food service, security, transportation, and building operations, for instance
- business services—for example, human resources, payroll, and purchasing

Because of the complexity of their jobs, Superintendents delegate areas of responsibility to their subordinate administrators. For example: a Superintendent delegates the responsibility of human resources and financial services to an assistant superintendent. The assistant oversees the different programs (such as personnel, payroll, and purchasing) within those areas. The size and makeup of a Superintendent's staff varies, depending on the types and number of programs, the district budget, the size of the district, and so forth.

Superintendents handle many different duties and tasks each day, which they perform with assistance from their administrative support staff as well as subordinate administrators. One major duty is coordinating school board meetings. They schedule meetings as often as the school board desires, inform members and the general public of the time and place for board meetings, and prepare meeting agendas. In addition, they prepare reports of all school business that they will present at the meetings. Most Superintendents communicate with the individual board members before each meeting.

Some other major duties of Superintendents are:

- overseeing the development, implementation, and evaluation of instructional programs and support services in the schools
- preparing monthly financial reports and annual budgets for the school district
- developing plans for the maintenance, improvement, or expansion of buildings and site facilities as needed
- managing human resources—hiring and firing staff for all schools, negotiating contracts, resolving personnel complaints, staff development, and so on
- supervising all school principals
- preparing accurate records and reports for compliance with federal, state, and county educational agencies
- performing fund-raising activities

Superintendents are also responsible for maintaining community relations. As advocates for the children and staff of their schools, Superintendents keep the community aware of what is happening in the schools through correspondence, local media, and presentations to local community organizations. Superintendents also network with community leaders, business leaders, social service agencies, community groups, and so on. In addition, they participate in community events, and serve on boards, task forces, and committees of local agencies and organizations.

As part of their jobs, Superintendents join professional associations to keep up with current educational issues, trends, and developments as well as to network with colleagues. Representing their school districts, they participate in conferences, seminars, and workshops sponsored by professional associations, state and federal educational agencies, universities and colleges, as well as private industries.

Superintendents work on a 12-month schedule. They put in long hours each day to complete their duties. Many evenings and weekends are filled with meetings, school functions, community events, and other work-related activities.

Superintendents do not receive tenure. They are appointed to renewable, term-limit contracts, usually for three to four years.

Salaries

Salaries vary, depending on factors such as education, experience, school budget, and location. In general, salaries are higher in public schools than in private schools. According to a 1998–99 salary survey by the Educational Research Service, the average annual salary ranged from $88,590 for Superintendents of very small public school districts to $133,702 for Superintendents of large public school districts. The Council of the Great City Schools, a nonprofit group representing large public school systems, reports that Superintendents for the 58 largest U.S. city public school districts earned between $103,000 and $199,800.

Superintendents also receive fringe benefits such as sick leave, medical insurance, life insurance, and retirement benefits. They receive additional compensation that varies from district to district. For example, a Superintendent may be provided with an expense account, use of an automobile, a moving allowance, housing allowance, and membership dues for professional organizations.

Employment Prospects

Most job opportunities become available as Superintendents retire, resign, or accept another appointment upon the completion of their contracts. In the 1990s, the American Association of School Administrators estimated that more than 50 percent of the Superintendents in the United States are expected to retire by 2003.

Advancement Prospects

School Superintendents realize advancement through higher pay, professional recognition, and appointments to larger school districts.

Superintendents can also follow other career paths in state and federal education agencies, professional associations, and other educational organizations. They might become program administrators, specialists, consultants, and so on.

Licensure/Certification

Superintendents must hold a valid school administrator credential with a superintendent endorsement for the state in which they work. Licensure requirements vary from state to state. (For information, contact the state board of education for the state where you wish to work.)

Private schools may require state licensure or professional certification from school accreditation organizations, professional associations, or other recognized organizations.

Education and Training

Education requirements vary from district to district. Most districts require that Superintendents have a master's degree in educational administration. Some districts require that Superintendents have either an education specialist's or a doctoral degree.

In addition, School Superintendents must have completed an educational administrator program at an accredited university. They have completed courses such as educational leadership, school administration, school law, curriculum development, school finance, school board relations, and special services, in addition to a one-year internship, which may be substituted with qualifying school administrative experience.

Most Superintendents continue their own professional development through continuing education and professional development sponsored by professional organizations, such as the American Association of School Administrators.

Experience, Skills, and Personality Traits

School boards look for candidates with extensive experience in classroom teaching, building (or school) administration, and central office administration. They have experience in curriculum, staff development, and school fiscal management. In addition, they have experience working at the school levels that the school district covers, and are knowledgeable of the educational programs and services that are provided in the schools.

To handle their job effectively, Supervisors must have superior management, supervisory, and executive skills. They also need excellent communication, interpersonal, team building, and social skills.

Successful Superintendents share several personality traits, such as being patient, flexible, honest, trustworthy, compassionate, analytical, creative, courageous, and energetic. They are able to motivate and inspire their staff, parents, school board, and the community, earning their trust and loyalty. Furthermore, Superintendents are passionate about providing quality education to students of all backgrounds and abilities.

Unions/Associations

Superintendents join different local, state, and national professional organizations to take advantage of services such as professional resources, continuing education programs, and networking opportunities. Some associations that they might join are:

- American Association of School Administrators
- Association for Supervision and Curriculum Development
- Urban Superintendents Association of America
- National Association of Elementary School Principals
- National Middle School Association
- National Association of Secondary School Principals

Tips for Entry

1. Many Superintendents recommend that individuals prepare for the profession by holding a variety of teaching and administrative positions in schools.
2. You can find nationwide job listings for Superintendents on the Internet. For example, the following organizations list available vacancies on their on-line job bulletin boards at their web sites: the American Association of School Administrators (*http://www.aasa.org*) and the National School Boards Association—click on the link for "Resources" (*http://www.nsba.org*). To learn about positions in private schools, visit the web page for the Independent School Management's Career Corner (*http://www.isminc.com/pubs/mart/mm.html*).

ASSISTANT SUPERINTENDENT

CAREER PROFILE

Duties: Provide administrative support to the chief executive officer of a school system; be responsible for managing assigned administrative programs; perform duties as required

Alternate Titles: Associate Superintendent, Deputy Superintendent

Salary Range: $70,000 to $100,000

Employment Prospects: Fair

Advancement Prospects: Fair

Prerequisites:
　Licensure/Certification—School administrator credential with superintendent endorsement
　Education/Training—An advanced degree; completion of an educational administration program
　Experience—Classroom teacher, principal, and central office administrator experience
　Special Skills and Personality Traits—Management, supervisory, communication, interpersonal, and teamwork skills; patient, flexible, loyal, honest, analytical, creative, resourceful, compassionate

CAREER LADDER

Associate Superintendent or Superintendent of Schools

↑

Assistant Superintendent

↑

School Principal or a central office Program Director

Position Description

Assistant Superintendents contribute to the overall instructional leadership and administrative management of public school districts. Under the direction of superintendents (the chief executive officers), Assistant Superintendents have the authority to make administrative decisions that best execute the policies and standards established by the superintendents and the school boards of education.

Generally, Assistant Superintendents are assigned specific areas of responsibility, depending on the needs of the school districts. These areas include, but are not limited to:

- curriculum and instruction—core academic curriculum, vocational education, and special programs such as remedial reading programs, special education, and bilingual education
- support services—such as pupil services, health services, and psychological services
- noninstructional services—for example, school security, food service, and transportation
- business services—human resources, payroll, accounting, purchasing, material handling, and so on

In some school districts, Assistant Superintendents manage instructional and administrative responsibilities for assigned schools. In K–12 (kindergarten through 12th grade) school districts, Assistant Superintendents might be assigned to oversee all elementary schools or all secondary schools. Some large K–12 districts divide their schools into geographical areas; thus, they are assigned as Area Assistant Superintendents.

The duties of Assistant Superintendents vary, according to the administrative areas for which they are responsible. Some duties, however, are the same regardless of the administrative area. For example, Assistant Superintendents:

- coordinate and prepare budgets for programs and activities that are under their authority

- recruit, select, supervise, and evaluate staff members
- assist in the development, implementation, and evaluation of programs and activities
- advise department and program managers with personnel, budgets, and other administrative matters
- interpret and enforce district policies and regulations as well as federal, state, and local laws and guidelines
- represent school district at meetings with community organizations, educational agencies, and professional organizations

In addition, Assistant Superintendents contribute to maintaining community relations for the superintendent's office. Like other central office administrators, Assistant Superintendents network with community leaders, business leaders, social service agencies, community groups, and so on. They also serve on community boards, task forces, and committees as well as attend community functions.

Some school districts have two or more Assistant Superintendents, each of whom is assigned to different areas. Some districts have several levels of assistants—Assistant Superintendent, Associate Superintendent, and Deputy Superintendent.

Assistant Superintendents work more than 40 hours a week, including evenings and weekends. They are appointed to renewable, term-limit contracts.

Salaries

Salaries vary, and depend on factors such as individual's education and experience, job responsibilities, size of school, and location. Assistant Superintendents in large school systems in urban areas can expect to earn salaries between $70,000 and $100,000.

In addition to a salary, Assistant Superintendents receive fringe benefits such as sick leave, health plans, life insurance, and retirement benefits.

Employment Prospects

Most job opportunities become available as Assistant Superintendents retire, resign, or advance to higher positions. From time to time, a school district may create a new Assistant Superintendent position to fill a need if funding is available.

Advancement Prospects

With additional education and training, Assistant Superintendents can become school superintendents. Most work their way up through the ranks from assistant to associate superintendent to deputy superintendent to, finally, superintendent. Some Assistant Superintendents make this administrative level their ultimate career goal; they realize advancement through pay increases, achievements, and receiving assignments of their choice.

Assistant Superintendents can also pursue other career paths. For example, they can become program administrators, researchers, and consultants with state or national educational agencies, educational research laboratories, or private educational consultant firms.

Licensure/Certification

Assistant Superintendents must hold a valid school administrator credential with a superintendent endorsement for the state in which they work. Licensure requirements vary from state to state. For specific information, contact the state board of education for the state where you wish to work.

Private schools may require state licensure or professional certification from school accreditation organizations, professional associations, or other recognized organizations.

Education and Training

Education requirements vary from district to district. Most districts require that Assistant Superintendents have a master's degree in educational administration. Some districts require an education specialist's or doctoral degree.

In addition, Assistant Superintendents must have completed an educational administrator program at an accredited college or university. They have completed courses such as school administration, school law, curriculum development, school finance, special services and federal programs, and student behavior management. In addition, they have completed a one-year internship.

Assistant Superintendents usually receive in-service training. Many also participate in professional conferences and workshops to improve skills, obtain new skills, and keep up with current developments in education and educational administration.

Experience, Skills, and Personality Traits

School boards look for candidates with extensive experience in classroom teaching, building (or school) administration, and central office administration. They also have experience in curriculum and staff development, as well as with school budgeting and financial management.

To handle their job effectively, Assistant Superintendents must have strong management, supervisory, communication, interpersonal, teamwork, and social skills.

Successful Assistant Superintendents share several personality traits, such as being patient, flexible, loyal, honest, analytical, creative, resourceful, and compassionate. They also have a strong commitment to provide the best educational opportunities to students of all backgrounds and abilities.

Unions/Associations

Assistant Superintendents join different local, state, and national professional organizations to take advantage of services such as networking opportunities, professional resources, and professional development programs. Some organizations are:

- American Association of School Administrators
- Association for Supervision and Curriculum Development
- National Association of Elementary School Principals
- National Middle School Association
- National Association of Secondary School Principals

Tips for Entry

1. Many school districts have a residency requirement, in which Assistant Superintendents (and superintendents) must live within the boundaries of the school districts or the city where they work.
2. Most Assistant Superintendents continue their own professional development through continuing education programs sponsored by professional organizations, such as the American Association of School Administrators.
3. The Internet is a valuable tool for your job search, especially if you are willing to relocate to another area of the country. Most school districts have web sites which may include information about the school board, central office administration, and the individual schools. E-mail addresses for different school officials are often provided.

PROGRAM DIRECTOR

CAREER PROFILE

Duties: Manage an instructional program (such as curriculum), noninstructional program (such as school transportation), or business service program (such as human resources) that serves all schools in a system; perform duties as required

Alternate Title: A title that reflects a program area, such as Director of Curriculum or Human Resources Director

Salary Range: $30,000 to $93,000

Employment Prospects: Good

Advancement Prospects: Good

Prerequisites:
 Licensure/Certification—School administrator or school business officer licensure
 Education/Training—Bachelor's or master's degree; completion of an educational administration program
 Experience—Qualifying work experience
 Special Skills and Personality Traits—Leadership, supervisory, management, interpersonal, team building, and communication; energetic, self-motivated, organized, decisive, flexible, creative

CAREER LADDER

Assistant Superintendent

Program Director

Program Coordinator or Specialist

Position Description

In public and private schools, various instructional programs, noninstructional programs, and business services are required to fulfill the educational missions and goals established by the governing school boards. Program Directors manage the different individual programs and departments. In public schools, Program Directors work under the direction of superintendents or assistant superintendents in school district central offices. In most private schools, Program Directors are supervised by school headmasters.

At any school office or school district central office, Program Directors are responsible for a variety of programs. Some Program Directors manage instructional programs and support services such as curriculum, elementary education, secondary education, vocational education, special education, technology, pupil personnel services, guidance, assessment and evaluation, or professional development. They plan, organize, and coordinate educational programs and activities that are implemented at the building, or school, level. Program Directors also act as leaders, consultants, and advisers to teachers, educational specialists, and building administrators.

Some Program Directors manage noninstructional programs that support the administrative services in schools. These include programs in transportation, food service, security, custodial services, athletics, and so on. Other Program Directors are in charge of business service programs that are essential to the day-to-day operations, such as human resources, fiscal services, purchasing, or risk management. Private schools also have Program Directors that manage programs for school admissions, financial aid, and development (or fund-raising activities).

The different Program Directors have duties that are specific to their area. However, all perform general duties that include, but are not limited to:

- developing departmental plans, setting program goals, and setting deadlines
- implementing programs and activities
- preparing and administering program budgets

- conducting program reviews and evaluations
- supervising and evaluating program staff members
- enforcing district policies and regulations as well as federal, state, and local laws and guidelines
- representing schools or school districts at meetings with community organizations, educational agencies, and professional organizations

In addition, Program Directors contribute to positive community relations for their schools or school districts. They network with community leaders, business leaders, social service agencies, community groups, and so on. Many serve on community boards, task forces, and committees as well as attend community functions.

Program Directors typically work more than 40 hours a week. They often work evenings and weekends to complete tasks, attend meetings, appear at school and community events, participate in professional conferences, and so forth.

Salaries

Salaries vary with the different positions, and generally depend on factors such as experience, education, school budgets, and geographical location. According to the U.S. Bureau of Labor Statistics, the estimated annual salary for most Program Directors in 1998 ranged from $30,480 to $92,680.

Program Directors also receive fringe benefits, such as sick leave, vacation leave, health plans, life insurance, and retirement benefits.

Employment Prospects

Most job opportunities become available as Program Directors retire, resign, or advance to higher positions. On occasion, school districts create new administrative positions to fill particular needs if funds are available.

Advancement Prospects

Many Program Directors realize advancement through higher pay and more complex assignments. Some administrators pursue positions with larger school districts while others pursue positions such as assistant superintendents and, eventually, superintendents.

Licensure/Certification

In public schools, Program Directors must hold a valid educational administrator credential with an endorsement for either a program director or school business officer. Types of licensure and requirements vary from state to state. (To find out the requirements for the state where you wish to work, contact the state board of education.) Private schools may require state licensure or professional certification from school accreditation organizations, professional associations, or other recognized organizations.

Education and Training

Education requirements vary from school to school, as well as depend on the type of position. Program Directors need at least a master's degree in educational administration or other related field. School business officers need either a bachelor's or master's degree related to their specialty, such as accounting or human resources. Schools sometimes accept qualifying work experience to substitute for some or all education requirements.

Licensed Program Directors have completed an approved educational administrator program (or other related program) from an accredited institution that leads to the appropriate licensure endorsement.

Experience, Skills, and Personality Traits

Qualifying experience requirements vary, and depend on the position. Many Program Directors have years of experience at both the building and district levels. For example, a Curriculum Director may have been a middle school teacher, reading teacher, assistant principal, instructional supervisor, and curriculum coordinator. School business officers may not have worked previously in the education field, but have qualified work experience in their specialty.

To do their jobs effectively, Program Directors need leadership, supervisory, management, interpersonal, team building, and communication skills. Also, they must be proficient in skills that are related to their area. For example, development directors need grant writing, fund-raising, and public relations skills.

Successful Program Directors share several common personality traits, such as being energetic, self-motivated, organized, decisive, flexible, and creative. In addition, they are committed to providing quality resources and services that can help all students succeed in school.

Unions/Associations

Program Directors join different local, state, and national professional organizations to obtain professional services such as continuing education programs, professional certification, and networking opportunities. Many belong to school administrator associations such as the American Association of School Administrators and the American Federation of School Administrators.

Program Directors also join organizations that serve their particular areas, such as the Association for Supervision and Curriculum Development, the Council for Exceptional Children, or the National Middle School Association. School business officers might join the Association of School Business Officials, as well as organizations that serve their specific areas. For example:

- human resource directors might join the American Association of School Personnel Administrators

- food service directors might join the American School Food Service Association
- pupil transportation directors might join the National Association for Pupil Transportation

Tips for Entry

1. Job descriptions for Program Directors differ and vary from school to school, so be sure to get detailed job descriptions from the human resources offices.
2. To enhance your qualifications, you may want to obtain certification from a professional association or other organization that is recognized in your profession.
3. You can use the Internet to research information about school districts where you would like to work. Most school districts post job listings on their web site. To find a particular school district, enter its name in any search engine. For example: "San Francisco school district." (For best results, enter the phrase between quotation marks.)

INSTRUCTIONAL SUPERVISOR

CAREER PROFILE

Duties: Provide guidance and support to teachers in particular subject areas or educational services; perform teacher evaluations; plan professional development programs; perform other duties as required

Alternate Title: Instructional Specialist

Salary Range: $55,000 to $65,000

Employment Prospects: Fair

Advancement Prospects: Limited

Prerequisites:
　Licensure/Certification—School administrator credential with an instructional supervision endorsement
　Education/Training—Master's degree
　Experience—Three to five years classroom teaching experience; some supervisory experience
　Special Skills and Personality Traits—Leadership, interpersonal, teamwork, communication, organizational, and management skills; confident, steadfast, decisive, innovative, creative

CAREER LADDER

Lead Area Instructional Supervisor or Curriculum and Instruction Coordinator

↑

Instructional Supervisor

↑

School Teacher

Position Description

In public schools, Instructional Supervisors are administrators at the school district central office level. They are specialists in subject areas, such as mathematics, social studies, science, foreign language, music, physical education, vocational education. Some are specialists in educational services, such as special education, bilingual education, and guidance services. Their jobs are to coordinate the curriculum for their specialty in their school district. For example, in a K–12 school district, a math Instructional Supervisor is responsible for coordinating the mathematics curriculum from kindergarten to 12th grade. She or he is able to assist all K–12 teachers who teach arithmetic, remedial math, algebra, geometry, calculus, and other math courses.

Instructional Supervisors fill several roles. As instructional leaders, they provide guidance and support to teachers in the classroom. They also evaluate teachers' performance by observing them in the classroom. In written or oral reports, Instructional Supervisors give teachers feedback on their performance and recommend ways to improve their instruction.

Instructional Supervisors are also resources and consultants. They can provide teachers with information, references, and resources on specific topics in their specialty. They can discuss different teaching techniques and teaching methods that teachers might try in their classroom. In addition, they can recommend supplementary materials and instructional aids that would be helpful for instruction.

Being an administrator is another role that Instructional Supervisors fulfill. They perform administrative duties that include, but are not limited to:

- evaluating curriculum programs
- distributing information about content, teaching methods, and so on to teachers and administrators
- planning professional development programs
- conducting in-service workshops
- coordinating or conducting research for experimental educational programs
- enforcing school district policies as well as state and federal laws and guidelines

Instructional Supervisors are also responsible for keeping up with developments in the content, curriculum, and teaching methods of their particular specialties. They enroll in continuing education programs and participate in professional conferences. In addition, they network with colleagues and read professional journals, reports, and books.

Instructional Supervisors spend much of their time at the different schools where they are assigned. They have a 40-hour work schedule, but sometimes work additional hours to complete their many different tasks.

Salaries

Salaries vary, depending on factors such as experience, education, level of responsibility, and school budgets. Instructional Supervisors generally earn between $55,000 and $65,000. According to a 1997–98 survey by the Educational Resources Services, the average annual salary for Instructional Supervisors was $60,359.

In addition to a salary, Instructional Supervisors receive fringe benefits, such as sick leave, vacation leave, health insurance, and retirement benefits.

Employment Prospects

Most job opportunities become available as Instructional Supervisors retire, resign, or advance to higher positions. School districts may create additional positions to fill needs as long as funding is available.

Advancement Prospects

Instructional Supervisors can advance to higher administrative positions such as coordinators and directors of curriculum and instruction, assistant superintendents, and superintendents. Many Instructional Supervisors choose to pursue advancement through higher pay and more complex responsibilities.

Instructional Supervisors can also pursue other career paths. For example, they can become curriculum developers and program directors in state and federal education agencies; editors, authors, and software developers in educational publishing companies; or curriculum and instruction consultants for private educational firms.

Licensure/Certification

Instructional Supervisors must hold a teacher's license in addition to a school administrator credential with an instructional supervisor endorsement. Licensure requirements vary from state to state. (For specific information, contact the state board of education in the state where you wish to work.) Completion of continuing education units may be required for licensure renewal.

Education and Training

Instructional Supervisors must have either bachelor's or master's degrees in their disciplines. They also require a master's degree in education administration with an emphasis in instructional supervision from an accredited university. They have completed courses such as human relations, curriculum development, research, and advanced pedagogy courses, as well as a supervised field practicum.

Experience, Skills, and Personality Traits

In general, Instructional Supervisors need three to five years of teaching experience in their subject area. Many schools also require that they have previous supervisory experience or knowledge of management principles and practices.

Instructional Supervisors need strong leadership, interpersonal, teamwork, and communication skills, as they must meet with teachers, administrators, parents, and others every day. In addition, they need adequate organizational and management skills to perform their work effectively.

Successful Instructional Supervisors share several personality traits, such as being confident, steadfast, decisive, innovative, and creative. In addition, they are passionate about providing children with quality education.

Unions/Associations

Instructional Supervisors join different local, state, and national professional organizations to take advantage of services such as research data, continuing education programs, professional certifications, job listings, and networking opportunities. Many join organizations that serve their particular subject area, such as the International Reading Association, the National Business Education Association, the National Council for the Social Studies, or the Council for Exceptional Children.

Many Instructional Supervisors also join school administrator organizations such as the Association for Supervision and Curriculum Development and the American Association of School Administrators.

Tips for Entry

1. As a teacher, you might obtain experience by participating on school committees that review textbooks or becoming a teacher consultant to educational publishers.
2. Job titles, as well as job descriptions, vary from employer to employer. When applying for a position, obtain the current job description from the personnel office.
3. To learn more about curriculum and instruction development on the Internet, visit the web site for the Association for Supervision and Curriculum Development (*http://www.ascd.org*).

COLLEGE AND UNIVERSITY ADMINISTRATORS

DIRECTOR OF ADMISSIONS

CAREER PROFILE

Duties: Oversee the process of admissions and enrollment of new students; supervise and evaluate staff; may coordinate student recruitment programs; perform other duties as required

Salary Range: $41,000 to $74,000

Employment Prospects: Good

Advancement Prospects: Limited

Prerequisites:
  Licensure/Certification—None is required
  Education/Training—Master's degree
  Experience—Five or more years of work experience in admissions, preferably in higher education settings
  Special Skills and Personality Traits—Leadership, supervisory, management, communication, interpersonal, team building, conflict resolution, and computer skills; independent, self-motivated, ethical, creative, dedicated, energetic, organized

CAREER LADDER

Vice President of Enrollment Management

Director of Admissions

Assistant Director of Admissions

Position Description

The admissions office is usually the first college or university office that most students contact. This office is part of the enrollment management department, which oversees all recruitment, admission, enrollment, and student records programs for an institution. From an admissions office, prospective students can obtain general information about an institution as well as learn how to apply for admission. Applications for entry to an institution are sent to the admissions office where they are processed and a selection of new students is made.

The Director of Admissions is responsible for the administration of the admissions office. He or she develops and implements admissions policies and procedures that are consistent with an institution's mission, enrollment goals, and administrative policies. At universities and comprehensive colleges, undergraduate and graduate admissions may be handled separately by different Directors of Admissions.

Most colleges and universities have three entrance terms—fall, spring, and summer. For each entrance term, Directors oversee the processing of admissions applications, which includes financial aid applications and campus housing applications. They direct a staff of admissions counselors who review the applications and select new students based on factors such as their completion of basic high school requirements, school grades, standardized test scores, extracurricular activities, academic interests, application essays, and personal recommendations. All applicants are sent a letter from the Office of Admissions informing them whether or not they have been accepted to their institution.

Many Directors of Admissions are also responsible for the recruitment of new students. In some institutions, Directors coordinate or assist with the recruitment of student athletes. Along with their staff, other enrollment management teams, campus committees, and other college personnel, Directors of Admissions develop and implement strategic recruitment and marketing plans to attract a diverse population of prospective students—incoming freshmen, transfer students, graduate students, adult students, students of different ethnic and cultural backgrounds, international students, and so on. Many higher education institutions have special admissions programs for prospective students who do not have basic entry requirements but show the potential of succeeding in a college environment.

Another major area of responsibility is the evaluation of admission and enrollment data to improve recruitment and admissions services. Directors conduct various forms of analyses, such as student needs analyses, trend analyses, and satisfaction surveys. Based on the feedback, Directors make adjustments where needed in staffing, customer services, or recruitment programs, as well as make recommendations to the administration for addressing market changes.

As leaders of admissions offices, Directors are responsible for building a supportive and efficient team that provides high quality services to students, parents, faculty, and others. Directors of Admissions supervise all activities performed by their professional and administrative support staff members. (Some part-time staff members are students from the institution.) Directors also provide ongoing training for staff to update or learn new skills, procedures, computer applications, and so on. In addition to performing job evaluations of staff members, Directors make recommendations for staff promotions, demotions, or terminations to the administration.

Directors of Admissions perform a variety of administrative duties. For example, they:

- prepare and administer department budgets
- recruit and select new staff members
- manage student information databases and admissions records
- direct the distribution of general information to prospective students, parents, guidance counselors, community agencies, and other groups
- develop and maintain professional contacts with academic units and other administrative departments
- serve on administrative committees
- represent the college or university through membership in appropriate professional and community organizations

In some institutions, Directors of Admissions are also responsible for overseeing financial aid programs. They help students obtain scholarships, loans, fellowships, or other financial assistance for their school tuition and living expenses.

A Director of Admissions reports to the chief officer of enrollment management who may be a dean, vice president, or other executive-level administrator.

Directors work 40 hours a week, sometimes working additional hours on evenings and weekends to complete their duties.

Salaries

Salaries vary and depend on factors such as education, experience, type of institution, size of budget, and location. According to a 1998–99 salary survey by the College and University Personnel Association, Directors of Admissions receive a median salary that ranges from $40,788 to $74,024.

Directors of Admissions also receive fringe benefits such as health plans, sick leave, vacation leave, tuition benefits, and retirement benefits.

Employment Prospects

Directors of Admissions are employed by public and private higher education institutions, as well as by private K–12 schools, technical schools, and vocational schools.

Job opportunities in student admissions are generally available for staff positions and assistant administrators. At the Director level, most opportunities become available as individuals retire, advance to higher positions, or transfer to other institutions.

Advancement Prospects

Directors of Admissions can become administrative deans, vice presidents, and college or university presidents. At the executive levels, advanced degrees are required. Directors also have the option to pursue careers in other areas of enrollment management services, as well as other administrative departments in higher education institutions.

Licensure/Certification

No state licensure or professional certification is required for this profession.

Education and Training

Education qualifications vary, but most employers require that Directors of Admissions have a master's degree in student personnel, higher education administration, business administration, or other related field. Some employers prefer that Directors have doctoral degrees. Employers sometimes choose candidates with bachelor's degrees if they have qualifying work experience.

Directors receive training on the job. Many pursue their own professional development through individual study, by enrolling in continuing education classes and professional seminars, and by participating in professional conferences.

Experience, Skills, and Personality Traits

Depending on the institution, candidates need a minimum of five to eight years of work experience, preferably in a higher education setting. They should have a work history that demonstrates increasingly responsible supervisory and management experience in admissions or enrollment management.

Directors of Admissions should have strong leadership, supervisory, and management skills along with superior communication, interpersonal, team building, and conflict resolution skills. In addition, they need computer skills, including a knowledge of databases.

Successful Directors of Admissions share several personality traits such as being independent, self-motivated, ethical, creative, dedicated, energetic, and organized. They are committed to providing high quality services to potential and current students of their institutions.

Unions/Associations

Directors of Admissions join local, state, and national associations to take advantage of professional services such as continuing education programs, training programs, professional publications, job listings, and networking opportunities. They might join organizations that specifically service enrollment management officers, such as the American Association of Collegiate Registrars and Admissions Officers. They also join organizations that generally serve higher education administrators such as the Association of College Administration Professionals or the American Association of University Administrators.

Tips for Entry

1. To find out if the field of enrollment management is right for you, obtain part-time work in the admissions office at the college that you attend. You might also network with Directors of Admissions and admissions staff members to learn more about the field.
2. Experts say that job seekers willing to relocate to another city or region may have better opportunities for securing a position.
3. You can learn about admissions offices at different colleges and universities on the Internet. To get a list of web pages to read, enter the keyword "admissions office" in any search engine.

REGISTRAR

CAREER PROFILE

Duties: Administer student registration services; manage and maintain student academic records; oversee staff; perform other duties as required

Salary Range: $48,000 to $74,000

Employment Prospects: Good

Advancement Prospects: Limited

Prerequisites:
　Licensure/Certification—None is required
　Education/Training—Bachelor's or master's degree
　Experience—Three to eight years of management and supervisory experience in the enrollment management field
　Special Skills and Personality Traits—Leadership, administrative, management, computer, communication, interpersonal, and team building skills; analytical, organized, honest, reliable, flexible

CAREER LADDER

Vice President of Enrollment Management

↑

Registrar

↑

Assistant Registrar

Position Description

Every higher education institution has a Registrar's Office that provides student enrollment services and maintains all records of admissions, registration, and student academic records. Overseeing the day-to-day administration of this office is the Registrar.

Registrars have several areas of responsibility that are generally the same regardless of the type of institution (two-year college, four-year college, or university) or whether an institution is public or private. One major responsibility is managing the student registration process for each school term—fall, spring, or summer. (Many campuses also have a short term between the fall and spring terms.) Under the Registrar's direction, staff members obtain proposed class offerings and schedules from each department on campus. The staff assigns classrooms and creates a master schedule; they then prepare a class schedule and distribute it to students near the end of the current term. The schedule announces the courses that each department plans to offer for the forthcoming term. Relevant information is given about each course, such as the name of the course, the number of units, the name of the instructor, if available, and the days and time a class would be held.

Most students preregister for classes, forwarding completed registration forms and their tuition fees to the Registrar's Office. The office processes the forms and fees, then mails individual class schedules to students before the new term begins.

Another major responsibility is managing student records of current and former students. Most campuses now keep student records on computer databases which include information such as grades, attendance, transfer evaluations, admissions applications, enrollment records, and graduation certifications. The Registrar is responsible for the integrity and security of all student records for an institution.

Registrars are also responsible for directing the activities of the professional and support staff in their departments. (Staff may also include students who work part time.) Providing leadership, Registrars are expected to develop a strong collaborative team that offers superior service to students, faculty, administrators, and others. Registrars also provide in-service programs to help staff improve skills as well as learn new ones. In addition, they evaluate the job performance of their staff members, and make recommendations for staff promotions, demotions, or terminations to the administration.

Registrars work closely with faculty and administrators on their campuses. They communicate with appropriate personnel about changes in enrollment policies and procedures. On occasion, Registrars are asked to compile statistical data that administrators would use for accreditation compliance requirements, institutional planning, preparing annual reports, and so on. Registrars may also be asked to prepare data that might assist faculty in curriculum development.

Registrars perform many other duties, with the assistance of their staff. For example, Registrars:

- prepare and administer the budget for the Registrar's Office
- recruit and select new staff
- oversee the preparation of college catalogs
- respond to student requests for certification of academic status
- provide former students with transcripts and other student records
- provide faculty with class rosters
- process grades upon the completion of each term
- audit students' grades and credits to ensure that they have the requirements for graduation

Registrars work 40 hours a week, sometimes working evenings and weekends to complete their various tasks.

Salaries

Salaries vary, depending on factors such as experience, education, type and size of college, and location. According to a 1998–99 salary survey by the College and University Personnel Association, the median annual salary for Registrars ranges from $48,499 to $74,400.

Registrars also receive fringe benefits such as sick leave, vacation leave, medical plans, and retirement benefits. Many institutions also offer benefits such as flexible four-day work weeks during summer and free tuition for employees and their spouses and children.

Employment Prospects

Employment of education administrators, including Registrars, is expected to grow about as fast as the average for all occupations through 2008. Most opportunities, however, become available as administrators retire, resign, or advance to other positions.

Advancement Prospects

Registrars can become administrative deans, vice presidents, and college (or university) presidents. For executive administrator positions, advanced degrees are required. Registrars also have the option to pursue careers in other areas of enrollment management services, as well as other administrative departments in higher education institutions.

Licensure/Certification

No state licensure or professional certification is required for this profession.

Education and Training

Generally, candidates need either a bachelor's or master's degree in business administration, student personnel services, or a related field. Employers may consider candidates who have degrees in unrelated fields if they have qualifying work experience. Specialty colleges often give preference to qualified candidates who have degrees in their specialized fields. For example, a fine arts college might choose a qualified candidate who has a degree in one of the visual arts.

Experience, Skills, and Personality Traits

Depending on the size and type of college, candidates generally need three to eight years of management and supervisory experience in registration or student records functions, preferably in higher education environments. Employers look for candidates who have knowledge of academic regulations and issues in higher education, as well as technical experience with computerized registration systems.

To do their work effectively, Registrars must have strong leadership, administrative, and management skills along with computer, communication, interpersonal, and team building skills. Successful Registrars share several personality traits, such as being analytical, organized, honest, reliable, and flexible.

Unions/Associations

Registrars join local, state, and national associations to take advantage of professional services such as continuing education programs, professional publications, and networking opportunities. They might join organizations that specifically service enrollment management officers, such as the American Association of Collegiate Registrars and Admissions Officers. They also join organizations that generally serve higher education administrators such as the Association of College Administration Professionals or the American Association of University Administrators.

Tips for Entry

1. To find job listings for Registrars and other nonacademic job opportunities, check out professional journals, national newspapers, and major metropolitan newspapers. Also contact professional associations for higher education administrators.
2. You can learn about the Registrar's Office at different colleges and universities on the Internet. To get a list of web pages to read, enter the keyword "registrar's office" in any search engine.

DIRECTOR OF STUDENT ACTIVITIES

CAREER PROFILE

Duties: Plan, implement, and evaluate student activity programs; oversee the operations of the student union; advise student organizations; manage staff, budgets, and schedules; perform other duties as required

Alternate Titles: Director of Student Life; Director of Campus Life; Assistant Dean/Director

Salary Range: $43,000 to $93,000

Employment Prospects: Good

Advancement Prospects: Limited

Prerequisites:
  Licensure/Certification—None required
  Education/Training—Master's degree
  Experience—At least three years of managerial or supervisory experience in student affairs
  Special Skills and Personality Traits—Report writing, communication, decision making, computer, leadership, management, interpersonal, and team building skills; tactful, organized, energetic, self-motivated, creative

CAREER LADDER

Dean of Students

Director of Student Activities

Assistant Director of Student Activities

Position Description

Every college and university has a student activities office that provides its student body with a variety of extracurricular programs and leisure activities. The office is usually found in an institution's student union (or student center) where many activities take place. The Director of Student Activities is in charge of this office.

Directors of Student Activities oversee the planning and organizing of a wide variety of educational, social, cultural, and recreational programs and activities that meet students' interests and needs. Activities may include, for example:

- community service programs, such as blood drives and adult literacy tutoring programs
- student newspapers and other publications
- cultural activities such as movies, concerts, and art shows
- lectures, presentations, or talks by well-known politicians, educators, artists, and other personalities
- dances and other social events
- educational programs and events—for example, career days and health fairs
- student leadership development programs
- recreational and outdoor activities
- intramural sports programs

A program or activity may be sponsored by the student activities office, a student organization, or an academic department. Activities and programs are sometimes sponsored by campus organizations in collaboration with community organizations, local schools, or other outside groups. Directors ensure that all programs and activities are in compliance with the policies and regulations of their institutions.

Most programs and activities are held at an institution's student union. It is also the place where many students go between and after classes. At student unions, students (as well as faculty and other college employees) have access to food services, bookstores, recreational facilities, student organization offices, conference rooms, lounges, and so on. Staff members of the student activities office manage the student union, under the direction of the Director of Student Activities.

Supervising campus-sponsored student organizations is another responsibility of Directors of Student Activities. These organizations include student government councils; honor societies; academic organizations; sororities and fraternities; musical groups, dance groups, and other performance organizations; political and issue-oriented groups; sports clubs; religious organizations; special interest organizations; and so on. Directors advise student organizations about their financial status, on planning activities, and on methods for improving their organizations. Directors also maintain contact with faculty advisers.

Directors of Student Activities are also responsible for administering budgets for their offices. Each term, student activities offices receive funds raised by student activity fees which Directors allocate accordingly to the student union, student organizations, student publications, cultural activities, intramural programs, and so forth. Furthermore, Directors prepare budgets for their offices that they submit to executive-level administrators.

Another major responsibility is supervising the student activities office staff. The staff is made up of professionals and support workers. Some members are students who work part time. Directors are responsible for providing staff with job training and professional development programs. They also perform job evaluations and make recommendations for staff promotions, demotions, and terminations to the administration.

Directors of Student Activities have many other duties that include, but are not limited to:

- keeping a master schedule of events and activities
- assigning conference rooms and other space within the student union
- coordinating campus orientation programs for new students
- recruiting and selecting staff members
- producing and distributing information about upcoming programs and events
- assisting in development, or fund-raising activities, for community-based programs
- serving on campus councils and committees as representatives of the office of student activities
- representing the college at professional conferences related to student services or student affairs
- providing individual or group counseling regarding which social activities to choose or how to use leisure time

The Director of Student Activities reports to the dean of students or other senior-level administrator at his or her institution.

Directors often work more than 40 hours a week. They typically work many evenings and weekends to attend meetings, participate in professional conferences, supervise student activities, appear at student functions, and so on.

Salaries

Salaries vary, depending on factors such as experience, education, responsibilities, type of college, and budget. According to the U.S. Bureau of Labor Statistics, the estimated annual salary in 1998 for most education administrators, including Directors of Student Activities, ranged from $43,870 to $92,680.

In addition to a salary, Directors of Student Activities receive fringe benefits such as sick leave, vacation leave, medical plans, and retirement benefits.

Employment Prospects

Directors of Student Activities are employed by public and private higher education institutions.

Employment for education administrators, including Directors, is expected to grow about as fast as the average for all occupations through 2008. Most opportunities, however, become available as individuals advance to other positions, transfer to other institutions, retire, or resign.

Advancement Prospects

Directors of Student Affairs can become deans of students, vice presidents of student affairs, and college or university presidents. Master's or doctoral degrees are usually required for executive-level positions.

Many Directors of Student Affairs realize advancement through increased pay, with professional recognition, and by transfers to other institutions with complex responsibilities.

Licensure/Certification

No state licensure or professional certification is required for this profession.

Education and Training

The education requirement varies with the different institutions. In general, Directors of Student Activities should have a master's degree, preferably in student personnel, counseling, or related field. Candidates with a doctoral degree in college student personnel, higher education administration, or related fields are preferred by many employers.

Directors generally receive on-the-job training. Many pursue professional development through individualized study, by enrolling in continuing education courses and professional workshops, and by participating in professional conferences.

Experience, Skills, and Personality Traits

Employers generally require a minimum of three years of professional experience with student activities. Some employers allow candidates to substitute a combination of training and experience in student affairs administration, counseling, policy analysis, or equivalent experience.

Employers look for candidates who have experience with budget management and human resource management. Candidates also demonstrate a knowledge and sensitivity to issues and behaviors that shape and affect students' college experience.

Directors of Student Activities need strong report writing, communication, decision making, and computer skills along with skills in leadership, management, interpersonal, and team building skills.

Being tactful, organized, energetic, self-motivated, and creative are some personality traits that successful Directors of Student Activities share. They also have a desire to provide quality service to students, faculty, administrators, and others.

Unions/Associations

Directors of Student Activities join local, state, and national professional organizations to take advantage of services such as training programs, networking opportunities, professional resources, and job listings. Some organizations that they might join are:

- College and University Personnel Association
- American College Personnel Association
- National Association of Student Personnel Administrators
- Association of College Administration Professionals
- American Association of University Administrators

Tips for Entry
1. As a college student, find out if the field of student affairs might interest you. Volunteer or obtain part-time jobs in the student affairs office.
2. You can learn about different college student activity offices on the Internet. To get a list of relevant web sites, enter the keyword "office of student activities" in any search engine. If you would like to learn more about student affairs in general, use the keyword "student affairs" to find pertinent web sites.

ATHLETIC DIRECTOR

CAREER PROFILE

Duties: Plan and direct intercollegiate athletic programs; perform departmental administrative duties; supervise coaches; perform other duties as required

Alternate Title: Athletic Administrator

Salary Range: $43,000 to $93,000 or more

Employment Prospects: Fair

Advancement Prospects: Limited

Prerequisites:
　　Licensure/Certification—None required
　　Education/Training—Master's degree
　　Experience—Supervisory and management experience in college athletic departments; coaching experience preferred
　　Special Skills and Personality Traits—Leadership, supervisory, communication, interpersonal, team building, report writing, financial management, computer, fund-raising, and community relations skills; fair, honest, open-minded, optimistic, even-tempered, dedicated

CAREER LADDER

Administrative Dean or Vice President

↑

Athletic Director

↑

Assistant Athletic Director

Position Description

Most two-year colleges, four-year colleges, and universities offer intercollegiate sports as extracurricular activities. College or university athletic teams compete in regional intercollegiate athletic leagues or conferences, which are governed by the National Collegiate Athletic Association or other intercollegiate athletic association. Both female and male students can participate on school teams for football, basketball, baseball, softball, soccer, lacrosse, golf, fencing, tennis, gymnastics, swimming, diving, rowing, cross country, track and field, and other competitive intercollegiate sports.

All intercollegiate sports at higher education institutions are under the guidance of athletic departments that are administered by Athletic Directors. Some Athletic Departments have two Athletic Directors—one for women's sports, and the other for men's sports. On some campuses, the women's athletic administrator is a senior executive under the Athletic Director.

Athletic Directors are responsible for planning, administering, and evaluating all intercollegiate athletic programs. Working with the coaching staff, Directors develop objectives and strategic plans to meet the goals (such as gender equity) of their departments. They also make sure that the athletic departments are compatible with the missions, policies, and regulations of their institutions. In addition, Directors ensure that all athletic programs comply with the regulations and standards of the athletic conferences in which their institutions are members.

Athletic Directors are also responsible for overseeing the activities of the coaching staffs of the different sports. Additionally, they supervise administrative staffs that may include assistant athletic directors, support workers, business managers, publicists, and others. On a regular basis, Athletic Directors conduct performance reviews of the different personnel. They also make recommendations for promotions, demotions, or terminations of coaching and administrative staff to the administration.

Athletic Directors are also business managers. Their duties include, but are not limited to:

- managing and preparing budgets
- coordinating student athlete recruiting plans
- recruiting and selecting coaching and other athletic department staff

- overseeing development, or fund-raising, plans to raise resources for the various athletic programs
- scheduling games, meets, and other sports events
- overseeing ticket sales for athletic events
- supervising public relations
- supervising the maintenance of gymnasiums, playing fields, swimming pools, and other facilities
- reviewing purchase requisitions, travel requests, and other expenditures from coaches

As representatives of their institutions, Athletic Directors participate in meetings held by intercollegiate conferences and professional organizations. They also actively participate in community activities and projects, serving on committees, boards, and task forces.

Some Athletic Directors are also responsible for planning and administering intramural sports programs. (In an intramural program, students on campus form coeducational or single-sex teams, such as in volleyball, and play against each other.) Some Athletic Directors assume teaching responsibilities, teaching one or more classes in physical education, health education, teacher education, or other departments.

Athletic Directors report to different executive administrators at different campuses. An Athletic Director, for example, might report to the vice president for student affairs at one campus, while the Athletic Director at another campus reports directly to the president.

Athletic Directors often put in more than 40 hours a week to complete their various tasks. They spend many evenings and weekends attending meetings, participating in professional conferences, meeting with boosters and donors, appearing at school and community functions, and so forth.

Salaries

Salaries vary, depending on factors such as experience, education, size of athletic program, and financial support. At institutions with strong and successful athletic departments, Athletic Directors may be able to earn salaries up to $200,000 per year. According to the U.S. Bureau of Labor Statistics, the estimated annual salary in 1998 for most education administrators, including Athletic Directors, ranged from $43,870 to $92,680.

Athletic Directors also receive fringe benefits such as sick leave, vacation leave, medical plans, tuition benefits, and retirement benefits.

Employment Prospects

In addition to being employed by higher education institutions, Athletic Directors are also hired by public and private schools.

Employment of education administrators, including Athletic Directors, is expected to grow about as fast as the average for all occupations through 2008. Most opportunities, however, become available as administrators retire, resign, or transfer to other institutions.

Advancement Prospects

Athletic Directors can become administrative deans, vice presidents, and college or university presidents. Becoming an executive administrator requires an advanced degree. Many Athletic Directors realize advancement through salary increases, with professional recognition, and by obtaining positions in institutions of their choice.

Athletic Directors can also pursue other career paths, such as becoming coaches and administrators in professional sports organizations.

Licensure/Certification

No special licensure or professional certification is required for this profession.

Education and Training

Depending on the institution, Athletic Directors must have a minimum of either a bachelor's or master's degree, preferably in athletic administration or a related field. Most four-year colleges and universities prefer that candidates have an advanced degree.

Directors generally receive on-the-job training. Many pursue professional development through individualized study, with continuing education courses and professional workshops; and by participating in professional conferences.

Experience, Skills, and Personality Traits

Requirements vary with the different employers. In general, Athletic Directors have previous management and supervisory experience in positions of increasing responsibility. They have demonstrated success in handling gender equity, financial management, and other matters related to running a successful athletic department. Many employers prefer that prospective Athletic Directors have coaching or athletic administrative experience at the intercollegiate conference level in which their institutions participate.

Because they work with students, coaches, administrators, boosters, and others, Athletic Directors need superior leadership, supervisory, communication, interpersonal, and team building skills. They also need strong report writing, financial management, computer, fund-raising, and community relations skills to perform their jobs effectively.

Successful Athletic Directors share several personality traits, such as being fair, honest, open-minded, optimistic, even-tempered, and dedicated. They also share a fine sense of humor. Furthermore, they are committed to increasing the quality and competitiveness of their teams in addition to encouraging and assisting student athletes to academic excellence.

Unions/Associations

Athletic Directors join local, state, regional, and national professional organizations to take advantage of networking opportunities, training programs, and other professional services. Two national organizations are the National Association of Collegiate Directors of Athletics and the National Association of Collegiate Women Athletic Administrators. Many Athletic Directors also join professional organizations that serve specific sports.

Athletic Directors also belong to organizations that generally serve higher education administrators, such as the Association of College Administration Professionals and the American Association for Higher Education.

Tips for Entry

1. As you develop your career toward becoming an Athletic Director, obtain practical experience in the different areas of running a college athletic department. This includes coaching, fund-raising, booster club activities, public relations, facilities management, enforcement and compliance, and so forth.
2. Network with colleagues to learn about job openings that may be coming up in the near future. Also talk with colleagues who are familiar with the athletic departments in which you are interested. You may be able to learn about people, issues, politics, and so on within the department as well as within the overall college administration and the campus.
3. To learn more about intercollegiate athletics on the Internet, visit the web site for the National Collegiate Athletic Association (*http://www.ncaa.org*).

DIRECTOR OF PUBLIC SAFETY

CAREER PROFILE

Duties: Develop, implement, and evaluate programs and activities for the security and safety of the campus; supervise staff; perform other duties as required

Alternate Titles: Director of Campus Security, Director of Campus Safety, Chief

Salary Range: $40,000 to $65,000

Employment Prospects: Good

Advancement Prospects: Limited

Prerequisites:
  Licensure/Certification—May require police certification; professional security certification desirable
  Education/Training—Associate, bachelor's or master's degree
  Experience—Law enforcement or security background, preferably in campus settings; supervisory and management experience
  Special Skills and Personality Traits—Leadership, communication, interpersonal, team building, report writing, computer, supervisory, and program management skills; honest, dedicated, organized, personable, innovative, flexible

CAREER LADDER

Director of Public Safety (for larger or more complex public safety departments)

↑

Director of Public Safety

↑

Assistant Director of Public Safety

Position Description

Every higher education institution has a public safety department that ensures the safety and security of the campus environment for all students, faculty, administrators, employees, and visitors. The head of this department is the Director of Public Safety. He or she is responsible for coordinating all campus safety and security programs and activities.

Public safety departments differ from campus to campus. Some departments are composed of security officers. They enforce the campus rules and regulations. Any individuals suspected of criminal or illegal activities can be questioned and held by security officers until local law enforcement officers arrive on the scene. Other campus public safety departments are composed of police officers who enforce local, state, and/or federal laws in addition to institutional rules and regulations. Campus police officers have the authority to arrest people suspected of criminal or illegal activities. They also can conduct criminal investigations for prosecution. Some public safety departments have both law enforcement and security forces. A Director of Public Safety who oversees law enforcement officers is also known as the chief of (campus) police.

Directors of Public Safety are responsible for the development, implementation, and evaluation of all safety and security programs and activities. Most campus public safety departments provide the following protective services:

- patrol units (vehicle, foot, bicycle, and other types) that check the grounds and buildings for security as well as for suspicious and illegal activities
- security services for campus facilities (such as art museums and science laboratories), construction projects, special campus events, visiting dignitaries, and so on
- security technology systems, such as burglar alarm systems and access card systems
- crime prevention programs and services such as a campus escort service, a bicycle registration program, and a rape prevention program

- traffic and parking enforcement as well as general assistance to motorists
- emergency services during medical emergencies, fires, floods, civil disturbances, and other crises
- safety and environmental health inspections of campus facilities and grounds in compliance with government laws and regulations
- repository for lost and found property

Directors of Public Safety oversee all field operations. They may supervise armed or unarmed officers. (On many campuses, the security staff includes students who work part time.) Directors also supervise unit supervisors, dispatch staff, and support staff. As part of their responsibilities, Directors provide staff members with in-service training. Furthermore, Directors evaluate job performances of their staff members.

They perform many administrative duties, which vary with the different Directors. One general task that most Directors do is the management and preparation of department budgets. Many Directors also assist in the recruitment and selection of staff members. Another general duty is overseeing the recordkeeping of criminal and security incident statistics. As mandated by law, Directors of Public Safety prepare annual crime reports for their campuses.

Their responsibilities also include maintaining a working relationship with local, state, and federal law enforcement agencies. In addition, Directors of Public Safety represent their institutions at meetings with community organizations, law enforcement agencies, professional associations, and other groups.

The Director of Public Safety reports to the dean of students, vice president for administrative services, or other executive-level administrator.

Directors of Public Safety are on call 24 hours a day.

Salaries

Salaries vary from employer to employer, and depend on factors such as education, experience, type and size of educational institution, and location. Generally, directors in larger institutions earn higher salaries. According to the American Society for Industrial Security, the salary range for campus security professionals, including Directors of Public Safety, is between $40,000 and $65,000 per year.

In addition to a salary, Directors of Public Safety receive fringe benefits such as sick leave, vacation leave, medical plans, retirement benefits, and tuition benefits.

Employment Prospects

Directors of campus public safety or security are employed by two-year colleges as well as four-year colleges and universities. Most opportunities become available as Directors retire, resign, or transfer to other campuses.

Advancement Prospects

Directors of Public Safety realize advancement through pay increases, professional recognition, and transfers to other institutions.

Other careers that they might pursue include becoming private campus security consultants. They might also become community college instructors or university professors in criminal justice, police science, or other related field.

Licensure/Certification

Requirements vary from employer to employer, and depend on the type of protective services provided by a campus public safety department. Directors in charge of campus enforcement officers must be certified as police officers or be certifiable within a certain time period after their appointments. For campus security programs, Directors may be required to obtain professional certification as a Certified Protection Professional (CPP).

Directors may also be required to have a valid driver's license as well as certification in standard first aid and cardiopulmonary resuscitation (CPR).

Education and Training

Education requirements vary from employer to employer, and generally depend on the type and size of the public safety department. Most employers require an associate or bachelor's degree along with qualifying work experience. Some employers prefer that candidates have a master's degree. Degrees may be in any field, although most employers prefer a degree in criminal justice, police science, industrial security, business management, public management, or a related field.

Directors of campus police forces are usually required to have completed police academy training.

New directors usually receive on-the-job training during their first few months in employment. Directors typically participate in professional training workshops and continuing education classes to improve skills as well as to learn new skills and knowledge of new advancements in security, equipment, management, and so on.

Experience, Skills, and Personality Traits

In general, candidates must have several years of experience in law enforcement, industrial security, the military, or a combination in such fields. Their work history should also show progressively responsible managerial or supervisory experience.

Directors of Public Safety must have strong leadership, communication, interpersonal, and team building skills to establish effective relationships with their staff as well as students, faculty, administrators, and others. In addition,

Directors need report writing and computer skills along with supervisory and program management skills.

Successful Directors of Public Safety share several personality traits, such as being honest, dedicated, organized, personable, innovative, and flexible. Furthermore, they are committed to provide a safe and secure campus environment.

Unions/Associations

Many campus Directors of Public Safety join local, state, and national professional organizations to take advantage of services such as training programs, professional resources, publications, and networking opportunities. National security and law enforcement organizations that they might join are the International Association of Campus Law Enforcement Administrators, the American Society for Industrial Security, the International Association of Chiefs of Police, and the National Sheriffs Association.

Campus Directors of Public Safety are also eligible to join organizations for higher education administrators such as the Association of College Administration Professionals.

Tips for Entry

1. As a college student, you can start gaining work experience by obtaining part-time work as a campus security officer.
2. The International Association of Campus Law Enforcement Administrators provides nationwide job listings on its web site. Go to: *http://www.iaclea.org*, then click on the link "employment opportunities."
3. You can learn more about campus security and read about different campus public safety departments on the Internet. To get a list of web pages to read, enter any of these keywords in a search engine: "campus public safety," "campus security," "university police," or "college police."

DEAN OF STUDENTS

CAREER PROFILE

Duties: Oversee the administration of all student services; provide leadership and supervision to program directors and their staffs; recommend student personnel policies; perform other duties as required

Salary Range: $40,000 to $100,000

Employment Prospects: Fair

Advancement Prospects: Limited

Prerequisites:
  Licensure/Certification—None required
  Education/Training—Master's or doctoral degree
  Experience—Extensive administrative, management, and supervisory experience in student affairs programs
  Special Skills and Personality Traits—Leadership, management, supervisory, computer, communication, mediation, interpersonal, and team building skills; energetic, creative, innovative, self-motivated, organized

CAREER LADDER

Vice President of Student Affairs

↓

Dean of Students

↑

Assistant Dean of Students or Program Director (such as Director of Student Life, Student Union Director, or Director of Student Affairs)

Position Description

Every higher education institution has an administrative department that is responsible for the well-being of the student body and for providing a supportive learning environment. On most campuses, this department is called the *Office of Dean of Students.* As administrator of this office, the Dean of Students oversees different student services that assist students with handling campus life so that they can successfully complete their academic and personal goals. The types of student services vary from campus to campus. They include (but are not limited to):

- enrollment services—recruitment, admissions, enrollment, registration, and student records
- financial aid services
- "new student" orientation programs
- housing services
- academic and personal support services—such as academic counseling, personal counseling, career service programs, and study skills programs
- student health services
- student judicial affairs
- student activities, which includes the development of social, cultural, educational, and recreational programs and activities; supervision of student organizations, sororities, and fraternities; and direction of the student union
- intercollegiate sports programs for both men and women
- public safety departments

The various student services are run by different directors who are under the leadership and direction of the Dean of Students. The Dean of Students meets with directors on a regular basis to stay up-to-date with what is happening with the different operations. The Dean of Students also advises and assists directors on numerous policy, administrative, and program matters such as student personnel policies, fiscal management, human resources management, and program development.

Deans of Students are responsible for the quality of student services. Thus, they conduct reviews of the various student services and individual programs on a regular basis to ensure they are providing satisfactory services to students, faculty, and others. Deans also make sure that the services and programs are in compliance with the missions, policies, and regulations of their institutions, as well as with any local, state, and federal laws. Deans also do a continuing assessment of each service and program to evaluate whether the need for and cost of a service or program is justified.

Other general responsibilities of Deans of Students include: administering and preparing budgets for the overall operation of student services; directing the activities of the professional and support staff within the Office of Dean of Students; and assisting in the recruitment and selection of student service directors and the office administrative staff.

As representative of student service operations, Deans of Students serve on various administrative committees and councils on campus. They recommend and assist in the development of effective student personnel policies for their campuses. On occasion, Deans of Students speak to community organizations on behalf of their institutions regarding student programs and activities. They may also represent their institutions at meetings and conferences with educational agencies and professional associations.

Deans work more than 40 hours a week. They work many evenings and weekends to attend meetings, appear at student activities and functions, participate in professional conferences, complete reports, and so on.

Salaries

Salaries vary, depending on factors such as experience, education, the type and size of an institution, and the institution's budget. According to the Association of College Administration Professionals, the annual salary range for administrators, including Dean of Students, ranges from $40,000 to $100,000.

Deans of Students also receive fringe benefits such as sick leave, vacation leave, medical plans, retirement benefits, and tuition benefits.

Employment Prospects

Deans of Students are employed by two-year colleges, four-year colleges, and universities. Private and independent K–12 schools also employ Deans of Students.

Employment for education administrators, including Deans, is expected to grow about as fast as the average for all occupations through 2008. Most opportunities, however, become available as administrators advance to other positions, transfer to other institutions, retire, or resign.

Advancement Prospects

Deans of Students can advance to such policy-making positions as vice presidents of student affairs, which generally require doctoral degrees. They can also become, if desired, presidents of higher education institutions. Many Deans of Students realize advancement through pay increases, with professional recognition, and by transferring to other institutions.

Licensure/Certification

No special state licensure or professional certification is required for this profession.

Education and Training

Employers generally require that Deans of Students have at least a master's degree in college student personnel, higher education administration, or related field. Many employers, however, prefer candidates with doctoral degrees.

Many Deans of Students pursue professional development through individual study, enrollment in continuing education classes and professional workshops, and participation in professional conferences.

Experience, Skills, and Personality Traits

Deans of Students have extensive administrative, management, and supervisory experience. Generally, employers look for candidates who have held positions with increasing levels of responsibility in student affairs. The qualifying number of years (about six to 10 years) varies with the different institutions.

To perform their work effectively, Deans of Students must have excellent skills in leadership, management, and supervision. They should also have good computer skills, as well as communication, mediation, interpersonal, and team building skills. Being energetic, creative, innovative, self-motivated, and organized are some personality traits that successful Deans of Students share.

Unions/Associations

Deans of Students join local, state, and national professional organizations to take advantage of services such as training programs, networking opportunities, professional resources, and job listings. Some of the organizations that they might join are:

- American College Personnel Association
- National Association of Student Personnel Administrators
- College and University Personnel Association
- National Association for Women in Education
- Association of College Administration Professionals

Tips for Entry

1. Talk with current and former Deans of Students and find out what different career paths they traveled to arrive at the Dean of Students position.
2. Job descriptions for the Dean of Students positions differ from one campus to the next. Be sure to get a job description from the human resources department for the position for which you wish to apply.
3. On the Internet, you can visit web pages of college and university Dean of Students offices. To get a list of web pages to read, enter the keyword "Dean of Students office" in any search engine.

DIRECTOR OF DEVELOPMENT

CAREER PROFILE

Duties: Develop and implement fund-raising programs and activities; manage day-to-day operations; supervise staff; perform duties as required

Alternate Title: Director of Annual Giving, or other title that reflects a fund-raising program

Salary Range: $45,000 to $84,000

Employment Prospects: Good

Advancement Prospects: Limited

Prerequisites:
    Licensure/Certification—None required
    Education/Training—Bachelor's or master's degree
    Experience—Three to five years experience in increasingly responsible positions, preferably in higher education settings
    Special Skills and Personality Traits—Organization, management, team building, computer, grant-writing, interpersonal, communication, and social skills; honest, caring, enthusiastic, persistent, loyal, flexible, creative

CAREER LADDER

Vice President of Development or Vice President of Advancement

↑

Director of Development

↑

Assistant Director

Position Description

Most private and public higher education institutions use private endowments to help pay for general operations, employee salaries, construction projects, academic programs, student scholarships, student services, athletic programs, laboratory equipment, and so on. Thus, institutions must continually acquire resources through donations from alumni, parents, and other supporters as well as through grants from philanthropic foundations.

On most campuses, all development (or fund-raising) programs and activities are coordinated by a special department, usually called the *Office of Development*. Within this office, the Directors of Development are responsible for creating and implementing strategic fund-raising plans for their institutions.

Depending on the complexity of the fund-raising programs and activities, a development office may have one or more Directors of Development. The Executive Director of Development is responsible for overseeing the total operations of the development department. He or she also supervises a staff that includes several Directors of Development who each have particular roles. Some Directors are in charge of different fund-raising programs for the institutions. Other Directors are in charge of all fund-raising programs and activities for individual colleges (such as the college of engineering) or major student services (such as library services or intercollegiate sports programs).

Development offices coordinate a variety of fund-raising programs throughout the year. The following are some types of programs that Directors of Development oversee.

- Annual giving programs solicit gift donations on a yearly basis from alumni, parents, businesses, and other donors.
- Corporate and foundation relations programs develop relations with corporations and nonprofit foundations for major grants.
- Major gifts and planned gifts programs solicit donations, such as large cash gifts, real estate, securities, and property. These gifts may be donated to an institution all at once, given in increments over several years, or distributed upon the death of the donors. For example, a couple might give their alma mater $20 million to be distributed in equal amounts over five years.

- Capital campaigns raise a specific dollar amount over a certain period of time. For example, a college may hope to raise a total of $100 million in seven years in its 10th capital campaign.

In addition, Directors of Development oversee the planning and organizing of fund-raising activities, such as dinners, dances, auctions, and sports tournaments.

The different Directors of Development perform general duties that are the same regardless of their roles. They evaluate the potential amount of money that can be raised with a fund-raising activity. They identify potential donors, as well as meet with donors in either a business or social setting.

In addition, Directors of Development coordinate and direct all marketing and public relations activities for their fund-raising programs or activities. For example, they might develop seminars and information packets for potential donors, or produce newsletters to keep donors up-to-date with campus activities. Directors of Development are also responsible for managing the day-to-day activities of the development offices. They develop, implement, and evaluate administrative operating plans. They administer and prepare program budgets. In addition, they represent their institutions at community meetings and professional conferences.

Another major responsibility is overseeing the office personnel, which includes professional and support staff, as well as volunteers. Directors provide leadership and supervision as they direct the activities of their staff members. They also plan and conduct in-service training for staff members and volunteers. In addition, Directors assist in the recruitment and selection of their staffs. They also recruit on an ongoing basis for volunteer leaders, especially before major fund-raising campaigns.

Directors of Development report to an executive administrator (such as the vice president of institutional advancement). They typically work more than 40 hours a week. They often work evenings and weekends, meeting with donors, attending fund-raising events, conducting training workshops, or completing other tasks.

Salaries

Salaries vary, depending on factors such as experience, education, area of fund-raising responsibility, and an institution's budget. According to a 1998–99 salary survey by the College and University Personnel Association, the median annual salary for the different Directors of Development were:

- $45,900 for Director of Development/Alumni Affairs
- $52,958 for Director of Corporate/Foundation Relations
- $59,258 for Director of Planned Giving
- $60,000 for Director of Major Gifts
- $83,941 for Chief Development Officer

Directors of Development also receive fringe benefits such as sick leave, vacation leave, medical plans, retirement benefits, and tuition benefits.

Employment Prospects

In addition to being employed by colleges and universities, Development Directors are employed by hospitals, schools, churches, and nonprofit organizations.

According to some career experts, there is a growing demand for experienced development officers in higher education settings, particularly in the areas of major gifts and planned giving.

Advancement Prospects

With advanced education and experience, Directors of Development can become executive vice presidents of development in higher education institutions. Many Directors of Development realize advancement through pay increases, professional recognition, and transfers to other institutions.

Directors of Development can also continue their careers in other settings, such as schools, hospitals, museums, and nonprofit organizations.

Licensure/Certification

No special state licensure or professional certification is required for this profession.

Education and Training

Depending on the institution, a Director of Development must have either a bachelor's or a master's degree, in any field. Employers may waive the education requirement if a candidate has excellent qualifying experience.

Directors of Development generally receive on-the-job training. Many Directors generally pursue professional development through individual study, enrollment in continuing education classes and professional workshops, and participation in professional conferences.

Experience, Skills, and Personality Traits

Requirements vary with the different institutions. Many employers cite a minimum of three to five years of relevant, and successful, fund-raising experience in positions of increasing responsibility.

To handle their work effectively Directors of Development need strong organization, management, and team building skills. They also need good computer and grant writing skills. In addition, they should have outstanding interpersonal, communication, and social skills as they must be able to build positive relationships with alumni, donors, faculty, administrators, and others.

Some personality traits that successful Directors of Development share are: being honest, caring, enthusiastic, persistent, loyal, flexible, and creative. They also have a strong belief in the mission and goals of the universities and colleges for which they work.

Unions/Associations

Many Directors of Development join local, state, and national professional organizations, such as the National Society of Fund Raising Executives, that serve development officers. Directors might also join organizations for higher education administrators such as the Association of College Administration Professionals or the American Association for Higher Education. By joining professional associations, Directors of Development can take advantage of training workshops, networking opportunities, job listings, and other professional services.

Tips for Entry

1. As a middle school and high school student, you can get an idea if a profession in fund-raising might interest you. Participate in fund-raising activities for your school or for nonprofit organizations in your community. As a college student, you might volunteer or obtain part-time work in your college development department.
2. To enhance your employability, obtain professional certification, such as Certified Fund Raising Executive (CFRE) or Advanced Certified Fund Raising Executive (ACFRE). For more information, contact the National Society of Fund Raising Executives, 1101 King Street, Suite 700, Alexandria, Va., 22314. Phone: (703) 684-0410, or fax: (703) 684-0540. On the Internet, you can also find information at its web site (*http://www.nsfre.org*).
3. You can learn more about the field of development or fund-raising on the Internet. One place to start is the web site of *Philanthropy Journal Online* (*http://www.nonprofitnews.org/index.html*). Or get a list of relevant web sites to read by entering any of the following keywords in a search engine: "fund-raising," "philanthropy," or "development."

DEAN (ACADEMIC)

CAREER PROFILE

Duties: Provide academic and administrative leadership to an academic division or college in a higher education institution; oversee daily operations and personnel; participate in academic policy making for the institution

Alternate Title: A title that reflects the school or college being administered, such as Dean of College of Liberal Arts or Dean, College of Architecture

Salary Range: $43,000 to $93,000

Employment Prospects: Fair

Advancement Prospects: Limited

Prerequisites:
　Licensure/Certification—None required
　Education/Training—Doctoral degree
　Experience—Be a full professor; have administrative experience as a department chair or higher
　Special Skills and Personality Traits—Leadership, administrative, management, fund-raising, communication, interpersonal, team building, and computer skills; organized, analytical, honest, fair, innovative, energetic, flexible

CAREER LADDER

```
Provost or Vice President
of Academic Affairs
```

```
Dean (Academic)
```

```
Department Chair or Assistant Dean
```

Position Description

In higher education institutions, academic Deans provide leadership and supervision to academic units, which are composed of departments and schools. In community colleges, the academic units are called *divisions.* In four-year colleges and universities, the academic units are called *colleges.* For example, a university might be comprised of four colleges, the college of letters and science, college of education and human service, college of nursing, and college of business administration. An academic Dean is usually known by the name of the college that he or she leads—such as *Dean of College of Education and Human Service.*

The responsibilities and duties of Deans vary from one institution to the next. In general, Deans are responsible for overseeing all personnel, programs, and services related to their academic units. They direct and coordinate activities of department chairs in matters such as curriculum and personnel. Deans review the different academic programs within their units. On occasion, they recommend additional courses to be taught in a department.

Deans also perform evaluations of faculty members, assessing their performances and achievements. Deans make recommendations to the administration about faculty appointments, promotions, tenure, and sabbatical leaves. Furthermore, Deans are responsible for providing professional development for the faculty.

Deans also lead and encourage fund-raising efforts for their academic units. For example, they inspire (and assist) faculty members to write proposals for research grants. Deans also participate in fund-raising activities for their academic units, which may include meeting with prospective donors in business or social settings.

Deans perform various administrative duties that include (but are not limited to):

- supervising support staff in their office
- managing and developing annual budgets
- coordinating the scheduling of courses
- administering collective bargaining agreements
- recruiting and selecting faculty members and administrative staff

- coordinating student recruitment activities
- enforcing institutional policies and regulations, as well as local, state, and federal laws and guidelines

Additionally, academic Deans serve on various faculty, student, and administrative committees. Most academic Deans are part of a provost's council that develops and recommends academic polices for the institution. Furthermore, as representatives of their institutions, Deans participate in meetings with community organizations, educational agencies, and professional associations.

Academic Deans generally work long days. They attend frequent meetings and social engagements connected to their academic units and institutions in the evenings and on weekends.

Salaries

Salaries vary, depending on factors such as experience, education, type and size of college, and location. According to the U.S. Bureau of Labor Statistics, the estimated annual salary in 1998 for most education administrators, including academic Deans, was between $43,870 and $92,680.

In addition to a salary, Deans receive fringe benefits such as sick leave, medical plans, and retirement benefits.

Employment Prospects

Employment of education administrators, including academic Deans, is expected to grow about as fast as the average for all occupations through 2008. Most opportunities, however, become available as administrators retire, resign, or advance to other positions.

Advancement Prospects

Academic Deans are part of a traditional career ladder, in which Deans can advance to assistant provost, provost, and president. Many Deans realize advancement through increases in salary and with professional recognition. Some Deans choose to return to teaching and researching after serving one or more terms in this position.

Other career options for Deans include becoming consultants, administrators, and professionals with government agencies, private industry, professional associations, and nonprofit institutions.

Licensure/Certification

No state licensure or professional certification is required for this profession.

Education and Training

Academic Deans usually have doctoral degrees in their disciplines. For example, the Dean who oversees his or her university's college of business administration might have a doctoral degree in economics.

Deans typically learn their duties and tasks on the job. Many Deans participate in professional development workshops and classes.

Experience, Skills, and Personality Traits

Candidates must hold the academic rank of full professor and have academic tenure, or have the appropriate academic credentials to be granted tenure. Academic credentials include classroom teaching experience, recognized scholarly and professional accomplishments, along with successful administrative experience. Furthermore, candidates should have considerable administrative experience at the level of department chair or higher. Employers typically prefer candidates with a successful record of working with a diversified population, encouraging faculty development and scholarship, and performing successful fund-raising.

To do their work effectively, academic Deans must have strong leadership, administrative, management, and fund-raising skills along with communication, interpersonal, and team building skills. In addition, they should have computer skills. Successful academic Deans share several personality traits, such as being organized, analytical, honest, fair, innovative, energetic, and flexible. They are committed to providing the best academic opportunities for all students.

Unions/Associations

Academic Deans join local, state, regional, and national higher education organizations to take advantage of professional services such as continuing education programs, professional publications, and networking opportunities. Some organizations that Deans belong to are:

- American Association of University Administrators
- Association of College Administration Professionals
- American Association for Higher Education
- National Association for Women in Education
- American Conference of Academic Deans
- National Association of Scholars

Tips for Entry

1. As you begin your teaching career in higher education, volunteer to serve on administrative committees in your department, academic unit, and institution.
2. Use your network to help you learn about job opportunities, as well as about key people, issues, political climate, and so forth, regarding an institution where you may be interested in applying for a position.
3. Learn more about the academic Dean profession on the Internet. Enter the keyword "academic dean" in any search engine to get a list of relevant web pages.

PROVOST

CAREER PROFILE

Duties: Provide overall academic leadership for an institution; oversee the administration of all academic programs; develop and implement academic policies; supervise faculty and administrative staff; perform other duties as required

Alternate Title: Executive Vice President and Provost

Salary Range: $77,000 to $155,000

Employment Prospects: Fair

Advancement Prospects: Limited

Prerequisites:
  Licensure/Certification—None required
  Education/Training—A doctoral degree
  Experience—Extensive instructional and administrative experience; be a full professor
  Special Skills and Personality Traits—Leadership, administrative, supervisory, communication, interpersonal, team building, and computer skills; honest, fair, innovative, energetic, patient, flexible, decisive, organized

CAREER LADDER

President

↑

Provost

↑

Dean, Assistant Provost, or Vice President of Academic Affairs

Position Description

The chief academic officers at two-year colleges, four-year colleges, and universities are called *Provosts*. As executive vice presidents, Provosts report directly to the presidents of colleges and universities. Their role is to manage the overall academic programs and to advise presidents on academic matters. Provosts also assist presidents in making both academic and administrative policies, which are based on the missions and goals established by the governing board of trustees. When presidents must be absent from their duties, Provosts usually serve as acting chief executive officers.

Provosts are responsible for the overall design and implementation of curriculum and academic standards for the various programs that are offered at their institutions. Depending on the missions of their institutions, Provosts oversee programs that may include (but are not limited to):

- associate degree programs
- bachelor's degree programs
- master's degree programs
- doctoral degree programs
- continuing education programs
- vocational programs
- professional certificate programs
- nondegree programs

Provosts are also responsible for building and supporting positive environments that encourage superior teaching and scholarship. They are generally expected to raise and expand their institutions' academic standing statewide, regionally, nationally, and internationally. Thus, they continually look for ways to improve existing academic programs and to introduce new academic offerings that would benefit the student body. Many Provosts also develop educational partnerships with local educational institutions, community organizations, businesses, and industries. For example, a community college Provost and local school superintendents might develop a program that allows qualifying high school senior students to enroll in one or more courses at the community college for their elective classes.

Another major responsibility is providing support and guidance to academic deans. Provosts coordinate and direct the activities of the various academic deans. They also advise deans about instructional programs, academic policies, and administrative matters such as personnel and fiscal management. In addition, Provosts provide academic leadership and advocacy to the faculty.

Provosts are also responsible for the day-to-day administration of the academic operations at their institutions. This includes all academic units (departments, divisions, schools, and colleges), libraries, museums, and other cultural and educational units. Their administrative duties include, but are not limited to:

- overseeing central administration planning and fiscal management
- developing annual academic budgets
- directing the process of faculty appointments, evaluation, and professional development
- ensuring that academic programs are in compliance with institutional policies and regulations, as well as with any government laws and guidelines
- serving as liaison officers with accreditation agencies which evaluate academic programs
- performing fund-raising duties
- representing their institutions at educational, legislative, and professional meetings, conferences, and events

In some institutions, Provosts are in charge of overseeing the administration of student support and student affairs services. This includes enrollment services (recruitment, admissions, registration, school records), student organizations, health services, instructional resources, and so on.

Provosts are also responsible for maintaining positive relationships with the local communities. Provosts network with community leaders, business leaders, social service agencies, community groups, and so on. In addition, they participate in community events, as well as serve on boards, task forces, and committees of local agencies and organizations.

Provosts put in long hours in order to fulfill their duties and responsibilities. They often spend evenings and weekends attending meetings, participating in conferences, meeting with donors, making presentations at conferences, appearing at social or political functions, and so on.

Salaries

Salaries vary and depend on factors such as experience, education, size and type of institution, and an institution's budget. According to a 1998–99 salary survey by the College and University Personnel Association, the median annual salary for executive vice presidents, including Provosts, ranged from $77,367 to $155,075.

In addition to their salaries, Provosts receive fringe benefits, such as sick leave, medical plans, life insurance, and retirement benefits. They usually receive additional compensation in the form of moving allowances, expense accounts, tuition benefits for their spouses and children, payment for professional organization dues, and so forth.

Employment Prospects

Most job opportunities become available when Provosts retire, resign, or transfer to other institutions. Those willing to relocate to another city or region may have better chances of obtaining positions.

Advancement Prospects

Provosts can become presidents of single institutions or college systems. Those who have chosen the Provost position as their highest career goal realize advancement through pay increases, with professional recognition, and by transfers to other institutions with more complex responsibilities and challenges.

Provosts can pursue other career paths such as becoming consultants and chief executive officers with government agencies, private industry, educational organizations, and professional associations.

Licensure/Certification

No state licensure or professional certification is required for this profession.

Education and Training

Most higher education institutions require that Provosts hold doctoral degrees.

Provosts generally pursue professional development through individual study, enrollment in continuing education classes and professional workshops, and participation in professional conferences.

Experience, Skills, and Personality Traits

Employers choose candidates who have a distinguished record of teaching, research, and scholarship as well as successful senior-level administrative experience. Candidates for Provosts at the four-year college and university level should also be full professors or have the qualifications to be appointed as such.

To perform their work well, Provosts must have outstanding leadership, administrative, and supervisory skills. They should also have superior communication, interpersonal, and team building skills. In addition, they should be proficient with computers.

Being honest, fair, innovative, energetic, patient, flexible, decisive, and organized are some of the personality traits that successful Provosts share. In addition, they have integrity and a sense of humor. They are dedicated to encouraging and motivating faculty and administrators to contribute to the academic excellence of themselves and their students.

Unions/Associations

Provosts join local, state, and national organizations to take advantage of professional services such as continuing education programs, professional publications, networking opportunities, and professional resources. Some of the organizations they might join are:

- American Association of University Administrators
- Association of College Administration Professionals
- American Association for Higher Education
- National Association of Scholars
- National Association for Women in Education

Tips for Entry

1. Read biographies about different Provosts, as well as network with current and past Provosts. Learn what different career paths they traveled to reach the position of Provost.
2. Use the Internet to learn about job announcements for Provost positions nationwide. One source is the web site for the *Chronicle of Higher Education* (*http://chronicle.com*). Also, check web sites for professional associations, as many have web pages for job listings. (For web addresses of some organizations, see Appendix 2.)
3. You can learn about different Provost offices on the Internet. To find relevant web pages, enter the keyword "provost office" or "office of the Provost" in any search engine.

PRESIDENT

CAREER PROFILE

Duties: Provide educational leadership for an institution; oversee the administration of all academic, administrative, and other operations; develop and implement operational plans; develop and manage budgets

Alternate Titles: Chief Executive Officer (CEO), Chancellor

Salary Range: $100,000 to $187,000

Employment Prospects: Fair

Advancement Prospects: Limited

Prerequisites:
  Licensure/Certification—None required
  Education/Training—Doctoral degree
  Experience—Extensive administrative experiences in progressively responsible executive-level positions
  Special Skills and Personality Traits—Administrative, leadership, team building, communication, interpersonal, and social skills; dedicated, honest, ethical, analytical, approachable, flexible, creative, and resourceful

CAREER LADDER

Chancellor, college system

President

Provost

Position Description

The chief executive officer of a higher education institution is its President, who is responsible for the overall operations of the college or university. He or she is given the authority to develop and implement policies and programs that would best fulfill the missions and goals established by the governing board of trustees.

Whether administering a two-year college, four-year college, or university, a President oversees several major areas of operations that include (but are not limited to):

- academic programs (all degree and nondegree programs)
- student services—such as admissions, registration, housing services, student health services, and extracurricular programs
- administrative services—such as human resources, financial services, legal relations, facilities management, and information systems
- external affairs—such as development (or fund-raising), alumni relations, and community relations

Presidents have many different responsibilities that vary from one institution to the next. The priority of responsibilities also varies, depending on the needs of their campuses. One general responsibility of all Presidents is developing plans to meet the needs of their institutions. This includes long-range and short-term plans for instruction, student enrollment, human resources, new facilities, and so on.

Another general responsibility is overseeing the development and management of institutional budgets, which typically involve millions of dollars. The budgets cover salaries, operation costs, academic programs, student services, athletic programs, and so forth. In addition, Presidents are responsible for broadening their institution's financial base. This includes overseeing development, or fund-raising, activities such as capital campaigns, annual fund-raising drives, major gifts from prospective donors, and grants from corporations and philanthropic foundations.

Presidents perform many administrative duties that vary with the different institutions. Some general duties are:

- recruiting and selecting qualified executive-level administrators
- supervising the recruitment and selection of all other personnel

- ensuring that all programs and services are in compliance with institutional policies and standards, state and federal regulations, and requirements of accreditation agencies
- building collaborative partnerships with business, industry, and other educational institutions
- representing their institutions at educational conferences, professional meetings, community events, and so on

Their job also involves promoting positive community relations. Presidents network with community leaders, business leaders, social service agencies, community groups, and so on. In addition, they participate on boards, task forces, and committees for community organizations, educational agencies, and professional associations.

To assist Presidents with their responsibilities, most institutions have executive-level administrators—provosts (chief academic officers) and academic deans as well as nonacademic vice presidents, deans, program directors, and specialists. Presidents also have their own professional and support staffs. The administrators and Presidents' staffs perform their designated responsibilities under the direction and guidance of the Presidents.

The executive-level administrators (provosts, vice presidents, and some directors) typically form a President's executive council to advise the President as well as offer policy and program recommendations. Presidents are generally encouraged to develop a collaborative decision-making environment among students, faculty, administrators, and staff. However, the ultimate decision making rests upon the Presidents, who are held accountable by the governing boards of trustees.

In private colleges and universities, most Presidents report directly to boards of trustees (or boards of directors), while in public institutions, Presidents report to chancellors and/or boards of trustees.

Presidents work very long hours each day. They often work evenings and weekends completing their various tasks, participating in meetings, attending conferences, meeting with donors, appearing at community functions, and so on.

Salaries

Salaries vary and depend on factors such as experience, education, size and type of institution, and an institution's budget. According to a 1998–99 salary survey by the College and University Personnel Association, the median annual salary for Presidents—chief executive officers of single institutions—ranged from $100,000 to $186,174.

Presidents also receive fringe benefits, such as sick leave, medical plans, life insurance, and retirement benefits. They receive additional compensation in the form of expense accounts, free housing or housing allowance, payment for professional organization dues, and so on.

Employment Prospects

Most job opportunities become available when Presidents retire, resign, or transfer to other institutions. Those willing to relocate to other cities and regions may have better chances of obtaining positions.

Advancement Prospects

Presidents can become chancellors who administer college systems. Most Presidents realize advancement through pay increases, with professional recognition, and by transfers to other institutions with more complex responsibilities and challenges.

Other career paths available for Presidents include becoming consultants and chief executive officers with government agencies, educational organizations, professional associations, and private industry.

Licensure/Certification

No state licensure or professional certification is required for this profession.

Education and Training

Most higher education institutions require or prefer that Presidents have doctoral degrees. Many community colleges allow a minimum of a master's degree for the President position.

Many Presidents pursue professional development through individual study, enrollment in continuing education classes and professional workshops, and with participation in professional conferences.

Experience, Skills, and Personality Traits

Presidents have extensive administrative, management, and academic experiences, proven educational leadership ability, and successful working relationships with boards of trustees. In addition, their work history shows successful progression in executive-level administration roles, performing major administrative responsibilities in planning, fiscal management, human resource management, fundraising, and so forth.

To do their work effectively, Presidents must have superior administrative skills along with excellent leadership skills. Team building, communication, interpersonal, and social skills are also important as they must be able to relate well with boards, staff, administrators, faculty, students, alumni, local communities, educational agencies, and other constituents.

Being dedicated, honest, ethical, analytical, approachable, flexible, creative, and resourceful are some personality traits that successful college and university Presidents share. They also have sound personal judgment and a fine sense of humor. In addition, they are sensitive to the differing needs and diversity of the student body, faculty, administration, and staff of their institutions. Furthermore, they are strongly committed to provide and promote academic excellence.

Unions/Associations

Presidents join local, state, regional, and national higher education organizations to take advantage of professional services such as continuing education programs, professional publications, and networking opportunities. Some organizations that many Presidents join are the:

- American Association of University Administrators
- Association of College Administration Professionals
- American Association for Higher Education
- National Association of Scholars

Tips for Entry

1. Learn what career paths various Presidents have traveled to reach their positions. You might read biographies about college and university Presidents, as well as network with current and past Presidents.
2. The traditional career ladder for Presidents is to rise through the ranks of professors, department chairs, academic deans, and provosts. In recent years, more Presidents are being appointed who have risen within the ranks of nonacademic administrators.
3. You can learn more about college and university Presidents and their offices on the Internet. To get a list of relevant web pages to read, enter either of these keywords in any search engine: "college president" or "university president."

COUNSELORS

SCHOOL COUNSELOR

CAREER PROFILE

Duties: Provide academic, vocational, and personal counseling services to students; provide consultation and case management services; perform other duties as required

Alternate Titles: Guidance Counselor; a title, such as Elementary School Counselor or High School Counselor, that reflects a school level

Salary Range: $21,000 to $74,000

Employment Prospects: Good

Advancement Prospects: Limited

Prerequisites:
  Licensure/Certification—A school counseling credential; a teaching credential may be required
  Education/Training—Bachelor's or master's degree; for licensed School Counselors, completion of an educational administration program
  Experience—One to five years of classroom teaching experience
  Special Skills and Personality Traits—Organizational, time management, writing, communication, interpersonal, teamwork, conflict resolution, and computer skills; caring, gentle, firm, nonjudgmental, tolerant, patient, flexible

CAREER LADDER

Senior School Counselor

School Counselor

Classroom Teacher

Position Description

In public and private schools, School Counselors work with teachers, administrators, and families to help students of all backgrounds succeed in school. They address the educational, vocational, social, and personal needs of students at all school levels—elementary school, middle school, junior high school, and high school. Their work involves individual and small group counseling.

Because students' development and interests differ with age, School Counselors at the different school levels focus on different needs. Elementary and middle school counselors do more individual and small group counseling around personal and social matters. They also do large group guidance activities in the classrooms, covering topics such as life skills, coping skills, and career exploration.

High School Counselors mostly address academic and vocational needs. In particular, they help high school students explore vocational and career options. For example, they might advise students about different types of colleges, technical schools, and apprenticeships; arrange for job shadowing or college tours; or assist with admissions applications and financial aid forms. High school counselors also help students develop job search skills such as resume writing and interviewing techniques.

Another major responsibility of School Counselors is to provide consultation services to teachers, administrators, school psychologists, school social workers, and other school staff. They conduct consultations with families, community agencies, social service agencies, and others. In addition, School Counselors provide in-service training to teachers and administrators on child development issues, behavioral management techniques, and other topics.

Case management is another area of responsibility for most School Counselors. This includes coordinating meetings between parents, teachers, and other school personnel regarding individual children. It also involves helping families obtain services for their children through referrals to social service agencies, community agencies, health care professionals, and other agencies.

Counselors perform many other duties that may include:

- providing special services, such as alcohol and drug prevention programs or peer mediation programs
- providing crisis counseling to students and school staff when critical events occur
- developing a network of therapists, health care professionals, social service agencies, and others to refer students and their families
- performing student assessments as part of pupil services or special services teams
- coordinating and administering standard tests
- operating career guidance centers
- following up on students with attendance problems
- registering and scheduling new students
- writing required correspondence and reports, as well as filling out required paperwork
- participating in school meetings and on school committees
- sponsoring extracurricular activities
- continuing professional development through self-study, continuing education courses, networking with colleagues, and so on

Most School Counselors have a 10-month school schedule, usually from September to June. They frequently work long days, and sometimes on weekends, to complete their many tasks.

Salaries

Salaries vary, and depend on such factors as education, experience, job responsibilities, and school budget. According to the U.S. Bureau of Labor Statistics, the 1998 estimated annual salary for most vocational and educational counselors ranged from $21,230 to $73,920.

In addition to their salary, School Counselors receive a benefits package that includes sick leave, vacation leave, health insurance, retirement benefits, and so on.

Employment Prospects

Most School Counselor jobs become available as individuals retire, resign, or advance to other positions.

Job opportunities for School Counselors are expected to grow due to the increasing rate of student enrollment, as well as state laws requiring counselors in elementary schools. However, the creation of additional jobs in a public or private school depends on available school funding.

Advancement Prospects

School Counselors can advance to supervisory and management positions as instructional supervisors in counseling, directors of guidance and counseling, and directors of pupil services.

With additional education and licensure, they can become school psychologists, school social workers, or school administrators. Other options include specializing in other counseling fields such as rehabilitation counseling, career counseling, and marriage and family therapy.

Licensure/Certification

In public schools, School Counselors must hold a valid school counselor credential. Some states require that public School Counselors also hold a teaching credential. Licensure requirements vary from state to state. (For specific information, contact the state board of education in the state where you wish to work.)

Many private schools require state licensure or professional certification from school accreditation organizations, professional associations, or other recognized organizations.

Education and Training

School Counselors must have either a bachelor's or master's degree. According to the American School Counselors Association, most School Counselors have master's or doctoral degrees.

Licensed School Counselors must have completed an approved school guidance and counseling program which leads to licensure in the state where they practice. The program includes course work in developmental guidance and counseling, child psychology, individual and group counseling techniques, and pupil appraisal and evaluation techniques. It also includes a supervised field practicum in school settings.

Experience, Skills, and Personality Traits

Generally, schools require that School Counselors have one to five years of classroom teaching experience. Employers may accept previous school counseling experience or supervised school counseling internship as a substitution for some or all of the teaching requirement.

To perform their jobs effectively, School Counselors need adequate organizational, time management, and writing skills. They also need strong communication, interpersonal, teamwork, and conflict resolution skills to work well with students, teachers, administrators, parents, and others. In addition, School Counselors should have sufficient computer skills, including knowledge of computer databases and the Internet.

Successful School Counselors share several personality traits, such as being caring, gentle, firm, nonjudgmental, tolerant, patient, and flexible. They are able to stay positive and think fast on their feet. Furthermore, they are committed to helping students of all backgrounds succeed in their school careers.

Unions/Associations

School Counselors join different local, state, and national professional organizations to take advantage of services such as professional resources, continuing education programs, and networking opportunities. One national counseling organization that many School Counselors join is the American School Counselor Association, a division of American Counseling Association.

Many School Counselors also join educator organizations that serve their particular interests, such as the Council for Exceptional Children, the National Association for the Education of Young Children, or the National Middle School Association.

School Counselors in public schools are eligible to join their school's teacher union, such as the American Federation of Teachers or the National Education Association.

Tips for Entry

1. In high school and college, you can gain valuable experience by participating in peer counseling programs sponsored by your school, community center, church, youth agency, or other community organization.
2. Join professional associations, and network with members to learn about current or upcoming job vacancies. Many organizations have student memberships.
3. To enhance your employability, obtain the National Certified Counselor and/or National Certified School Counselor certification granted by the National Board for Certified Counselors (NBCC). For more information contact NBCC. Write to: 3 Terrace Way, Suite D, Greensboro, N.C. 27403-3660. Phone: (336) 547-0607 Fax: (336) 547-0017. Or visit its web site on the Internet at *http://www.nbcc.org*.
4. Many school counseling departments have web pages on the Internet. To get a list of web pages to read, enter the keyword "school counseling department" in any search engine.

COLLEGE CAREER COUNSELOR

CAREER PROFILE

Duties: Provide career development counseling to students and alumni; provide job search coaching; help develop and implement programs and activities for the college career center; perform other duties as required

Alternative Titles: Career Adviser, Career Development Counselor

Salary Range: $21,000 to $74,000

Employment Prospects: Fair

Advancement Prospects: Limited

Prerequisites:
 Licensure/Certification—None is required
 Education/Training—Master's degree
 Experience—Prior experience in career counseling and career programs; experience working in college settings
 Special Skills and Personality Traits—Organizational, project management, writing, communication, presentation, interpersonal, teamwork, customer service, and computer skills; patient, objective, friendly, tactful, sincere, trustworthy, flexible, creative

CAREER LADDER

Senior College Career Counselor

College Career Counselor

Intern

Position Description

Almost every college and university has a career center that provides career resources and job placement services to students and alumni. (Most centers also allow the general public to take advantage of their services.) One of the services offered is career development counseling by professional College Career Counselors. The counselors work with students and alumni on career development issues in individual or group sessions.

College Career Counselors advise many students who are unsure of what career choices to make. The counselors interview them to learn about their education, training, work history, skills, interests, and personality. Counselors may also have students take career tests, interest inventories, and other self-assessment tools to determine aptitude, talents, and skills of which they may be unaware.

Upon analyzing tests and evaluating information about individuals, College Career Counselors discuss the results with them and offer suggestions of possible career choices. When students have made their career choices, College Career Counselors can help them develop a career plan to meet their career objectives.

College Career Counselors also provide students, alumni, and others with information about occupations, careers, job markets, job trends, employers, graduate programs, financial aid, and so on. In addition, they show individuals how to use the resources that are available in the college career centers so that they can research on their own about careers, occupations, employers, and so forth. (More and more career centers are including technology-based resources such as computer databases and the Internet.)

Developing job search plans for full-time employment is another area in which College Career Counselors provide assistance. They might advise students on how to focus their job search in order to reach employers for whom they wish to work. They might review students' resumes and make suggestions for improvements. They might conduct mock job interviews to help students prepare and practice for their real-life interviews. College Career Counselors can also help individuals evaluate actual job offers.

Another aspect of the College Career Counselor's job is to help with the development and implementation of programs and services for their career centers. For example, many four-year colleges and universities offer internship and cooperative education programs that provide students with the opportunity to gain work experience in their chosen fields. College Career Counselors also plan and coordinate campus-wide events such as job recruitment fairs and career information days. This usually involves working with other staff members, faculty, other campus organizations, and employers.

College Career Counselors perform many other duties. For example, they might:

- conduct job skills workshops
- facilitate seminars in career trends, self-assessment, job skills, and other career-related topics
- develop instructional aids and marketing materials
- develop job opportunities both on and off campus
- help students find appropriate part-time and temporary jobs on or off campus
- prepare and distribute surveys
- write reports and correspondence and complete required paperwork
- maintain resources in the career library, including technology-based resources

College Career Counselors are also responsible for staying current with information on education, occupations, labor market, and job trends. In addition, they keep up with trends in career development counseling and hone their computer skills through continuing education courses, self-study, and networking with colleagues.

In many career centers, College Career Counselors are assigned to provide services to certain majors or to certain schools and colleges (such as a school of business or college of architecture). In small colleges, one full-time College Career Counselor may be responsible for providing all services offered by the career centers.

College Career Counselors work full time or part time. Some counselors work early evening hours to accommodate individuals who work or attend classes during the day.

Salaries

Salaries vary, and depend on factors such as type of employer, location, and a counselor's education, experience, and job duties. According to the U.S. Bureau of Labor Statistics, the estimated annual salary in 1998 for most education and vocational counselors ranged from $21,230 to $73,920.

In addition to a salary, full-time College Career Counselors receive fringe benefits such as medical insurance, vacation pay, and retirement benefits.

Employment Prospects

College Career Counselors work for public and private two-year colleges, four-year colleges, and universities. Most job opportunities become available as counselors retire, resign, or advance to other positions.

Opportunities vary from institution to institution. Generally, an increase in student enrollment often goes hand in hand with the addition of full-time and part-time counseling positions. However, the creation of new positions is dependent on available funding.

Advancement Prospects

College Career Counselors can advance to supervisory and administrative positions within career centers. With advanced degrees and extensive experience, they can pursue positions such as directors of student affairs, deans of students, vice presidents of student affairs, and college or university presidents.

They can also follow other paths such as becoming college professors, consultants, or private career counselors.

Licensure/Certification

No state licensure or professional certification is required for this profession.

Education and Training

Most employers prefer that Career College Counselors have a master's degree in counseling, higher education, student affairs, or a related field. Some employers accept candidates with bachelor's degrees if they are currently enrolled in an appropriate master's program.

Experience, Skills, and Personality Traits

Employers usually prefer that candidates have previous experience in career development counseling as well as in career programs. They also prefer that candidates have experience working in college settings.

To perform their work effectively, College Career Counselors must have strong organizational, project management, writing, communication, and presentation skills. They also need strong interpersonal, teamwork, and customer service skills. In addition, they should have adequate computer skills including the ability to utilize databases and the Internet.

Successful College Career Counselors share several personality traits such as being patient, objective, friendly, tactful, sincere, trustworthy, flexible, and creative. They are emotionally stable and have a good sense of humor. Furthermore, they have an understanding of college students and an empathy for their career issues.

Unions/Associations

College Career Counselors might join the American Counseling Association, the National Career Development

Association, and other national, local, and state professional organizations. By joining such organizations, they can take advantage of professional services such as continuing education programs, professional resources, and networking opportunities.

Tips for Entry

1. In college, volunteer or work in career centers, residential life, and/or other student affairs programs to gain experience working in college settings.
2. Contact the career center or personnel department of each institution where you would like to work. Find out if positions are currently available or will be in the near future. Also find out to whom you can submit a resume or application.
3. To enhance your employability, become certified as a National Certified Counselor and/or National Certified Career Counselor which is granted by the National Board for Certified Counselors (NBCC). For more information, write to NBCC at: 3 Terrace Way, Suite D, Greensboro, N.C. 27403-3660. Or call: (336) 547-0607; or fax: (336) 547-0017. Or visit its web site: *http://www.nbcc.org*.
4. Many college career centers have web pages on the Internet. To obtain a list of web pages, enter these keywords in a search engine: "career services" or "career center."

EMPLOYMENT COUNSELOR

CAREER PROFILE

Duties: Help clients develop career and job search plans; provide career development and employment counseling; perform other duties as required

Alternate Titles: Job Counselor, Employment Specialist, Career Counselor

Salary Range: $21,000 to $74,000

Employment Prospects: Fair

Advancement Prospects: Limited

Prerequisites:
  Licensure/Certification—None is required
  Education/Training—Master's or bachelor's degree
  Experience—Previous vocational counseling or related experience
  Special Skills and Personality Traits—Organizational, time management, writing, communication, interpersonal, teamwork, customer service, and computer skills; patient, objective, friendly, tactful, sincere, trustworthy, flexible, creative

CAREER LADDER

Senior Employment Counselor

Employment Counselor

Trainee

Position Description

Employment Counselors help individuals identify and pursue their career goals, as well as find jobs that match their goals. In public job service offices, community agencies, private practices, and other settings, Employment Counselors work with people of all ages, backgrounds, and circumstances. For example, clients may be high school dropouts with no job skills, recent college graduates, wives who are reentering the workforce, retirees looking for part-time work, parolees, laid-off workers wishing to learn new job skills, recent immigrants, part-time workers looking for full-time employment, full-time workers wanting to change careers, and so on.

As trained professionals, Employment Counselors establish a trusting and open relationship with each of their clients. Through individual and group counseling sessions, Employment Counselors support, encourage, and motivate their clients to achieve their career and job goals.

Because they handle many different clients at the same time who may require different services, Employment Counselors' jobs involve case management. For example, Employment Counselors in public employment services may manage a caseload of 200 or more clients. The counselors coordinate services with appropriate representatives of social service agencies, health centers, community agencies, and so on to help their clients achieve their goals.

In initial meetings with clients, Employment Counselors determine their eligibility for services and what types of services they would need. In addition, Employment Counselors learn about clients' job backgrounds—job interests, work experience, education and training, work attitudes, personality, and so on. They also recognize special needs that clients may have such as physical or mental disabilities, limited English proficiency, health problems, and so on. In addition, Employment Counselors provide clients with educational, occupational, and labor market information to help them decide on their immediate job and career goals.

With clients who are unsure of their career or job goals, Employment Counselors may have them take several standard tests and inventories to identify their interests, skills, aptitudes, and needs. Employment Counselors interpret the tests and explain the results to the clients.

Together, Employment Counselors and clients develop a realistic job and career plan for the clients. This includes obtaining any education, training, and services (such as rehabilitative, psychological, or social services) that would help them attain their goals. For example, an Employment Counselor might refer a client with emotional problems to a mental health counselor.

As part of their services, Employment Counselors provide clients with suitable job referrals. They review job orders at their agencies for job vacancies that match their clients' interests and experiences. They give their clients information about particular jobs—name of employer, address, and phone number—so that they can contact the employers about the openings.

Employment Counselors also help clients through the job search process. They may help clients prepare resumes and cover letters or conduct mock job interviews. Clients with little or no job search skills may be referred to workshops or training programs within the counselors' agencies or in the community.

Employment Counselors perform many other duties that vary from one agency to the next. These duties might include:

- developing job and job training opportunities
- receiving job orders from employers
- performing outreach activities to let people know of the services their agencies provide
- conducting in-service workshops for staff
- participating in staff meetings
- maintaining client files
- writing correspondence, preparing reports, and completing required paperwork

Employment Counselors are also responsible for keeping up with current regulations and laws that affect employment and training, job service, and employee rights. In addition, they keep up with current information about occupations, labor markets, and job trends. Furthermore, they are responsible for developing a network of public agencies, community agencies, institutions, business organizations, and other groups for client referrals.

Employment Counselors generally work 40 hours per week. They may work extra hours in the evenings and on weekends to attend meetings, conduct workshops, or perform other job tasks. Some counselors have evening and weekend counseling hours to accommodate clients who may work or attend school during the day.

Salaries

Salaries vary, and depend on factors such as type of employer and an Employment Counselor's education, experience, and responsibilities. According to the U.S. Bureau of Labor Statistics, the estimated annual salary in 1998 for vocational and educational counselors ranged from $21,230 to $73,920.

In addition to their salary, Employment Counselors typically receive fringe benefits such as medical insurance, vacation pay, and retirement benefits.

Employment Prospects

Employment Counselors work for public job service offices, community agencies, military facilities, and private practices. Most job opportunities become available as Employment Counselors retire, resign, or advance to other positions.

Advancement Prospects

Advancement opportunities are limited to supervisory and administrative positions. Many counselors realize advancement through higher pay and more complex assignments.

Employment Counselors can also pursue other options such as becoming consultants, rehabilitation counselors, or counselor educators.

Licensure/Certification

No state licensure or professional certification is required for this profession.

Education and Training

Depending on an employer's requirements, Employment Counselors need either a master's or bachelor's degree in counseling or a related field. Some employers accept candidates with bachelor's degrees in any field as long as they have completed appropriate counseling courses on human behavior and development, counseling strategies, ethical practice, and other core knowledge areas.

Experience, Skills, and Personality Traits

Employers generally require that Employment Counselors have previous vocational counseling or related experience with employment services. New counselors should be familiar with the principles and techniques of vocational guidance, as well as be able to interpret labor market information and laws and regulations regarding employment and training.

To perform their work effectively, Employment Counselors need adequate organizational, time management, writing, and communication skills. They also need strong interpersonal and teamwork skills in order to establish and maintain positive working relationships with clients, coworkers, and others. Having good customer service skills and computer skills is also essential.

Successful Employment Counselors share personality traits such as being patient, objective, friendly, tactful, sincere, trustworthy, flexible, and creative. They are emotionally stable and have a good sense of humor. In addition, they have the desire to help others and enjoy working with all people of different backgrounds.

Unions/Associations

Employment Counselors join local, state, and national professional organizations to take advantage of professional services such as continuing education programs, professional certification, and networking opportunities. Many Employment Counselors belong to the National Employment Counseling Association, a division of American Counseling Association.

Tips for Entry

1. Obtain experience by volunteering or working in your school or college career center.
2. Talk with Employment Counselors to learn more about their work. Ask for permission to follow an Employment Counselor at work to gain firsthand knowledge about what they do.
3. The selection process for positions with government agencies typically involves several steps. Selection requirements may include an examination, oral interview, medical exam, background investigation, and so on.
4. To enhance your employability, you might obtain the nationally recognized National Certified Counselor and/or National Certified Career Counselor certifications. These are voluntary certifications granted by the National Board for Certified Counselors (NBCC). For more information, write to NBCC, 3 Terrace Way, Suite D, Greensboro, N.C. 27403-3660. Or call at (336) 547-0607; or fax at (336) 547-0017. Or visit its web site at *http://www.nbcc.org*.
5. Learn more about employment counseling on the Internet. One web site you might visit belongs to the National Employment Counseling Association (*http://www.geocities.com/Athens/Acropolis/6491/neca.html*). To get a list of other relevant web sites to read, enter the keyword "employment counseling" in a search engine.

HEALTH EDUCATORS

HEALTH EDUCATOR

CAREER PROFILE

Duties: Perform needs assessments; develop, implement, and evaluate health education programs; provide instruction on health and health-related issues; act as a resource; coordinate community outreach activities; develop educational materials; perform other duties as required

Alternate Titles: Health Education Specialist; Prevention Educator; Health Education Teacher; a title, such as Substance Abuse Educator or Violence Prevention Specialist, that reflects an area of specialization

Salary Range: $20,000 to $35,000

Employment Prospects: Fair

Advancement Prospects: Limited

Prerequisites:

    Licensure/Certification—May require a teaching credential or other certification for teaching in public and private schools

    Education/Training—Bachelor's or master's degree; for licensed school teachers, completion of an accredited teacher education program

    Experience—Previous experience working with the target clientele (such as teenagers, elderly, immigrants, or pregnant women) in the appropriate settings

    Special Skills and Personality Traits—Organizational, management, writing, computer, public speaking, interpersonal, teamwork, leadership, and communication skills; caring, friendly, confident, tactful, respectful

CAREER LADDER

Senior Health Educator or Program Coordinator

↑

Health Educator

↑

Student

Position Description

Health Educators help people make informed decisions that affect their personal health as well as the health of their family and community. As advocates of health-related issues, Health Educators' goals are to promote healthy lifestyles and to prevent diseases, disabilities, and premature deaths through educational activities. Throughout their careers, Health Educators provide education on a wide range of health issues to people of different ages, backgrounds, and circumstances. For example, Health Educators address topics such as nutrition, physical fitness, stress management, substance abuse, sexually transmitted diseases, prenatal care, preventative health care, disease prevention, environmental health, patients' rights, and safety and disaster preparedness.

Health Educators work on health programs in a variety of settings. They work for government agencies (such as public health departments) and community organizations. Many work in health care settings such as hospitals and health centers. Some Health Educators are health education teachers and curriculum specialists in public and private schools. Others hold Health Educator positions in colleges and universities. Some Health Educators are employed in business and industry agencies.

Their tasks vary according to their positions, but some duties are the same regardless of their work setting. For instance, Health Educators:

- perform individual and/or community needs assessments
- develop and implement health education programs
- evaluate the effectiveness of health education programs
- provide instruction on health and health-related issues to their clientele—students, workers, the elderly, patients, and so on—through individual counseling, workshops, seminars, and classes
- be resources for individuals, employers, health care professionals, organizations, and so on
- provide clients with referrals to medical professionals, health care organizations, community agencies, and other groups that may help individuals with their health-related concerns
- coordinate community outreach activities to promote wellness, program services, or special program activities
- provide training and supervision to peer counselors, volunteers, and others who assist in outreach and educational activities
- develop audio, visual, and print educational materials—brochures, pamphlets, books, multimedia software, and so on
- write grant proposals for proposed or existing health education programs
- maintain accurate records, prepare reports, write correspondence, and complete required paperwork

In addition, Health Educators keep up with current developments in their field as well as nurture their professional growth. They read professional journals and books, enroll in continuing education courses, attend professional training workshops, participate in professional conferences, network with colleagues, and so on.

Health Educators work part time or full time. At times they work evenings and weekends to complete paperwork, conduct research, attend meetings, give presentations, facilitate workshops, participate in conferences, and so on.

Salaries

Salaries vary, and depend on factors such as education, experience, job responsibilities, type of employer, and location. The annual salary for most Health Educators is between $20,000 and $35,000 per year.

In addition to their salary, Health Educators receive fringe benefits that include sick pay, vacation leave, medical insurance, and retirement benefits.

Employment Prospects

Some of the employers that hire Health Educators are local and state health departments; community agencies and nonprofit organizations; schools, colleges and universities; business and industry; and hospitals and health centers.

Job opportunities are generally available for Health Educators. An agency or organization often creates new positions for newly funded projects. However, these positions usually last only for the duration of the available funding. Openings for permanent positions typically become available as Health Educators retire, resign, or transfer to other positions.

Advancement Prospects

Health Educators can advance to supervisory and administrative positions such as program coordinators and directors. With advanced degrees and extensive experience, ambitious Health Educators can pursue such positions as health department managers and directors.

Health Educators might also follow other paths such as to become college instructors, researchers, curriculum developers, or public health inspectors.

Licensure/Certification

Health Educators who plan to teach in public school systems are required to have teaching credentials. Licensure requirements differ from state to state. For specific information, contact the state board of education for the state where you wish to teach.

Many private schools require certification from state boards of education, school accreditation groups, professional associations, or other recognized organizations.

Education and Training

Education requirements vary with the different employers. The minimum requirement is a bachelor's degree in health education or other related field. Many employers require or prefer that Health Educators have master's degrees.

Health Educators who plan to obtain a teaching license must complete an accredited teacher education program that includes course work in pedagogy and instruction, as well as a supervised field practicum.

Experience, Skills, and Personality Traits

Requirements vary from job to job. For entry-level positions, employers generally look for candidates who have previous experience working with their target clientele—such as teenagers, the elderly, immigrants, pregnant women, etc. Employers also prefer that candidates have experience working in appropriate settings. Candidates' experience may have been in the form of paid employment, volunteer work, internship, or field practicum.

To do their work effectively, Health Educators need organizational, management, writing, computer, and public speaking skills. They also need interpersonal, teamwork, leadership, and communication skills in order to work well with the many different people they meet on the job.

Being caring, friendly, confident, tactful, and respectful are some personality traits that successful Health Educators share. In addition, they are dedicated to helping people make informed decisions about their health.

Unions/Associations

Health Educators belong to different local, state, and national professional associations to take advantage of professional resources, training workshops, continuing education programs, job listings, and networking opportunities. Some organizations are:

- American Public Health Association
- American Association for Health Education
- Society for Public Health Education
- American College Health Association
- American School Health Association

Tips for Entry

1. You can obtain valuable work experience in college as a volunteer or employee for the health education services on your college campus. Many colleges, for example, have peer health educator programs.
2. Keep a portfolio of examples of your work from school projects and volunteer and paid experience. Also keep letters of recommendation from professors and employers in your portfolio. Bring your portfolio to show prospective employers when you meet them.
3. To enhance your employability, obtain the voluntary Certified Health Education Specialist (CHES) certification that is granted by the National Commission for Health Education Credentialing, Inc. (NCHEC). For more information, write to: NCHEC, 944 Marcon Boulevard, #310, Allentown, Pa. 18103. Or call: (610) 264-8200. Or visit its web site (*www.nchec.org*).
4. Use the Internet to learn more about Health Educators. To get a list of relevant web sites to read, enter either of these keywords in a search engine: "health educator" or "health education."

NUTRITIONIST

CAREER PROFILE

Duties: Perform needs assessments; develop, implement, and evaluate nutrition programs; provide information and advice about food and nutrition; develop educational and promotional materials about nutrition; conduct research; perform other duties as required

Alternate Title: Nutritionist Specialist

Salary Range: $20,000 to $51,000

Employment Prospects: Good

Advancement Prospects: Limited

Prerequisites:
  Licensure/Certification—Nutritionist license, certification, or registration may be required; Registered Dietitian certification may be required
  Education/Training—Bachelor's degree
  Experience—Experience working with target clientele in appropriate work settings; many employers prefer Nutritionists who are registered dietitians
  Special Skills and Personality Traits—Organizational, management, writing, research, computer, interpersonal, counseling, and communication skills; small business skills (if self-employed or a business owner); friendly, tactful, trustworthy, tolerant, caring

CAREER LADDER

Senior Nutritionist or Program Coordinator

Nutritionist

Trainee

Position Description

Nutritionists are experts in the science of nutrition—the way humans, animals, and plants need and use food. With their knowledge and skills about foods and nutrition, Nutritionists work in many different settings to help people make wise choices about the food they eat. Many work in hospitals, day care facilities, educational institutions, or public lunch programs to oversee the preparation of healthy, balanced meals. Some Nutritionists plan and implement the nutrition education programs that are sponsored by public health departments and community agencies.

Some Nutritionists work for food companies, providing analysis and testing of food products and recipes. Some Nutritionists are independent (or self-employed) nutrition counselors who help individuals design realistic food plans to lose or gain weight, deal with food allergies, or control diabetes, high blood pressure, high cholesterol levels, and other health conditions.

Regardless of where they work, Nutritionists attend to many of the same duties.

- They perform needs assessments. For example, an independent Nutritionist performs a nutrition screening of his or her teenage client's diet to find out what nutrients the teenager may be lacking. Or, a Nutritionist in a public health agency surveys the elderly community to learn what nutrition programs they might need.
- They develop, implement, and evaluate nutrition programs for individuals or for groups. For example, one Nutritionist creates a food plan for a client with high blood pressure, while a Nutritionist in a school district plans weekly lunch menus.
- They provide information about food and nutrition to individuals, health professionals, organizations, companies, and communities. Nutritionists may act as resources, consultants, teachers, or trainers.

- They conduct outreach activities to promote nutrition, healthy nutrition practices, and nutrition-related programs and events.
- They write about nutrition-related topics for newspapers, magazines, radio programs, and other media sources. For example, a Nutritionist might write a newspaper article about the nutritional content found in different packaged foods.
- They develop educational materials about nutrition—brochures, pamphlets, books, multimedia software, and so on.
- They conduct research for their employers (such as educational institutions, health departments, and food companies). This includes evaluating food products, analyzing food dishes or recipes, developing new menus, and so on.

Additionally, their job includes preparing and maintaining accurate records. They write correspondence, prepare reports, and complete required paperwork. Many write grant proposals to fund proposed or existing nutrition education programs.

Nutritionists are also responsible for keeping up with current developments in their field as well as for nurturing their professional growth. They accomplish this by reading professional journals and books, enrolling in continuing education courses, participating in professional conferences, networking with colleagues, and so on.

Depending on the nature of their job description, Nutritionists may work in offices as well as in kitchens. Their job may involve traveling to other locations.

Nutritionists work part time or full time. They sometimes work evenings and weekends to attend meetings, give presentations, facilitate workshops, and participate in conferences.

Salaries

Salaries vary, and depend on such factors as education, experience, job responsibilities, and type of employer. According to the U.S. Bureau of Labor Statistics, the estimated annual salary in 1998 for most nutritionists and dietitians ranged from $20,300 to $51,370.

In addition to their salary, Nutritionists typically receive fringe benefits such as medical insurance, vacation pay, and retirement benefits.

Employment Prospects

Among the employers of Nutritionists are hospitals, public health departments, schools, colleges, senior centers, health food stores, weight loss clinics, food companies, sports teams, food associations, and private nutritional services. Many Nutritionists are self-employed consultants or business owners.

According to the U.S. Bureau of Labor Statistics, employment within the nutrition field is expected to grow about as fast as the average for all occupations in the United States through 2008. Most opportunities will become available as Nutritionists retire, resign, or advance to other positions.

Advancement Prospects

Advancement opportunities are limited to supervisory and administrative positions. Advanced degrees are required for higher-level executive positions. The ultimate goal for some Nutritionists is to become self-employed consultants or business owners.

Licensure/Certification

Many states require Nutritionists who provide nutritional counseling to be licensed, certified, or registered. Requirements vary with the different states. (For more information, contact the state licensing board for nutritionists and dietitians in the state where you wish to practice.)

Many employers require or prefer that Nutritionists hold a Registered Dietitian credential. This is a voluntary certification granted by the American Dietetic Association. (For more information about the Registered Dietitian credential, write to: American Dietetic Association, 216 West Jackson Boulevard, Suite 800, Chicago, Ill. 60606. Phone: (800) 877-1600. Or visit its web site: *http://www.eatright.org*.)

Education and Training

Nutritionists need at least a bachelor's degree in food and nutrition or other related field. Their studies include course work in foods, nutrition, chemistry, microbiology, physiology, statistics, and institutional food service management.

Nutritionists who are registered dietitians must have earned their degrees from accredited institutions approved by the American Dietetic Association.

Experience, Skills, and Personality Traits

Employers generally hire entry-level Nutritionists who have previous experience working with the target clientele as well as in the employers' settings. Many employers prefer candidates who are registered dietitians. (Registered dietitians have completed a six- to 12-month supervised practice program.)

To perform their work effectively, Nutritionists need organizational, management, writing, research, and computer skills. They also need interpersonal, counseling, and communication skills to maintain positive working relationships with clients, coworkers, and others. Self-employed Nutritionists should have adequate small business skills.

Being friendly, tactful, trustworthy, tolerant, and caring are a few personality traits that successful Nutritionists share with each other. In addition, they have the desire to help people make wise decisions about their health.

Unions/Associations

Nutritionists belong to local, state, and national professional organizations to take advantage of professional services such as training programs, continuing education programs, professional certification, networking opportunities, job listings, and professional resources. Some national organizations that Nutritionists might join are:

- American Dietetic Association
- American Public Health Association
- American Society for Nutritional Sciences
- International and American Associations of Clinical Nutritionists

Tips for Entry

1. Obtain work as a dietary aide or nutrition assistant in hospitals, health care facilities, schools, and other settings to learn if the nutrition field is right for you.

2. One valuable source for job announcements are professional associations. Many professional associations have job listings that they send by mail or E-mail to members, as well as job hotlines that are available to the general public. Some organizations also post job vacancies on their web sites.

3. Use the Internet to learn more about the Nutritionist profession. One place to start is a visit to the American Dietetic Association's web site (*http://www.eatright.org*). To get a list of relevant web sites to read, enter either of these keywords in a search engine: "nutrition" or "nutritionist."

CHILDBIRTH EDUCATOR

CAREER PROFILE

Duties: Provide information on and support of the childbirthing process to expectant women and their families; perform other duties as required

Alternate Title: Childbirth Instructor

Salary Range: $60 to $200 per couple for a class series (earnings usually based on class fees)

Employment Prospects: Good

Advancement Prospects: Limited

Prerequisites:
  Licensure/Certification—No license is required; a Childbirth Educator certification may be required
  Education/Training—Completion of a certified Childbirth Educator training program is required or preferred
  Experience—Previous experience in the childbirth process preferred, including one's own experience of giving birth
  Special Skills and Personality Traits—Communication, presentation, interpersonal, organizational, and management skills; small business skills (if an independent instructor); friendly, enthusiastic, caring, sympathetic, confident, patient

CAREER LADDER

Lead Childbirth Educator or Independent Instructor

Childbirth Educator

Trainee

Position Description

In a series of classes, Childbirth Educators provide information about the birthing process to expectant women and their families to help them prepare for the eventful labor and delivery of their babies. Educators also present information about the different delivery methods so that women can make well-informed decisions for themselves.

Many Childbirth Educators teach classes as staff members in hospitals, health departments, birthing centers, and obstetricians' offices. Many are independent (or self-employed) instructors who hold classes in their homes or offices, as well as in community centers, health centers, and other locations.

Childbirth Educators who are employed by hospitals, health departments, and other organizations generally follow the curriculum guidelines established by their employers. Independent instructors may develop their own curriculum or follow the guidelines of the childbirth-educator organization, such as the International Association of Childbirth Educators, under which they were trained. All Childbirth Educators bring their own philosophy and teaching style into the classroom.

In general, childbirth instruction is taught in a series of four to 12 classes that are held once a week for two hours. Classes are small; they usually range from six to 10 couples who are made up of pregnant women and their labor coaches. (Coaches are husbands or other loved ones who will be in the delivery room to give the women support as they give birth.)

Childbirth Educators cover basic topics that include:

- the conditions of pregnancy
- signs of labor and labor management
- delivery and anesthesia options (for example, cesarean delivery or natural birthing without drugs)
- hospital and delivery room procedures
- parenting of newborn babies

They also teach coping and relaxation skills (such as breathing exercises) that can help women through the pain and discomfort of labor and the delivery.

Childbirth Educators use a variety of teaching strategies—short lectures, slides, videos, guest speakers, and, if possible, a tour through a hospital labor room. They arrange their classrooms so that the students feel comfortable and secure to ask questions and discuss their concerns, as well as to socialize and provide emotional support for each other.

Many Childbirth Educators hold the last class of the series several months later when all the mothers have given birth. Often known as the reunion class, mothers and coaches, with their newborn babies, return to share their experiences as well as to bring up questions and concerns about caring for their newborn babies.

Many Childbirth Educators assist their employers with the development of educational programs, as well as help in the assessment and evaluation of current programs. These staff Childbirth Educators also perform administrative tasks such as collecting class fees and maintaining attendance records.

Independent instructors are responsible for operating their businesses, and this includes tasks such as collecting clients' fees, paying bills and taxes, bookkeeping, finding classroom facilities, and so on. In addition, they continually look for ways to generate income through advertising, networking, and other means.

Childbirth Educators work part time or full time. Most classes are usually taught in the evenings and on weekends to accommodate parents' schedules.

Salaries

Earnings for many Childbirth Educators are based on class fees that generally range from $60 to $200 per couple for a class series. So, for example, different Childbirth Educators who teach 10 couples for one class series might earn between $600 and $2,000. Annual earnings depend on the total number of series of classes and the total number of who are taught during a year. As small business owners, independent instructors subtract business costs from their annual earnings.

Staff Childbirth Educators generally earn less than independent instructors. However, staff personnel may receive fringe benefits such as medical insurance and retirement benefits.

Employment Prospects

In general, childbirth education is a growing field. Job opportunities in hospitals, childbirth centers, health centers, and medical offices are dependent on the availability of funds as well as the demand for childbirth education within communities. Most staff positions become available as Childbirth Educators retire, resign, or transfer to other positions.

Advancement Prospects

Staff Childbirth Educators are limited to few supervisory and management positions. For many Childbirth Educators, the ultimate goal is to become successful independent instructors.

Licensure/Certification

No state Childbirth Educator licensure or certification is required for this profession. However, many employers require or prefer that Childbirth Educators be certified by professional childbirth-educator organizations, such as Lamaze International or the American Academy of Husband-Coached Childbirth (the Bradley method). Many independent instructors also obtain certification to enhance their professional credibility.

Instructors must renew certification every few years.

Education and Training

Education requirements vary from employer to employer. In some work settings, Childbirth Educators must be registered nurses or other health care professionals, thus needing either an associate, bachelor's, or higher degree. In some settings, Childbirth Educators may need only a high school diploma if they have the appropriate training.

Many Childbirth Educators are initially trained in a specific methodology by a childbirth educator organization. Training programs are comprehensive and intense. Some training programs can be completed in a three- to four-day period. The programs combine academic and practical experience, covering topics such as anatomy, methodology, pedagogy, exercises for the pregnant woman, alternative birthing methods, and care of the newborn.

Childbirth Educators are also responsible for maintaining their professional development. They read professional books and journals, join professional organizations, network with colleagues, attend continuing education classes and training workshops, and so on.

Experience, Skills, and Personality Traits

Employers typically choose candidates whose childbirth philosophy is in tune with theirs. Although candidates may not have previous childbirth teaching experience, they often have experience with childbirth that may include the birth of their own babies.

For their work, Childbirth Educators need effective communication, presentation, and interpersonal skills. Having adequate organizational and management skills is also useful. Independent instructors should have adequate small business skills.

Successful Childbirth Educators share several personality traits such as being friendly, enthusiastic, caring, sympathetic, confident, and patient. In addition, they are committed to helping women make well-informed personal choices about childbirth.

Unions/Associations

Childbirth Educators join local, state, and national professional organizations to take advantage of services such as professional journals, continuing education programs, training workshops, and networking opportunities. Some organizations are:

- Lamaze International
- International Childbirth Education Association, Inc.
- Birthworks, Inc.
- Association of Labor Assistants and Childbirth Educators
- American Academy of Husband-Coached Childbirth

Tips for Entry

1. Contact employers for whom you would like to work. Be sure your philosophies are similar to those of an employer before taking a position.
2. Stay in contact with former students and be in touch with obstetricians, midwives, and other childbirth professionals and health care personnel. Many Childbirth Educators get new students through personal recommendations.
3. You can learn more about the Childbirth Educator profession on the Internet. To get a list of relevant web sites to read, enter these keywords in a search engine: "childbirth education" or "childbirth educator."

CPR/FIRST AID INSTRUCTOR

CAREER PROFILE

Duties: Provide instruction of standard first aid and cardiopulmonary resuscitation (CPR) procedures for emergency situations; perform other duties as required

Salary Range: $10 to $20 per hour

Employment Prospects: Limited for full-time positions

Advancement Prospects: Limited

Prerequisites:
  Licensure/Certification—Standard first aid and CPR certificates; instructor certificate
  Education/Training—Completion of a certified training program
  Experience—Knowledge of CPR and first aid techniques
  Special Skills and Personality Traits—Communication, interpersonal, and presentation skills; small business skills (if an independent instructor or a business owner); friendly, enthusiastic confident, patient, flexible, organized

CAREER LADDER

Lead Instructor, Independent Instructor, or Business Owner

First Aid and CPR Instructor

Student

Position Description

CPR/First Aid Instructors teach standard first aid and cardiopulmonary resuscitation (CPR) procedures to individuals of all ages so that they can respond to emergency situations. Instructors also teach them basic knowledge for assessing an emergency situation, calling for immediate emergency medical services, and applying lifesaving techniques that are appropriate for the baby, child, or adult. With these skills, individuals can attend to injuries, burns, wounds, hypothermia, poisoning, choking, drowning, heart attacks, and seizures until emergency medical service professionals arrive on the scene.

Many CPR/First Aid Instructors are volunteer teachers for the American Red Cross, the American Heart Association, or other organizations. Some instructors are employed by protective services training centers, medical facilities, or private safety training companies. Others are independent (or self-employed) instructors.

CPR/First Aid Instructors teach courses that are designed to meet the needs of different audiences, such as schoolchildren or the general public. Many instructors train medical and other health care professionals, and protective service professionals (such as firefighters, search and rescue technicians, emergency medical technicians, and police officers). Many CPR/First Aid Instructors specialize in training personnel in business, industry, and the government. They teach courses that meet OSHA requirements. (OSHA stands for Occupational Safety and Health Administration, which is a regulatory agency at both the federal and state levels.)

Some CPR/First Aid Instructors also teach first aid and CPR courses that include the use of an automated external defibrillator (AED). The AED is a device used to administer an electric shock through the chest wall to the heart.

Classes are usually two to eight hours long, depending on the type of course. Instructors follow course outlines that are specifically developed by their employers or the organization from which they received their certified training. CPR/First Aid Instructors bring their own teaching style to the classroom. As part of their teaching role, Instructors build students' confidence so that they can successfully learn the class material and be able to respond to emergency situations when they actually occur.

CPR/First Aid Instructors use a variety of teaching techniques that include lecturing and using instructional films. They also give students mock emergency scenarios in which to practice the various skills. In addition, instructors provide students with pamphlets and other handouts to take with them when the class ends.

CPR/First Aid Instructors perform other tasks that include:

- gathering all equipment and instructional materials and setting them up properly before classes begin
- performing administrative tasks such as collecting class fees, keeping attendance records, and completing all required paperwork
- maintaining equipment, such as cleaning mannequins according to approved standards
- attending instructor meetings
- keeping instructor certification up to date

Most CPR/First Aid Instructors teach on a part-time basis. Many have part-time or full-time jobs within the health and protective services fields.

Salaries

Many CPR/First Aid Instructors teach courses on a part-time or voluntary basis, and have other sources of income. Staff CPR/First Aid Instructors generally earn $10 to $20 per hour. They may receive fringe benefits such as medical insurance, sick pay, and retirement benefits.

Earnings for independent CPR/First Aid Instructors are based on class fees. They charge $20 to $50 for each student in a course, depending on their location.

Employment Prospects

CPR/First Aid Instructors are employed by hospitals, protective services training centers, community colleges, and private safety training companies. Some CPR/First Aid Instructors are independent instructors.

CPR/First Aid Instructors are generally in demand to train (and retrain) employees in business, industry, and government. They are also needed to train protective services and health care professionals as well as the general public. However, most opportunities are for voluntary or part-time positions.

Advancement Prospects

There are no direct advancement opportunities for CPR/First Aid Instructors. Some may become independent instructors or business owners that offer CPR/First Aid instruction to companies, agencies, or other organizations.

Most CPR/First Aid Instructors teach classes on a part time or voluntary basis while pursuing careers in teaching, medicine, protective services, and other fields.

Licensure/Certification

CPR/First Aid Instructors are required to obtain certification from one of the following nationally recognized organizations: American Red Cross, American Heart Association, National Safety Council, Medic First Aid, and American Safety and Health Institute.

Each organization has its own requirements and selection process for obtaining certification. (For more information, contact the local office of a national organization.) Instructors must renew certification every one or two years.

Education and Training

There is no minimum education requirement to become a CPR/First Aid Instructor. However, instructors must have successfully completed a certified instructor training program. Training programs are usually short, but comprehensive and intense, providing for both academic instruction and hands-on teaching practice.

Experience, Skills, and Personality Traits

New CPR/First Aid Instructors should have competent knowledge of CPR and first aid techniques. They should also have the ability to teach others. In addition, they should have good communication, interpersonal, and presentation skills. Independent instructors should have adequate small business skills.

Successful CPR/First Aid Instructors share personality traits such as being friendly, enthusiastic, confident, patient, flexible, and organized.

Unions/Associations

CPR/First Aid Instructors join local, state, and national professional organizations to take advantage of resources, continuing education programs, networking opportunities, and other professional services. Many become members of the organizations (listed above) from which they earned their certification.

Tips for Entry

1. Learn basic CPR/First Aid skills from a local chapter of the American Red Cross, American Heart Association, or other organization.
2. Part-time and voluntary positions for CPR/First Aid Instructors are generally available in any community. Some places to contact are: community centers, community agencies, continuing education programs, and the local chapters of the organizations that certify instructors.
3. Learn more about CPR/First Aid Instructors on the Internet. To get a list of pertinent web sites, enter the keywords "first aid and CPR" in a search engine.

LIBRARIANS

PUBLIC LIBRARIAN (CITY OR COUNTY)

CAREER PROFILE

Duties: Help library patrons access and use print and nonprint resources; develop and maintain library collections; plan and coordinate library programs for patrons; do technical and administrative tasks; perform other duties as required

Alternate Title: A title that reflects an area of specialty, such as Reference Librarian, Technical Service Librarian, Children's Librarian, or Special Collections Librarian

Salary Range: $9,000 to $55,000

Employment Prospects: Fair

Advancement Prospects: Good

Prerequisites:
   Licensure/Certification—State or local Public Librarian certification may be required; a driver's license may be required
   Education/Training—Master's degree in library science
   Experience—Work experience in public library settings preferred
   Special Skills and Personality Traits—Writing, communication, self-management; interpersonal, public service, teamwork, computer, and on-line skills; courteous, friendly, enthusiastic, energetic, organized, resourceful, patient, tolerant

CAREER LADDER

Senior Librarian or Library Director

Librarian

Intern or Assistant Librarian

Position Description

Most communities in the United States have a public library that offers patrons free access to library collections of books, magazines, newspapers, videos, recordings, computer databases, and other print and nonprint materials. Public Librarians manage all library collections and ensure that they are readily available to library patrons.

Public Librarians perform many different duties that are generally divided into public, technical, or administrative services. In the area of public services, one of their duties is to provide reference services to library patrons. Being familiar with a wide variety of scholarly and public information sources, librarians can direct patrons to print and nonprint resources that may have the information that patrons want. Public Librarians also provide search services that range from looking up a fact in an encyclopedia to an in-depth search of Internet resources. Public Librarians might assist patrons in person, over the telephone, by fax, or by E-mail.

Public Librarians also teach patrons how to use the library facilities. They give tours, describing the various collections that are available. They explain how to look up book titles, subjects, and authors in the library catalog, which most libraries now have on computer systems. Public Librarians also demonstrate how to use microfilm and microfiche machines as well as how to access CD-ROM and on-line databases and the Internet.

Many Public Librarians plan and coordinate programs and special events to promote reading and the use of library resources. These might include such programs as children's story times and reading programs, author readings, literacy programs, video or film programs, reading groups, and workshops on using the Internet. Many Public Librarians solicit the help and input of parents, teachers, community organizations, and the general public to develop programs that meet the needs of children, teenagers, and adults in their communities.

Public Librarians assist patrons directly in many other ways, such as recommending books to read, checking out and checking in books, and borrowing books from other libraries for patrons through an interlibrary loan system.

In the area of technical services, Public Librarians maintain adequate and up-to-date library collections that support the needs of their patrons. Their duties include:

- analyzing library collections and recommending materials that should be discarded as well as new materials that should be acquired
- reading book reviews, software reviews, publishers' catalogs, and other sources to learn about new materials to add to collections
- purchasing print and nonprint materials for library collections
- classifying and cataloging materials so that they can be easily found by patrons
- compiling lists of the different print and nonprint materials in the library

Public Librarians are also responsible for performing a variety of administrative services. They develop, implement, and evaluate information systems. They negotiate contracts with various vendors for materials, equipment, and services. They select, train, and supervise library assistants, library clerks, and other support staff. Many librarians train and supervise volunteers. Public Librarians also prepare budgets, financial reports, and other reports that library directors or library boards may request. Additionally, librarians maintain accurate records of circulation, materials, and personnel. Many librarians have fund-raising duties that include writing grant proposals, soliciting gifts from donors, and participating in fund-raising activities.

In addition, Public Librarians are responsible for updating their technical skills and keeping up with developments in their field. They read professional journals, enroll in professional workshops, participate in professional conferences, network with colleagues, and so on.

In small libraries, Public Librarians usually handle all aspects of library work. In large library systems, many librarians specialize in the different public, technical, or administrative services. Public Librarians may also specialize in overseeing particular collections such as children's services, audiovisual collections, government documents collections, special collections, or bookmobile services.

Public libraries may be part of city or county government services. A large library system is typically composed of a main library and library branches in different city neighborhoods or different cities within a county. Public Librarians may be assigned to work at more than one branch.

Public Librarians work full time or part time. Their work schedules may include evening and weekend hours.

Salaries

Salaries vary, and depend on such factors as education, experience, responsibilities, library budget, and location. According to a 1998 salary survey done by *Library Journal*, a professional journal, the annual salary for Public Librarians ranged from $9,200 to $55,000.

In addition to a salary, Public Librarians receive fringe benefits such as vacation leave, sick pay, medical insurance, and retirement benefits.

Employment Prospects

Public Librarians work for either city or county libraries. Most opportunities become available as Public Librarians retire, resign, or transfer to other positions. The competition for librarian jobs in urban and suburban areas is high with job opportunities usually better in rural areas.

Advancement Prospects

Public Librarians can pursue supervisory and administrative positions all the way up to the top position of public library director. Public Librarians can also follow other librarian career paths by becoming academic librarians, research librarians, law librarians, or specialist librarians (in private corporations). Public Librarians can pursue other related careers such as systems analysts, database specialists, web developers, network administrators, information brokers, archivists, museum curators, or research analysts.

Licensure/Certification

In some states, Public Librarians are required to hold state or local certification. The requirements for certification vary with the different states. For specific information, contact the state board or commission that oversees public libraries in the state where you wish to work.

Depending on their responsibilities, Public Librarians may be required to hold valid driver's licenses.

Education and Training

Education requirements vary from library to library. Most employers require or prefer that Public Librarians have a master's degree in library science from a library school accredited by the American Library Association (ALA). Some employers hire Public Librarians with bachelor's or associate degrees as long as they have qualifying work experience and have completed required courses in librarianship. They may also be required to complete a master's degree in library science within a certain time period.

Experience, Skills, and Personality Traits

Employers hire candidates for entry-level positions who demonstrate a knowledge of professional library principles, methods, and techniques that include print and electronic resources. Having work experience in public library settings is generally preferred.

To do their work effectively, Public Librarians need strong writing, communication, and self-management skills (such as the ability to manage multiple tasks, set priorities, plan and organize work, and meet deadlines). They also need excellent interpersonal, public service, and teamwork skills for their job. Furthermore, they need excellent computer skills along with effective on-line skills for searching CD-ROM and Internet databases.

Being courteous, friendly, enthusiastic, energetic, organized, resourceful, patient, and tolerant are some personality traits that Public Librarians share. They also take pleasure in reading. In addition, they are dedicated to helping the general public use library resources effectively.

Unions/Associations

Most Public Librarians join local, state, and national professional associations to take advantage of professional resources, training workshops, continuing education programs, job listings, and networking opportunities. Some national organizations are:

- American Library Association
- Public Library Association, a division of the American Library Association
- American Society for Information Science

Tips for Entry

1. Volunteer or obtain library assistant jobs in public libraries to gain work experience.
2. Many colleges and universities offer graduate library science programs but not all are accredited by the ALA. Keep in mind that more and more employers prefer candidates who have graduated from ALA-approved library schools. For more information, write to: ALA, 50 East Huron Street, Chicago, Ill. 60611. Or call: (800) 545-2433. Or visit its web site: *http://www.ala.org*.
3. Many public library systems need on-call librarians to substitute for staff members who must be absent. Contact public library personnel departments for information and job applications.
4. The selection process for Public Librarians may take several weeks to establish eligibility. You must be able to pass all steps of the selection process that includes an application, oral interview, examination, background investigation, and so on.
5. Use the Internet to explore the array of services that various public libraries provide throughout the United States. To get a list of relevant web sites, enter the keyword "public library" in any search engine.

CHILDREN'S LIBRARIAN

CAREER PROFILE

Duties: Help children and other patrons access and use library resources; develop and maintain library collections in the children's department; plan and coordinate children's programs for patrons; perform other duties as required

Alternate Title: Children Services Librarian

Salary Range: $9,000 to $55,000

Employment Prospects: Fair

Advancement Prospects: Good

Prerequisites:
   Licensure/Certification—State or local Public Librarian certification may be required; a driver's license may be required
   Education/Training—Master's degree in library science
   Experience—Professional librarian with experience working with child patrons; knowledgeable about children's literature and about children's services in public libraries
   Special Skills and Personality Traits—Interpersonal, communication, public service, writing, organizational, management, teamwork, computer, and on-line skills; courteous, patient, creative, enthusiastic, friendly, energetic, dependable

CAREER LADDER

Senior Librarian or Library Director

Children's Librarian

Graduate Student or Librarian

Position Description

Children's Librarians specialize in managing the library collections in the children's department of public libraries. The children's collection includes both print and nonprint materials such as books, magazines, pamphlets, recordings, videos, and CD-ROM databases. In many libraries, the collection includes materials in different foreign languages. Some children's collections also include toys and games. Many Children's Librarians also maintain lists of appropriate web sites on the Internet of various topics that might interest child patrons.

Children's Librarians have many responsibilities, which include providing children's reference services to library patrons. They assist children and other patrons with their research needs, using resources in both the children's and adult sections. They direct patrons to possible sources in books, magazines, microfilm, microfiche, computer databases, and the Internet. Children's Librarians also provide search services for their patrons, using both print and electronic resources. In addition, these librarians teach children and other patrons how to use the library resources. For example, a Children's Librarian might show a patron how to use the children's catalog on the library's computer system.

Children's Librarians are also responsible for developing quality collections that meet the developmental, cultural, recreational, and educational needs of the children in their communities. Many Children's Librarians confer with local teachers so that they can select materials that would support class assignments and projects. Furthermore, Children's Librarians regularly evaluate the children's collections to make sure that materials are up-to-date and useful to their patrons.

Another responsibility of Children's Librarians is planning and coordinating programs that develop children's enjoyment of reading as well as promote the use of library resources. Some types of children's programs that public libraries offer are:

- storytelling programs for infants, toddlers, and preschoolers
- puppet shows
- author readings
- reading programs
- film or video programs
- arts and crafts programs

Many Children's Librarians work closely with parents, teachers, social agencies, and other community organizations to develop programs that serve the educational, health, and other needs of children and their families. Thus, many public libraries also offer homework tutoring programs, family literacy programs, and children's workshops on topics such as first aid and safety.

Children's Librarians perform many other duties, which vary from one librarian to the next. For example, they:

- read book reviews, software reviews, publishers' catalogs, and other sources to learn about new materials that should be acquired
- classify and catalog new children's materials so that they can be easily found by library patrons
- assist in the selection, training, and supervision of library clerks, library assistants, and other support staff
- train and supervise junior and adult volunteers
- prepare reading lists for particular subjects—such as United States presidents, fairy tales, or 20th-century inventions
- conduct multimedia publicity campaigns to promote reading, children's programs, or special events
- assist the branch or head librarian with developing budgets, improving work procedures, writing grant proposals, and other tasks
- prepare required reports and paperwork
- act as a library liaison to schools, child care centers, community organizations, social agencies, and other groups

In addition, Children's Librarians stay informed about the curriculum needs in local schools. They also keep up with current trends in children's literature and developments in the field of librarianship through self-study, networking with colleagues, professional conferences, and other means.

In some public libraries, Children's Librarians are responsible for the youth services department, which provides resources that meet the specific needs of teenagers. Some Children's Librarians provide support for adult reference services, filling in for reference librarians when needed.

Children's Librarians work full time or part time. They have flexible work schedules that include evening and weekend hours. Children's Librarians in large public library systems may be assigned to work at more than one branch library.

Salaries

Salaries vary, and depend on factors such as education, experience, and the library budget. According to a 1998 salary survey done by the *Library Journal,* a professional journal, the annual salary for public librarians was between $9,200 and $55,000.

In addition to a salary, Children's Librarians receive fringe benefits such as vacation leave, medical insurance, and retirement benefits.

Employment Prospects

Children's Librarians work for city and county public libraries. Most opportunities become available as Children's Librarians retire, resign, or transfer to other positions. The creation of additional full-time or part-time positions depends upon the availability of funds.

The competition for librarian jobs is high and especially keen in urban and suburban areas.

Advancement Prospects

Advancement opportunities are usually better in large public library systems. With experience and ambition, Children's Librarians can advance to supervisory and administrative positions as department managers, branch library managers, division heads, assistant library directors, and library directors.

Children's Librarians can follow other librarian career paths by becoming specialists in technical services or cataloging. They can also become school library media specialists, academic librarians, research librarians, or specialist librarians. Additionally, they can pursue related careers by becoming systems analysts, web developers, curriculum developers, or children's book authors.

Licensure/Certification

Children's Librarians may be required to hold state or local certification for public librarians, depending on the state where they live. The requirements for certification vary with the different states. For information, contact the state board or commission that oversees public libraries in the state where you wish to work.

Children's Librarians may be also required to hold valid driver's licenses.

Education and Training

Children's Librarians need either a bachelor's or master's degree in library science or other related field. However, more and more employers are requiring or preferring that candidates have a master's degree in library science from an institution accredited by the American Library Association.

Public libraries generally require that new employees complete orientation and training programs. Many public libraries provide ongoing in service training.

Experience, Skills, and Personality Traits

Employers typically look for professional librarians who have experience working with child patrons. They also demonstrate knowledge of children's literature and are familiar with the different children's services that are offered in public libraries.

In order to relate well with children, parents, library staff, and others, Children's Librarians need superior interpersonal, communication, and public service skills. They also need effective writing, organizational, management, and teamwork skills for their job. In addition, they need excellent computer skills along with strong on-line skills for searching CD-ROM and Internet databases.

Successful Children's Librarians share personality traits such as being courteous, patient, creative, enthusiastic, friendly, energetic, and dependable. In addition, they are passionate about children's literature and about promoting the joy of reading to children of all backgrounds and circumstances.

Unions/Associations

Many Children's Librarians join local, state, and national professional associations to take advantage of training programs, continuing education programs, networking opportunities, and other professional services. A national organization specifically for Children's Librarians is the Association for Library Services to Children, a division of the American Library Association.

Tips for Entry

1. As college students, obtain internships with children's departments in public libraries.
2. To learn about job vacancies, contact library science schools, professional associations, and state employment offices. Also contact the personnel office of the public libraries where you would like to work.
3. Enroll in classes about child development, teaching reading to children, and other such subjects to advance your professional growth.
4. Use the Internet to learn about different children's departments in public libraries. To get a list of web sites to read, enter the keyword "children's library services" in any search engine.

LIBRARY MEDIA SPECIALIST

CAREER PROFILE

Duties: Manage the school library media center; instruct students, teachers, and others on how to access and use library resources; provide consultation services to teachers; develop and maintain collections of print and nonprint materials; perform other duties as required

Alternate Title: School Librarian

Salary Range: $12,000 to $65,000

Employment Prospects: Fair to Good

Advancement Prospects: Fair

Prerequisites:
  Licensure/Certification—A library media specialist credential; a teaching credential may be required
  Education/Training—Master's degree; completion of an accredited teacher education program
  Experience—Classroom teaching experience
  Special Skills and Personality Traits—Teaching, communication, interpersonal management, organizational, problem solving, computer, and on-line skills; caring, patient, curious, enthusiastic, flexible, creative, resourceful

CAREER LADDER

Library Supervisor or Coordinator (district or central office level)

↑

Library Media Specialist

↑

Teacher

Position Description

In most public and private schools, the school library is known as the library media center. Along with book collections and other print collections, the library media center holds video, software, CD-ROM and other nonprint collections for students to use for their assignments and projects as well as for their personal pleasure. The library media center also has multimedia workstations available so that students can take advantage of electronic resources such as access to the Internet. Library Media Specialists, who are professional librarians, manage these centers.

Library Media Specialists have many different responsibilities. One responsibility is providing reference services to students, such as helping them locate appropriate resources for research projects. Specialists also teach students essential library skills such as searching for information in print and technology resources and evaluating the information they find. In addition, Library Media Specialists instruct students on how to properly use and care for computers, copiers, and other equipment in the library media centers.

Library Media Specialists also provide consulting services to teachers about how to use the various print and electronic resources in the library media centers. Many collaborate with teachers on lesson plans to reinforce and enhance class lessons with library materials. Specialists also provide in-service training to teachers, administrators, and other school staff.

Another major duty is developing and maintaining the library media center collections of print and nonprint materials. Library Media Specialists continually review collections and discard materials that are outdated or no longer have any useful value. They select and purchase new materials that support the school curriculum as well as the diverse backgrounds, learning styles, abilities, and interests of the students.

Also part of their job is making sure that center policies such as hours of operation, library rules, circulation procedures, and rules for Internet access are in place and are being followed by students, teachers, and others. Additionally, Library Media Specialists check out and check in books. Furthermore, they perform many administrative duties such as evaluating their centers' goals; overseeing budgets; writing reports and completing required paperwork; keeping inventory of hardware and other equipment; and maintaining accurate records on circulation, work schedules, and other matters. In addition, specialists train and supervise support staff, student aides, and volunteers.

Library Media Specialists perform many other tasks, which vary from school to school. For example, they:

- classify and catalog new materials
- arrange their centers so they are welcoming, attractive, and conducive to studying
- maintain media and computer equipment
- repair books
- conduct public relations activities to educate parents and the community about their centers
- sponsor extracurricular activities
- participate in faculty meetings and serve on school committees
- continue professional development through self-study, networking with colleagues, attending professional conferences, enrolling in continuing education courses, and so on.

Library Media Specialists work part time or full time. They typically have a 10-month work schedule, usually from September to June.

Salaries

Salaries vary and depend on factors such as education, experience, job responsibilities, and school budget. According to a 1998 salary survey done by *Library Journal*, a professional library journal, Library Media Specialists earned an annual salary between $12,459 and $65,000.

Library Media Specialists also receive fringe benefits packages that include holiday pay, sick leave, health benefits, retirement benefits, and so on.

Employment Prospects

Library Media Specialists are employed by public and private schools. Most job opportunities become available as Library Media Specialists retire, resign, or transfer to other positions. The creation of additional school library staff positions is dependent upon the availability of school funds.

Advancement Prospects

Most Library Media Specialists realize advancement through increases in pay. In library media centers with more than one staff member, Library Media Specialists can advance to supervisory and managerial positions. With additional licensure, specialists can become library supervisors or coordinators at the district (or central office) level. Those with higher administrative ambitions can pursue positions as principals, program directors, assistant superintendents, and school superintendents.

Library Media Specialists can pursue other librarian careers by becoming academic librarians, public librarians, research librarians, or special librarians (in corporate settings). They can also pursue related careers by becoming systems analysts, webmasters, information scientists, information brokers, or museum curators.

Licensure/Certification

In public schools, Library Media Specialists must hold a valid Library Media Specialist credential. They may also be required to hold a teaching credential in some states. Licensure requirements vary from state to state. For specific information, contact the state board of education in the state where you wish to work.

Many private schools require state licensure or professional certification from school accreditation organizations or other recognized organizations.

Education and Training

Library Media Specialists must have either a bachelor's or master's degree. Many employers require or prefer that candidates have master's degrees in library science from schools accredited by the American Library Association.

Licensed Library Media Specialists must have completed an approved school library media program that leads to licensure in the state where they practice. The program also includes a supervised field practicum.

Experience, Skills, and Personality Traits

Most public schools require that Library Media Specialists have previous classroom teaching experience. The minimum number of years varies among different schools. Both public and private schools look for candidates who have traditional library skills as well as knowledge about technology to support curriculum and instruction programs.

To do their work effectively, Library Media Specialists need excellent teaching, communication, interpersonal, management, organizational, and problem-solving skills. They also need superior computer skills and effective on-line skills for searching CD-ROM and Internet databases.

Successful Library Media Specialists share several personality traits such as being caring, patient, curious, enthusiastic, flexible, creative, and resourceful. Furthermore, they are committed to instilling the enjoyment of reading in students, as well as helping them become independent information seekers.

Unions/Associations

Library Media Specialists can join local, state, and national professional organizations to take advantage of professional services such as continuing education programs and networking opportunities. Two organizations that many Library Media Specialists join are:

- American Association of School Librarians, a division of the American Library Association

- Association for Educational Communications and Technology

Library Media Specialists in public schools are eligible to join teacher unions, such as the American Federation of Teachers or the National Education Association.

Tips for Entry

1. To learn more about the profession, visit school library media centers at the different school levels. Talk with Library Media Specialists about their jobs. Also volunteer or intern at a school library media center during your undergraduate years in college.
2. Contact public and private schools where you would like to work. Be ready to complete job applications with all your information—education, work history, references, and so on. Also have your resume at hand to submit with your application.
3. Use the Internet to learn more about the Library Media Specialist profession. To get a list of relevant web sites to read, enter the keyword "library media specialist" in any search engine.

ACADEMIC LIBRARIAN

CAREER PROFILE

Duties: Develop library collections; provide consultation services to faculty; teach students library research skills; perform public services, technical, and administrative duties

Alternate Title: A title that reflects a specialized area such as Public Services Librarian, Technical Services Librarian, Computer Services Librarian, or Special Collections Librarian

Salary Range: $12,000 to $60,000

Employment Prospects: Fair

Advancement Prospects: Good

Prerequisites:
  Licensure/Certification—None is required
  Education/Training—Master's degree in library science
  Experience—Previous work experience in an academic library setting; teaching experience preferred
  Special Skills and Personality Traits—Analytical, writing, presentation, supervisory, teaching, organizational, communication, interpersonal, computer, and on-line skills; courteous, energetic, organized, patient, flexible, resourceful

CAREER LADDER

Senior Librarian

Academic Librarian

Intern

Position Description

In large institutions, the academic library may be composed of a central library and branch libraries that are located throughout the campus. All academic libraries hold a vast number of diverse collections of print and nonprint materials that support the many different degree programs at their institutions. Most, if not all, academic libraries are part of integrated on-line library systems that allow access to library catalogs at other college and university libraries as well as other public and private library systems.

The responsibility of managing an academic library's various collections is shared by a staff of academic librarians. They work closely with faculty to develop collections that offer primary and secondary sources for research projects. Also in collaboration with the faculty, Academic Librarians develop educational programs that provide students with effective information literacy skills.

Like all professional librarians, Academic Librarians perform duties in three basic areas. One area is public services (or user services). Essentially, Academic Librarians provide reference services to students, faculty, and others, using the available print and electronic resources in their libraries. They also explain and demonstrate how to use the library resources and equipment. In addition, they teach students library research skills through seminars, workshops, and individual consultations.

Technical services is another area of responsibility that Academic Librarians have. Their duties include acquiring new library materials in all media formats (print, audio, video, software, and so on). They also classify and catalog materials so that patrons can easily find them, prepare new materials for distribution, compile reading lists, and so on.

Academic Librarians are also responsible for administrative services. These duties include: coordinating library activities; supervising support staff; preparing budgets; negotiating contracts for materials and equipment; administrating public relations activities and so forth.

Academic Librarians usually specialize in specific types of public, technical, or administrative services. For example:

- *Reference Librarians* help students find appropriate print and electronic resources for their research projects.
- *Acquisition Librarians* select and purchase print and nonprint materials for the libraries.
- *Technical Services Librarians* process new library materials, such as cataloging and classifying materials.
- *Computer Services Librarians* administer and maintain library's computer systems and other computer resources.
- *Special Collections Librarians* develop and promote use of their institutions' rare book and manuscript holdings.

In many higher education institutions, Academic Librarians' jobs are tenure-track positions. With tenure, Academic Librarians are assured of a job at an institution until they retire or resign.

Academic Librarians work part time or full time. Their work schedules may include evening and weekend hours.

Salaries

Salaries vary, and depend on factors such as education, experience, the library budget, and location. According to a 1998 salary survey done by *Library Journal,* a professional journal, the annual salary for librarians in college and university settings was between $12,000 and $60,000.

In addition to a salary, Academic Librarians receive fringe benefits such as vacation leave, sick pay, medical insurance, and retirement benefits.

Employment Prospects

Academic Librarians are employed by two-year colleges, four-year colleges, and universities. Most opportunities become available as Academic Librarians retire, resign, or transfer to other positions. The creation of additional jobs is dependent upon the availability of funding.

Advancement Prospects

Academic Librarians can advance to such supervisory and administrative positions as department heads and library directors. To obtain faculty or higher administrative positions (such as deans), a doctoral degree in library science is usually required.

Academic Librarians can follow other librarian career paths by becoming research librarians, law librarians, or specialist librarians (in private corporations). Academic Librarians can also pursue other related careers such as archivists, research analysts, information brokers, systems analysts, or network administrators.

Licensure/Certification

No licensure or certification is required for this profession.

Education and Training

Academic Librarians are required to have a master's degree in library science from a program accredited by the American Library Association.

Experience, Skills, and Personality Traits

In general, employers look for candidates who have previous experience in the academic library setting, and prefer those with some teaching experience. Candidates should have a strong background with electronic information and instructional technologies. Other requirements vary and depend on the type of position (such as special collections librarian, reference librarian, or technical services librarian) for which a candidate is applying.

Academic Librarians need adequate analytical, writing, presentation, supervisory, teaching, and organizational skills. They also need good communication and interpersonal skillss. In addition, they need excellent computer skills and on-line skills that include searching computer databases and the Internet.

Successful Academic Librarians share various personality traits such as being courteous, energetic, organized, patient, flexible, and resourceful.

Unions/Associations

Many Academic Librarians belong to local, state, and national professional associations to take advantage of professional resources, training workshops, continuing education programs, job listings, and networking opportunities. Two national organizations that many Academic Librarians join are the Association of College and Research Libraries (a division of the American Library Association) and the American Society for Information Science.

Tips for Entry

1. As an undergraduate student, find out what courses you can take to prepare for the graduate program in library science. If you will be working part time while in college, try to obtain jobs at your campus library.
2. You can use the Internet to help you with your job search. Check out job listings posted at professional associations for librarians as well as for higher education faculty and administrators. Some web sites are:

    - American Library Association (*http://www.ala.org*)
    - The *Chronicle of Higher Education* career network page (*http://chronicle.com/jobs*)—library jobs are listed under both faculty and administration listings
    - HigherEdJobs.com (*http://www.higheredjobs.com*)— library jobs are listed under staff listings

EDUCATIONAL AND INSTRUCTIONAL TECHNOLOGY SPECIALISTS

TECHNOLOGY DIRECTOR
(DISTRICT, OR SCHOOL-WIDE, LEVEL)

CAREER PROFILE

Duties: Develop and implement a school-wide educational technology plan; provide consultations to teachers, administrators, and others; execute administrative tasks; perform other duties as required

Alternate Title: Technology Coordinator (District Level)

Salary Range: $30,000 to $80,000

Employment Prospects: Good

Advancement Prospects: Limited

Prerequisites:
  Licensure/Certification—A teaching or school administrator credential may be required
  Education/Training—Bachelor's or master's degree
  Experience—Knowledgeable of educational technology; have supervisory and management experience; having teaching experience is preferred
  Special Skills and Personality Traits—Organizational, supervisory, management, writing, leadership, communication, interpersonal, and presentation skills; patient, positive, enthusiastic, self-motivated, energetic, flexible, creative

CAREER LADDER

Assistant Superintendent of Technology or Chief Information Officer

↑

Technology Director

↑

Instructional Technology Specialist or Classroom Teacher

Position Description

In public and private schools, Technology Directors are responsible for administering school-wide technology plans that provide strategies for academic and administrative use of technology (such as computers, software, and the Internet) in the schools. Additionally, they are in charge of managing the school-wide technology resources that include technology infrastructure (hardware, networks, telephone systems, and so on), professional development, technical support systems, and technology-related curriculum materials.

Technology Directors are responsible for performing a wide variety of duties. As educational technology managers, they continually evaluate the effectiveness of technology plans and make recommendations for improvements and modifications to superintendents or school boards. Technology Directors also oversee the daily maintenance of technology infrastructure throughout all schools. For example, directors coordinate the installation of new technology (computers, software, networks, and so on); arrange for the repair and maintenance of equipment; manage accounts for Internet access; troubleshoot problems with hardware, software, networks, and so forth; and provide administrators, teachers, and others with technical support as requested.

Technology Directors also provide consultations on technology-related issues and problems to teachers, administrators, school boards, and others. Upon request, they provide individual assistance. They also plan and conduct in-service workshops, covering a wide range of topics—creating spreadsheets for daily recordkeeping, using E-mail, editing desktop videos, and so on. In addition, Technology Directors keep teachers and administrators informed of current technology developments that may be useful for curriculum or instruction.

Completing a wide variety of administrative tasks each day is another major part of their work. For example, Technology Directors:

- oversee (and develop) technology budgets
- maintain an inventory of all software and hardware in the schools

- secure specs and bids from vendors for telephone systems, copiers, software, and other equipment
- coordinate purchase requisitions for instructional computing materials from the various schools
- make purchases with the appropriate vendors
- coordinate and supervise the distribution of hardware and software to schools
- organize the storage of instructional computing materials
- conduct researches for available funding opportunities
- prepare grant proposals
- write daily correspondence and E-mail responses; complete reports; maintain accurate records; and fill out required paperwork
- serve as technology liaisons between their school systems and other school systems, businesses, educational agencies, or other organizations

In addition, Technology Directors oversee a staff that may include computer technicians, computer specialists, and administrative support staff. Many Technology Directors also supervise instructional technology specialists who provide training and support to teachers and administrators at individual schools. All Technology Directors provide staff members with ongoing technology training.

Technology Directors are also responsible for keeping up with new technologies as well as with their professional development. They read books, magazines, and journals about technology as well as about education. They join professional associations, participate in professional conferences, and network with colleagues. In addition, they enroll in training workshops and continuing education courses.

Technology Directors typically work more than 40 hours a week, often working evening and weekend hours to meet all the demands of their jobs.

Salaries

Salaries vary, and depend on education, experience, the school budget, and other factors. Technology Directors generally earn between $30,000 and $80,000 per year. In addition to a salary, they receive fringe benefits such as sick pay, vacation leave, medical insurance, and retirement benefits.

Employment Prospects

Technology Directors are employed by public and private school systems.

Most opportunities become available as Technology Directors retire, resign, or transfer to other schools. As more public and private schools integrate technology into their systems, the demand for experienced educational technology managers should grow as well.

Advancement Prospects

With advanced degrees and appropriate licensure, Technology Directors can advance to the positions of chief information officers and assistant superintendents of technology. Many Technology Directors realize advancement by way of receiving higher salaries, gaining professional recognition, and becoming educational technology managers in larger school systems.

Technology Directors can follow other career paths that lead to positions in state departments of education or educational service agencies. Other options are to pursue information systems careers in business, industry, government, and other nonschool settings.

Licensure/Certification

Public school districts may require Technology Directors to hold a valid teaching or school administrator credential. For specific licensure requirements, contact the central office for the school district where you would like to work.

Education and Training

Employers require either a bachelor's or master's degree. The degree may be in any discipline as long as Technology Directors have qualifying work experience. Many employers prefer that Technology Directors have master's or higher degrees in technical or management disciplines.

Experience, Skills, and Personality Traits

Employers look for candidates who have an overall knowledge of educational technology, and whose work history shows increasingly responsible supervisory and management experience. Many employers prefer that candidates have teaching experience.

To perform their work effectively, Technology Directors need excellent organizational, supervisory, management, and writing skills. They also need effective leadership, communication, interpersonal, and presentation skills as they must work well with teachers, students, administrators, staff, and others.

Successful Technology Directors share several personality traits, such as being patient, positive, enthusiastic, self-motivated, energetic, flexible, and creative. Furthermore, they have a strong interest in computers and technology as well as being committed to the education of future leaders.

Unions/Associations

Local, state, and national professional associations provide many professional services such as training workshops, continuing education programs, job listings, and networking opportunities. Some organizations that Technology Directors might join are:

- International Society for Technology in Education
- Association for Educational Communications and Technology

- Association for the Advancement of Computing in Education
- American Association of School Administrators

Tips for Entry
1. To get an idea of what it is like to work in school settings, obtain work—or volunteer—as computer technicians.
2. Join professional organizations to take advantage of their services. Many organizations have student memberships. Attend local or regional conferences and network with Technology Directors and other professionals.
3. Some Technology Directors advise that you learn a little about everything in technology that you can, including programming, networks, software, wiring, computer troubleshooting, basic repairs, and so on.
4. You can learn more about educational technology on the Internet. To get a list of relevant web sites to read, enter the keyword "educational technology" in any search engine.

INSTRUCTIONAL TECHNOLOGY SPECIALIST (K–12 SCHOOLS)

CAREER PROFILE

Duties: Provide training and support to teachers for integrating technology into the curriculum; may manage computer lab; may provide technical support; perform other duties as required

Alternate Titles: Educational Technologist, Technology Facilitator, Technology Coordinator (Building Level), Computer Teacher, Technology Resource Specialist, Lab Administrator

Salary Range: $27,000 to $52,000

Employment Prospects: Fair

Advancement Prospects: Limited

Prerequisites:
  Licensure/Certification—A teaching credential
  Education/Training—Master's degree
  Experience—Classroom teaching experience integrating technology with curriculum and instruction
  Special Skills and Personality Traits—Organizational, management, problem solving, communication, interpersonal, and leadership skills; patient, courteous, flexible, adaptable, creative, positive

CAREER LADDER

Technology Director

↑

Instructional Technology Specialist

↑

Classroom Teacher

Position Description

Instructional Technology Specialists are professional teachers with expertise in integrating technology (computers, software, Internet, and so on) into the curriculum. They provide training and support to teachers on how to use technology as tools to enhance their lessons and instruction.

Instructional Technology Specialists are based in computer labs at public and private elementary schools, middle schools, junior high schools, and high schools. They are responsible for the coordination of technology training in their schools. Working with teachers and administrators, they evaluate the technology training needs of teachers and plan training workshops accordingly. They also provide teachers with individual coaching for their specific needs. For example, an Instructional Technology Specialist in a middle school might demonstrate how different instructional software works to an eighth grade math teacher.

Instructional Technology Specialists also provide consultation services to teachers in designing effective technology strategies for their instruction. For example, an Instructional Technology Specialist and a fifth grade teacher might brainstorm ways that students can use a digital camera for classroom assignments. They often collaborate with teachers on preparing lesson plans, showing how teachers can integrate various technologies to teach, reinforce, and enrich their lessons. Sometimes, Instructional Technology Specialists coteach classes in order to model the use of technology for the teachers.

In many schools, Instructional Technology Specialists manage the computer labs. This includes overseeing the use of the Internet by teachers, students, and other staff members. Specialists also make sure all hardware, networks, providers, and so on are running correctly, and that they are maintained and repaired as needed. They also set up equipment and install software, as well as troubleshoot hardware, software, or network problems. Additionally, they organize, store, and maintain an inventory of hardware, software, manuals, computer supplies, and other materials. Instructional Technology Specialists may also supervise and train student aides.

Many Instructional Technology Specialists are responsible for providing technical support to teachers and administrators as the need arises. Some schools have computer specialists who provide technical support so that Instructional Technology Specialists may focus on curriculum and instruction.

Some Instructional Technology Specialists are also part-time computer teachers at their schools. They are responsible for teaching one or more technology classes in a grading period. Some computer teachers/Instructional Technology Specialists collaborate with other teachers to develop technology projects that combine both subject area and computer lab curriculum.

All Instructional Technology Specialists perform many administrative tasks. For example, they submit requisitions for hardware, software, and other products; complete required reports and paperwork; and assist in the preparation of grant proposals. Other duties vary from one school to the next. For example, they might:

- oversee technology needs for administrative, guidance, and business networks
- provide training and support to teachers in the use of assistive technology equipment for special education students
- design school web pages
- serve as technology liaisons between their school and district (or central) offices, community organizations, businesses, educational agencies, and other organizations

In public schools, many Instructional Technology Specialists serve on district technology committees. They participate in the development and evaluation of school-wide technology plans that include strategies for the technology budget, professional development, and academic and administrative use of the various technologies.

Instructional Technology Specialists stay current with new instructional technologies as well as keep up with their professional development. They attend training workshops and continuing education classes; network with colleagues; read professional journals, technology magazines; join professional associations, and so on.

Most Instructional Technology Specialists report to Technology Directors based in the district (or central) office. Instructional Technology Specialists may hold full-time or part-time positions. Some Instructional Technology Specialists are assigned to two or more schools. In some schools, teachers provide instructional technology services on a volunteer basis.

Salaries

Salaries vary, and depend on factors such as education, experience, job responsibilities, and the school budget. The annual salary for Instructional Technology Specialists is usually based on a teacher salary schedule. According to the 1997–98 teacher salary survey by the American Federation of Teachers, the average annual salaries for public school teachers ranged from $27,839 to $51,727.

In addition to a salary, Instructional Technology Specialists receive fringe benefits such as sick pay, medical insurance, and retirement benefits.

Employment Prospects

Instructional Technology Specialists are employed by public and private schools. This is a profession that is still emerging. Job opportunities, in general, are dependent upon the availability of funds. Most full-time positions are found in larger school districts.

Advancement Prospects

Instructional Technology Specialists can advance to district level (or central office) positions such as technology directors, chief information officers, and assistant superintendents for technology. Advanced degrees and school administrator licensure may be required for executive-level positions.

Other career options are to obtain Instructional Technology Specialist positions in other settings, such colleges, universities, business, industry, government, or health institutions.

Licensure/Certification

Instructional Technology Specialists are generally required to hold valid teaching credentials. State licensure requirements vary from state to state. For specific information, contact the state board of education for the state in which you wish to teach.

Education and Training

Most employers require or prefer that Instructional Technology Specialists have a master's degree in instructional technology or a related field with acceptable course work in instructional technology.

Experience, Skills, and Personality Traits

Most employers require that Instructional Technology Specialists have previous classroom teaching experience that includes the integration of technology into their lesson plans and teaching.

To perform their jobs effectively, Instructional Technology Specialists need strong organizational, management, problem solving, communication, interpersonal, and leadership skills.

Successful Technology Specialists have several personality traits in common, such as being patient, courteous, flexible, adaptable, creative, and positive. They are also self-starters, and have a good sense of humor. Furthermore, they are committed to helping teachers use technology as tools for enhancing curriculum and instruction.

Unions/Associations

Many Instructional Technology Specialists join local, state, and national professional associations to take advantage of training workshops, networking opportunities, professional resources, and so on. Some organizations that they might join are:

- International Society for Technology in Education
- International Technology Education Association
- Association for Educational Communications and Technology
- Association for the Advancement of Computing in Education

Instructional Technology Specialists who are classified as teachers in public schools are eligible to join teacher unions, such as the American Federation of Teachers or the National Education Association.

Tips for Entry

1. Get experience working in school computer labs. While in high school, you might become a student aide. While in college, you might become a volunteer, intern, or paid assistant.
2. As a teacher, keep a portfolio of lesson plans, class projects, videotapes, and other items that show how you have used technology in the classroom. You can then show your portfolio to prospective employers when you are ready to apply for Instructional Technology Specialist positions.
3. Use the Internet to learn more about the field of instructional technology. To get a list of relevant web sites, enter the keyword "instructional technology" in any search engine.

SPECIAL EDUCATION TECHNOLOGY SPECIALIST

CAREER PROFILE

Duties: Provide assistive technology services to special education students; perform other duties as required

Alternate Title: Assistive Technology Specialist

Salary Range: $25,000 to $35,000 (starting salary)

Employment Prospects: Good

Advancement Prospects: Limited

Prerequisites:
  Licensure/Certification—A teaching credential may be required
  Education/Training—Bachelor's or master's degree
  Experience—Previous experience working with disabled children in school or other settings
  Special Skills and Personality Traits—Organizational, management, problem solving, observation, communication, interpersonal, and computer skills; analytical, patient, self-motivated, resourceful, patient, creative

CAREER LADDER

Lead Assistive Technology Specialist or Program Coordinator

Assistive Technology Specialist

Trainee

Position Description

Public and private schools are mandated by law to provide special education programs and related services to students with learning, emotional, and physical disabilities to help them succeed in school. Special Education Technology Specialists provide one type of related service that is called *assistive technology services*. Assistive technology is any item, device, or equipment that helps special education students function independently in the school environment. For example, a special education student with a speech impairment may be accommodated with a special electronic communication device so that he or she can communicate in class with his or her teacher and classmates.

Technology Specialists are usually part of student assessment teams that are composed of general education teachers, special education teachers, parents, school psychologists, and other school specialists. The teams develop Individualized Education Programs (IEPs) that outline the goals and objectives for instruction and related services such as those offered by Special Education Technology Specialists.

As members of student assessment teams, Special Education Technology Specialists provide expertise in assessing and evaluating whether students with disabilities need assistive technology. They observe students in classrooms as well as interview their teachers to learn about the daily activities and tasks that students do. Specialists may also administer tests to assist them with their assessments.

When it is determined that special education students require assistive technology, Technology Specialists consider possible accommodations that range from no-technology solutions to high-technology solutions. A no-technology solution may be a referral to services such as occupational therapy, or it may be a modification of a student's environment or the way a student performs his or her tasks. For example, a learning disabled student's work area is rearranged so that he or she can better focus on his or her lessons. Low-technology solutions include the use of items such as adapted spoon handles, pencil grips, special-lined paper, or Velcro fasteners. Medium-technology solutions include the use of equipment such as wheelchairs, while high-technology solutions include the use of computers, talking calculators, and other electronic technology.

Any assistive technologies that special education students need are provided by the schools. Thus, Special Education Technology Specialists are responsible for conducting a thorough research on every assistive device that they might recommend. They learn information such as the cost of operating a device, its reliability, and how much training time may be required.

Technology Specialists are responsible for ordering assistive devices as well as installing them or providing for their installation. They also train students how to use their assistive devices properly. Specialists also train the students' teachers, parents, and others who work with them.

Accurate record keeping is an important part of Special Education Technology Specialists' work. They maintain daily records of their staff meetings, in-service sessions, and training sessions with students, teachers, and parents. They also keep statistics on the number of students that are referred to them, as well as maintain an inventory of assistive devices on hand. In addition, Technology Specialists write correspondence, progress reports, and evaluation reports. They also complete forms and other paperwork in compliance with federal and state laws as well as with local education agency policies and procedures.

Special Education Technology Specialists perform many other tasks that include:

- assisting with the development and evaluation of assistive technology services, policies, procedures, and services
- troubleshooting problems with wheelchairs, computers, and other assistive devices
- keeping parents informed of their children's progress
- preparing grant proposals
- keeping up with developments in their field through self-study, networking with colleagues, attending professional conferences, and through other means

Special Education Technology Specialists may be assigned to work at one or more schools. They may be part-time or full-time employees. Some specialists work for private companies and so provide their services on a contractual basis.

Salaries

Salaries depend on factors such as education and experience. The starting salary for Rehabilitation Technology Practitioners (which includes Special Education Technology Specialists) is $25,000 to $35,000 per year.

Technology Specialists may also receive fringe benefits such as vacation leave, medical insurance, and retirement benefits.

Employment Prospects

Special Education Technology Specialists are employed by private and public schools. Some work for consulting services or are self-employed consultants.

This is a relatively new profession. The number of special education students is expected to increase in the coming years; this should contribute to the demand for more Special Education Technology Specialists. The creation of new positions, however, is dependent on the availability of funds.

Advancement Prospects

Promotions are limited to lead and supervisory positions. With continuing education and additional licensure, Special Education Technology Specialists can become special education directors and other school administrators.

Another option is to work in other settings such as hospitals, developmental centers, and vocational rehabilitation agencies. Technology Specialists can also pursue careers as university professors, researchers, or private consultants.

Licensure/Certification

Some states may require that Special Education Technology Specialists hold valid teaching credentials. For specific information, contact the state board of education for the state where you wish to work.

Education and Training

Education requirements vary from one employer to the next. In general, Special Education Technology Specialists possess either a bachelor's or master's degree in such disciplines as special education, vocational counseling, and adaptive physical education. Several colleges and universities now offer undergraduate classes in special education technology.

Experience, Skills, and Personality Traits

Employers typically look for candidates who have previous experience working with special education children in schools or other settings. Specialists with backgrounds in special education as teachers, school occupational therapists, school speech language pathologists, or other related professions have the best chances of being hired.

To do their work effectively, Special Education Technology Specialists need excellent organizational, management, problem solving, observation, communication, and interpersonal skills. In addition, they need strong computer skills.

Successful Special Education Technology Specialists share several personality traits such as being analytical, patient, self-motivated, resourceful, patient, and creative. They are dedicated to helping children with disabilities become confident users of technology so that they can succeed in school and other endeavors.

Unions/Associations

Local, state, and national professional associations provide many professional services such as training workshops, continuing education programs, job listings, and networking opportunities. Some organizations that many Special Education Technology Specialists join are:

- Technology and Media, a division of the Council for Exceptional Children
- Alliance for Technology Access
- Rehabilitation Engineering and Assistive Technology of North America

Tips for Entry
1. You can prepare for a career in assistive technology while in high school by taking classes in some or all of these courses—science, math, English, technology, business, and industrial arts.
2. Get experience working with children with disabilities. For example, you might volunteer in special education classrooms and with groups such as the Special Olympics.
3. To enhance their employability, many Assistive Technology Specialists obtain the Assistive Technology Practitioner certificate. This is a voluntary, professional credential granted by the Rehabilitation Engineering and Assistive Technology Society of North America (RESNA). For more information, write to: RESNA, 1700 North Moore Street, Suite 1540, Arlington, Va. 22209. Or call: (703) 524-6686. Or visit its web site (*http://www.resna.org*).
4. You can learn more about assistive technology on the Internet. To get a list of relevant web sites, enter the keyword "assistive technology" in any search engine.

INSTRUCTIONAL TECHNOLOGY SPECIALIST (HIGHER EDUCATION)

CAREER PROFILE

Duties: Provide training and support to higher education faculty for integrating technology into curriculum and instruction; assist in the development and design of computer-based instructional materials; perform other duties as required

Alternate Titles: Educational Technology Specialist, Instructional Technology Consultant, Academic Technology Specialist, Instructional Designer

Salary Range: $30,000 to $50,000

Employment Prospects: Good

Advancement Prospects: Limited

Prerequisites:
  Licensure/Certification—None is required
  Education/Training—Bachelor's or master's degree
  Experience—One or more years of work experience in instructional technology in academic settings; teaching experience is preferred
  Special Skills and Personality Traits—Communication, interpersonal, customer service, organizational, management, teamwork, writing, and presentation skills; patient, tactful, energetic, enthusiastic, creative, flexible

CAREER LADDER

Department Coordinator or Director

Instructional Technology Specialist

Intern

Position Description

In higher education institutions, more and more faculty are learning how to use technology to enhance their instruction. For example, an English professor might have a web site for his or her courses, while a history instructor might have his or her students use the Internet to complete assignments. On many campuses, Instructional Technology Specialists are available to provide faculty—professors, instructors, lecturers, teaching assistants, and other academic professionals—with the necessary technology support.

Instructional Technology Specialists are usually based in information technology services centers on academic campuses. Most specialists are assigned to work with faculty from the various academic departments on campus. Some are assigned to work with faculty in specific departments (such as history) or individual schools (such as liberal arts).

In higher education settings, Instructional Technology Specialists generally work in a consultant role, providing assistance to individual faculty members with their teaching projects. Upon assessing the faculty member's interests and project needs, Instructional Technology Specialists advise on appropriate hardware, software, and peripherals (such as scanners and digital cameras) to use for completing teaching projects. They also help faculty develop and design computer-assisted instruction and presentations, which may include the use of interactive web-based applications.

Instructional Technology Specialists are also available to brainstorm about technology solutions to instructional problems. For example, a specialist and architecture lecturer might consider the use of electronic mail or video conferencing to improve communication with the lecturer's students. Furthermore, faculty members may request Instructional Technology Specialists to coteach a class session (in the computer lab or regular classroom) to instruct students on how to use the Internet, software databases, or other technology to perform specific tasks for student assignments.

Instructional Technology Specialists perform many other duties, such as:

- assisting with the development and design of new services and procedures for their centers
- supervising interns
- developing and conducting training workshops and individual training sessions for faculty
- reviewing and evaluating articles and other information about new software and hardware
- maintaining equipment in their centers
- providing faculty with technical support

Instructional Technology Specialists work 40 hours a week, sometimes working additional hours to complete projects.

Salaries

Salaries vary, and depend on factors such as education, experience, and an institution's budget. In general, Instructional Technology Specialists can earn $30,000 to $50,000 per year. In addition to a salary, they receive fringe benefits such as sick pay, medical insurance, and retirement benefits.

Employment Prospects

Instructional Technology Specialists work for public and private two-year colleges, four-year colleges, and universities. This position is relatively new in academic settings. Until the 1990's, Instructional Technology Specialists were mostly employed in business and industry.

The demand for qualified Instructional Technology Specialists in academic settings is high throughout the United States. Many campuses find it difficult to recruit and retain specialists because of the growing demand for this profession in business and industry, where the salary rate is much higher.

Advancement Prospects

Advancement opportunities are limited to coordinator or director positions. With advanced degrees, Instructional Technology Specialists can pursue faculty and higher-level administrative positions on campus.

Licensure/Certification

No licensure or certification is required for this profession in academic settings.

Education and Training

Instructional Technology Specialists have either bachelor's or master's degrees in instructional technology, educational media, or other related field. Most employers prefer candidates with master's or higher degrees. Many employers accept candidates who have degrees in unrelated fields as long as they have qualifying work experience.

Experience, Skills, and Personality Traits

Requirements vary from employer to employer. In general candidates need one or more years of experience in instructional technology in academic settings. Many employers require or prefer that candidates have some teaching experience.

Instructional Technology Specialists need excellent communication, interpersonal, and customer service skills to work well with faculty, staff, and others. They also need strong organizational, management, teamwork, writing, and presentation skills. Successful Instructional Technology Specialists share several personality traits such as being patient, tactful, energetic, enthusiastic, creative, and flexible.

Unions/Associations

Instructional Technology Specialists join local, state, and national professional associations to take advantage of professional resources, continuing education programs, networking opportunities, and other professional services. Some of the organizations that they might join are:

- Association for Educational Communications and Technology
- American Society for Training and Development
- Association for the Advancement of Computing in Education
- International Society for Performance Improvement

Tips for Entry

1. As a college student, obtain part-time jobs with the instructional technology center.
2. Get as much teaching experience as possible so you have an understanding of what faculty want to accomplish with their instruction.
3. To learn about job listings, contact professional organizations that serve Instructional Technology Specialists. Many organizations have job hotlines as well as job banks on their web sites. Another source for job listings can be found in the *Chronicle of Higher Education,* a professional journal. The journal also provides job listings on its web site (*http://chronicle.com/jobs*).
4. You can use the Internet to learn more about instructional technology in higher education. For a list of web sites of different instructional technology centers, enter the keyword "instructional technology center" in a search engine.

LANGUAGE TECHNOLOGY SPECIALIST (HIGHER EDUCATION)

CAREER PROFILE

Duties: Help foreign language faculty integrate technology into their curriculum and instruction; conduct training workshops; provide technical support; perform other duties as required

Alternate Titles: Language Technology Consultant, Modern Languages Instructional Technology Specialist, Language Lab Director (or Lab Coordinator)

Salary Range: $30,000 to $60,000

Employment Prospects: Good

Advancement Prospects: Limited

Prerequisites:
  Licensure/Certification—None is required
  Education/Training—Bachelor's degree or higher
  Experience—Previous work experience in higher education language labs; one or more years of teaching a foreign language; instructional technology experience
  Special Skills and Personality Traits—Proficient in a foreign language; communication, interpersonal, teamwork, leadership, organizational, and writing skills; analytical, energetic, creative, patient, respectful

CAREER LADDER

Language Lab Director

Language Technology Specialist

Language Lab Staff Member

Position Description

Since the 1990's, foreign language departments in higher education institutions have been upgrading their language labs to take advantage of technology. In addition, an increasing number of foreign language department faculty are exploring ways to use the different types of technology to enhance their instruction. For example, a Spanish language professor might have students communicate with native speakers in Spanish-speaking countries through the Internet.

On many college and university campuses, Language Technology Specialists are available to assist foreign language faculty use technology effectively in their instruction. Language Technology Specialists are experts in instructional technology, and are knowledgeable of second-language acquisition principles, methods, and techniques. Many specialists are proficient in one or more foreign languages.

Usually based in language lab centers, Language Technology Specialists provide several roles. One role is that of instructional technology consultant. Upon request, Language Technology Specialists meet with individual faculty members and assess their needs for appropriate academic technologies, such as using specific instructional software in the classroom or developing web sites for their courses. Specialists also assist faculty with developing and designing computer-based and multimedia instructional materials. In addition, they help faculty identify appropriate technical resources (such as hardware, digital cameras, and application software) for their teaching projects. Furthermore, Language Technology Specialists provide faculty members with general information on trends and innovations in instructional technology as it relates to language instruction.

Being trainers is another role that Language Technology Specialists perform. They plan and conduct individual training sessions and group training workshops on various topics that meet the needs of the faculty. For example, specialists might hold individual sessions on using a type of instructional software; conduct small workshops about using new computer operating systems in the language lab; or provide longer workshops about such topics as the integration of multimedia technology with instruction.

Many Language Technology Specialists provide technical support in language labs. They assist with the installation and maintenance of software, operating systems, and microcomputer workstations; provide technical assistance to support staff, faculty, and students; provide technical troubleshooting; and so on.

Some Language Technology Specialists are foreign language department faculty members, and thus responsible for teaching one or more classes per semester. Other Language Technology Specialists hold the position of language lab director (or coordinator), and are responsible for administering the daily operations of the lab. Their administrative duties include developing and evaluating policies and procedures for the daily use of the language lab. They also select, train, and supervise student assistants. Additionally, they maintain an inventory of equipment, software, supplies, and other materials; repair and service equipment; maintain accurate records of student attendance; prepare required reports and paperwork; and so on.

Language Technology Specialists typically work 40 hours a week. Some positions are based on one-year or longer contracts, which are usually renewable.

Salaries

Salaries vary, and depend on factors such as education, experience, and job responsibilities. Salaries, in general, range between $30,000 to $60,000 per year. In addition, Language Technology Specialists receive fringe benefits that include sick pay, vacation leave, medical insurance, retirement benefits, and so on.

Employment Prospects

Language Technology Specialists work for foreign language institutes, two-year colleges, four-year colleges, and universities. This is a relatively new profession. It should grow in the coming years as more higher education institutions convert from analog language labs to computer-assisted language learning centers, and as more faculty choose to integrate technology into their instruction.

Advancement Prospects

Promotions are limited to language lab coordinator and director positions. Finding work in these administrative positions may require transferring to other institutions.

With doctoral degrees, Language Technology Specialists can become professors in foreign language, instructional technology, or other disciplines in which they are interested.

Licensure/Certification

No state licensure or professional certification is required for this profession.

Education and Training

The education requirement varies from one employer to the next. Most employers prefer that Language Technology Specialists have advanced degrees in a foreign language, educational technology, or a related field. Many employers accept candidates with bachelor's degrees if they have qualifying work experience.

Experience, Skills, and Personality Traits

Language Technology Specialists generally have previous work experience in higher education foreign language labs, and have one or more years of experience teaching a foreign language. In addition, they have experience in integrating instructional technologies into the foreign language curriculum. Many specialists are proficient in a foreign language that is taught at their institutions.

Having excellent communication, interpersonal, teamwork, and leadership skills are essential to Language Technology Specialists as they must be able to work well with staff, faculty, and students. They also have strong organizational and writing skills.

Successful Language Technology Specialists share several personality traits such as being analytical, energetic, creative, patient, and respectful.

Unions/Associations

Many Language Technology Specialists belong to local, state, and national associations to take advantage of professional services such as continuing education programs, professional publications, and networking opportunities. Some organizations that many specialists join are:

- International Association for Language Learning Technology
- Computer Assisted Language Instruction Consortium (CALICO)
- Computer-Assisted Language Learning Interest Section, a special interest group of TESOL, Inc. (Teachers of English to Speakers of Other Languages, Inc.)

Tips for Entry

1. Become proficient in a second language.
2. Gain experience working in language labs while you are in college as part-time lab assistants.
3. Contact foreign language departments or foreign language labs directly to learn about job openings.
4. Many foreign language labs have web pages on the Internet. To get a list of relevant web pages to read, enter any of these keywords in a search engine: "college language lab," "university language lab," or "foreign language lab."

CURRICULUM AND INSTRUCTION DEVELOPERS

CURRICULUM SPECIALIST

CAREER PROFILE

Duties: Develop curriculum frameworks for a subject area such as language arts, science, music, or physical education; be a resource to teachers and administrators regarding curriculum and instruction for subject area; perform other duties as required

Alternate Titles: Curriculum Supervisor, Curriculum Coordinator

Salary Range: $30,000 to $80,000

Employment Prospects: Fair

Advancement Prospects: Limited

Prerequisites:
   Licensure/Certification—School administrator credential with a curriculum specialist endorsement; teaching credential
   Education/Training—Master's degree
   Experience—Classroom teaching experience
   Special Skills and Personality Traits—Writing, analytical, organizational, management, leadership, communication, interpersonal, and team building skills; confident, dedicated, creative, energetic, enthusiastic

CAREER LADDER

Curriculum Coordinator (District Level)

↑

Curriculum Specialist

↑

Department Head or Classroom Teacher

Position Description

In public schools, Curriculum Specialists are district-level administrators who develop curriculum standards for all the subjects that are taught in their schools. Teachers use these standards as guidelines for creating units of study and daily lesson plans for their classes.

Curriculum Specialists are assigned to subject areas—such as mathematics, social studies, foreign language, art, technology, or language arts—in which they had taught as classroom teachers. They are responsible for developing curriculum standards for each subject taught in their subject area; for example, Spanish and French might be taught in the area of foreign language in a K–12 school district. Curriculum Specialists describe the concepts and skills that students should learn in a subject throughout the school year as well as from one grade level to the next. They also define the student learning objectives that should be accomplished in a subject.

Curriculum Specialists base district curriculum standards on curriculum frameworks established by state and federal educational agencies. Specialists are continually modifying district curriculum standards because of changes in educational programs and priorities.

Curriculum Specialists also serve as resources to teachers and administrators. They are available to assist on curriculum and instruction questions related to their subject areas. For example, a Social Studies Curriculum Specialist in a K–8 school system helps teachers from kindergarten through eighth grade who teach social studies classes.

Curriculum Specialists perform many other duties, such as:

- training teachers in the newest teaching methods
- evaluating teachers in their subject area
- evaluating new textbooks, supplementary materials, and other instructional materials
- administering budget for assigned subject areas
- processing orders for instructional supplies, equipment, and textbooks
- coordinating with community organizations and agencies about specific activities related to a subject area

(such as essay contests, science fairs, field trips, and guest speakers)
- planning special school-wide events such as math contests, knowledge bowls, art contests, and band performances

Furthermore, Curriculum Specialists are responsible for staying current with developments in the content of their particular subject areas as well as with curriculum and instruction trends.

Curriculum Specialists work 40 hours a week on a 12-month schedule. Most Curriculum Specialists travel a lot, going from school to school. In some school districts, Curriculum Specialists are assigned to cover all subject areas at one school.

Salaries

Salaries vary, depending on factors such as experience, education, job responsibilities, and location. Curriculum Specialists with managerial and administrative duties earn higher wages. According to the U.S. Bureau of Labor Statistics, the estimated annual salary in 1998 for most education administrators (including Curriculum Specialists) was between $30,480 and $80,030.

In addition to a salary, Curriculum Specialists receive fringe benefits, such as vacation leave, medical insurance, and retirement benefits.

Employment Prospects

Most job opportunities become available as Curriculum Specialists retire, resign, or advance to higher positions. School districts may create additional positions as long as funding is available.

Advancement Prospects

Curriculum Specialists can advance to higher administrative positions such as district-level curriculum coordinators, directors of curriculum and instruction, assistant superintendents, and superintendents. Another career option is to become school principals or assistant principals. Many Curriculum Specialists choose to pursue advancement through higher pay and more complex responsibilities, which may require transferring to other school districts.

Curriculum Supervisors can also follow other career paths such as becoming instructional technologists, software developers, textbook editors, or textbook authors. Another option is to become curriculum developers for publishers, software companies, businesses, corporations, or state or federal education agencies.

Licensure/Certification

Curriculum Specialists hold a school administrator credential with a curriculum specialist endorsement. Licensure requirements vary from state to state. (For specific information, contact the state board of education in the state where you wish to work.) Completion of continuing education units may be required for licensure renewal.

Education and Training

Most Curriculum Specialists have a master's degree or higher in education. They have also completed an approved education program leading to licensure, which includes classes in curriculum and instruction, group dynamics, human resource development, instructional technology, and a supervised field practicum.

Experience, Skills, and Personality Traits

Curriculum Specialists generally are selected from the ranks of classroom teachers who have taught several years. In addition, they are experts in the curriculum and instruction of their subject areas.

Curriculum Specialists need superior writing, analytical, organizational, management, and leadership skills to do their work effectively. Additionally, they need excellent communication, interpersonal, and team building skills.

Successful Curriculum Specialists share several personality traits such as being confident, dedicated, creative, energetic, and enthusiastic.

Unions/Associations

Curriculum Specialists join different local, state, and national professional organizations to take advantage of professional resources, continuing education programs, networking opportunities, and other professional services. Many join organizations that serve their particular subject area, such as the International Reading Association, the National Council for the Social Studies, the Council for Exceptional Children, or MENC: The National Association for Music Education.

Curriculum Specialists also join school administrator organizations such as:

- Association for Supervision and Curriculum Development
- American Association of School Administrators
- National Association of Elementary School Principals
- National Association of Secondary School Principals
- National Middle School Association

Tips for Entry

1. As teachers, participate on curriculum committees.
2. You can read about different state and local curriculum frameworks on the Internet. To find a list of relevant sites, enter the keyword "curriculum framework" in any search engine.

TEXTBOOK EDITOR

CAREER PROFILE

Duties: Manage textbook projects through editorial development; provide guidance to authors; edit manuscripts for content and for publisher's formats, house styles, and standards; perform other duties as required

Alternate Titles: Development Editor; Acquisition Editor; a title (such as ESL Editor, Elementary Math Editor, or College Social Science Editor) that reflects subject areas

Salary Range: $19,000 to $48,000

Employment Prospects: Fair

Advancement Prospects: Good

Prerequisites:
　Licensure/Certification—None required
　Education/Training—Bachelor's degree
　Experience—Publishing experience is desirable; teaching experience in subject matter usually preferred
　Special Skills and Personality Traits—Writing, analytical, problem solving, communication, interpersonal, teamwork, organizational, and project management skills; tactful, friendly, enthusiastic, energetic, self-motivated, creative

CAREER LADDER

Senior Editor

↑

Textbook Editor

↑

Assistant Editor

Position Description

Most textbooks, workbooks, and other instructional materials used by students in schools, colleges, and universities are developed and produced by educational publishers. Textbook Editors are responsible for developing ideas into manuscripts that are ready to be prepared for printing into textbooks. Ideas for textbooks are proposed by Textbook Editors, marketing staff, vice presidents, or other staff within a publishing house. Textbook Editors also acquire book proposals from authors who submit original ideas that fit publishers' needs.

Textbook Editors specialize in subject areas, such as elementary language arts, secondary mathematics, college biology, special education, and adult ESL (English as a second language). Most editors manage one or more editorial projects at a time, with each project usually at a different point in its development. A project may be one proposed textbook title or a series of several proposed titles.

For each project, editors determine the goals, objectives, and contents for textbooks and ancillary materials, such as teacher's guides, student workbooks, and teacher resource books. Textbook Editors also find and assign authors to write all or parts of manuscripts. They provide authors with working guidelines from which to develop manuscripts. Textbook Editors keep in constant communication with authors to track their progress and to ensure that they are able to make writing deadlines.

Manuscripts usually go through draft and revision stages. Textbook Editors review manuscript drafts carefully, providing authors with detailed comments and suggestions for necessary revisions. If needed, Textbook Editors send manuscript drafts to subject experts to review content for accuracy.

When authors have finished writing manuscripts, Textbook Editors then edit manuscripts for content as well as for adherence to the publisher's own styles, formats, and standards. When needed, a Textbook Editor rewrites parts or all of a manuscript. Edited manuscripts are released to production departments where manuscripts are physically prepared for printing. (During the production stage, the book design, page design and layout, illustrations, and other physical features of textbooks are created.) Textbook Editors usually review manuscripts again, but in the form of galley and page proofs which show how actual book pages will look. Textbook Editors make sure that manuscript copy has been transferred completely and accurately. They also edit text further on pages where the text runs too long. Textbook Editors may also send proofs to authors to review to make corrections and comments.

Textbook Editors perform various other tasks, which differ from one editor to the next. For example, they:

- assist in new product development that includes proposing ideas or acquiring book ideas from authors
- hire and supervise outside staff, such as freelance editors, writers, and artists
- maintain relationships with authors
- perform photo research
- obtain permission from other publishers to reprint artwork and passages from magazines, books, or other materials
- give presentations at educator conferences and conventions
- assist sales and marketing departments—for example, editors might facilitate meetings with focus groups or write promotional copy for new books

Many Editors work more than 40 hours a week, often staying late or bringing work home in the evenings and on weekends.

Salaries

Salaries vary, and depend on experience, education, job responsibilities, and other factors. According to the U.S. Bureau of Labor Statistics, the estimated annual salary for most editors in 1998 ranged from $19,720 to $47,670. (Note: This salary range includes book editors, magazine editors, newspaper editors, and other editors that develop different types of materials for publication.)

In addition to a salary, Textbook Editors receive fringe benefits, such as sick leave, vacation leave, health insurance, and retirement benefits.

Employment Prospects

Educational publishers can be found in and around major cities such as New York City, Boston, Los Angeles, Chicago, Seattle, and San Francisco, as well as in smaller cities and rural areas throughout the United States.

The competition for jobs in the book publishing industry is keen. Most opportunities for Textbook Editors become available as editors retire, resign, or advance to other positions. Turnover in general is relatively high for book editors as they move from one publishing house to another to pursue higher pay and advancement opportunities.

Advancement Prospects

Textbook Editors can advance to supervisory and administrative positions as senior editors, managing editors, executive editors, editorial directors, and up to executive-level positions as vice presidents and publishers. Many editors pursue advancement by accepting jobs at different publishing houses. Some editors choose to become freelance editors or to start their own businesses offering editorial development services to publishers.

Textbook Editors might also follow paths for other editor careers by becoming children's book editors, reference book editors, acquisitions editors, technical editors, magazine editors, newspaper editors, multimedia editors, and so on. Other options are to pursue related careers such as instructional designers, software developers, librarians, and teachers.

Licensure/Certification

No professional licenses or certificates are required to become a Textbook Editor.

Education and Training

Employers generally require that Textbook Editors have a bachelor's degree, preferably in the field in which they would be working. For example, an Editor who edits college math textbooks has a bachelor's degree in mathematics. Publishers may waive the requirement if candidates have qualifying work experience.

Experience, Skills, and Personality Traits

In general, employers require that Textbook Editors have one or more years of teaching experience, preferably in the subject areas for which they are applying. Alternatively, they should be knowledgeable with the subject matter as well as familiar with the pedagogy, curriculum, and instruction for a subject area. In addition, candidates should have editorial or publishing experience that may be in the form of writing newsletters, working on student publications, freelance editing, and so on.

Textbook Editors need excellent writing, analytical, and problem-solving skills to do their work effectively. Strong communication, interpersonal, and teamwork skills are needed as they must work well with authors, editors, production staff, freelancers, and others. In addition, Textbook Editors should have good organizational and project management skills.

Being tactful, friendly, enthusiastic, energetic, self-motivated, and creative are some personality traits that successful Textbook Editors share. They also have a fine sense of humor.

Unions/Associations

Textbook Editors might join local or regional professional organizations for publishing professionals to take advantage of conferences, networking opportunities, job listings, and so on. Many freelance textbook editors belong to the Editorial Freelancers Association, a national organization.

Many Textbook Editors join professional associations for instructors that serve their subject area, such as:

- National Council of Teachers of English
- TESOL, Inc. (Teachers of English to Speakers of Other Languages, Inc.)
- American Association for Adult and Continuing Education
- American Chemical Society

Tips for Entry

1. Obtain as much teaching experience as you can, especially in the subject area in which you are interested in working. You might be a tutor, teacher aide, or teacher. Taking education courses can also be helpful.
2. Many educational publishers hire teachers on a freelance basis to write specific lessons, exercises, and activities for projects. Many also use teachers to review manuscript drafts. Find out who the editorial directors are at publishing houses for whom you'd like to offer your writing or consulting services. Then send query letters and your resume to them.
3. Use the Internet to learn about various educational publishers. To find relevant web sites, enter the keyword "educational publisher" in a search engine.

INSTRUCTIONAL DESIGNER

CAREER PROFILE

Duties: Develop and design technology-based instructional materials; work with other experts to complete projects; conduct needs assessments; manage instructional projects; perform other duties as required

Alternate Titles: Courseware Developer, Distance Education Specialist

Salary Range: $21,000 to $77,000

Employment Prospects: Good

Advancement Prospects: Limited

Prerequisites:
  Licensure/Certification—None required
  Education/Training—Bachelor's or master's degree
  Experience—Prior experience in the design and delivery of distance education in appropriate work settings; teaching experience is preferred
  Special Skills and Personality Traits—Analytical, writing, organizational, project management, communication, interpersonal, and teamwork skills; patient, tolerant, tactful, flexible, self-motivated, energetic, enthusiastic, creative

CAREER LADDER

Senior Instructional Designer

Instructional Designer

Intern

Position Description

Instructional Designers provide the basic framework for the development and design of training videotapes, satellite television courses, on-line courses, and other instructional materials. Many Instructional Designers are part of training departments of businesses, corporations, government agencies, and other organizations where they help in the creation of instructional materials (and sometimes curriculum) for technical training programs. Many Instructional Designers work in higher educational institutions where they help faculty with creating technology resources (such as web pages) for their courses as well as assist in the design and development of on-line courses. Some Instructional Designers work in educational publishing companies and software companies, providing instructional expertise for the development of software and courseware projects.

Most Instructional Designers work as part of a team of experts, each responsible for different aspects of the project. Other team members would include editorial, graphic design, and technical personnel. The team also includes one or more subject matter experts who are responsible for providing the content matter. When the content is highly technical, subject matter experts provide instructional objectives and other instructional guidance. For example, if an art professor asks an Instructional Designer to design an on-line course on 16th-century Italian art, the professor would provide him or her with content materials, learning objectives, lesson activities, and so on.

When developing materials, Instructional Designers look at instruction from the perspective of the learners in order to meet their specific needs. A project usually begins with a needs assessment to determine the direction and design of the project. Instructional Designers identify important information, such as:

- the target audience
- the settings in which the proposed material would be used
- the educational goals and objectives
- the appropriate instructional strategies to use
- the most effective media and formats for presenting instruction

Instructional Designers also work on the creation of instructional projects. They might write or edit text, develop layouts, make videotapes, write programming codes, and so on. Instructional Designers often have the responsibility of managing projects through completion. This includes creating deadline schedules, answering questions from outsiders about the project, and tracking the project's progress. Furthermore, it involves testing the instruction with sample learners to evaluate whether it has met learning objectives. The material is revised and retested until the evaluation is satisfactory.

Instructional Designers' responsibilities vary according to their expertise. Beginning developers generally work on parts of a project under the direction of senior instructional designers. As they become more experienced, they are given the responsibility of developing entire courses and becoming team project leaders. Senior Instructional Designers have higher-level responsibilities that include supervising team project leaders, managing projects, and directing needs assessments.

Instructional Designers are also responsible for keeping up with new technologies as well as with their professional development. They read books, magazines, and journals about technology as well as about education. They join professional associations, participate in professional conferences, and network with colleagues. In addition, they enroll in training workshops and continuing education courses.

They work 40 hours a week, and often work evening and weekend hours in order to meet deadlines.

Salaries

Salaries vary, and depend on factors such as education, experience, and school budget. According to the U.S. Bureau of Labor Statistics, the estimated annual salary in 1998 for most instructional coordinators, including Instructional Designers, ranged from $20,980 to $77,250.

In addition to a salary, Instructional Designers receive fringe benefits, such as vacation leave, medical insurance, and retirement benefits.

Employment Prospects

Instructional Designers work for colleges and universities, educational publishers, businesses, corporations, government, the military, nonprofit organizations, and various other types of organizations and agencies. Many Instructional Designers also work for courseware development businesses that provide contractual services to different organizations. Some Instructional Designers are self-employed.

Job opportunities are readily available for experienced Instructional Designers. This field is expected to continue growing due to the public interest in on-line distance education programs. Educational institutions, businesses, and corporations in particular have need for Instructional Designers to create new on-line courses as well as redesign existing on-line courses.

Advancement Prospects

Instructional Designers can advance to become lead developers, project managers or other administrative positions. They can also become self-employed, as well as start their own software companies.

Licensure/Certification

No licensure or certification is required for this profession.

Education and Training

The education requirement varies from one employer to the next. In general, the minimum requirement for Instructional Designers is a bachelor's degree in instructional technology, instructional design, educational media, or other related field. More and more employers, however, are requiring or preferring candidates with master's degrees.

Experience, Skills, and Personality Traits

Requirements vary among the different types of employers. In general, employers look for candidates who have prior experience in their particular work settings. They also prefer candidates who have teaching experience and are knowledgeable about educational multimedia design principles. Furthermore, candidates have working knowledge of appropriate technology such as HTML programming, authoring software, and web-based instructional systems.

To perform their work effectively, Instructional Designers need superior analytical, writing, organizational, and project management skills. In addition, they need excellent communication, interpersonal, and teamwork skills as they must work well with faculty, project team members, and others on a daily basis.

Successful Instructional Designers share several personality traits such as being patient, tolerant, tactful, flexible, self-motivated, energetic, enthusiastic, and creative.

Unions/Associations

Instructional Designers join local, state, and national professional associations to take advantage of professional resources, continuing education programs, networking opportunities, and other professional services. Some organizations might be the:

- International Society for Performance Improvement
- Association for Educational Communications and Technology
- American Society for Training and Development
- Association for the Advancement of Computing in Education
- Association of Internet Professionals

Tips for Entry

1. In middle school or high school, you can start gaining teaching experience by volunteering or getting part-

time jobs as a tutor, coach, teacher aide, summer camp counselor, Sunday school teacher, and so on.
2. To gain instructional design work experience, get intern positions. Ask professors and college career counselors for help in finding appropriate internships.
3. Keep up with advances in technology and update your skills as needed.
4. You can learn more about the field of courseware development on the Internet. To get a list of relevant web sites, enter either of these keywords in any search engine: "courseware," "courseware development," or "Instructional Designer."

EDUCATIONAL SOFTWARE DEVELOPER

CAREER PROFILE

Duties: Coordinate the management of software projects; define the parameters of a project, including its goals and objectives, content matter, teaching strategies, and so on; perform other duties as required

Alternate Title: Courseware Developer

Salary Range: $25,000 to $75,000

Employment Prospects: Good

Advancement Prospects: Fair

Prerequisites:
  Licensure/Certification—None is required
  Education/Training—Bachelor's degree
  Experience—One or more years experience with specific programming languages; a background in education
  Special Skills and Personality Traits—Organizational, management, interpersonal, teamwork, self-management skills; patient, tolerant, flexible, self-motivated, confident, energetic, enthusiastic

CAREER LADDER

Senior Software Developer

Educational Software Developer

Intern

Position Description

From preschool to college, instructors are integrating computers into their curriculum and instruction. In classrooms or in computer labs, instructors have their students use educational software which reinforces, supplements, or enriches their daily lessons. For example, a preschool teacher might have children access software that introduces them to letters and numbers. Or, a high school general math teacher might have students work with software that teaches about essential language and math skills for work settings.

The development of educational software is the primary job of Educational Software Developers. Many work for publishers or software companies. Some, who are self-employed, work on software projects on a contractual basis. Many create courseware on their own time, whether they are staff members, self-employed, or working in another profession. (Courseware is another name for educational software.)

Educational Software Developers generally are responsible for managing a project from start to finish. They take an idea for a software program—such as teaching simple fractions by showing equal segments of pizza pies—and begin to define the product from the eyes of the learners. Software Developers ask questions, such as: What type of students would be using the software? What concepts and skills should the students be learning? What are the learning objectives that should be achieved with the software? What types of activities and exercises can be used to motivate students, and to keep their interest throughout the whole program?

Most educational software today is multimedia, meaning that a combination of text, sounds, animation, graphic arts, and video is used. Educational software also allows for users to interact with the content. Thus Software Developers determine how the software should look, how the user should move around in the program, and what type of interactions the user should be doing. (Software Developers may also research the marketability of the proposed product as well as the competition it would be facing.)

Once the parameters of the product are defined, the development of the product begins. In staff positions, most Educational Software Developers are part of teams, in which each team member (such as a graphic artist, software engineer, writer, instructional designer, or video artist) brings his or her own expertise to the project.

Software Developers are sometimes designated the project managers. They are responsible for tasks such as creating deadline schedules, preparing budgets, and keeping track of the project's progress. They also coordinate testing sessions with sample users to evaluate the products, reviewing and retesting them until evaluations are satisfactory.

Educational Software Developers also contribute to the creative development of projects. Depending on their interests and skills, they might write text, design exercises and tests, write programming codes, create graphics, and so on. On simple projects, Software Developers who have the expertise might create the products all by themselves.

Software Educational Developers typically work long hours to meet deadlines.

Salaries

Salaries vary, and depend on factors such as experience, size of employer, and location. In general, software developers earn between $25,000 and $75,000 per year. Employed Educational Software Developers usually receive fringe benefits such as sick leave, vacation pay, medical insurance, and retirement benefits.

Employment Prospects

Computer-related jobs, including those of software developers, are projected to grow rapidly through 2008, according to the U.S. Bureau of Labor Statistics. In addition, educational software is one of the fastest-growing categories of software, which is partly due to the growing number of schools that are integrating technology into the curriculum, and thus purchasing instructional software.

Advancement Prospects

Educational Software Developers can advance to become lead developers, project managers, or other administrative positions. Another option is to pursue careers in the other areas of educational software development, such as programming, graphic arts, or curriculum development. They can also become self-employed educational software developers or consultants, as well as start their own software companies.

With their skills and experience, Educational Software Developers can become developers of games and other types of software.

Licensure/Certification

No state licensure or certification is required to become an Educational Software Developer.

Education and Training

Most employers require that Educational Software Developers have a bachelor's degree, preferably in computer science. However, employers usually waive the education requirement if candidates have qualifying experience.

Educational Software Developers are expected to keep up with their skills and professional development. They may do so through self-study, continuing education courses, networking with colleagues, participating in professional conventions, and so on.

Experience, Skills, and Personality Traits

In general, educational software companies require that candidates have one or more years experience with specific programming languages such as C, C++, or Java. Candidates should also have a background in education, or at the minimum a basic understanding of educational theory for the target audiences of the software they would be developing.

To do their work effectively, Educational Software Developers need adequate organizational, management, interpersonal, and teamwork skills. They also should have superior self-management skills—the ability to meet deadlines, manage several duties at the same time, take the initiative to seek new work and update skills, work well under pressure, and so on.

Successful Educational Software Developers share several personality traits, such as being patient, tolerant, flexible, self-motivated, confident, energetic, and enthusiastic.

Unions/Associations

Many Educational Software Developers belong to professional organizations that allow them to take advantage of professional services such as training seminars, networking opportunities, and professional resources. Some general computing associations that they might join are the Association for Computing Machinery and IEEE Computer Society, a society of the Institute of Electrical and Electronics Engineers.

Many self-employed developers and business owners belong to the Educational Software Cooperative. Educational Software Developers who sell their own software might join the Association of Shareware Professionals.

Tips for Entry

1. To gain experience, obtain internships with educational software companies or educational publishers that develop software.
2. Take courses in education. Also, volunteer or get a job as a tutor, teacher aide, recreation leader, CPR instructor, or other similar position to get an idea of what teaching is about.
3. You can learn more about various educational software companies on the Internet. To find pertinent web sites, enter either of these keywords in any search engine: "educational software" or "educational software company."

EMPLOYEE TRAINING SPECIALISTS

TRAINER (IN-HOUSE)

CAREER PROFILE

Duties: Provide instruction to employees on various work and work-related topics and skills; assist in developing and evaluating in-house training programs; perform other duties as required

Alternate Title: Technical Trainer

Salary Range: $20,000 to $30,000 (starting salary)

Employment Prospects: Good

Advancement Prospects: Good

Prerequisites:
    Licensure/Certification—None required
    Education/Training—Bachelor's degree
    Experience—Hands-on experience required; teaching experience desirable
    Special Skills and Personality Traits—Communication, interpersonal, motivational, presentation, public speaking, organizational, teamwork, writing, computer skills; patient, enthusiastic, energetic, flexible, creative

CAREER LADDER

Training Specialist

Trainer

Trainee

Position Description

In most workplaces, employers have in-house training departments to develop and implement training programs that improve the performance of their various employees. The departmental staff members who provide instruction are called Trainers. Those who provide technology-based instruction are generally known as *Technical Trainers*.

Along with conducting training sessions, Trainers assist with assessing the training needs within an organization; planning new training programs; and updating courses. They also help develop print and technology-based instructional materials. In addition, they maintain training equipment.

Different training programs are set up to meet various needs of employees. The following are some programs for which Trainers conduct individual or group training sessions:

- orientation training for new employees, in which Trainers explain employers' mission and policies, organizational structure and services, compensation plans and benefits, work requirements and rules, and so on
- technical training programs for different computer hardware, software, networks, and so on
- professional skills workshops, in which Trainers teach job-specific technical skills that are specific to a particular department (such as the accounting department) or to a particular type of employee within the organization (such as department supervisors)
- safety training workshops, which includes training that meets government-mandated health and safety training
- informational workshops on employer policies and practices, such as workplace diversity, sexual harassment, and health issues
- basic skills classes, in which Trainers provide remedial instruction in reading, writing, math, and—in some workplaces—English as a second language

Trainers are assigned to provide instruction for one or more training programs, according to their expertise. Depending on the size of their training departments, Trainers may be also responsible for managing individual training programs.

When teaching a course, Trainers follow a prescribed curriculum and use established instructional materials. However, Trainers bring their own teaching styles to the training sessions. Like all teachers, Trainers plan for the most effective means of delivering instruction based on the topic, learning objectives, number of participants, length of training, and so on. Often a combination of teaching methods is used, such as lectures, videotapes, computer-based instruction, and web-based instruction. In preparation for their training sessions, Trainers gather all materials, equipment, and supplies needed for instruction, and set up the classrooms appropriately.

Trainers manage the learning environment so that employees can learn successfully. They provide learners with various activities and exercises to reinforce learning. Trainers also answer questions and provide employees with positive feedback on their learning progress. After the completion of a training session, they evaluate the participants' performances and the effectiveness of their instruction, then present the information to their superiors.

In-house Trainers work part time or full time. Some Trainers are contractual employees, working for a designated length of time which can be several weeks, months, or years.

Salaries

Salaries vary, and depend on factors such as education, experience, job responsibilities, and the size and type of employer. Technical Trainers usually earn higher wages. Entry-level Trainers generally earn between $20,000 and $30,000 per year.

In addition to their salaries, Trainers receive fringe benefits such as vacation pay, sick leave, health insurance, life insurance, and retirement benefits.

Employment Prospects

In-house Trainers work for financial institutions, retail corporations, computer companies, manufacturing firms, transportation companies, government agencies, health care organizations, educational institutions, nonprofit organizations, and many other public sector and private sector organizations. Trainers are also employed by training organizations that provide services to employers on a contractual basis.

In general, Trainer positions are available nationwide. Most job opportunities become available as Trainers retire, resign, or transfer to higher positions or to other organizations.

As long as companies and organizations need to train and retrain employees on new procedures, equipment, and technology skills, Trainers shall be in demand. Companies may cut in-house training staffs, but jobs would still be available with outsource providers.

Advancement Prospects

Trainers can advance to supervisory and management positions within an organization as well as advance by seeking positions in other organizations. They can also become self-employed consultants or training company owners that provide training and development services to companies and organizations.

Trainers can also pursue other related careers such as by becoming schoolteachers, community college instructors, curriculum developers, software developers, or instructional technologists.

Licensure/Certification

No state licensure or certification is required to become a Trainer.

Education and Training

Most employers require that Trainers have bachelor's degrees in instructional technology, organizational development, human resources, education, or some other related field that is appropriate to a particular work setting. Many employers will accept candidates with high school diplomas or associate degrees if they have qualifying work experience.

Trainers receive training on the job. In addition, most Trainers continue developing their own professional growth through independent study, networking with colleagues, enrollment in continuing education programs, participating in professional organizations, and so forth.

Experience, Skills, and Personality Traits

Requirements vary, according to job responsibilities, type of training program, size of employer, and so on. Previous teaching experience is usually preferred; but many employers waive the teaching requirement if candidates have the necessary hands-on technical experience. Candidates also demonstrate the ability to teach the necessary content and skills to adult learners. For technical training positions, candidates should have the appropriate technical experience.

To facilitate classes and seminars effectively, Trainers should have communication, interpersonal, motivational, presentation, and public speaking skills. Trainers also need strong organizational, teamwork, and writing skills for their work. In addition, they should have appropriate computer skills. Being patient, enthusiastic, energetic, flexible, and creative are some personality traits that successful Trainers share.

Unions/Associations

Many Trainers belong to local, state, and national professional associations to take advantage of professional services such as networking opportunities, job listings, training programs, and professional resources. The American Society for Training and Development and the International Society for Performance Improvement are two professional associations that many Trainers join. Technical Trainers might join the Information Technology Training Association.

Tips for Entry

1. To become a technical instructor, obtain technical training and on-the-job experience first. For entry-level technical instructor jobs, many employers hire

candidates without teaching experience if they have the appropriate technical experience.
2. Keep up with developments in the training field. Also maintain your computer skills as technology is continually changing.
3. Post your resume at strategic web sites for employers to read. Check with different professional associations to see if they offer that service.
4. You can learn more about the field of employee training and development on the Internet. You might begin by visiting American Society for Training and Development's web site (*http://www.astd.org*). Or, to get a list of other relevant web sites, enter the keywords "training and development" in any search engine.

TRAINING DEVELOPER

CAREER PROFILE

Duties: Develop and design various training programs for employees in the workplace; manage training projects; create print and technology-based instructional materials; perform other duties as required

Alternate Titles: Instructional Designer, Training Specialist

Salary Range: $20,000 to $75,000

Employment Prospects: Good

Advancement Prospects: Fair

Prerequisites:
  Licensure/Certification—None required
  Education/Training—Bachelor's degree
  Experience—Previous experience developing training programs and materials
  Special Skills and Personality Traits—Communication, interpersonal, teamwork, organizational, management, writing, presentation, and computer skills; patient, tactful, energetic, enthusiastic, creative, flexible

CAREER LADDER

Training Manager

↑

Training Developer

↑

Trainer or Intern

Position Description

Training Developers are specialists in the training and development departments of hospitals, department stores, computer companies, banks, colleges, bus companies, distribution centers, government agencies, nonprofit organizations, and other private and public sector organizations. As experts in instructional design, they develop and design effective training programs for their employers, such as:

- new employee orientation training
- employee safety training
- technical training
- professional skills training for specific departments (such as customer service, sales, or warehouse) or specific employee positions (such as department supervisors, division managers, or sales representatives)
- basic skills training (remediation of literacy and math skills)
- informational workshops on work-related topics, such as sexual harassment in the workplace

Training Developers usually act as project managers of training projects. They are responsible for defining the project and coordinating it from start to finish. They also ensure that a project is completed on time and within a given budget.

When starting a training project, Training Developers first conduct a needs assessment. They gather information such as relevant characteristics of trainees, and different job procedures, by talking with appropriate personnel, observing workers, reviewing work materials, and so on.

Training Developers work closely with subject matter experts—department managers, supervisors, and other personnel—as they design specific instructional programs. Together, they determine the content of the program—information to be taught, learning objectives, sequence of teaching, types of activities and exercises, and so on. They also discuss evaluation strategies for measuring employee performance upon completion of training. In addition, they determine the most effective way to deliver the instruction—such as classroom training, conferences, individual coaching, on-the-job training, interactive video training, or intranet instruction.

Depending on the complexity of a training project, Training Developers may work alone or as part of a team. Training Developers design training programs that integrate adult learning principles, as well as take into account the different abilities and learning styles of the program participants.

Many Training Developers also develop and produce print, visual, and/or technology-based instructional materials that include both trainer and participant guides.

Training Developers are also responsible for maintaining training programs. On a regular basis, they review and evaluate the effectiveness of current programs. When necessary, they update current courses and instructional materials.

Some Training Developers are responsible for managing the development of all training programs within their organization. This includes coordinating and administering contracts with outside vendors who provide specific training programs.

Training Developers are expected to update and improve their skills as well as keep up with current training and development research. They might join professional associations and network with colleagues. They might also enroll in training seminars and continuing education courses, read professional books and journals, participate in professional conferences, and so on.

Furthermore, Training Developers perform other duties, which vary from one employer to the next. For example, they might:

- train instructional staff
- conduct employee training workshops and classes
- develop training programs and/or design training materials and user documents for their employers' customers
- help develop marketing and sales materials
- attend professional meetings and conferences as employers' representatives

Training Developers are either in-house staff members or consultants working on a contractual basis. They generally work 40 hours a week, sometimes working additional hours to meet deadlines.

Salaries

Salaries vary, and depend on factors such as education, experience, job responsibilities, and the size and type of employer. Training Developers in large organizations can expect to earn higher wages. According to the U.S. Bureau of Labor Statistics, the estimated annual salary in 1998 for most personnel, training, and labor relations specialists ranged from $20,310 to $75,440.

In addition to their salaries, Training Developers receive fringe benefits, such as vacation pay, sick leave, medical insurance, and retirement benefits.

Employment Prospects

Training Developers work in a wide variety of settings, such as financial institutions, retail companies, manufacturing firms, government agencies, health care organizations, educational institutions, nonprofit organizations. They are also employed by training and development companies who provide their services to employers on a contractual basis.

The demand for Training Developers is constant, as employers continually need to train and retrain employees. Most job opportunities for Training Developers become available as developers retire, resign, or transfer to higher positions or to other organizations.

Advancement Prospects

Training Developers can advance to senior, supervisory, and management positions within an organization as well as by seeking positions in other organizations. They can also become training consultants or training company owners who provide training and development services to companies and organizations.

Training Developers can pursue other related careers in such positions as college professors, community college instructors, software developers, and desktop publishing specialists.

Licensure/Certification

No state licensure or certification is required to become a Training Developer.

Education and Training

The minimum requirement for most Training Developers positions is a bachelor's degree in instructional technology, education, organizational development, or other related field. For some positions, employers require or prefer candidates with master's degrees, but will often waive the requirement if candidates have qualifying work experience.

Experience, Skills, and Personality Traits

In general, Training Developers have previous experience developing training programs and materials. (Entry-level developers may have gained experience through internships or work-study programs while in college.) They are also knowledgeable about basic adult learning principles, course development methodology, and creating learning materials that are computer-based or technology-based.

Training Developers need excellent communication, interpersonal, and teamwork skills to work well with training staff, as well as with other employees within their organizations. They also need strong organizational, management, writing, and presentation skills. In addition, they have appropriate computer skills needed to perform their work.

Successful Training Developers share several personality traits such as being patient, tactful, energetic, enthusiastic, creative, and flexible.

Unions/Associations

Many Training Developers join local, state, and national professional associations to take advantage of continuing education programs, networking opportunities, and other professional services. Two organizations that they might join are:

- American Society for Training and Development
- International Society for Performance Improvement

Tips for Entry

1. As a college student, join professional organizations and begin networking with professionals in the field. They may be able to provide you with job leads when you are ready to begin your job search after graduation.
2. While in college, obtain internships in different work settings to get an idea of the type of environment in which you would like to work.
3. Get experience teaching adult learners. You might tutor adult students in college settings or volunteer to teach adults in adult literacy programs. Or, you might teach adult classes in continuing education programs sponsored by community centers, community colleges, and other organizations.
4. Learn more about the field of instructional technology on the Internet. To get a list of pertinent web sites, enter either of these keywords in a search engine: "instructional technology" or "instructional designer."

TRAINING MANAGER

CAREER PROFILE

Duties: Manage and coordinate all training programs provided by an employer to its employees; oversee the development and implementation of training programs; execute administrative duties; perform other duties as required

Alternate Titles: Training Director, Training and Development Manager

Salary Range: $25,000 to $91,000

Employment Prospects: Good

Advancement Prospects: Limited

Prerequisites:
  Licensure/Certification—None Required
  Education/Training—Bachelor's degree
  Experience—Several years of training and development experience in appropriate work settings; have supervisory and management experience
  Special Skills and Personality Traits—Leadership, project management, writing, communication, interpersonal, team building, teamwork, presentation, public speaking, and computer skills; organized, flexible, adaptable, analytical, creative, self-motivated

CAREER LADDER

Training Director or Training Consultant

↑

Training Manager

↑

Training Specialist

Position Description

Training Managers are in charge of administering the training departments of public and private sector employers. (The training department is also known as the *training and development department,* and is usually part of a human resources department.) Training Managers manage and coordinate all training programs that employers provide to their employees so that they can perform their jobs effectively and efficiently. Some of the various types of programs that Training Managers oversee are:

- orientation and on-the-job training for new employees
- safety training
- workshops on employer's policies and practices regarding work-related topics such as equal employment opportunities
- reinforcement of general work skills, such as teamwork, interpersonal, communication, and conflict resolution skills
- technical training on computer software applications, such as word proccessors, spreadsheets, graphics, and databases
- specific job skills training for particular departments (such as the marketing department) or for particular employees (such as department supervisors)
- basic skills classes, or remedial instruction in reading, writing, math, and—in some workplaces—English as a second language
- training programs for clients, customers, or users of products and services

Training Managers work closely with human resource and departmental managers to determine the training needs for the overall organization as well as for the various departments. Training Managers then plan training strategies, and oversee the development and implementation of appropriate training programs.

Depending on the size of their staff, Training Managers may conduct needs assessments for new training projects. They may develop and design instructional programs, and may assist in the development of print, visual, and/or technology-based materials. Some Training Managers teach classes or workshops and/or provide individual coaching of employees.

Training Managers are also responsible for identifying and evaluating external, or outside, resources that may offer training programs. These sources include vendors, independent consultants, training companies, higher education institutions, professional associations, and trade unions. Training Managers assist human resource managers and various departmental managers in choosing appropriate external training programs that meet their specific needs. In addition, Training Managers make contracts with vendors, consultants, and training companies and coordinate the logistics of providing instruction. Managers may also form partnerships with community colleges, technical colleges, and university and college continuing education programs to develop specialized training programs.

Training Managers monitor all training programs to ensure that they meet employer standards as well as comply with any government requirements. They also evaluate the curriculum, instructional materials, and instructors' presentations, and make recommendations for changes and improvements.

In addition, Training Managers are responsible for performing various administrative tasks. For example, they:

- train and supervise training staff and support staff
- develop and manage budgets
- oversee contracts for equipment, consultants, and services
- determine work priorities and procedures
- schedule training courses
- locate facilities for training courses
- write correspondence and reports, maintain accurate records, and complete all necessary paperwork

In many organizations, Training Managers assume the role of internal consultants, assisting managers with specific employee problems that may be alleviated with appropriate training. For example, a department manager has two employees who are not getting along. The Training Manager may suggest that the employees be given training in conflict resolution and team building skills.

Training Managers work 40 hours a week, and sometimes work additional hours to complete their various tasks.

Salaries

Salaries vary, and depend on factors such as education, experience, job responsibilities, and the size and type of employer. Training Managers in large organizations can expect to earn higher wages. According to the U.S. Bureau of Labor Statistics, the 1998 estimated annual salary for all personnel, training, and labor relations managers ranged from $25,750 to $91,040.

In addition to their salaries, Training Managers receive fringe benefits such as vacation pay, sick leave, health insurance, life insurance, and retirement benefits.

Employment Prospects

Training Managers are employed by financial institutions, business services companies, retail companies, manufacturing firms, transportation corporations, government agencies, utilities companies, hospitals, health care organizations, educational institutions, nonprofit organizations, and many other corporations and organizations.

Most job opportunities become available as managers retire, resign, or advance to higher positions. Employers may create new training management positions to meet additional training needs.

Advancement Prospects

In small and mid-size organizations, Training Managers are usually the top administrative positions for the training departments. In larger organizations, they can usually pursue executive positions such as training directors and vice presidents of training and development.

Many Training Managers pursue higher pay and more complex responsibilities by seeking positions with other employers. They can also become consultants or owners of businesses that provide training and development services to companies and organizations on a contractual basis.

Licensure/Certification

No state licensure or certification is required to become a Training Manager.

Education and Training

A bachelor's degree is the minimum requirement for most Training Manager positions. Many employers, however, prefer candidates with master's degrees. College degrees should be in business administration, education, organizational development, instructional technology, or other related fields.

Training Managers are expected to pursue their own professional development through self-study, networking with colleagues, attending professional conferences, enrolling in continuing education courses, and so on.

Experience, Skills, and Personality Traits

Requirements vary depending on the size of the training department, job responsibilities, and other factors. In general, candidates should have several years of experience providing instruction and developing training programs in appropriate work settings. Additionally, they should have supervisory and management experience.

To do their jobs effectively, Training Managers need leadership, project management, and writing skills. They also need communication, interpersonal, team building, and teamwork skills as they work daily with various people within their organizations. In addition, they should have presentation and public speaking skills, as well as computer skills that include the use of word processing, spreadsheet, and presentation software.

Successful Training Managers share several personality traits such as being organized, flexible, adaptable, analytical, creative, and self-motivated.

Unions/Associations

Training Managers can join local, state, and national professional associations to take advantage of professional resources, training programs, networking opportunities, and other services. Two organizations that many training professionals join are:

- American Society for Training and Development
- International Society for Performance Improvement

Tips for Entry

1. Before going to a job interview, learn all that you can about the employer and its training department. Think of a few things you could do to strengthen or improve the department.
2. Network with colleagues and employers (including former employers) to learn about current and upcoming job vacancies.
3. You can use the Internet to learn about job vacancies throughout the United States. One source for job listings is the American Society for Training and Development web site (*http:www.astd.org*). Other sources are on-line job banks such as America's Job Bank (*http://www.careerkit.org/seeker*). To find specific information about an employer, enter the employer's name in a search engine to see if it has its own web site. On an employer's web site, look for a link such as "employment opportunities" or "human resources department."

INDEPENDENT INSTRUCTORS

MUSIC TEACHER (STUDIO OWNER)

CAREER PROFILE

Duties: Teach private music instrument or vocal lessons to children and adults; develop curriculum and lesson plans; perform small business responsibilities; perform other duties as required

Alternate Titles: Voice Teacher; a title, such as Piano Teacher, Flute Teacher, or Accordion Teacher, that reflects the type of instrument being taught

Salary Range: $13,000 to $47,000

Employment Prospects: Good

Advancement Prospects: Limited

Prerequisites:
　Licensure/Certification—None required
　Education/Training—Extensive music training in the types of vocal and instrumental instruction being offered
　Experience—Broad background in music with performance skills; teaching experience is helpful
　Special Skills and Personality Traits—Communication, interpersonal, motivational, organizational, time management, public relations, customer services, and small business skills; friendly, patient, calm, flexible, enthusiastic, trustworthy, creative, resourceful

CAREER LADDER

Owner of Larger Studio or School Music Teacher or Professor

↑

Independent Music Teacher

↑

Music Teacher

Position Description

Independent Music Teachers operate their own studios, offering private music lessons to children and adults. Many different independent Music Teachers provide instruction for the various types of instruments—violin, bass, guitar, flute, clarinet, saxophone, trumpet, trombone, tuba, percussion, accordion, harp, organ, electronic keyboards, and so on. Some private teachers offer vocal or singing instruction. In addition, many instructors specialize in teaching particular types of music such as jazz, classical, country, Afro-Cuban, or Latin. Some also offer instruction in music theory or music history.

Music Teachers provide individual and group lessons to beginning, intermediate, and advanced students. In group lessons, students are generally at the same skill level. Most teachers work out of their homes or in rented facilities. Some provide lessons in students' homes.

Independent Music Teachers are responsible for developing their own curriculum—the skills that they teach, the order for teaching the skills, the musical pieces that students practice, and so on. Teachers also create lesson plans and compile a repertoire of musical pieces which they assign to their students. Many instructors base their instruction on one or more method books, which consist of established, graded curriculum developed by recognized music educators. (For example, one method book that some piano teachers use is the *Frances Clark Library for Piano Students*.) Some Music Teachers also integrate technology, such as electronic keyboards and music instruction software, into their curriculum.

Students receive weekly lessons that are usually 30 to 60 minutes long. Within a lesson, Music Teachers review the previous week's lesson and teach a new lesson which builds on students' prior learning. They assign students new musical pieces that best match students' abilities, skill levels, and personal interests.

Music Teachers encourage their students to practice as much as possible during the week, and may help them establish a workable practice schedule. Many Music Teachers hold student recitals so that students can experience performing their music before the public. With intermediate and advanced students, Music Teachers might schedule performances for senior centers, child care centers, or other organizations.

As music studio owners, independent Music Teachers establish policies for their businesses. For example, they determine:

- the maximum number of students they will teach
- the number of weeks for a class term
- what ages, skill levels, and other criteria by which they will accept new students
- how students should pay their fees
- when students must notify them to cancel lessons
- how many make-up lessons they will allow, if any, for absent students
- if they will accept new students on an ongoing basis or at the start of class terms
- specific reasons why they would drop students

Furthermore, independent Music Teachers are responsible for running their own businesses. This includes scheduling students, collecting students' fees, keeping accurate records, doing bookkeeping, paying bills, cleaning and maintaining studio space, locating rental space, if necessary, and so on. They also continually look for ways to bring in new students. In addition, they need to set time aside for answering phone calls from prospective students.

Making a steady income from private instruction is difficult, thus many Music Teachers look for additional means of income. For example, some teachers offer music classes through continuing education programs sponsored by community centers, schools, and colleges. Many teach music classes for public and private schools, colleges, music schools, music stores, or other music studios. Furthermore, some Music Teachers have part-time or full-time jobs as secretaries, bus drivers, sales clerks, customer service representatives, warehouse workers, and so on.

Music Teachers have flexible work hours. They determine which days and the number of hours each day that they wish to work. They often schedule lessons during evenings and on weekends to accommodate the work or school schedules of their pupils.

Salaries

An independent Music Teacher's earnings are based on lesson fees, which generally range from $10 to $80 or more per lesson. The rates depend on their geographic location, the demand for their type of music instruction, and what the local community is willing to pay for lessons. For example, a private piano teacher in Cincinnati might charge $25 per lesson while a piano teacher in Washington, D.C., might charge $85 per lesson.

Annual earnings would depend on the total number of lessons and students who are taught during a year. As small business owners, independent instructors subtract business costs from their annual earnings. According to the U.S. Bureau of Labor Statistics, the 1998 estimated annual salary for most nonvocational educational instructors (which includes independent Music Teachers) ranged from $13,080 to $47,430.

Employment Prospects

Within any given community, opportunities for independent Music Teachers depend on the local demand for the types of music lessons that they offer, as well as the number of teachers within the area who provide similar music lessons. Private Music Teachers are usually in greater demand in rural areas, areas that are experiencing a rapid increase in population, and in communities that lack comprehensive music programs within their public schools.

Advancement Prospects

Advancement opportunities are defined by an individual's own interests and ambitions. Many independent Music Teachers realize advancement through job satisfaction, professional recognition, and the growth of their music studios.

Those wishing more job and financial security can pursue music education careers in public or private schools, music schools, colleges, and universities. Depending on the institutional setting, they may need to obtain additional education and teaching credentials.

Licensure/Certification

No state licensure or professional certification is required to become a private Music Teacher.

Education and Training

College degrees are not required to become an independent Music Teacher; however, many instructors have bachelor's or advanced degrees in music, education, or other related fields. Music Teachers without degrees should have an expansive knowledge of music. In addition they have extensive music training in the types of vocal and instrumental instruction they plan to offer.

Independent instructors are responsible for their own professional development in both the study of music and in teaching. They read music education journals and books, enroll in music classes and workshops, join professional associations, network with colleagues, and so on.

Experience, Skills, and Personality Traits

Independent Music Teachers should have a broad music background that includes several years of experience performing their instruments in public or private settings. Having teaching experience is helpful, whether formally or informally. For example, Music Teachers may have taught music classes for music stores. In addition, Music Teachers who plan to teach children should have a genuine love of children.

To work well with students, independent Music Teachers should have excellent communication, interpersonal, and motivational skills. As business owners, they should have adequate organizational, time management, public relations, customer services, and small business skills.

Successful independent Music Teachers have several personality traits in common, such as being friendly, patient, calm, flexible, enthusiastic, trustworthy, creative, and resourceful. Above all, they are passionate about teaching the joy of music to children and adults.

Unions/Associations

Independent Music Teachers join the Music Teachers National Association and other national, state, or local professional organizations to take advantage of continuing education programs, networking opportunities, and other services. Many also join professional organizations that serve their specific music fields.

Tips for Entry

1. To enhance your credibility as a professional music educator, you might obtain the Nationally Certified Teacher of Music certification, granted by the Music Teachers National Association (MTNA). For more information, contact: MTNA, The Carew Tower, 441 Vine Street, Suite 505, Cincinnati, Ohio 45202-2814. Or call: (513) 421-1420. Or visit its web site at *http://www.mtna.org*.
2. Define your teaching philosophy. Knowing why you want to teach and what you want your students to achieve and to learn is important to your business. Your teaching philosophy guides the development of your curriculum, teaching methods, and teaching styles. It also becomes part of how you advertise your business.
3. Some Music Teachers suggest that one way of advertising your business is to do this: expose your musical talent to your community. Many people are more likely to take music lessons from a teacher whom they have heard perform. Thus, for example, you might volunteer to play for your church or to perform at local community events.
4. The Internet has many resources available for independent Music Teachers, including the ability to network with colleagues across the nation. To get a list of relevant web sites, enter any of these keywords in a search engine: "private music teacher," "private music teaching," or "private music instruction."

DANCE INSTRUCTOR

CAREER PROFILE

Duties: Provide private dance lessons to children and adults; prepare lessons; perform duties of operating a business (if a studio owner); perform other duties as required

Alternate Title: A title, such as Ballroom Dance Teacher, that reflects the form of dance being taught

Salary Range: $13,000 to $47,000

Employment Prospects: Good

Advancement Prospects: Limited

Prerequisites:
    Licensure/Certification—None required
    Education/Training—Several years of dance training in chosen discipline; apprenticeship as a dance teacher
    Experience—Solid performance foundation; broad life experiences; teaching experience or equivalent training
    Special Skills and Personality Traits—Communication, interpersonal, motivational, customer services, organizational, management, and leadership skills; small business and public relations skills (if studio owners); friendly, positive, caring, enthusiastic, energetic, calm, patient, creative

CAREER LADDER

Dance Studio Owner

↑

Independent Dance Teacher

↑

Apprentice or Teaching Assistant

Position Description

Independent Dance Teachers provide dance lessons to students of all ages, from preschoolers to senior citizens. Working for themselves or for private dance studios or schools, Dance Teachers teach one of more forms of dance—ballet, tap dance, jazz dance, line dancing, ballroom dancing, social dancing, Hawaiian dance, country Scottish dancing, belly dancing, Latin dances, swing dance, square dancing, modern dance, folk dances, and so on. Many independent Dance Teachers also offer dance classes to adults through continuing education programs sponsored by community centers, adult schools, colleges, or other organizations.

Instructors teach beginning, intermediate, and advanced students on a group basis. Dance instruction is once a week, and may be 30 to 90 minutes long, depending on the skill level of the students. Upon request, Dance Teachers provide individual coaching to amateur and professional dancers, as well as offer private lessons to students of all abilities.

Dance Teachers create curriculum plans for their studios, or, if they are employees, assist in curriculum development. All Dance Teachers prepare for their classes, creating formal or informal lesson plans. They choose dances and music that match the ages, abilities, and interests of their students, and gather all necessary materials and equipment for their lessons. If musicians will be providing music for the lessons, then teachers must let the musicians know what songs to play, and may need to provide them with music scores.

Instructors teach classes according to the methods and philosophy of their studios, but Dance Teachers each bring their own teaching styles to their lessons. In general, lessons begin with warm-ups and a review of learned skills. Teachers then demonstrate new steps and movements, which are built upon their students' previous lessons.

Dance Teachers observe students as they practice, giving them individual attention to help them execute new steps and movements correctly. Teachers also make sure that students are standing and moving properly so as to prevent injuries.

Dance Teachers give students positive feedback throughout their lessons. Teachers also encourage students to practice their steps as often as they can throughout the week.

Independent Dance Teachers who own studios have the responsibility of operating their businesses. Whether they run their studios from their homes or rented facilities, they develop studio policies on matters such as tuition payments and make-up classes for absent students. As business owners, Dance Teachers are in charge of arranging class schedules, collecting fees, paying bills, keeping accurate records, cleaning and maintaining studio space, and so on. If they have additional teachers working for them, they provide them with ongoing supervision and training. Studio owners also continually look for ways to bring in new students.

Independent Dance Teachers have flexible hours, often teaching classes on evenings and weekends to accommodate the work and school schedules of their students.

Salaries

Independent teachers who own studios generally earn more than those working for other studios. According to the U.S. Bureau of Labor Statistics, the 1998 estimated annual salary for most nonvocational educational instructors, including independent Dance Teachers ranged from $13,080 to $47,430.

Employment Prospects

In general, the competition for teaching positions in private dance studios is high. The opportunities are better for Dance Teachers who own studios. Their success as studio owners depends on factors such as the local demand for the types of dance lessons that they offer, the number of teachers within the area who provide similar dance lessons, and how well individual teachers run their businesses.

Advancement Prospects

Dance Instructors can become instructors in public and private schools, colleges, and universities with the appropriate educational training. To teach in public schools may require teaching credentials. Instructors who are interested in more administrative duties can pursue management positions in larger dance studios. For many Dance Instructors, the ultimate goal is to have their own dance studios.

Licensure/Certification

No state licensure or certification is required to become a Dance Instructor.

Education and Training

College degrees are not required for becoming independent Dance Teachers; however, many do have bachelor's or advanced degrees in dance or related fields. In general, Dance Teachers have had several years of serious training in their discipline. In addition, most had served as apprentice teachers or obtained the appropriate training to teach their particular forms of dance.

Dance Teachers are responsible for continuing their professional growth. This includes maintaining their dance skills, as well as keeping up with developments in dance teaching pedagogy.

Experience, Skills, and Personality Traits

Along with a solid foundation in the performance of their discipline, Dance Teachers have broad life experiences upon which to draw in order to reach the different abilities and personalities of their students. In addition, Dance Instructors have previous teaching experience or appropriate training in dance education.

To do their work effectively, Dance Teachers need excellent communication, interpersonal, motivational, customer services, organizational, management, and leadership skills. As studio owners, they should also have adequate small business and public relations skills.

Successful Dance Teachers have several personality traits in common, such as being friendly, positive, caring, enthusiastic, energetic, calm, patient, and creative.

Unions/Associations

The Dance Educators of America, the National Dance Association, and the American Dance Guild are some national professional organizations that many independent Dance Teachers join. By joining these national associations and other national, state, or local professional organizations, Dance Teachers can take advantage of continuing education programs, networking opportunities, and other professional services. Dancing Teachers also join professional organizations that serve their particular dance discipline.

Tips for Entry

1. Contact dance studios directly to learn about possible upcoming job vacancies. Also check out advertisements and want ads in local newspapers, including free newspapers published by community centers, art centers, and other organizations.
2. If you plan on becoming a studio owner, take one or two small business courses. Many dance studios fail because Dance Teachers could not handle the business end effectively.
3. You can use the Internet to find general information about dance education, private dance studios, education programs, and so on. To get a list of relevant web sites, enter any of these keywords in a search engine: "dance education," "dance teacher," or "dance studio."

RIDING INSTRUCTOR

CAREER PROFILE

Duties: Provide riding and horsemanship lessons to children and adults; perform duties of operating a business (if a business owner); perform other duties as required

Salary Range: $13,000 to $47,000

Employment Prospects: Good

Advancement Prospects: Limited

Prerequisites:
  Licensure/Certification—None required
  Education/Training—Apprenticeship under experienced instructors
  Experience—Competent rider; solid foundation in horsemanship and horse care
  Special Skills and Personality Traits—Leadership, organizational, management, communication, interpersonal, and customer service skills; if owners—small business and public relations skills; friendly, enthusiastic, flexible, patient, caring, energetic, responsible

CAREER LADDER

Riding School Manager or Owner

Riding Instructor

Apprentice or Intern

Position Description

Independent Riding Instructors provide private horseback riding lessons to children, teenagers, and adults. In group or individual sessions, Riding Instructors teach students of all riding skill levels—beginning, intermediate, and advanced. They teach individuals how to ride their horses properly and safely, and how to give their horses the appropriate commands to go, stop, walk, change directions, trot, gallop, jump, and so forth. Riding Instructors teach lessons for one or more different types of riding activities—such as English-style or Western-style pleasure riding, trail riding, long distance riding, dressage, hunt seat riding, vaulting, barrel racing. Some instructors also teach carriage driving.

Riding Instructors might work for riding schools, horse farms, horse stables, dude ranches, or other horse-related businesses. Many Riding Instructors have their own establishments. Some Riding Instructors consider teaching their primary focus, while others teach riding lessons as part of the overall horse training services that they provide customers. (Many Riding Instructors also continue to participate in horse shows and riding competitions.)

Riding Instructors develop a teaching philosophy upon which they build their curriculum and lessons as well as their teaching methods and techniques. They teach lessons that are appropriate to the skill levels and abilities of their students. Beginning students, for example, learn basic horsemanship skills, such as correct riding posture; proper mounting and dismounting; and hand, leg, and voice commands. They also learn how to saddle their horses and prepare them for riding as well as to care for their horses and equipment afterward. Riding Instructors build up students' riding skills slowly and ensure that students learn proper and safe practices and use them as they develop their riding proficiency.

Many Riding Instructors perform other nonteaching duties. They help with the feeding, grooming, exercising, and care of horses. They may help with maintaining stables and grounds. They may also assist with administrative tasks such as answering phones and keeping accurate records of their students' progress.

Independent Riding Instructors who own riding schools have the responsibility of operating their businesses. They develop school policies on matters such as student requirements, tuition payments, and make-up classes for absent students. As business owners, they are in charge of arranging schedules, collecting fees, paying bills and taxes, cleaning and maintaining stables and office space, and so on. They are also responsible for providing staff members with ongoing training and supervision. In addition, Riding Instructors continually look for ways to bring in new students.

Riding Instructors work part time or full time, often teaching classes on weekends to accommodate students' work or school schedules.

Salaries

Salaries vary and depend on such factors as job duties and geographical location. Salaried instructors generally earn between $7 to $15 per hour while business owners may earn up to $50 or more per hour. According to the U.S. Bureau of Labor Statistics, most nonvocational educational instructors (which includes independent Riding Instructors) earned an estimated annual salary between $13,080 and $47,430 in 1998.

Employment Prospects

Job opportunities for staff positions become available as individuals retire, resign, or advance to other positions. In general employment is good for part-time Riding Instructors due to the high turnover rate.

The success rate for Riding Instructors who wish to open riding schools depends on factors such as the local demand for the types of riding lessons that they offer; the number of teachers within the area who provide similar lessons; and how well individual teachers run their businesses.

Advancement Prospects

Advancement opportunities are limited. In large riding schools or stables, Riding Instructors may advance to lead and administrative positions. The ultimate goal for some Riding Instructors is to have their own riding schools or riding stables.

Riding Instructors can pursue other careers in the horse industry, by becoming horse trainers, farriers, or equine veterinarians, for example.

Licensure/Certification

No state licensure or certification is required for Riding Instructors at the recreational or show ring competition level.

Education and Training

There is no minimum educational requirement to become Riding Instructors, although they should have at least a high school diploma or general equivalency diploma. However, Riding Instructors typically complete internships or apprenticeships under experienced Riding Instructors.

Riding Instructors are responsible for their own professional growth through self-study and further training under master Riding Instructors. In addition, Riding Instructors participate in professional associations, attend professional conferences, and network with colleagues.

Experience, Skills, and Personality Traits

Riding Instructors are competent riders and have a solid foundation in horsemanship, including stable management, basic veterinary care, and an understanding of the psychology of the horse. Additionally, they are physically fit and have the stamina and endurance to perform their work well.

To do their work well, Riding Instructors need leadership, organizational, management communication, interpersonal, and customer service skills. If they are business owners, they also need strong small business and public relations skills.

Successful Riding Instructors share several personality traits such as being friendly, enthusiastic, flexible, patient, caring, energetic, and responsible. They love horses and enjoy teaching people how to ride and handle horses.

Unions/Associations

Many Riding Instructors join local, state, and national professional organizations to take advantage of professional resources, certification programs, networking opportunities, and other professional services. Two national organizations that serve Riding Instructors are the American Association of Riding Schools and the American Riding Instructors Association. Additionally, Riding Instructors join various other organizations that serve the horse industry such as the American Horse Council or the Horse Industry Alliance. Many also join organizations that provide support to riders of specific horse breeds or riding activities.

Tips for Entry

1. Many 4-H organizations provide opportunities for young people to obtain academic and practical training in horsemanship, as well as experience in competition activities.
2. Contact local riding stables or horse farms directly about internship or apprenticeship positions.
3. To enhance your professional status, you might obtain instructor certification that is granted by a nationally recognized professional organization. One such organization is the American Riding Instructors Association. For more information, write to: 28801 Trenton Court, Bonita Springs, FL 34134. Or call: (941) 948-3232. Or visit its web site at *http://www.win.net/~aria.*
4. Use the Internet to learn more about the Riding Instructors, as well as the horse industry, in general. To get a list of pertinent web sites, enter any of these key words in a search engine: "riding instruction," "riding instructor," or "horse industry."

FLIGHT INSTRUCTOR (FREELANCE)

CAREER PROFILE

Duties: Provide instruction for private flying lessons; perform duties of operating a freelance business; perform other duties as required

Alternative Titles: Certified Flight Instructor, Authorized Flight Instructor

Salary Range: $12,000 to $41,000

Employment Prospects: Good

Advancement Prospects: Good

Prerequisites:

    Licensure/Certification—FAA flight instructor certification; certified endorsement for each type of instruction being provided

    Education/Training—High school diploma; flight training as a commercial pilot with instrument ranking or as an airline transport pilot

    Experience—Experienced pilot; teaching experience or equivalent training

    Special Skills and Personality Traits—Communication, interpersonal, motivational, leadership, public relations, small business, organizational, management, and self-management skills; patient, calm, flexible, responsible, creative, enthusiastic, energetic, independent

CAREER LADDER

```
┌─────────────────────────────────┐
│      Commercial Pilot           │
│   or Flight School Owner        │
│  or Career with flight schools  │
│    or fixed base operators      │
└─────────────────────────────────┘

┌─────────────────────────────────┐
│   Freelance Flight Instructor   │
└─────────────────────────────────┘

┌─────────────────────────────────┐
│             Pilot               │
└─────────────────────────────────┘
```

Position Description

Freelance Flight Instructors teach private flying lessons to people who want to become pilots. Normally working in small airports, they teach students how to fly single-engine planes, multiengine planes, helicopters, seaplanes, gliders, balloons, or airships. They provide both ground and flight instruction that students must complete to obtain pilot certificates, which are granted by the Federal Aviation Administration (FAA).

The instructors develop their own course outlines, using FAA *Practice Test Standards* as their guidelines. They teach essential concepts and skills that individuals must know and master in order to become safe and competent pilots. In general, Flight Instructors cover subjects such as aerodynamics, aircraft construction, airport operations, navigation, weather, preflight preparation, cockpit management, safety, and federal aviation regulations. They teach students specific procedures and maneuvers such as preflight procedures, taxiing, takeoff, landing, turns, instrument maneuvers, navigating by landmarks, and postflight procedures. They create simulated emergency situations (such as becoming lost or going into a tailspin) so that students can recognize problems and know what emergency procedures to perform.

Like all teachers, Flight Instructors prepare lesson plans, instructional activities, and study materials. They provide instruction at a pace that fits the abilities and learning styles of their students, as well as use a variety of teaching methods to reinforce students' learning.

Flight Instructors sign off on the appropriate document for students to obtain their student pilot certificates when they are ready for solo flights. Flight Instructors monitor each student's progress and determine when a student is competent to pass the required test for the pilot certificate or rating that the student is seeking.

Furthermore, freelance Flight Instructors are responsible for running their own businesses. This includes collecting students' fees, keeping accurate records, doing bookkeeping, paying bills, and so on. They also continually look for ways to bring in new students.

Flight Instructors work long and irregular hours. They schedule ground school classes and flight lessons at times that are convenient for their students. In addition, instructors' work hours are dependent on the weather. They generally work more hours during the summer months and on any weekend when the weather is clear and calm for flying.

Salaries

Earnings are based on students' fees which Flight Instructors usually charge by the hour. Their annual earnings depend on such factors as student fees, their total number of instructional hours, and geographical location. According to Airline Employment Assistance Corps, Flight Instructors earn between $12,300 and $40,530 per year.

Employment Prospects

Besides being freelancers, Flight Instructors can be salaried employees of flight schools or of fixed base operators, retail firms that sell general aviation products or services at airports, such as gas, aircraft service.

Currently, the airline industry is experiencing an increasing demand for qualified airline pilots, which is expected to continue for several years. As more Flight Instructors become airline pilots, the demand for experienced Flight Instructors should increase as well. (While they teach, Flight Instructors accumulate the required minimum number of flight hours for entry-level pilot positions with airlines and corporations.)

Advancement Prospects

Flight Instructors can advance according to their interests and ambition. Many become airline or commercial pilots. Those wishing to work in flight schools or fixed base operators can advance to management and administrative positions. With additional education, Flight Instructors may teach in aviation programs at colleges and universities. Airlines also have training departments in which Flight Instructors can pursue their careers. For many career Flight Instructors, the ultimate goal is to become freelancers or to have their own flight schools.

Licensure/Certification

Instructors must hold the appropriate FAA flight-instructor certificate for each type of flight instruction—such as multiengine, instrument, commercial, glider, or helicopter instruction—that they wish to offer students. To learn more about the specific requirements for the different types of flight-instructor certificates, contact the FAA. Write to: 800 Independence Avenue SW, Washington, D.C. 20591. Or visit its web site at *http://www.faa.gov*

Education and Training

The minimum educational requirement for Flight Instructors is a high school diploma, but many Flight Instructors do have bachelor's or advanced degrees in various fields. (A college degree is generally required or preferred for commercial and airline pilot positions.)

In order to become a Flight Instructor, an individual must first complete required flight training for becoming a commercial pilot with instrument ranking or an airline transport pilot. Having a teaching background or training is helpful.

Freelance Flight Instructors are responsible for their own professional development. They participate in professional associations, network with colleagues, enroll in training workshops, read professional journals, and so on.

Experience, Skills, and Personality Traits

Flight Instructors are experienced pilots. They have the appropriate knowledge and skills proficiency in the flight rankings that they are teaching—such as recreational pilot, commercial pilot, multiple engine, or glider.

To work well with students, Flight Instructors need excellent communication, interpersonal, motivational, and leadership skills. To be successful freelancers, they need adequate small business, public relations, organizational, and management skills. In addition, they have solid self-management skills—the ability to work well under pressure, make sound judgments, follow directions, and so on.

Successful Certified Flight Instructors share several personality traits such as being patient, calm, flexible, responsible, creative, enthusiastic, and energetic.

Unions/Associations

Many Flight Instructors join national, state, and local professional organizations to take advantage of networking opportunities, training programs, and other professional services. The National Association of Flight Instructors and the Aircraft Owners and Pilots Association are two national associations available to Flight Instructors.

Tips for Entry

1. You can start gaining experience working in the aviation field at an early age. Many airlines and fixed base operators hire young people for part-time and summer jobs.
2. The Internet offers many resources. To find relevant web sites, enter any of these keywords into a search engine: "flight instructor," "flight instruction," or "flying lessons."

FITNESS AND RECREATION PROFESSIONALS

AEROBICS INSTRUCTOR

CAREER PROFILE

Duties: Teach group exercise classes; design exercise routines set to music; provide students with encouragement and motivation; perform other duties as required

Alternate Titles: Group Exercise Instructor, Fitness Instructor, Dance Exercise Instructor, Aqua Aerobics Instructor

Salary Range: $12,000 to $48,000

Employment Prospects: Good

Advancement Prospects: Limited

Prerequisites:

Licensure/Certification—Certified by an employer or nationally recognized professional fitness association; CPR certification may be required

Education/Training—Bachelor's degree is desirable; completion of a training program that leads to certification

Experience—One or more years taking aerobics classes; aerobic instructor internship or apprenticeship

Special Skills and Personality Traits—Leadership, communication, interpersonal, motivational, public speaking, organizational, management, and customer service skills; friendly, caring, enthusiastic, observant, confident, energetic, creative

CAREER LADDER

Program Director or Owner

↑

Aerobics Instructor

↑

Intern or Assistant Instructor

Position Description

Every day, hundreds of women and men throughout the United States attend aerobics classes to maintain or improve their fitness and health. These are group exercise classes in which Aerobics Instructors, fitness professionals, lead students through exercise routines that are set to music. The exercises are especially designed to exercise the body's large muscle groups (such as those of the stomach and legs) and to increase the cardiovascular system's ability to deliver oxygen more quickly and efficiently to the body.

Aerobics Instructors teach different types of group exercise classes. The most familiar is the aerobics class, which includes common exercises and dance movements. Many instructors also teach classes that include the use of step platforms or slide boards with the exercises. Some Aerobics Instructors incorporate boxing or martial arts movements into exercise routines. Some instructors teach classes that involve a different type of aerobic exercise such as yoga. Others may lead group exercise classes in swimming pools.

Designing exercise classes is usually the responsibility of individual Aerobics Instructors. They make sure the classes are fun and safe, as well as interesting and challenging. They create exercise routines that students of different abilities can perform and can easily follow. Additionally, they choose different kinds of music that match the movements or steps of the different exercises, and that motivate students to perform the exercises. Some Aerobics Instructors specialize in developing aerobics classes for special groups such as pregnant women, elderly persons, or physically disabled individuals.

Aerobic classes are 30 to 90 minutes long, depending on the class level—beginning, intermediate, or advanced—and the type of students. The format is generally the same for all classes, with exercises divided into the following segments:

- warm-up exercises, which include stretching exercises and full body movements to prepare muscles for aerobics
- aerobic exercises—knee lifts, leg kicks, light jogging, calisthenics, dance movements, and so on
- muscle toning and strength exercises for large muscle groups such as legs and stomach
- cool-down exercises, which are less intense movements, and stretches to reduce the heart rate and decrease the flow of blood to the heart

Instructors introduce each new exercise by explaining its benefits to the body and demonstrating the proper way to do it. They watch students do the steps to ensure that they are doing them correctly. Instructors then lead students through the exercise routine, giving students verbal and nonverbal cues for what to do, how to do it, and when to do it. For example, an instructor might direct students to do four more leg lifts on the right leg, then turn and do leg lifts on the left leg.

Aerobics Instructors also monitor students' progress to make sure they are doing techniques safely and properly. During the aerobics segment, Instructors have students monitor their heart rates to ensure that they are not overworking their hearts. In addition, Aerobics Instructors give out constant encouragement and positive feedback to their students to motivate them onward to finish one more repetition, one more exercise, and finally one more class.

Many Aerobics Instructors are self-employed. They might work for one or more organizations on a contractual basis. Some teach private classes in rented facilities or through continuing education programs sponsored by schools, colleges, or community centers. As independent contractors, Aerobics Instructors perform various administrative tasks such as collecting student fees, sending out invoices, paying bills and taxes, keeping accurate business records, doing bookkeeping, and so on.

Aerobics Instructors work part time or full time. Their hours are flexible to accommodate the schedules of their students. Instructors may teach classes in the early morning, evenings, and on the weekends.

Salaries

Salaries vary, depending on factors such as type of employer and geographic location.

According to the U.S. Bureau of Labor Statistics, the 1998 estimated annual salary for most sports and physical training instructors and coaches ranged from $11,850 to $48,050.

Salaried employees may receive fringe benefits such as sick leave and medical insurance.

Employment Prospects

Aerobics Instructors work for various employers such as health clubs, aerobic exercise companies, resorts, community centers and senior centers. Some instructors work for large residential complexes or corporations that have fitness facilities. Many Aerobics Instructors are independent contractors or own aerobics instruction companies.

The job market for Aerobics Instructors is favorable due to people's increasing interest in the benefits of preventative health measures through sensible nutrition and exercise plans.

Advancement Prospects

Advancement opportunities are limited to program managers and directors. Many Aerobics Instructors realize advancement through job satisfaction and professional reputation.

Aerobics Instructors can also pursue other fitness careers by becoming exercise physiologists, physical therapists, physical education teachers, athletic trainers, or fitness consultants.

Licensure/Certification

No state licensure or certification is required to become an Aerobics Instructor.

Most employers require that Aerobics Instructors hold proper certification for each type of aerobics that they teach. Instructors may be required to hold certification from a specific professional fitness organization, such as the American Fitness Professionals and Associates, or pass their employers' own certification process.

To obtain certification or employment, Aerobics Instructors may be required to obtain CPR (cardiopulmonary resuscitation) certification.

Education and Training

The minimum educational requirement varies from employer to employer. However, more employers are preferring or requiring that Instructors have bachelor's degrees in exercise science, physical education, or other related fields.

To become certified professionals, Aerobics Instructors must successfully complete all training programs that lead to certification. Training workshops cover theoretical knowledge and practical skills that instructors need to teach a particular form of aerobic instruction. Anatomy, physiology, injury prevention, sequencing, and cueing are some topics that are covered within training programs.

Employers provide training on the job. In addition, Aerobics Instructors pursue their own professional growth through self-study, networking with colleagues, joining professional associations, participating in professional conferences, and so on.

Experience, Skills, and Personality Traits

In general, Aerobics Instructors should have at least one year of experience taking aerobics classes, dance, or related fitness activities. They should also have completed an internship or apprenticeship under experienced, certified Aerobics Instructors.

In order to work well with their students, Aerobics Instructors need excellent leadership, communication, interpersonal, motivational, and public speaking skills. They should also have strong organizational, management, and customer service skills.

Successful Aerobics Instructors share several personality traits such as being friendly, caring, enthusiastic, observant, confident, energetic, and creative.

Unions/Associations

Aerobics Instructors usually join local, state, and national professional associations to take advantage of professional resources, certification programs, continuing education programs, networking opportunities, and other professional services. Some of the various professional associations are:

- Aerobics and Fitness Association of America
- American Council on Exercise
- American Fitness Professionals and Associates
- IDEA, The Health and Fitness Source
- Aquatic Exercise Association
- National Dance-Exercise Instructors Training Association

Tips for Entry

1. Broaden your experiences to stay competitive in your field. Learn yoga, kickboxing, or other types of aerobic activities that interest you. Also take dance classes to pick up new dance steps and choreography skills. In addition, improve your teaching skills through self-study, networking, or classes.
2. There are different certification programs available. Be sure to choose one that best fits your needs. Talk with different Aerobics Instructors for their opinions about the different programs. Also talk to employers for whom you would like to work. Find out what kind of certification each employer would require.
3. Use the Internet to learn more about aerobics instruction. To get a list of relevant web sites to read, enter the keyword "aerobics" in any search engine.

PERSONAL TRAINER

CAREER PROFILE

Duties: Design personal fitness programs that meet individuals' fitness goals, skill levels, and interests; provide personalized training and support to clients; perform administrative duties (as independent consultants); perform other duties as required

Salary Range: $12,000 to $48,000

Employment Prospects: Good

Advancement Prospects: Limited

Prerequisites:
  Licensure/Certification—Personal Trainer certificate; state licensure, certification, or registration as a nutritionist may be required; CPR certification may be required
  Education/Training—Bachelor's degree is preferred
  Experience—An internship or apprenticeship; experience designing personal exercise plans and providing one-on-one training
  Special Skills and Personality Traits—Leadership, communication, interpersonal, motivational, organizational, management, and public speaking skills; (if independent consultants) public relations and small business skills; patient, friendly, caring, diplomatic, enthusiastic, observant, flexible, trustworthy

CAREER LADDER

Training Director or Business Owner

Personal Trainer

Intern or Trainee

Position Description

Personal Trainers are fitness professionals who help clients develop safe exercise programs that meet their individual goals for health and fitness; they also help clients stay motivated to reach their goals. Their clients may include business professionals, teachers, health care professionals, secretaries, athletes, senior citizens, pregnant women, and so on.

Personal Trainers start their working relationship with their clients by conducting an assessment interview. They discuss fitness goals, exercise history, and their clients' favorite fitness activities. They also discuss any health problems and health conditions—such as diabetes or heart disease—for which their clients may be at risk. (Personal Trainers normally request that their clients with existing health conditions provide them with a medical clearance from their physicians.) Personal Trainers also evaluate their clients' body composition and test their flexibility, strength, and endurance.

Individualized fitness programs are then designed with their clients' health, personal interests, abilities, and goals in mind. Programs may include training with free weights and resistance machines, as well as one or more forms of aerobics instruction (such as kickboxing, yoga, aerobic dance, low impact aerobics, or aqua aerobics).

To help their clients integrate fitness activity into their lifestyle, many Personal Trainers also incorporate their clients' favorite fitness activities into their exercise programs. These activities may include hiking, rollerblading, skiing, mountain climbing, cycling, kayaking, swimming, and so on.

Some Personal Trainers also provide nutritional counseling and design nutrition programs that fit their clients' goals. Usually these Personal Trainers are experienced nutritionists or registered dietitians.

Personal Trainers schedule hour-long training sessions with their clients, at least once or twice a week. They may work with clients in small groups or on an individual basis.

Some clients prefer to schedule training sessions in the privacy of their homes.

In training sessions, Personal Trainers demonstrate correct exercise techniques to avoid injury. They show their clients how to use free weights and equipment safely and properly. In addition, they answer general questions about exercise, fitness, health, and nutrition. For specific medical information, Personal Trainers refer their clients to the appropriate health professionals. Furthermore, Personal Trainers provide the right motivation to keep their various clients interested so that they come to their training sessions, complete their workouts, and successfully meet their fitness goals.

Personal Trainers are responsible for keeping up with new research and trends in the fitness field. They attend professional conferences and network with colleagues. They also enroll in continuing education classes and training workshops as well as read professional journals, magazines, and books.

Most Personal Trainers are independent consultants, and so perform various duties to successfully run their small businesses. They develop policies regarding payments, cancellations, and other important matters. They perform administrative duties such as collecting payments, paying bills and taxes, obtaining liability insurance, doing bookkeeping, and maintaining accurate business records. Furthermore, they continue to look for ways to bring in new clients.

Personal Trainers work flexible hours to accommodate their clients' schedules. Thus, they may hold training sessions during early mornings, late evenings, and weekends.

Salaries

Personal Trainers generally earn an hourly rate which depends on factors such as experience, location, and what their clients are willing to pay. Most Personal Trainers earn $25 to $100 or more per hour. According to the U.S. Bureau of Labor Statistics, the 1998 estimated annual salary for most physical training instructors and coaches (including personal trainers) ranged from $11,850 to $48,050.

Employment Prospects

Personal Trainers work for health clubs, gyms, resorts, community centers, residential complexes, corporations, and other employers as salaried employees or on a contractual basis. Many Personal Trainers have their own training facilities or work from their homes or clients' homes.

The job market for Personal Trainers is favorable, and may expand further due to the increasing number of people who want personal trainers to help them develop and maintain effective individualized exercise programs.

Advancement Prospects

As employees, Personal Trainers can advance to supervisory and management positions. The ultimate goal for many Personal Trainers is to become high-salaried independent contractors or have their own fitness facilities.

Many Personal Trainers realize advancement through job satisfaction, professional recognition, and higher earnings.

Licensure/Certification

No state licensure or certification is required to become Personal Trainers. In some states, Personal Trainers who provide nutritional counseling may be required to obtain state licensure, certification, or registration. (For specific information, contact your state licensing board for nutritionists and dietitians.)

Most employers require that Personal Trainers be certified by a recognized professional fitness organization, such as the American College of Sports Medicine. Completion of continuing education units is usually required to renew certifications.

To obtain certification or employment, Personal Trainers may be required to obtain CPR (cardiopulmonary resuscitation) certification.

Education and Training

The educational requirement varies from employer to employer. More and more employers are preferring or requiring that Personal Trainers have a bachelor's degree in exercise physiology, exercise science, physical education, or related fields. Also some professional associations require that applicants for certification have college degrees.

To become certified professionals, Personal Trainers must complete a training program that leads to certification. The training program generally covers both theoretical knowledge and practical skills on topics such as anatomy, exercise physiology, kinesiology, fitness assessments, exercise technique, nutrition, and injury prevention.

Experience, Skills, and Personality Traits

Personal Trainers generally complete an apprenticeship or internship under the tutelage of experienced, certified Personal Trainers. Novice Personal Trainers should have experience in designing safe exercise programs that meet individuals' needs, abilities, and interests. In addition, they should have experience providing one-on-one training, including the safe and proper use of free weights and resistance equipment.

To work well with their clients. Personal Trainers need excellent leadership, communication, interpersonal, motivational, organizational, management, and public speaking skills. Independent consultants also need strong public relations and small business skills to run a successful business.

Successful Personal Trainers share several personality traits such as being patient, friendly, caring, diplomatic, enthusiastic, observant, flexible, and trustworthy.

Unions/Associations

Most Personal Trainers join local, state, and national professional associations to take advantage of professional services such as resources, training programs, continuing education programs, and networking opportunities. Some of the various professional associations available to Personal Trainers are:

- Aerobics and Fitness Association of America
- American College of Sports Medicine
- American Council on Exercise
- IDEA, The Health and Fitness Source
- National Strength and Conditioning Association

Tips for Entry

1. Do your research about a gym before taking a job there. Spend some time there to see what the facilities are like as well as what the customers and the staff are like. Also be sure to find out if the gym would be covering you under its liability insurance plan, or if you need to get your own.
2. Use the Internet to learn more about the Personal Trainers profession. To find relevant web sites, enter the keywords "personal training fitness" or "personal trainer" in any search engine.

GUIDE

CAREER PROFILE

Duties: Conduct tours of an establishment or area; ensure the safety and comfort of a tour group; oversee all necessary arrangements for tour meals, lodging, and transportation; perform other duties as required

Alternate Titles: Tour Guide, Establishment Guide, Sightseeing Guide, Travel Guide, Travel Manager, Outdoors Guide, Adventure Guide, Fishing Guide

Salary Range: $12,000 to $60,000 or more per year

Employment Prospects: Good

Advancement Prospects: Limited

Prerequisites:
  Licensure/Certification—None required
  Education/Training—High school diploma or college degree
  Experience—Knowledgeable in the subject matter or locations where tours are led; have experience planning, managing, and supervising tour programs and activities
  Special Skills and Personality Traits—Leadership, interpersonal, conflict resolution, presentation, public speaking, organizational, and management skills; friendly, enthusiastic, patient, calm, tactful, diplomatic, reliable, energetic, resourceful, flexible, confident

CAREER LADDER

Senior Guide, or Business Owner

↑

Guide

↑

Trainee

Position Description

Guides conduct tours of a specific place for individuals and groups who are interested in learning more about it. Tours may be of a particular establishment, such as a candy factory, or of a specific area, such as a city or wilderness area. Guides follow specific routes, or itineraries, and stop at interesting points to tell participants facts and anecdotes about people, places, things, and events that are related to the establishment or locale.

Different Guides lead different types of tours. *Establishment Guides* lead short indoor or outdoor tours. They guide tourists through museums, zoos, gardens, parks, underground caves, historical houses, manufacturing plants, and other places of interest. At the end of their tours, they may recommend other interesting places to visit or special events that are happening in the area.

Sightseeing Guides conduct walking, limousine, or bus tours of a city or region, showing points of interest to tourists. For example, a Guide may lead a walking tour through his or her city's Chinatown, describing its history and pointing out important local landmarks.

Travel Guides (also known as *Tour Managers*) manage tours that cover several cities or countries over several days or weeks. For example, a Guide may supervise a group of tourists on a 10-day bus tour through northern Italy. Trips sometimes include a combination of cruise and land tours. In foreign tours, Guides may work with local guides.

Outdoor Guides conduct various types of day, overnight, and longer tours to parks, recreational areas, and the wilderness. Tours usually involve one or more outdoor activities such as bicycling, fishing, hunting, camping, backpacking, mountain climbing, kayaking, or rafting. For example, a Guide may be part of a week-long rafting tour down the Rio Grande. Outdoor Guides teach inexperienced members how to use equipment. They are also responsible for explaining relevant local hunting, fishing, and environmental laws and regulations to their tour groups. If they are camping in the wilderness, Outdoor Guides take care of all necessities such as preparing meals and disposing of waste.

Tour Guides are like hosts. They make sure that all group members are comfortable, safe, and enjoying themselves. They handle any unexpected situations that may arise such as injuries, discourteous group members, bad weather, or long lines. For overnight and long tours, Guides oversee all necessary arrangements and details for meals, lodging, and transportation.

Guides perform other duties, as required by their employers. For example, they might assist in planning new tours. They might help organize tours by making hotel reservations, contacting group members, or gathering information about special events. Guides might also write brochures or other written materials about the various tours that are offered.

They work part time or full time, and may be scheduled to work during weekends. Many sightseeing, outdoors, and travel guides work for one or more tour operators on a contractual basis. Independent contractors have the flexibility of choosing when they want to work and how many tours they wish to work in a year.

Salaries

Salaries vary, and depend on factors such as job responsibilities, type of employer, and job status (part time, full time, or freelance). According to the U.S. Bureau of Labor Statistics, the 1998 estimated annual salary for most Guides ranged from $11,540 to $24,830.

Tour managers of packaged and adventure tours may receive per diem wages, depending on whether they are employees, contractors, or business owners. Many earn between $60 to $200 per day, which includes gratuities (or tips). Skilled and popular Guides can make up to $60,000 or more per year. While on tours, Guides receive free lodging and meals.

Salaried employees may receive fringe benefits such as sick leave, health insurance, and pension plans.

Employment Prospects

Guides work for various employers including art galleries, museums, industrial establishments, historical sites, parks, tour bus companies, resorts, travel agencies, packaged tour operators, adventure tour companies, and so on. Many Guides work with tour operators on a contractual basis; some Guides operate their own businesses.

Most job opportunities become available to replace Guides who resign, advance to other positions, transfer to other locations, or retire.

According to the U.S. Bureau of Labor Statistics, travel is expected to grow through the year 2005 due to the increase in personal incomes and more people wishing to travel for recreation, education, and business reasons. In general, job opportunities in the travel industry fluctuate with the prosperity of the economy. For example, when the overall economy is in a recession, fewer people make travel plans.

Advancement Prospects

In major tour operations, Guides can advance to supervisory and management positions. For some Guides, the ultimate goal is to become freelancers or to have their own tour companies. Most Guides realize advancement through job satisfaction, professional reputation, and higher earnings.

Guides might also pursue other career paths in the travel industry by becoming travel agents, travel counselors, travel writers, resort social directors, or public relations officers with visitor and convention bureaus.

Licensure/Certification

No state licensure or certification is required to become a Guide.

Depending on the type of tour operations, employers may require that Guides have appropriate licensure, certification, or other documentation. For example, a Guide with a bus tour company may be required to hold a valid commercial driver's license in order to drive company vans during the tours. Guides who lead tours to foreign countries must have valid passports and may be required to hold appropriate work permits in the other countries.

Education and Training

Requirements vary from employer to employer. Some employers require only a high school diploma or high school equivalency diploma. Many employers prefer that Guides have bachelor's degrees in any field.

Employers provide Guides with training for their particular jobs.

Experience, Skills, and Personality Traits

Tour Guides generally have broad life experiences that enrich their abilities to provide participants with enjoyable and memorable tours. They are knowledgeable in the subject matter or locations for which they would be leading tours. In addition, they have experience in planning, managing, and supervising tour programs and activities.

Because they work with people extensively, Guides need strong leadership, interpersonal, conflict resolution, presentation, public-speaking, organizational, and management skills.

Successful Guides share several personality traits, such as being friendly, enthusiastic, patient, calm, tactful, diplomatic, reliable, energetic, resourceful, flexible, and confident.

Unions/Associations

Various local, state, and national professional associations are available for Guides, such as the National Tour Association, the International Association of Tour

Managers, the Ecotourism Society, and the Outdoor Guides Association. Through these different associations, members can take advantage of professional services such as professional resources, networking opportunities, and training programs.

Tips for Entry

1. Having a broad knowledge in art, history, geography, and literature is an advantage for obtaining jobs in this profession.
2. To gain work experience, you might volunteer as a guide with local museums or historical sites, or obtain internships with tour operators.
3. Learn a foreign language. Many employers particularly need Guides who speak French, German, Italian, Spanish, Japanese, Dutch, or Swedish.
4. Use the Internet to learn about various tour operators. To get a list of relevant web sites, enter any of these keywords in a search engine: "tour operator," "outdoor guides," or "ecotours."

ENVIRONMENTAL EDUCATORS AND ANIMAL TRAINERS

ENVIRONMENTAL EDUCATOR

CAREER PROFILE

Duties: Provide instruction about nature to the general public who visit zoos, nature centers, natural history museums, parks, and other informal settings; plan for classes, workshops, and presentations; perform other duties as required

Alternate Titles: Environmental Education Specialist, Naturalist, Park Interpreter

Salary Range: $16,000 to $28,000 (starting salary)

Employment Prospects: Fair

Advancement Prospects: Limited

Prerequisites:
  Licensure/Certification—None required
  Education/Training—Bachelor's degree; on-the-job training
  Experience—An environmental education background; teaching experience or training highly desired; have experience working with target audiences
  Special Skills and Personality Traits—Organizational, time management, writing, teamwork, communication, interpersonal, leadership, presentation, and computer skills; friendly, enthusiastic, responsible, reliable, flexible, self-motivated, creative

CAREER LADDER

Program Coordinator

↑

Environmental Educator

↑

Assistant Environmental Educator or Intern

Position Description

Environmental Educators work for environmental education programs in zoos, nature centers, natural history museums, biological gardens, parks, and other organizations. Their primary responsibility is to provide informal instruction about nature to the general public who visit their facilities. Environmental Educators also make guest presentations in school classrooms and community centers as well as at community events. Many Environmental Educators conduct hikes and nature walks in forests or deserts, through marshes or wetlands, along shorelines or reefs, on hillsides or mountains, and other natural settings.

Environmental Educators are responsible for planning their classes, workshops, and presentations. They try to provide their audiences with as much practical experience as possible. They use various multimedia tools, such as films, slide shows, and videos, to bring the world of nature alive to their lectures. They sometimes bring in rocks, fossils, plants, and animals for their audiences to experience. In addition, Environmental Educators plan hands-on activities that are age-appropriate and meet the interests and skill levels of their audiences.

Some environmental education programs offer curriculum and instruction support to schools, colleges, youth service groups, and community organizations. Public schools, for example, are mandated by federal law to provide students with instruction about the environment. Thus, some Environmental Educators conduct workshops for schoolteachers, demonstrating methods for enhancing their lessons about the environment.

Some Environmental Educators provide instruction to schoolchildren in week-long day camps or residential camps during the spring, summer, or fall. These camps may be based on land as well as on ships at sea. Environmental Educators teach about ecology, natural history, conservation, and other environmental topics. They lead students on hikes and nature walks as well as conduct recreational activities such as art, nature crafts, games, drama, and songs. Many Environmental Educators also provide instruction in outdoor living skills—reading a compass and map, building a fire, setting up a tent, using emergency procedures, and so forth.

Along with teaching, Environmental Educators perform many other tasks which vary from one educator to the next. For example, Environmental Educators might:

- set up and maintain educational exhibits
- answer general information inquiries about the facilities or environmental educational programs
- book and conduct tours of their facilities
- feed and water animals at their facilities
- clean animals' living areas
- maintain facilities and grounds
- assist with the development and evaluation of different classroom and field education programs
- assist with preparing grant proposals
- assist with training and supervising volunteers
- maintain records, and complete required reports and paperwork

Some Environmental Educators are required to reside at environmental centers to care for animals. Those working for residential environmental education programs are usually required to live at the camps as well.

Environmental Educators work part time or full time, which may include working evenings, weekends, and holidays.

Salaries

Salaries vary, and depend on such factors as experience, job responsibilities, and type of employer. Educators can generally earn more by working for employers in the private sector. Starting salaries typically range between $16,000 to $28,000 per year.

In addition, most Environmental Educators receive fringe benefits such as sick leave, vacation leave, medical insurance, and retirement benefits. Environmental Educators who work for residential environmental education programs receive room and board along with a weekly salary.

Employment Prospects

Environmental Educators work for environmental centers, zoos, museums, schools, colleges, universities, government agencies, conservation organizations, community organizations, corporations, and other institutions. Many also work for private enterprises that provide curriculum developmental services to schools and other organizations.

Environmental education is a relatively new field, and is still evolving. In general, the job market is competitive for both permanent and seasonal positions. Many jobs are based on the funding of grant proposals, and so may last only for a specific period of time.

Advancement Prospects

Environmental Educators can advance to supervisory and administrative positions, such as program coordinators and directors. Depending on their interests and ambitions, educators can pursue other environmental careers by becoming industrial hygienists, forest rangers, environmental engineers, researchers, environmental regulatory specialists, or environmental lawyers.

Licensure/Certification

No state licensure or certification is required to become Environmental Educators.

Education and Training

Most employers require that Environmental Educators hold a bachelor's degree in biology, animal sciences, natural resources, environmental science, education, outdoor education, or other related field. Some employers require or prefer candidates with master's degrees, but may waive the requirement if candidates have qualifying work experience.

Environmental Educators are trained on the job. They are also expected to continue their professional growth through self-study, enrollment in continuing education programs and training programs, networking with colleagues, participating in professional conferences, and so on.

Experience, Skills, and Personality Traits

In general, employers look for candidates who have a background in environmental education. Having teaching experience or training is highly desirable. Candidates should also have experience working with the target audience of the educational programs. (Most Environmental Educators work with K–12 students, so they should enjoy working with children.)

To do their work effectively, Environmental Educators need strong organizational, time management, writing, and teamwork skills. They also need excellent communication, interpersonal, leadership, and presentation skills to work well with the various people they meet. In addition, they should have computer skills, including the use of databases, spreadsheets, word processing, and desktop publishing.

Successful Environmental Educators share several personality traits, such as being friendly, enthusiastic, responsible, reliable, flexible, self-motivated, and creative.

Unions/Associations

Many Environmental Educators belong to local, state, and national professional organizations to take advantage of professional services such as training programs, networking opportunities, and professional resources. Some of the organizations that Environmental Educators might join are:

- North American Association for Environmental Education
- National Association of Environmental Professionals
- National Association for Humane and Environmental Education, a division of the Humane Society of the United States
- National Association for Interpretation

Environmental Educators also join conservation organizations, such as the Nature Conservancy, the National Wildlife Federation, or the Sierra Club.

Tips for Entry
1. Get involved in environmental projects at your school or college or in your community. Along with helping to maintain the environment, you will gain experience for a career in environmental education.
2. Start looking for summer positions in early spring. This is also the best time to search for post-graduation jobs, when you are a college senior.
3. Contact environmental organizations and professional associations in your area for job listings. Also check with college job placement centers and state employment agencies.
4. Enhance your employability by learning how to integrate technology into environmental education curriculum.
5. Learn more about environmental education on the Internet. To get a list of relevant web sites to read, enter any of these keywords in a search engine: "environment education" or "environment educator."

PARK NATURALIST

CAREER PROFILE

Duties: Plan, implement, and evaluate various interpretive programs and activities that teach about the geology, fauna, flora, and other natural features of city, county, state, and national parks; conduct presentations to park visitors; create exhibits and written materials; perform general park ranger duties; perform other duties as required

Alternate Title: Park Interpretive Naturalist

Salary Range: $19,000 to $33,000 (starting salaries in national parks)

Employment Prospects: Fair

Advancement Prospects: Limited

Prerequisites:
  Licensure/Certification—Driver's license and CPR and first aid certifications may be required
  Education/Training—Bachelor's degree
  Experience—One or more years providing naturalist interpretive work; knowledgeable of park flora and fauna
  Special Skills and Personality Traits—Teaching, organizational, project management, interpersonal, teamwork, writing, communication, presentation, public speaking, and leadership skills; outgoing, enthusiastic, calm, tolerant, flexible, observant, curious, creative, self-motivated, energetic

CAREER LADDER

Senior Naturalist

Park Naturalist

Seasonal Park Naturalist or Naturalist Aide or Intern

Position Description

Park Naturalists are park rangers who specialize in teaching the public about the natural resources in city, county, state, and national parks. As interpretive specialists, they use lectures, storytelling, displays of original objects, and audiovisual media to describe and discuss the geology, flora, fauna, and other natural wonders that are unique to their individual parks. Some Park Naturalists are responsible for operating and maintaining park nature centers.

Park Naturalists plan, implement, and evaluate various interpretive programs for park visitors. These include nature walks, trail hikes, nature crafts programs, campfire presentations, field trips, and so on. They also create natural exhibits in the museums, nature centers, or visitor centers that depict natural history and resources of their individual parks. They develop, create, and produce brochures, pamphlets, and other written materials about the fauna and flora of their parks, hiking trails, and so forth. Additionally, Park Naturalists prepare self-guiding trail markers to describe special features along the different park trails. To create accurate interpretations as well as develop educationally sound programs, Park Naturalists diligently conduct research on background materials.

Park Naturalists are also responsible for planning and conducting group presentations. Many give scheduled presentations at their park's visitor center or nature center. In addition, many Park Naturalists make guest presentations at schools, children's organizations, community clubs, senior citizen groups, conservation organizations, and other groups. During the summer, Park Naturalists who work in parks with campgrounds often give evening presentations to visiting campers.

Another duty is answering visitors' questions about their park's natural features, and sometimes historical features, on a daily basis. Park Naturalists answer individual questions in person, by phone, by mail, by fax, and by E-mail.

Park Naturalists also assist with park resource management. They help develop plans for new trails, additional campsites, landscaping, and so forth at their individual parks. Some Park Naturalists serve as technical advisers for area park agencies, which sometimes involves reviewing development and landscape plans for new and existing parks.

In addition, Park Naturalists perform a variety of administrative tasks. For example, they might maintain records and statistics about program participants and write required reports. Many Park Naturalists perform public relations duties to publicize park programs, activities, and special events. Some Park Naturalists hold supervisory positions, and thus provide training and guidance to other staff members, including park aides and volunteers.

Many Park Naturalists perform some of the duties of general park rangers. For example, they might:

- collect park entrance and camping fees
- provide visitors with general information about their parks including park laws, regulations, and rules; park services; water, air, or plant quality issues; appropriate camping practices; and so on
- conduct research projects, such as studying wildlife behavior or monitoring air quality in the park
- patrol a designated area in their parks, including the back country
- perform maintenance of trails and park grounds
- assist in emergency situations, such as firefighting and search and rescue missions

Park Naturalists may hold seasonal or permanent, part-time or full-time positions. They work flexible hours that may include evenings, weekends, and holidays.

Salaries

Salaries vary, and depend on factors such as education, experience, job responsibilities, type of employer, and geographical location. For example, the starting salaries for Park Naturalists in national parks ranged from $19,100 to $32,380 in 2000.

Depending on their job status, Park Naturalists may be able to receive fringe benefits such as sick leave, medical insurance, and retirement benefits. In addition, Park Naturalists may be eligible for overtime pay.

Employment Prospects

Park Naturalists work for city, county, state, and national park systems. Most parks hire seasonal employees, particularly during the summer months. Permanent positions typically become available as employees retire, resign, transfer to other locations, or advance to higher positions. The job market is highly competitive for permanent as well as seasonal positions.

Advancement Prospects

With appropriate training and education, Park Naturalists can advance to supervisory and administrative positions or pursue law enforcement ranger positions. Many Park Naturalists realize advancement in the form of job satisfaction, higher pay, and park assignments to locations of their choice.

Park Naturalists can also follow paths to other related careers by becoming schoolteachers, researchers, environmental consultants, or educational program managers for environmental and outdoor centers.

Licensure/Certification

No state licensure or certification is required to become Park Naturalists.

Park Naturalists may be required to hold a valid state driver's license and CPR (cardiopulmonary resuscitation) and first aid certifications. To work for some parks, Park Naturalists may be required to be U. S. citizens or obtain naturalization within a specific time after being hired.

Education and Training

In general, employers require or prefer Park Naturalists who have a bachelor's degree in botany, zoology, geology, forestry, outdoor education, environmental interpretation, natural resource management, or other related field. A bachelor's degree is typically required for permanent and seasonal employment. Some employers accept candidates with associate degrees or some college work if they have qualifying work experience.

Experience, Skills, and Personality Traits

Requirements vary from position to position. In general, candidates should have at least one year of experience providing naturalist interpretive work. It may have been gained as a seasonal Park Naturalist, naturalist aide, science teacher, naturalist intern, or nature program volunteer. (To get a full-time position with the National Park Service usually requires two to five years experience as a seasonal ranger.) Candidates should be knowledgeable about principles and methods pertaining to science education and environmental interpretation. They should also be familiar with the flora and fauna of the parks where they would be working.

Park Naturalists need various skills to do their work effectively. They should have strong teaching, organizational, project management, interpersonal, teamwork, and writing skills. Additionally, having excellent communication, presentation, public speaking, and leadership skills are important as they work with colleagues, administrators, park patrons, and others on a daily basis.

Successful Park Naturalists have several personality traits in common, such as being outgoing, enthusiastic, calm, tolerant, flexible, observant, curious, creative, self-motivated, and energetic.

Unions/Associations

Many Park Naturalists join local, state, and national professional organizations to take advantage of professional services such as networking opportunities, training programs, job listings, and professional resources. Some national organizations that they might join are:

- National Society for Park Resources, a branch of the National Recreation and Park Association
- Association of National Park Rangers
- National Association for Interpretation

Many Park Naturalists also join conservation organizations such as the National Audubon Society, the Nature Conservancy, or the National Wildlife Federation.

Tips for Entry

1. You can start planning while in high school for a career as a Park Naturalist. Take courses in biology, chemistry, physics, earth sciences, mathematics, social studies, history, and geography. Also valuable are classes in English, public speaking, and journalism.
2. Internships and volunteer positions with park systems are available for individuals to obtain hands-on training.
3. To enhance your employability, you might obtain certification as an emergency medical technician (EMT), first responder, or paramedic.
4. The National Park Service (NPS) has specific recruitment periods for seasonal positions. For more information about these particular time periods, job requirements, and how to apply, write to: Seasonal Employment Program, Human Resources Office, National Park Service, 1849 C Street NW, Mail Stop 2225, Washington, D.C. 20013-7127. Or call (202) 208-5074. Or visit the NPS seasonal employment program's web page at *http://www.sep.nps.gov*. (The NPS main web site is *http://www.nps.gov*.)
5. Many local, state, and national park systems have web sites on the Internet. Many also provide job listings or information on how to apply for jobs. To find a web site for a specific park, enter its name in any search engine. (Note: Enter a park's name between quotation marks to get better results. For example, if you want to find a web site for the Oregon Caves National Monument, enter the keyword as "Oregon Caves National Monument.")

HUMANE EDUCATOR

CAREER PROFILE

Duties: Provide humane education programs and activities that promote public awareness of compassionate and respectful treatment of animals; perform other duties as required

Alternate Title: Humane Education Specialist

Salary Range: $20,000 to $30,000

Employment Prospects: Limited

Advancement Prospects: Limited

Prerequisites:
　Licensure/Certification—None required
　Education/Training—A high school diploma or bachelor's degree
　Experience—Previous experience working with animals; teaching experience desirable; experience working with people of all ages
　Special Skills and Personality Traits—Writing, computer, organizational, project management, teaching, interpersonal, communication, classroom management, and public speaking skills; friendly, approachable, flexible, reliable, dedicated, energetic

CAREER LADDER

Humane Education Coordinator

↑

Humane Educator

↑

Intern, Shelter Technician, or Volunteer

Position Description

Humane Educators provide various educational programs and activities relating to the compassionate and respectful treatment and control of animals. Their primary responsibility is to educate children and adults so that they make wise decisions about how to interact with animals and the environment. In addition, Humane Educators promote responsible pet ownership by making people aware that their pets have the same needs of water, food, and shelter as humans and that pets should not be abused or neglected.

Working mostly for community animal shelters and humane societies, Humane Educators perform several duties. One major duty is developing effective humane education programs. Depending on the particular needs of their communities, Humane Educators plan programs that address topics such as animal control, pet overpopulation, animal ordinances, and basic animal care.

Human Educators deliver education programs in various forms. They give presentations to schools and civic organizations, often bringing in animals from the pet shelter. They set up booths at local community events. Humane Educators might also sponsor public events in which they promote animal licensing, immunization shots for pets, pet care, spay/neuter clinics, and so on.

Humane Educators are also responsible for developing brochures, pamphlets, and written information on various topics for the public. Many educators gather appropriate materials from national humane organizations and other resources to distribute to the public. Some educators create materials or modify existing materials to meet their specific needs. In addition, many Humane Educators develop a library of humane education materials for the general public.

Humane Educators also perform other duties, as required. For example, they might:

- conduct tours of animal shelters
- provide training and supervision to staff and volunteers
- write grant proposals
- maintain accurate records, prepare reports, write correspondence, and complete required paperwork

Depending on the size of their facilities, Humane Educators may be in charge of all or some of a facility's humane education program. In some organizations, Humane Educators are in charge of coordinating presentations, developing materials, and managing the volunteer coordinator. In other organizations, the Humane Educator may also be the volunteer coordinator and the contact person for public information. In small facilities, the Humane Educator may also perform duties as executive director, animal adoption counselor, or other staff position.

Many Humane Educators work on a volunteer basis. Salaried Humane Educators typically work a 40-hour week.

Salaries

Salaries vary, and depend on factors such as experience, education, job responsibilities, size of employer, and location. In general, most Humane Educators earn an annual salary in the $20,000 to $30,000 range. Additionally, they receive fringe benefits such as sick leave, vacation leave, medical insurance, and retirement benefits.

Employment Prospects

Most Humane Educators work for animal shelters and humane organizations as either employees or volunteers. Some Humane Educators are consultants, providing educational services to schools and other facilities.

The job market is limited for paid positions. They become available as Humane Educators resign, retire, advance to higher positions, or transfer to other jobs.

Advancement Prospects

Humane Educators can advance to administrative positions, such as program coordinators, education managers, and education directors. They can also become animal shelter directors. Most prospects are found in large facilities or with national organizations such as the American Humane Association. In many shelters, the Humane Educator is the only educator on staff.

Depending on their interests and ambitions, Humane Educators can also seek paths to related careers. For example, they might become environmental educators, schoolteachers, animal researchers, veterinarians, and zookeepers.

Licensure/Certification

No state licensure or certification is required to become a Humane Educator.

Education and Training

Some employers require that Humane Educators have a high school diploma or general equivalency diploma with qualifying work experience. Other employers require or prefer that Humane Educators have a bachelor's degree in animal sciences, natural resources, wildlife ecology, education, environmental education, or other related field. In addition, most employers require or prefer that Humane Educators have completed internships with animal shelters, nature centers, zoos, or similar institutions.

Experience, Skills, and Personality Traits

In general, Humane Educators should have previous experience working with animals and be knowledgeable about animal welfare issues. Some employers require that Humane Educators have at least one year of experience working with animal shelters, which may include volunteer work, if they do not meet educational requirements. In addition, Humane Educators should have teaching experience or appropriate training, as well as experience working with a variety of people in a variety of settings.

Humane Educators need strong writing, computer, organizational, project management, and teaching skills. Having strong interpersonal, communication, classroom management, and public speaking skills are also needed to provide effective presentations. Successful Humane Educators share several personality traits, such as being friendly, approachable, flexible, reliable, dedicated, and energetic.

Unions/Associations

Many Humane Educators belong to local, state, and national professional organizations to take advantage of professional resources, training workshops, networking opportunities, and other professional services. Some national organizations that many Humane Educators join are:

- American Society for the Prevention of Cruelty to Animals (ASPCA)
- American Humane Association
- Humane Society of the United States
- National Association for Humane and Environmental Education

Tips for Entry

1. In high school, start gaining experience working with animals. You might volunteer at your local animal shelter, zoo, nature center, museum, or other similar institution.
2. Having a degree or course work in education can enhance your employability as well as give you valuable skills for the job.
3. Learn more about humane education on the Internet. To get a list of relevant web sites, enter these keywords in a search engine: "humane education" or "humane educator."

DOG TRAINER

CAREER PROFILE

Duties: Train dogs to behave and obey specific commands; teach dog owners how to handle their dogs; design individualized training programs; operate a business, if an owner; perform other duties as required

Alternate Titles: Apprentice Trainer, Assistant Trainer, Master Trainer

Salary Range: $12,000 to $37,000

Employment Prospects: Good

Advancement Prospects: Limited

Prerequisites:
    Licensure/Certification—None required
    Education/Training—A combination of apprenticeship, independent study, workshops, seminars, and classes
    Experience—Several years of experience of training and handling various dog breeds
    Special Skills and Personality Traits—Leadership, interpersonal, communication, motivational, organizational, and management skills; (as business owners) public relations skills and small business skills; ethical, methodical, fair, kind, enthusiastic, patient, confident, self-motivated

CAREER LADDER

Senior Dog Trainer or Business Owner

↑

Dog Trainer

↑

Trainee

Position Description

Dog Trainers provide dog training services to dog owners who do not have the time or expertise to train their dogs. As experts in dogs and dog behavior, Dog Trainers teach dogs to behave and obey their owners by responding to proper voice and hand signal commands. Dog Trainers work with owners to design individual plans for their dogs, defining details such as the training goals, the length of training, and a daily work schedule for the dogs. The plans also include instruction for the dog owners. Dog Trainers teach owners how to work with their dogs so that the dogs know the owners are in control. Trainers also teach owners how to maintain their dogs' training so that they continue responding appropriately to the proper commands.

Many Dog Trainers specialize in training particular dog breeds. Many also specialize in providing one or more dog training programs, such as:

- obedience training for pet dogs
- protection training for guard dogs
- training of dogs for dog show competitions
- training for police service dogs that are used by law enforcement agencies

Dog Trainers train several dogs each day, holding individual training sessions. Training is slow and repetitive. Patiently, they teach dogs one skill at a time. In addition, no two dogs are alike: they learn in different ways as well as at different paces. Thus, most Dog Trainers use a variety of training methods, and try to find the most effective method for each dog.

Most Dog Trainers are independent trainers. Some train dogs from their homes, within their clients' homes, or in rented facilities. Others own dog training facilities, in which dogs may be boarded during their training. As small business owners, independent Dog Trainers are responsible for performing administrative duties. Some of their tasks include developing policies and rules; collecting client fees; bookkeeping, paying bills, and paying taxes; cleaning and maintaining facilities; and so on. If they have employees, Dog Trainers are responsible for paying salaries, as well as providing training and supervision. In addition, Dog Trainers continually look for ways to bring in new clients.

Many business owners provide other services besides training. For example, they might offer group dog obedience classes, boarding services, or breeding services.

Salaried Dog Trainers work part time or full time. For business owners, dog training is a 24-hour, seven-days-a-week job.

Salaries

Salaries vary, and depend on factors such as experience, work status, and location. Independent Dog Trainers typically earn more than salaried employees. According to the U.S. Bureau of Labor Statistics, the 1998 estimated annual salary for most animal trainers, which includes Dog Trainers, is between $12,400 and $36,540.

Salaried Dog Trainers may receive fringe benefits such as sick leave and medical insurance.

Employment Prospects

The job market for Dog Trainers is favorable. The pet industry is continually growing, and an increasing number of new dog owners need help training their dogs. Most job opportunities for salaried positions become available as Dog Trainers resign or transfer to other positions. Employers may create additional positions as their businesses grow.

Job prospects are better for independent Dog Trainers. However, their success depends on factors such as the local demand for the type of dog training that they offer; the number of trainers within the area who provide similar lessons; and how well individual trainers run their businesses.

Advancement Prospects

Advancement opportunities are defined by an individual's own interests and ambition. Salaried Dog Trainers in large organizations may advance to supervisory or management positions. For most Dog Trainers, the ultimate goal is to have their own businesses. Many Dog Trainers realize advancement by way of job satisfaction, professional recognition, and higher earnings.

Licensure/Certification

No state licensure or certification is required to become Dog Trainers.

Education and Training

Dog Trainers develop their own training program, which they continue throughout their careers. Their training includes one or more apprenticeships under experienced dog trainers. It also includes independent study; enrollment in professional training and animal behavior workshops, seminars, and classes; participation in professional conferences; and networking with colleagues. Dog Trainers study subjects such as: dog breeds, animal behavior, dog handling skills, training methods, canine anatomy, dog care, pet safety tips, animal control laws and regulations, and games and exercise for dogs.

Experience, Skills, and Personality Traits

To become Dog Trainers requires several years of hands-on experience as apprentices under experienced Dog Trainers. Dog Trainers need a broad background of training and handling various dog breeds, as well as knowledge of animal behavior. In addition, Dog Trainers should have a repertoire of training methods in order to accommodate the many different learning styles of dogs and their owners.

To do their work well, Dog Trainers need excellent leadership, interpersonal, communication, motivational, organizational, and management skills. As business owners, they also need public relations and small business skills.

Successful Dog Trainers have several personality traits in common, such as being ethical, methodical, fair, kind, enthusiastic, patient, confident, and self-motivated. They have a genuine love for and devotion to dogs.

Unions/Associations

Many Dog Trainers join local, state, and national professional associations to take advantage of training programs, professional resources, networking opportunities, and so on. Two national organizations that serve Dog Trainers are the Association of Pet Dog Trainers and the National Association of Dog Obedience Instructors.

In addition, many Dog Trainers belong to general organizations such as the Animal Behavior Society or the American Society for the Prevention of Cruelty of Animals (ASPCA). Many Dog Trainers also join organizations that support owners of particular dog breeds.

Tips for Entry

1. As a middle school or high school student, you can start gaining experience working with dogs. For example, you might volunteer at animal shelters, "pet-sit" for dog owners, or get part-time jobs at dog kennels.
2. Network with veterinarians, animal hospitals, dog owners, pet store owners, dog trainers, and other professionals in the dog field to learn about job opportunities. If you are willing to relocate or commute, you may have better chances of finding apprenticeships or salaried positions.
3. Use the Internet to learn more about the dog training field. To find a list of relevant web sites, enter the keyword "dog trainer" in any search engine.

GUIDE DOG INSTRUCTOR

CAREER PROFILE

Duties: Train dogs to become guide dogs for blind, or visually impaired, individuals; teach blind owners how to handle their new guide dogs; perform other tasks as required

Alternate Titles: Apprentice Trainer, Assistant Trainer, Guide Dog Trainer

Salary Range: $12,000 to $37,000

Employment Prospects: Limited

Advancement Prospects: Limited

Prerequisites:
  Licensure/Certification—State license required in California; certified by employer
  Education/Training—Associate or bachelor's degree is preferred or required; complete an apprenticeship
  Experience—Extensive background in animal training and handling; ability to teach or coach others; physically fit
  Special Skills and Personality Traits—Leadership, interpersonal, communication, writing, public speaking, problem solving, and self-management skills; patient, tactful, honest, reliable, responsible, dedicated, compassionate

CAREER LADDER

Guide Dog Instructor

Guide Dog Trainer

Apprentice or Assistant Trainer

Position Description

Many blind or visually impaired individuals use guide dogs to help them walk independently down crowded sidewalks, across busy streets, up and down stairs, into buildings, onto buses, and so forth. (In the United States, as well as other countries, blind persons with their guide dogs have the legal right to access stores, banks, restaurants, and all other public places.) Guide dogs and their blind owners receive special training from Guide Dog Instructors, who work in guide dog schools.

Guide Dog Instructors participate in every aspect of a guide dog's training. The training process begins several weeks after dogs are born. Guide dog schools place puppies with volunteers who can raise the puppies with lots of love, care, and attention. Instructors encourage volunteers to expose the puppies to new experiences—such as riding in cars, walking into unfamiliar buildings, and being in crowded places.

When dogs are between 14 and 22 months old, they return to the guide dog schools. Guide Dog Instructors screen the dogs critically to see if they would make good guide dogs. Instructors look for such things in a dog as excellent health, an even temperament, and a willingness to learn. Dogs who pass the evaluation are then placed in formal training for four to six months.

Guide Dog Instructors work with dogs on a daily basis. Dogs learn to respond to basic commands. For example, a guide dog should stop completely when his handler commands, "Halt."

With patience and diligence, Guide Dog Instructors train dogs to stop at street curbs, move around obstacles, board escalators, walk up and down stairs, and so forth. Instructors also train dogs to behave properly in any environment or situation. In addition, they train dogs to perform "intelligent disobedience" responses that keep the dogs and their blind handlers from dangerous situations. For example, a handler and a guide dog are stopped at an intersection. The handler commands the dog to go forward. But the guide dog does not move because it sees a car coming toward them.

When the dogs have completed their training, Guide Dog Instructors assist with matching dogs to new owners. Instructors then teach the new owners how to handle their guide dogs in a wide variety of situations and environments. Most schools require students to live in the facilities during their training session, which usually lasts four weeks.

Guide Dog Instructors provide students with both the theory and practice of handling their guide dogs. Each day, students practice working with their dogs in various simulated and real situations (such as crowded sidewalks, crossing busy streets, bus travel, obstacles in the path). Instructors also work with students individually on any special problems or particular needs. In addition, they teach students how to care for their dogs. After students go home, Guide Dog Instructors follow up on how they are doing. When needed, instructors provide refresher training.

Guide Dog Instructors perform many other tasks. For example, they:

- supervise and train apprentices and trainers
- assist the school's veterinary staff
- clean dog kennels
- transport puppies to volunteer homes, or drive students and their dogs to various places for training purposes
- give presentations at civic organizations or conventions to promote their schools
- assist in fundraising activities

Salaries

Salaries vary, and depend on factors such as experience, job responsibilities, and location. According to the U.S. Bureau of Labor Statistics, the 1998 estimated annual salary for most animal trainers, which includes Guide Dog Instructors, is between $12,400 and $36,540.

Guide Dog Instructors also receive fringe benefits such as sick leave and medical insurance.

Employment Prospects

The job market for Guide Dog Instructors is rather limited due to the small population that is served. Most job opportunities become available as instructors retire, resign, or transfer to other positions. However, competition for available positions is high.

Advancement Prospects

Guide Dog Instructors who wish to perform supervisory and administrative work can advance to positions, such as field supervisors, training managers, and directors of training. Many Guide Dog Instructors realize advancement by way of job satisfaction, professional recognition, and higher wages.

Licensure/Certification

As of 2000, California is the only state that requires licensure of Guide Dog Instructors. (For more information, contact the Board of Guide Dogs for the Blind, 2000 Evergreen Street, Sacramento, Calif. 95815. Or call: (916) 263-8956. Or visit its web site at *http://www.dca.ca.gov/r_r/guidedog.htm.*)

Education and Training

Most employers prefer or require that trainers have associate or bachelor's degrees. The degree may be in any field, but having a degree or course work in animal behavior, psychology, orientation and mobility, rehabilitation counseling, and related fields are helpful for this profession.

Guide Dog Instructors must first serve an apprenticeship at a licensed guide dog school for two and a half to four years, depending on the school program. Apprenticeships include self-study, supervised instruction, and practical experience working with guide dogs and blind students.

Experience, Skills, and Personality Traits

To become an apprentice, individuals should have an extensive background in animal training and handling, as well as the ability to teach or coach others. Apprentices must have good health, be physically fit, and have the stamina to work a physically demanding job.

Some skills that Guide Dog Instructors need to do their work effectively are leadership, interpersonal, communication, writing, and public speaking skills. They also have good problem solving and self-management skills.

Successful Guide Dog Instructors share several personality traits such as being patient, tactful, honest, reliable, responsible, dedicated, and compassionate. They are able to work well with both animals and people.

Unions/Associations

Many Guide Dog Instructors belong to local, state, and national professional organizations to take advantage of networking opportunities, professional resources, and other professional services. One national organization that many trainers join is the Guide Dog Users Inc.

Tips for Entry

1. As a middle school or high school student, you can begin gaining experience by volunteering to raise puppies for guide or service dog schools.
2. Gain experience teaching dogs to perform specific tasks. For example, you might work with dogs in an area such as dog sports or search and rescue.
3. You can learn more about the Guide Dog Instructor field on the Internet. To get a list of relevant web sites, enter any of these keywords in a search engine: "guide dog," "Guide Dog Instructor," or "training guide dogs."

K-9 TRAINER (POLICE DOGS)

CAREER PROFILE

Duties: Train police dogs to perform specific tasks, such as detaining suspects or detecting bombs; teach K-9 handlers (law enforcement officers) how to work with their dogs, care for them, and provide daily training; perform other duties as required

Alternate Titles: K-9 Instructor, Master Trainer

Salary Range: $12,000 to $75,000 or more (for civilian K-9 Trainers)

Employment Prospects: Limited for law enforcement K-9 Trainers; fair for civilian K-9 Trainers

Advancement Prospects: Limited

Prerequisites:
  Licensure/Certification—A nationally recognized professional certification
  Education/Training—Law enforcement K-9 trainers complete certified training programs; a combination of apprenticeship, independent study, classes, and workshops
  Experience—Extensive background in handling and training police service dogs; have basic knowledge of dog behavior and care; strong background in law enforcement for civilian K-9 Trainers
  Special Skills and Personality Traits—Leadership, teaching, writing, organizational, management, communication, and interpersonal skills; (as business owners) customer service, public relations, and small business skills; confident, tactful, tolerant, patient

CAREER LADDER

Business Owner; for Law Enforcement officers, the next rank up—sergeant, lieutenant, captain, and so on

K-9 Trainer

Apprentice or Assistant Trainer

Position Description

Canine (or K-9) Trainers teach dogs to obey commands so that they can be used as effective law enforcement tools to help prevent and detect crime. For example, police canines can be trained to pursue and detain suspects, track suspects, or search for physical evidence such as narcotics, explosives, or cadavers. K-9 Trainers train police canines and their handlers (who are law enforcement officers) to provide one or more services—such as patrol duty, tactical support, tracking, bomb detection, narcotics detection, or explosives detection.

K-9 Trainers begin training selected dogs when they are between 12 and 18 months old. The initial training requires at least 14 weeks for dogs to learn the proper obedience, motivation, balance, and conditioning needed for performing their specific tasks. K-9 Trainers teach dogs basic voice and hand-signal obedience and the special skills that they need to perform tasks such as detaining suspects. The work is slow and meticulous. Trainers teach skills one at a time and use training methods that suit the different learning styles of the dogs. Trainers usually create simulated real-life day and night scenarios for dogs to practice their skills.

Whenever possible, K-9 Trainers work with both the canines and their handlers throughout the initial training period. But many law enforcement agencies do not have the budget or staff to allow the handlers to attend the entire training session. In those cases, K-9 Trainers first train the dogs, then train the officers on how to handle their dogs as well as how to provide daily basic training to maintain the dogs' skills.

K-9 Trainers also provide K-9 handlers with instruction on topics such as basic animal behavior, police dog psychology, dog grooming, basic dog care, and proper tactical measures. In addition, they inform K-9 handlers about current law enforcement practices and laws regarding the use of police canines.

Furthermore, K-9 Trainers provide in-service training for K-9 teams. This is done on a regular basis to maintain and improve the effectiveness of the K-9 teams' skills.

Along with training, K-9 Trainers perform many different tasks. For example, they might:

- maintain daily training records for canines and handlers
- provide daily care for canines
- maintain kennels
- select canines
- keep up with developments in police canine training, current court cases regarding police canines, and relevant topics in their field
- continue their own professional development

Some K-9 Trainers work in law enforcement agencies. They usually perform canine training duty in addition to their primary duties as patrol officers, detectives, supervisors, and so on. Most officers perform regular duty as K-9 handlers. In general, most law enforcement K-9 Trainers provide in-service training for all K-9 teams. In larger agencies, K-9 Trainers provide initial training as well. These agencies often offer canine training services to other law enforcement agencies in the area.

Other K-9 Trainers work for or own private canine academies that provide training services to law enforcement. Many civilian K-9 Trainers are former or retired law enforcement officers who have years of experience as law enforcement K-9 handlers and K-9 Trainers.

As business owners, civilian K-9 Trainers perform many administrative tasks relevant to running a small business. Some of their tasks include developing policies and rules, collecting client fees, bookkeeping, paying bills, and so on. If they have employees, K-9 Trainers are responsible for paying salaries, as well as providing training and supervision. In addition, K-9 Trainers continually look for new ways to bring in new clients. Many business owners also provide dog training services to clients besides law enforcement agencies.

Salaried civilian K-9 Trainers work part time or full time. For business owners, dog training is a 24-hour, seven-days-a-week job.

Salaries

Salaries vary, and depend on such factors as experience, employer, and location. K-9 Trainers in law enforcement agencies receive a salary that is dependent on their departmental rank such as sergeant or lieutenant. Salaried civilian K-9 Trainers generally earn less than those in law enforcement. According to the U.S. Bureau of Labor Statistics, the 1998 estimated annual salary for most animal trainers, which includes K-9 Trainers, was between $12,400 and $36,540.

Civilian K-9 Trainers who own canine training schools can earn $50,000 to $75,000 or more per year.

Employment Prospects

K-9 Trainer positions in law enforcement agencies are limited, and generally based on the need of individual agencies as well as the size of the K-9 units. Job prospects are more favorable in law enforcement agencies that have in-house canine training facilities.

Most job opportunities for salaried civilian positions become available as K-9 Trainers resign or transfer to other positions. Employers may create additional positions as their businesses grow. Job prospects are good for K-9 Trainers who have their own businesses. Their success depends on various factors such as their reputation for providing quality work and how well they run their businesses. For many civilian K-9 Trainers, this profession is their second or third career. Most have backgrounds in law enforcement. Many also have backgrounds in dog training.

Advancement Prospects

Law enforcement K-9 Trainers can seek promotions in rank (sergeant, lieutenant, captain, and so forth); but they may be transferred out of the K-9 units to perform supervisory and administrative duties elsewhere in their agencies. Some law enforcement K-9 Trainers start businesses that provide canine training services to law enforcement agencies.

Most civilian and law enforcement K-9 Trainers realize advancement by way of job satisfaction, professional recognition, and higher wages.

Licensure/Certification

Most law enforcement agencies require internal K-9 Trainers to be certified by a nationally recognized professional organization such as the United States Police Canine Association or North American Police Work Dog Association. Trainers obtain certification for each area of training that they plan to provide.

Civilian K-9 Trainers obtain professional certification on a voluntary basis.

Education and Training

Education and training requirements for law enforcement K-9 Trainers vary from agency to agency. (Law enforcement officers who are interested in becoming K-9 Trainers should talk with their K-9 unit commanders.) In general, they complete certified training programs within their departments, other law enforcement agencies, or civilian canine academies.

Both civilian and law enforcement K-9 Trainers complete apprenticeships under experienced K-9 Trainers.

All K-9 Trainers are responsible for developing their own training program, which they continue throughout their careers. It generally includes a combination of independent study and apprenticeships under master K-9 trainers. K-9 Trainers also attend classes and workshops about dog obedience, animal behavior, dog care, training methods, and many other subjects relevant to their profession.

Experience, Skills, and Personality Traits

K-9 Trainers need an extensive background in handling and training dogs. They should be knowledgeable about dog behavior, especially regarding the variety of breeds that are used as police service dogs. Additionally, trainers should have basic knowledge of canine care and health care. Civilian K-9 Trainers should have a strong background in law enforcement; while law enforcement K-9 Trainers should have several years of experience as a K-9 Handler.

To perform their work effectively, K-9 Trainers need leadership, teaching, writing, organizational, management, communication, and interpersonal skills. Business owners should also have adequate customer service, public relations, and small business skills.

Successful Police K-9 Trainers share several personality traits such as being confident, tactful, tolerant, and patient.

Unions/Associations

Police K-9 Trainers might join local, state, and national professional organizations to take advantage of professional services such as certification programs, training programs, and networking opportunities. Two national organizations that many trainers join are the North American Police Work Dog Association and the United States Police Canine Association.

Tips for Entry

1. You can start gaining experience working with dogs as a middle school or high school student. Check out your local 4-H club or other youth groups to see what they might offer. Also volunteer or obtain part-time jobs at local animal shelters, humane societies, dog kennels, animal hospitals, or veterinarian offices.
2. Educational requirements for entry-level law enforcement officers vary from one agency to the next. Many agencies require a college degree (usually an associate or bachelor's degree) or a minimum number of college units in police science, criminal justice, or other related field. Contact law enforcement agencies for whom you would like to work and find out what their entry requirements are.
3. As a K-9 handler in a law enforcement agency, let your unit commander know that you are interested in becoming a trainer. Also learn if there are any particular requirements that you must satisfy in order to become a K-9 Trainer in your state.
4. To obtain an apprenticeship or internship, contact K-9 Trainers under whom you would like to learn. Be sure to have your resume ready that shows relevant education and experience in dog training and law enforcement.
5. Use the Internet to learn more about K-9 Trainers, civilian K-9 schools, and law enforcement K-9 units. For pertinent web sites, enter any of these keywords in a search engine: "training police service dogs," "police canine academy," or "K-9 unit."

HORSE TRAINER

CAREER PROFILE

Duties: Train horses for a specific type of riding activity such as pleasure riding, jumping, barrel racing, or carriage driving; provide riders with instruction for handling and training horses; operate a business, if an owner; perform other duties as required

Alternate Titles: Assistant Horse Trainer, Master Horse Trainer

Salary Range: $12,000 to $37,000

Employment Prospects: Good

Advancement Prospects: Limited

Prerequisites:
  Licensure/Certification—None required
  Education/Training—Apprenticeship under experienced Horse Trainers
  Experience—An extensive background in training and handling horses; a strong foundation in horsemanship and horse behavior
  Special Skills and Personality Traits—Leadership, communication, interpersonal, organizational, and management skills; (as independent trainers) customer service, writing, public relations, and small business skills; methodical, patient, dedicated, open-minded, calm, kind, gentle

CAREER LADDER

Business Owner

Horse Trainer

Assistant Horse Trainer

Position Description

Professional Horse Trainers offer horse training services to horse owners who do not have the time or expertise to do their own training. Owners usually want their horses trained for recreational purposes or horse competitions. Most Horse Trainers specialize in providing horse training for one or more types of riding activities, such as:

- pleasure riding—English style or Western style
- dressage competitions
- jumping competitions, such as cross-country jumping
- eventing, which is a competition involving dressage, cross-country jumping, and show jumping
- long distance or endurance riding
- barrel racing
- carriage driving
- horse racing

Horse Trainers work for horse training facilities, equestrian centers, horse farms, horse stables, dude ranches, and other horse-related businesses. Some Horse Trainers are self-employed, and may train horses at their customers' facilities. They sometimes live at their customers' facilities for the duration of the training. Many independent Horse Trainers have their own training facilities.

Before training any horse, Horse Trainers work with owners to determine what goals they wish their horses to achieve and create a workout schedule. Horses Trainers then begin their training by first gaining the horse's trust and forming a bond that is the basis of their working relationship. They determine what horses are capable of doing and develop the horses according to their abilities. Like people, horses learn in different ways and at different paces, thus most Horse Trainers use various techniques to match the learning styles and abilities of the horses. Horse Trainers work patiently with horses, building up their skills slowly.

Horse Trainers maintain accurate training records of horses and keep owners up-to-date with the progress of their horses. When training is complete, Horse Trainers then teach the riders (who may or may not be the owners) how to handle their horses. The Horse Trainers also instruct the riders on how to continue training the horses on a daily basis so that they maintain their skills.

Independent Horse Trainers perform necessary administrative tasks. For example, they determine client fees, arrange working schedules, collect fees, pay bills, buy supplies and equipment, do bookkeeping, promote their businesses, and so on. If they have employees, they are responsible for paying their salaries and providing them with proper training and supervision. Many facility owners also provide other services such as boarding for horses, horse breeding, or riding lessons.

After years of experience, some Horse Trainers become well-known for their training methods. They begin to supervise apprentice Horse Trainers as well as offer horse training clinics on topics such as problem horses, training techniques, and horse care.

Salaried Horse Trainers work part time or full time.

Salaries

Salaries vary, and depend on factors such as experience and location. According to the U.S. Bureau of Labor Statistics, the 1998 estimated annual salary for most animal trainers, which includes Horse Trainers, ranged from $12,400 to $36,540.

Salaried Horse Trainers may receive fringe benefits such as sick leave and medical insurance.

Employment Prospects

The horse industry is a healthy and growing field, and the job outlook, in general, is favorable.

Job opportunities for most staff positions become available as individuals retire, resign, or advance to other positions. Employers may create additional positions as their businesses grow. The success rate for independent trainers depends on such factors as how well the individual trainers run their businesses and the level of competition for their services in their area.

Advancement Prospects

Most Horse Trainers realize advancement with job satisfaction, professional recognition, and higher wages. The ultimate goal for most Horse Trainers is to become self-employed or to have their own training facilities.

Licensure/Certification

No state licensure or certification is required to train horses for pleasure or competition.

Education and Training

There is no minimum educational requirement to become a Horse Trainer. Some Horse Trainers do obtain associate or bachelor's degrees in equine science or a related field as part of their overall training toward becoming Horse Trainers. All Horse Trainers serve several years as an apprentice under one or more experienced (or master) Horse Trainers in which they receive hands-on training for the various breeds of horses.

All Horse Trainers are responsible for developing their own training program, which they continue throughout their careers. It typically includes a combination of independent study and networking with colleagues. They also attend professional conferences and enroll in horse clinics taught by master Horse Trainers in the United States and Europe.

Experience, Skills, and Personality Traits

Horse Trainers have an extensive background in the handling and training of various breeds. Additionally, they have a strong foundation in horse behavior and horsemanship.

Horse Trainers need good leadership, communication, interpersonal, organizational, and management skills. As independent trainers, they also need strong customer service, writing, public relations, and small business skills.

Being methodical, patient, dedicated, open-minded, calm, kind, and gentle are some personality traits that successful Horse Trainers share.

Unions/Associations

Horse Trainers might join local, state, and national professional associations that serve particular horse breeds or riding activities, such as dressage or training a specific breed. They might also join organizations such as the American Horse Council that serve the general horse industry. By joining professional organizations they can take advantage of professional resources, networking opportunities, job listings, and other professional services.

Tips for Entry

1. Many Horse Trainers started off by working on horse farms or in stables in exchange for training lessons.
2. If you plan on becoming an independent trainer, learn basic skills in running a small business.
3. To broaden your chances for apprenticeships or jobs of your choice, be willing to relocate or live temporarily in another location.
4. Many professionals in the horse industry use the Internet as a means to network with colleagues, as well as to advertise their services to potential customers. To begin a general search of relevant web sites, use any of these key words in a search engine: "horse trainer," "horse stables," or "horse farm."

APPENDIXES

APPENDIX I
EDUCATIONAL RESOURCES—COLLEGES AND UNIVERSITIES

Listed below are selected master's degree programs for professions that are discussed in this book. A few colleges and universities are given to get you started. To learn about other higher education institutions, or college degree programs, talk with school or career counselors and professionals. You can also look up schools in college directories produced by Peterson's, Barron's, or other publishers, which can be found in school or public libraries.

(Note: All web site addresses were current at the time this book was being written. If you come across an address that no longer works, then enter the name of the institution in a search engine to find its new web site.)

ART THERAPY—GRADUATE PROGRAMS

The following are some schools that were accredited by the American Art Therapy Association at the time this book was being written. Check with the individual schools about their current status.

CALIFORNIA

College Of Notre Dame
Art Therapy Program
1500 Ralston Avenue
Belmont, CA 94002-1997
http://www.cnd.edu

Loyola Marymount University
Department of Marital and Family Therapy
7900 Loyola Boulevard
Los Angeles, CA 90045-8217
http://www.lmu.edu

DISTRICT OF COLUMBIA

George Washington University
Art Therapy Program
2129 I Street NW
Washington, DC 20052
http://www.gwu.edu

KANSAS

Emporia State University
Division of Psychology and Special Education
1200 Commercial Street
Emporia, KS 66801-5087
http://www.emporia.edu

MASSACHUSETTS

Lesley College
Expressive Therapies Division
29 Everett Street
Cambridge, MA 02138-2790
http://www.lesley.edu/welcome.html

NEW YORK

College Of New Rochelle
Division of Graduate Art and Communication
29 Castle Place
New Rochelle, NY 10805
http://www.cnr.edu

Hofstra University
Counseling, Research, Special Education, and Rehabilitation Department
124 Hofstra University
1000 Fulton Avenue
Hempstead, NY 11549-1240
http://www.hofstra.edu

Long Island University—C. W. Post Campus
Art Department
720 Northern Boulevard
Brookville, NY 11548-1300
http://www.cwpost.liunet.edu/cwis/cwp/post.html

Nazareth College
4245 East Avenue
Rochester, NY 14618-3790
http://www.naz.edu

New York University
70 Washington Square South
New York, NY 10012
http://www.nyu.edu

Pratt Institute
Graduate Creative Arts Therapy Department
200 Willoughby Avenue
Brooklyn, NY 11205
http://www.pratt.edu

OREGON

Marylhurst University
Graduate Program in Art Therapy
17600 Pacific Highway (Hwy 43)
Marylhurst, OR 97036-0261
http://www.marylhurst.edu

PENNSYLVANIA

Marywood University
2300 Adams Avenue
Scranton, PA 18509
http://www.marywood.edu

**MCP Hahnemann University
of the Health Sciences**
School of Health Professions
Broad and Vine, Mail Stop 472
Philadelphia, PA 19102-1192
http://www.petersons.com/sites/gradinc/
28821002.html

VIRGINIA

Eastern Virginia Medical School
Graduate Art Therapy Program
P.O. Box 1980
Norfolk, VA 23501
http://www.evms.edu

WISCONSIN

Mount Mary College
2900 North Menomonee River Parkway
Milwaukee, WI 53222
http://www.mtmary.edu

EDUCATIONAL ADMINISTRATION—MASTER'S PROGRAM IN PRIVATE SCHOOL LEADERSHIP

The Klingenstein Center
Teachers College
Columbia University
204 Main Hall, Box 125
525 West 120th Street
New York, NY 10027-6696
http://www.klingenstein.org

LIBRARY AND INFORMATION SCIENCE—MASTER'S PROGRAMS

Note: The following are some schools that were accredited by the American Library Association at the time this book was being written. Check with the individual schools about their current status.

ALABAMA

The University of Alabama
School of Library and Information
 Studies
513 Main Library
Box 870252
Tuscaloosa, AL 35487-0252
http://www.slis.ua.edu

CALIFORNIA

San Jose State University
School of Library and Information Science
One Washington Square
San Jose, CA 95192
http://www.sjsu.edu

University of California, Los Angeles
Graduate School of Education and
 Information Studies
Box 951361
Los Angeles, CA 90095-1521
http://www.ucla.edu

CONNECTICUT

Southern Connecticut State University
Department of Library Science and
 Instructional Technology
501 Crescent Street
New Haven, CT 06515-1355
http://www.scsu.ctstate.edu

DISTRICT OF COLUMBIA

The Catholic University of America
School of Library and Information
 Science
620 Michigan Avenue
Washington, DC 20064
http://www.cua.edu

FLORIDA

Florida State University
School of Information Studies
P.O. Box 2100
Tallahassee, FL 32306-2100
http://www.fsu.edu

University of South Florida
School of Library and Information
 Science
4202 East Fowler Avenue
Tampa, FL 33620
http://www.cas.usf.edu

GEORGIA

Clark Atlanta University
School of Library and Information
 Studies
223 James P. Brawley Drive
Atlanta, GA 30314
http://www.cau.edu

ILLINOIS

Dominican University
Graduate School of Library and
 Information Science
7900 West Division Street
River Forest, IL 60305
http://www.dom.edu

IOWA

University of Iowa
School of Library and Information Science
Iowa City, IA 52242
http://www.uiowa.edu

KENTUCKY

University of Kentucky
School of Library and Information Science
502 King Library South
Lexington, KY 40506
http://www.uky.edu

LOUISIANA

Louisiana State University
School of Library and Information Science
Coates Hall Room 267
Baton Rouge, LA 70803-0100
http://www.lsu.edu

MARYLAND

University of Maryland
College of Library and Information
    Services
4105 Hornbake Library
College Park, MD 20742-4345
http://www.umd.edu

MASSACHUSETTS

Simmons College
Graduate School of Library and
    Information Science
300 The Fenway
Boston, MA 02115-5898
http://www.simmons.edu

MICHIGAN

University of Michigan
School of Information
550 East University Avenue
Ann Arbor, MI 48109-1092
http://www.umich.edu

Wayne State University
Library and Information Science Program
106 Kresse Library
Detroit, MI 48202-3939
http://www.wayne.edu

MISSISSIPPI

University of Southern Mississippi
School of Library and Information Science
Box 5146
Hattiesburg, MS 39406-5146
http://www.usm.edu

MISSOURI

University of Missouri at Columbia
School of Information Science and
    Learning Technologies
20 Rothwell Gymnasium
College of Education
Columbia, MO 65211
http://www.coe.missouri.edu

NEW JERSEY

Rutgers University
School of Communication, Information
    and Library Studies
4 Huntington Street
New Brunswick, NJ 08903
http://www.rutgers.edu

NEW YORK

Pratt Institute
School of Information and Library Science
200 Willoughby Avenue
Brooklyn, NY 11205
http://www.pratt.edu

Queens College
City University of New York
Graduate School of Library and
    Information Studies
65-30 Kissena Boulevard
Flushing, NY 11367
http://www.qc.edu

St. John's University
Division of Library and Information
    Science
8000 Utopia Parkway
Jamaica, NY 11439
http://www.stjohns.edu

Syracuse University
School of Information Studies
4-206 Center for Science and Technology
Syracuse, NY 13244-4100
http://www.syr.edu

University at Buffalo
State University of New York
Department of Library and Information
    Studies
534 Baldy Hall
Buffalo, NY 14260-1020
http://www.buffalo.edu

NORTH CAROLINA

North Carolina Central University
School of Library and Information
    Sciences
1801 Fayetteville Street
Durham, NC 27707
http://www.nccu.edu

OHIO

Kent State University
School of Library and Information Science
P.O. Box 5190
314 University Library
Kent, OH 44242
http://www.kent.edu

PENNSYLVANIA

Clarion University of Pennsylvania
Department of Library Science
840 Wood Street
Clarion, PA 16214-1232
http://www.clarion.edu

Drexel University
College of Information Science and
    Technology
3141 Chestnut Street
Philadelphia, PA 19104-2875
http://www.drexel.edu

University of Pittsburgh
School of Information Sciences
135 North Bellefield Avenue
Pittsburgh, PA 15260
http://www.pitt.edu

SOUTH CAROLINA

University of South Carolina
College of Library and Information
    Science
Columbia, SC 29208
http://www.sc.edu

TENNESSEE

University of Tennessee
School of Information Sciences
804 Volunteer Boulevard
Knoxville, TN 37996-4330
http://www.utk.edu

TEXAS

Texas Woman's University
School of Library and Information
  Studies
Denton, TX 76204-5438
http://www.twu.edu

University of North Texas
School of Library and Information
  Sciences
P.O. Box 311068
Denton, TX 76203
http://www.unt.edu

WASHINGTON

University of Washington
School of Library and Information Science
Box 352930
328 Old Electrical Engineering Building
Seattle, WA 98195-2930
http://www.washington.edu

WISCONSIN

University of Wisconsin at Milwaukee
School of Library and Information
  Science
Enders Hall, Room 1110
P.O. Box 413
Milwaukee, WI 53211
http://www.uwm.edu

SCHOOL PSYCHOLOGY—GRADUATE PROGRAMS

The following are some schools that were accredited by the American Psychological Association at the time this book was being written. Check with the individual schools about their current status.

ARIZONA

Arizona State University
College of Education
P.O. Box 870211
Tempe, AZ 85287-0611
http://www.asu.edu

FLORIDA

University of South Florida
Department of Psychological and Social
  Foundations of Education
Tampa, FL 33620
http://www.usfweb.usf.edu

GEORGIA

Georgia State University
Department of Counseling and
  Psychological Services
9th Floor, College of Education Building
Atlanta, GA 30303
http://www.gsu.edu

University of Georgia
Department of Educational Psychology
Alderhold Hall
Athens, GA 30602-5550
http://www.uga.edu

ILLINOIS

Illinois State University
Department of Psychology
Normal, IL 61790-4620
http://www.ilstu.edu

INDIANA

Indiana University
School of Education
107 S. Indiana Avenue
Bloomington, IN 47405
http://www.indiana.edu

Indiana State University
Department of Educational and School
  Psychology
School of Education
Room 108
Terre Haute, IN 47809
http://www.indstate.edu

MINNESOTA

University of Minnesota
College of Education
104 Burton Hall
178 Pillsbury Drive SE
Minneapolis, MN 55455
http://www.umn.edu

MISSISSIPPI

Mississippi State University
Department of Counselor Education and
  Educational Psychology
208 Montgomery Hall
Box 9727
Mississippi State, MS 39762
http://www.msstate.edu

University of Southern Mississippi
Department of Psychology
Box 5025
Hattiesburg, MS 39406-5025
http://www.usm.edu

MISSOURI

University of Missouri at Columbia
Department of Educational and
  Counseling Psychology
16 Hill Hall
Columbia, MO 65211
http://www.missouri.edu

NEBRASKA

University of Nebraska at Lincoln
Department of Educational Psychology
24 Henzlik Hall
Lincoln, NE 68588-0355
http://www.unl.edu

NEW JERSEY

Rutgers, The State University of New Jersey
Graduate School of Applied and Professional Psychology
152 Frelinghuysen Road
Piscataway, NJ 08854-8085
http://www.rutgers.edu

NEW YORK

Pace University
Department of Psychology
New York City Campus
New York, NY 10038
http://www.pace.edu

OREGON

University of Oregon
School Psychology Program
270 Education Building
Eugene, OR 97403-5261
http://www.uoregon.edu

PENNSYLVANIA

Lehigh University
Department of Education and Human Services
Bethlehem, PA 18015
http://www.lehigh.edu

Pennsylvania State University
Division of Educational and School Psychology and Special Education
University Park, PA 16802
http://www.psu.edu

Temple University
Department of Psychological Studies in Education
Ritter Annex, 2nd Floor
Philadelphia, PA 19122
http://www.temple.edu

RHODE ISLAND

University of Rhode Island
Psychology Department
Chafee Building
Kingston, RI 02881-0808
http://www.uri.edu

SOUTH CAROLINA

University of South Carolina
Department of Psychology
Barnswell College
Columbia, SC 29208
http://www.sc.edu

TEXAS

Texas A&M University
Department of Educational Psychology
4225 Tamu
College Station, TX 77843-4225
http://www.tamu.edu

University of Texas at Austin
Department of Educational Psychology
Austin, TX 78712
http://www.utexas.edu

UTAH

University of Utah
Department of Educational Psychology
1705 E. Campus Center Drive, Room 327
Salt Lake City, UT 84112
http://www.utah.edu

WISCONSIN

University of Wisconsin at Madison
Department of Educational Psychology
1025 W. Johnson Street
Madison, WI 53706-1796
http://www.wisc.edu

APPENDIX II
PROFESSIONAL UNIONS AND ASSOCIATIONS

Listed below are the main offices for the professional organizations that are mentioned in this book. You can contact these groups or visit their web sites to learn about careers, job opportunities, training programs, continuing education programs, professional certification programs, and so on. Many of these organizations have branch offices throughout the country. Contact an organization's headquarters to find out if a branch is in your area.

Other local, state, regional, and national professional organizations are also available. To learn about other relevant professional associations and unions, contact local professionals.

(Note: All web site addresses were current when this book was being written. If you come across an address that no longer works, you may be able find an organization's new web site by entering its name in a search engine.)

PROFESSIONALS IN EARLY CHILDHOOD CARE AND EDUCATION

American Federation of Teachers
555 New Jersey Avenue NW
Washington, DC 20001
(202) 879-4400
http://www.aft.org

Council for Exceptional Children
1920 Association Drive
Reston, VA 20191-1589
(888) CEC-SPED or (703) 620-3660;
TTY: (703) 264-9446;
fax: (703) 264-9494
http://www.cec.sped.org

National Association for the Education of Young Children
1509 16th Street NW
Washington, DC 20036
(800) 424-2460 or (202) 232-8777;
fax: (202) 328-1846
http://www.naeyc.org

National Child Care Association
1016 Rosser Street
Conyers, GA 30012
(800) 543-7161
http://www.nccanet.org

National Education Association
1201 16th Street NW
Washington, DC 20036
(202) 833-4000
http://www.nea.org

National Head Start Association
1651 Prince Street
Alexandria, VA 22314
703-739-0875; fax: 703-739-0878
http://www.nhsa.org

TEACHERS IN ELEMENTARY SCHOOLS, MIDDLE-LEVEL SCHOOLS, AND HIGH SCHOOLS

American Federation of Teachers
555 New Jersey Avenue NW
Washington, DC 20001
(202) 879-4400
http://www.aft.org

Council for Exceptional Children
1920 Association Drive
Reston, VA 20191-1589
(888) CEC-SPED or (703) 620-3660;
TTY: (703) 264-9446;
fax: (703) 264-9494
http://www.cec.sped.org

International Reading Association
800 Barksdale Road
P.O. Box 8139
Newark, DE 19714-8139
(302) 731-1600; fax: (302) 731-1057
http://www.reading.org

National Art Education Association
1916 Association Drive
Reston, VA 20191-1590
703-860-8000; fax: 703-860-2960
http://www.naea-reston.org

National Association for the Education of Young Children
1509 16th Street NW
Washington, DC 20036
(800) 424-2460 or (202) 232-8777;
fax: (202) 328-1846
http://www.naeyc.org

National Council for the Social Studies
3501 Newark Street NW
Washington, DC 20016
(202) 966-7840
http://www.ncss.org

National Council of Teachers of English
1111 W. Kenyon Road
Urbana, IL 61801-1096
(800) 369-6283
http://www.ncte.org

National Council of Teachers of Mathematics
1906 Association Drive
Reston, Virginia 20191-1593
(703) 620-9840; fax: (703) 476-2970
http://www.nctm.org

National Education Association
1201 16th Street NW
Washington, DC 20036
(202) 833-4000
http://www.nea.org

National Middle School Association
4151 Executive Parkway, Suite 300
Westerville, OH 43081
(800) 528-6672
http://www.nmsa.org

National Science Teachers Association
1840 Wilson Boulevard
Arlington, VA 22201-3000
(703) 243-7100
http://www.nsta.org

TEACHING SPECIALISTS

American Federation of Teachers
555 New Jersey Avenue NW
Washington, DC 20001
(202) 879-4400
http://www.aft.org

American String Teachers Association
1806 Robert Fulton Drive, Suite 300
Reston, VA 20191
(703) 476-1316; fax (703) 476-1317
http://www.astaweb.com

Council for Exceptional Children
1920 Association Drive
Reston, VA 20191-1589
(888) CEC-SPED or (703) 620-3660;
    TTY: (703) 264-9446;
    fax: (703) 264-9494
http://www.cec.sped.org

International Reading Association
800 Barksdale Road
P.O. Box 8139
Newark, DE 19714-8139
(302) 731-1600; fax: (302) 731-1057
http://www.reading.org

**Learning Disabilities Association
    of America**
4156 Library Road
Pittsburgh, PA 15234-1349
(412) 341-1515; fax: (412) 344-0224
http://www.ldanatl.org

**MENC: The National Association
    for Music Education**
1806 Robert Fulton Drive
Reston, VA 20191
(800) 336-3768 or (703) 860-4000;
    fax: (703) 860-9143
http://www.menc.org

**National Association for Bilingual
    Education**
1220 L Street NW, Suite 605
Washington, DC 20005-4018
(202) 898-1829; fax: (202) 789-2866
http://www.nabe.org

**National Association for Sport and
    Physical Education**
1900 Association Drive
Reston, VA 20191

(800) 213-7193 ext. 410;
    fax: (703) 476-8316
http://www.aahperd.org/naspe/naspe-
    main.html

National Education Association
1201 16th Street NW
Washington, DC 20036
(202) 833-4000
http://www.nea.org

**TESOL, Inc. (Teachers of English to
    Speakers of Other Languages, Inc.)**
700 South Washington Street, Suite 200
Alexandria, VA 22314
(703) 836-0774; fax: (703) 836-7864
http://www.tesol.edu

SPECIALISTS IN STUDENT SERVICES AND SPECIAL EDUCATION SERVICES

American Art Therapy Association
1202 Allanson Road
Mundelein, IL 60060-3808
(888) 290-0878 or (847) 949-6064;
    fax: (847) 566-4580
http://www.arttherapy.org

American Federation of Teachers
555 New Jersey Avenue NW
Washington, DC 20001
(202) 879-4400
http://www.aft.org

American Nurses Association
600 Maryland Avenue SW
Suite 100 West
Washington, DC 20024
(800) 274-4ANA
http://www.nursingworld.org

**American Occupational Therapy
    Association**
4720 Montgomery Lane
Bethesda, MD 20824-1220
(301) 652-2682
http://www.aota.org

American Psychological Association
750 First Street NE
Washington, DC 20002-4242
(800) 374-2721 or (202) 336-5500
http://www.apa.org

American School Health Association
7263 State Route 43
P.O. Box 708
Kent, OH 44240
(330) 678-1601; fax: (330) 678-4526
http://www.ashaweb.org

**American Speech-Language-Hearing
    Association**
10801 Rockville Pike
Rockville, MD 20852
(800) 638-8255; TTY: (301) 571-0457
http://www.asha.org

Council for Exceptional Children
1920 Association Drive
Reston, VA 20191-1589
(888) CEC-SPED or (703) 620-3660;
    TTY: (703) 264-9446;
    fax: (703) 264-9494
http://www.cec.sped.org

**Learning Disabilities Association of
    America**
4156 Library Road
Pittsburgh, PA 15234-1349
(412) 341-1515; fax: (412) 344-0224
http://www.ldanatl.org

National Association of School Nurses
P.O. Box 1300
Scarborough, ME 04070
(207) 883-2117; fax: (207) 883-2683
http://www.nasn.org

National Association of School Psychologists
4340 East West Highway, Suite 402
Bethesda, MD 20814
(301) 657-0270; TDD: (301) 657-4155; fax: (301) 657-0275
http://www.naspweb.org

National Association of Social Workers
750 First Street NE, Suite 700
Washington, DC 20002-4241
(800) 638-8799 or (202) 408-8600
http://www.naswdc.org

National Coalition of Arts Therapies Associations
8455 Colesville Road, Suite 1000
Silver Spring, MD 20910
(714) 751-0103
http://www.ncata.com

National Education Association
1201 16th Street NW
Washington, DC 20036
(202) 833-4000
http://www.nea.org

School Social Work Association of America
P.O. Box 2072
Northlake, IL 60164
(847) 289-4527
http://www.sswaa.org

SCHOOL SUPPORT STAFF

American Federation of Teachers
555 New Jersey Avenue NW
Washington, DC 20001
(202) 879-4400
http://www.aft.org
http://www.aft.org/psrp (home page for paraprofessionals and school-related personnel)

American School Food Service Association
700 S. Washington Street, Suite 300
Alexandria, VA 22314
(703) 739-3900; fax: (703) 739-3915
http://www.asfsa.org

Council for Exceptional Children
1920 Association Drive
Reston, VA 20191-1589
(888) CEC-SPED or (703) 620-3660; TTY: (703) 264-9446
fax: (703) 264-9494
http://www.cec.sped.org

National Association for Bilingual Education
1220 L Street NW, Suite 605
Washington, DC 20005-4018
(202) 898-1829; fax: (202) 789-2866
http://www.nabe.org

National Association for Pupil Transportation
1840 Western Avenue
Albany, NY 12203-0647
(800) 989-NAPT or (518) 452-3611; fax: (518) 218-0867
http://www.napt.org

National Association for the Education of Young Children
1509 16th Street NW
Washington, DC 20036
(800) 424-2460 or (202) 232-8777; fax: (202) 328-1846
http://www.naeyc.org

National Career Development Association
4700 Reed Road, Suite M
Columbus, Ohio 43220
(614) 326-1750; fax: (614) 326-1760
http://www.ncda.org

National Education Association
1201 16th Street NW
Washington, DC 20036
(202) 833-4000
http://www.nea.org
http://www.nea.org/esp (support personnel homepage)

Service Employees International Union
1313 L Street NW
Washington, DC 20005
http://www.seiu.org

COLLEGE AND UNIVERSITY FACULTY

American Association for Adult and Continuing Education
1200 19th Street NW, Suite 300
Washington, D.C. 20036
(202) 429-5131; fax: (202) 223-4579
http://www.albany.edu/aaace

American Association for Higher Education
1 Dupont Circle, Suite 360
Washington, DC 20036-1110
(202) 293-6440; fax: (202) 293-0073
http://www.aahe.org

American Association of University Professors
1012 Fourteenth Street NW, Suite 500
Washington, DC 20005-3465
(202) 737-5900; fax: (202) 737-5526
http://www.aaup.org

American Federation of Teachers
Higher Education Department
555 New Jersey Avenue NW
Washington, DC 20001
(202) 879-4426; fax: (202) 393-6386
http://www.aft.org
http://www.aft.org/higher_ed (home page for higher education division)

National Association of Scholars
221 Witherspoon Street
Second Floor
Princeton, New Jersey 08542-3215
(609) 683-7878; fax: (609) 683-0316
http://www.nas.org

National Education Association
1201 16th Street NW
Washington, DC 20036
(202) 833-4000
http://www.nea.org
http://www.nea.org/he (home page for higher education division)

INSTRUCTORS IN ADULT EDUCATION AND CONTINUING EDUCATION

American Association for Adult and Continuing Education
1200 19th Street NW, Suite 300
Washington, DC 20036
(202) 429-5131; fax: (202) 223-4579
http://www.albany.edu/aaace

American Association of Family and Consumer Sciences
1555 King Street
Alexandria, VA 22314
(703) 706-4600; fax: (703) 706-4663
http://www.aafcs.org

American Correctional Association
4380 Forbest Boulevard
Lanham, MD 20706-4322
(800) 222-5646
http://www.corrections.com/aca

American Dairy Science Association
1111 N. Dunlap Avenue
Savoy, IL 61874
(217) 356-3182; fax: (217) 398-4119
http://12.24.208.139

American Farm Bureau
225 Touhy Avenue
Park Ridge, IL 60068
(847) 685-8600
http://www.fb.com

American Federation of Teachers
555 New Jersey Avenue NW
Washington, DC 20001
(202) 879-4400
http://www.aft.org

American Jail Association
2053 Day Street, Suite 100
Hagerstown, MD 21740-9795
(301) 790-3930; fax: (301) 790-2941
http://www.corrections.com/aja

American Society for Training and Development
1640 King Street, Box 1443
Alexandria, VA 22313-2043
(800) 628-2783 or (703) 683-8100;
  fax: (703) 683-1523
http://www.astd.org

Association for Career and Technical Education
1410 King Street
Alexandria, VA 22314
(800) 826-9972
http://www.avaonline.org

Correctional Education Association
4380 Forbes Boulevard
Lanham, MD 20706
(301) 918-1915; fax: (301) 918-1846
http://metalab.unc.edu/icea

Council for Exceptional Children
1920 Association Drive
Reston, VA 20191-1589
(888) CEC-SPED or (703) 620-3660;
  TTY: (703) 264-9446;
  fax: (703) 264-9494
http://www.cec.sped.org

Epsilon Sigma Phi
http://165.95.58.60
(For more information, contact a local cooperative extension agent.)

International Reading Association
800 Barksdale Road
P.O. Box 8139
Newark, DE 19714-8139
(302) 731-1600; fax: (302) 731-1057
http://www.reading.org

National Association of County Agricultural Agents
252 N. Park Street
Decatur, IL 62523
tel: (217) 876-1220; fax: (217) 877-5382
http://www.cas.psu.edu/docs/coext/
  regions/southeast/cumberland/nacaa/
  nacaa.html

National Association of Extension 4-H Agents
http://www.nae4ha.org
(For more information, contact a local cooperative extension agent.)

National Association of Industrial and Technical Teacher Educators
School of Education
Oregon State University
Education Hall
Corvallis, OR 97331-3502
(541) 737-4661; fax: (541) 737-2040

http://www.orst.edu/dept/naitte

National Education Association
1201 16th Street NW
Washington, DC 20036
(202) 833-4000
http://www.nea.org

National Extension Association of Family and Consumer Sciences
740 B2 E. Flynn Lane
Phoenix, AZ 85014
(602) 212-0453; fax: (602) 212-9692
http://www.neafcs.org

SkillsUSA-VICA
P.O. Box 3000
Leesburg, VA 20177-0300
(703) 777-8810; fax: (703) 777-8999
http://www.skillsusa.org

TESOL, Inc. (Teaching English to Speakers of Other Languages, Inc.)
700 South Washington Street, Suite 200
Alexandria, VA 22314
(703) 836-0774; fax: (703) 836-7864
http://www.tesol.edu

APPENDIX II   279

OVERSEAS TEACHING PROFESSIONS

Association for the Advancement of International Education
Dr. Lewis A. Grell, Executive Director
Thompson House
Westminster College
New Wilmington, PA 16172
(724) 946-7172; fax: (724) 946-7194
http://www.aaie.org

International Association of Teachers of English as a Foreign Language
3 Kinsgdown Chambers
Whitstable, Kent UK, CT5 2FL
http://www.iatefl.org

International Reading Association
800 Barksdale Road
P.O. Box 8139
Newark, DE 19714-8139
(302) 731-1600; fax: (302) 731-1057
http://www.reading.org

National Council of Teachers of Mathematics
1906 Association Drive
Reston, Virginia 20191-1593
(703) 620-9840; fax: (703) 476-2970
http://www.nctm.org

TESOL, Inc. (Teaching English to Speakers of Other Languages)
700 South Washington Street, Suite 200
Alexandria, VA 22314
(703) 836-0774; fax: (703) 836-7864
http://www.tesol.edu

SCHOOL ADMINISTRATORS

American Association of School Administrators
1801 North Moore Street
Arlington, VA 22209-9988
(703) 875-0748
http://www.aasa.org

American Association of School Personnel Administrators
3080 Brickhouse Court
Virginia Beach, VA 23452
(757) 340-1217; fax: (757) 340-1889
http://www.aaspa.org

American Federation of School Administrators
1729 21st Street NW
Washington, DC 20009-1101
(202) 986-4209; fax: (202) 986-4211
http://www.admin.org

American School Food Service Association
700 S. Washington Street, Suite 300
Alexandria, VA 22314
(703) 739-3900; fax: (703) 739-3915
http://www.asfsa.org

Association for Supervision and Curriculum Development
1703 North Beauregard Street
Alexandria, VA 22311-1714
(800) 933-ASCD or (703) 578-9600;
  fax: (703) 575-5400
http://www.ascd.org

Association of School Business Officials
11401 North Shore Drive
Reston, VA 20190-4200
(703) 478-0405; fax: (703) 478-0205
http://www.asbointl.org

Council for Exceptional Children
1920 Association Drive
Reston, VA 20191-1589
(888) CEC-SPED or (703) 620-3660;
  TTY: (703) 264-9446;
  fax: (703) 264-9494
http://www.cec.sped.org

International Reading Association
800 Barksdale Road
P.O. Box 8139
Newark, DE 19714-8139
(302) 731-1600; fax: (302) 731-1057
http://www.reading.org

National Association for Pupil Transportation
1840 Western Avenue
Albany, NY 12203-0647
(800) 989-NAPT or (518) 452-3611;
  fax: (518) 218-0867
http://www.napt.org

National Association of Elementary School Principals
1615 Duke Street
Alexandria, VA 22314
(800) 38-NAESP; fax: (800) 39-NAESP
http://www.naesp.org

National Association of Secondary School Principals
1904 Association Drive
Reston, VA 20191-1537
(703) 860-0200; fax: (703) 476-5432
http://www.nassp.org

National Business Education Association
1914 Association Drive
Reston, VA 20191-1596
(703) 860-8300; fax: (703) 620-4483
http://www.nbea.org

National Council for the Social Studies
3501 Newark Street NW
Washington, DC 20016
(202) 966-7840
http://www.ncss.org

National Middle School Association
4151 Executive Parkway, Suite 300
Westerville, OH 43081
(800) 528-6672
http://www.nmsa.org

Phi Delta Kappa
408 N. Union Street
P.O. Box 789
Bloomington, IN 47402-0789
(800) 766-1156 or (812) 339-1156;
  fax: (812) 339-0018
http://www.pdkintl.org

Urban Superintendents Association of America
P.O. Box 1248
Chesapeake, VA 23327-1248
(757) 436-1032
http://www.usaa.org

COLLEGE AND UNIVERSITY ADMINISTRATORS

American Association for Higher Education
1 Dupont Circle, Suite 360
Washington, DC 20036-1110
(202) 293-6440; fax: (202) 293-0073
http://www.aahe.org

American Association of Collegiate Registrars and Admissions Officers
1 Dupont Circle NW, Suite 520
Washington, DC 20036
(202) 293-9161; fax: (202) 872-8857
http://www.aacrao.com

American Association of University Administrators
17103 Preston Road
LB 107, Suite 250
Dallas, TX 75248-1332
(972) 248-3957; fax: (972) 713-8209
http://www.aaua.org

American College Personnel Association
1 Dupont Circle, Suite 300
Washington, DC 20036
(202) 835-2272; fax: (202) 296-3286
http://www.acpa.nche.edu

American Conference of Academic Deans
1818 R Street NW
Washington, DC 20009
(202) 387-3760; fax: (202) 265-9532
http://www.acad-edu.org

American Society for Industrial Security
1625 Prince Street
Alexandria, VA 22314-2818
(703) 519-6200; fax: (703) 519-6299
http://www.asisonline.org

Association of College Administration Professionals
P.O. Box 1389
Staunton, VA 24402
(540) 885-1873; fax: (540) 885-6133
http://www.acap.org

College and University Personnel Association
1233 20th Street NW, Suite 301
Washington, DC 20036-1250
(202) 429-0311; fax: (202) 429-0149
http://www.cupa.org

International Association of Campus Law Enforcement Administrators
342 N. Main Street
West Hartford, CT 06117-2507
(860) 586-7517; fax: (860) 586-7550
http://www.iaclea.org

International Association of Chiefs of Police
515 North Washington Street
Alexandria, VA 22314
(800) THE-IACP or (703) 836-6767; fax: (703) 836-4543
http://www.theiacp.org

National Association for Women in Education
1325 18th Street NW, Suite 210
Washington, DC 20036
(202) 659-9330; fax: (202) 457-0946
http://www.nawe.org

National Association of Collegiate Directors of Athletics
P.O. Box 16428
Cleveland, OH 44116
(888) 967-2323
http://www.nacda.com

National Association of Collegiate Women Athletic Administrators
4701 Wrightsville Avenue
Oak Park D-1
Wilmington, NC 28403
(910) 793-8244; fax: 910-793-8299
http://www.nacwaa.org

National Association of Scholars
221 Witherspoon Street, Second Floor
Princeton, New Jersey 08542-3215
(609) 683-7878; fax: (609) 683-0316
http://www.nas.org

National Association of Student Personnel Administrators
1875 Connecticut Avenue NW, Suite 418
Washington, DC 20009
(202) 265-7500; fax: (202) 797-1157
http://www.naspa.org

National Sheriffs' Association
1450 Duke Street
Alexandria, VA 22314-3490
(703) 836-7827
http://www.sheriffs.org

National Society of Fund Raising Executives
1101 King Street, Suite 700
Alexandria, VA 22314
(703) 684-0410; fax (703) 684-0540
http://www.nsfre.org

COUNSELORS

American Counseling Association
5999 Stevenson Avenue
Alexandria, Virginia 22304
(800) 347-6647
http://www.counseling.org

American Federation of Teachers
555 New Jersey Avenue NW
Washington, DC 20001
(202) 879-4400
http://www.aft.org

American School Counselor Association
801 North Fairfax Street, Suite 310
Alexandria, VA 22314
(800) 306-4722 or (703) 683-2722; fax: (703) 683-1619
http://www.schoolcounselor.org

Council for Exceptional Children
1920 Association Drive
Reston, VA 20191-1589
(888) CEC-SPED or (703) 620-3660;
TTY: (703) 264-9446;
fax: (703) 264-9494
http://www.cec.sped.org

National Association for the Education of Young Children
1509 16th Street NW
Washington, DC 20036

(800) 424-2460 or (202) 232-8777;
fax: (202) 328-1846
http://www.naeyc.org

National Career Development Association
4700 Reed Road, Suite M
Columbus, Ohio 43220
(614) 326-1750; fax: (614) 326-1760
http://www.ncda.org

National Education Association
1201 16th Street NW
Washington, DC 20036
(202) 833-4000
http://www.nea.org

National Employment Counseling Association
5999 Stevenson Avenue
Alexandria, Virginia 22304

(800) 347-6647
http://www.geocities.com/Athens/Acropolis/6491/neca.html

National Middle School Association
4151 Executive Parkway, Suite 300
Westerville, OH 43081
(800) 528-6672
http://www.nmsa.org

HEALTH EDUCATORS

American Academy of Husband-Coached Childbirth
Box 5224
Sherman Oaks, CA 91413-5224
(800) 4-A-BIRTH or (818) 788-6662
http://www.bradleybirth.com

American Association for Health Education
1900 Association Drive
Reston, VA 20191
(800) 213-7193
http://www.aahperd.org/aahe.html

American College Health Association
P.O. Box 28937
Baltimore, MD 21240
(410) 859-1500
http://www.acha.org

American Dietetic Association
216 W. Jackson Boulevard
Chicago, IL 60606-6995
(800) 877-1600 or (312) 899-0040
http://www.eatright.org

American Heart Association
National Center
7272 Greenville Avenue
Dallas, TX 75231
http://www.americanheart.org

American Public Health Association
800 I Street NW
Washington, DC 20001
(202) 777-2742; TTY: (202) 777-2500;
fax: (202) 777-2534
http://www.apha.org

American Red Cross
Attn: Public Inquiry Office
431 18th Street
Washington, DC 20006
http://www.redcross.org
(Also contact a local Red Cross office for further information.)

American Safety and Health Institute
8324 Corporate Way, Suite A
New Port Richey, FL 34653
(800) 246-5101; fax: 1-727-817-0696
http://www.ashinstitute.com

American School Health Association
7263 State Route 43
P.O. Box 708
Kent, OH 44240
(330) 678-1601
http://www.ashaweb.org

American Society for Nutritional Sciences
American Society for Nutritional Sciences
9650 Rockville Pike
Bethesda, MD 20814
(301) 530-7050; fax: (301) 571-1892
http://www.faseb.org/asns

Association of Labor Assistants and Childbirth Educators
P.O. Box 382724
Cambridge, MA 02238
(617) 441-2500

Birthworks, Inc.
P.O. Box 2045
Medford, NJ 08055
888-TO-BIRTH (862-4784)
http://www.birthworks.org

International and American Associations of Clinical Nutritionists
5200 Keller Springs Road, Suite 410
Dallas, Texas 75248
(972) 250-2829; fax: (972) 250-0233
http://www.iaacn.org

International Childbirth Education Association, Inc.
P.O. Box 20048
Minneapolis, Minnesota 55420 USA
(612) 854-8660
http://www.icea.org

Lamaze International
1200 19th Street NW, Suite 300
Washington, DC 20036
(800) 368-4404; fax: (202) 857-1102
http://www.lamaze-childbirth.com

Medic First Aid
Mailing Address:
P.O. Box 21738
Eugene, Oregon 97402
Street Address:
500 S. Danebo Avenue
Eugene, Oregon 97402
(800) 800-7099 or (541) 344-7099;
fax: (541) 344-7429
http://www.medicfirstaid.com

National Safety Council
1121 Spring Lake Drive
Itasca, IL 60143-3201
(630) 285-1121; fax: (630) 285-1315
http://www.nsc.org

Society for Public Health Education
750 First Street NE, Suite 910
Washington, DC 20002
(202) 408-9804
http://www.sophe.org

LIBRARIANS

American Association of School Librarians
50 East Huron Street
Chicago, IL 60611
(800) 545-2433 or (312) 280-4386;
    fax: (312) 664-7459
http://www.ala.org/aasl/about.html

American Federation of Teachers
555 New Jersey Avenue NW
Washington, DC 20001
(202) 879-4400
http://www.aft.org

American Library Association
50 East Huron Street
Chicago, Illinois 60611
(800) 545-2433; TDD: (312) 944-7298;
    fax: (312) 440-9374
http://www.ala.org

American Society for Information Science
8720 Georgia Avenue, Suite 501
Silver Spring, MD 20910
(301) 495-0900; fax: (301) 495-0810
http://www.asis.org

Association for Educational Communications and Technology
1800 N. Stonelake Drive, Suite 2
Bloomington, IN 47404
(812) 335-7675; fax: (812) 335-7678
http://www.aect.org

Association for Library Services to Children
50 East Huron Street
Chicago, IL 60611-2795
(800) 545-2433, extension 2163;
    fax: (312) 944-7671
http://www.ala.org/alsc

Association of College and Research Libraries
50 East Huron Street
Chicago, IL 60611-2795
(800) 545-2433 or (312) 944-6780; fax:
    (312) 280-2520
http://www.ala.org/acrl

National Education Association
1201 16th Street NW
Washington, DC 20036
(202) 833-4000
http://www.nea.org

Public Library Association
50 East Huron Street
Chicago, IL 60611
(800) 545-2433, extension 5752; fax:
    (312) 280-5029
http://www.pla.org

EDUCATIONAL AND INSTRUCTIONAL TECHNOLOGY SPECIALISTS

Alliance for Technology Access
2175 East Francisco Boulevard, Suite L
San Rafael, CA 94901
(415) 455-4575
http://www.ataccess.org

American Association of School Administrators
1801 North Moore Street
Arlington, VA 22209-9988
(703) 875-0748
http://www.aasa.org

American Federation of Teachers
555 New Jersey Avenue NW
Washington, DC 20001
(202) 879-4400
http://www.aft.org

American Society for Training and Development
1640 King Street, Box 1443
Alexandria, VA 22313-2043
(800) 628-2783 or (703) 683-8100;
    fax: (703) 683-1523
http://www.astd.org

Association for Educational Communications and Technology
1800 North Stonelake Drive, Suite 2
Bloomington, IN 47404
(812) 335-7675; fax: (812) 335-7678
http://www.aect.org

Association for the Advancement of Computing in Education
P.O. Box 2966
Charlottesville, VA 22902
(804) 973-3987; fax: (804) 978-7449
http://www.aace.org

Computer Assisted Language Instruction Consortium
Southwest Texas State University
116 Centennial Hall
San Marcos, TX 78666
(512) 245-1417; fax: (512) 245-8298
http://calico.org

Computer-Assisted Language Learning Interest Section
TESOL (Teachers of English to Speakers
    of Other Languages, Inc.)
700 South Washington Street,
Suite 200
Alexandria, VA 22314
(703) 836-0774; fax: (703) 836-7864
http://darkwing.uoregon.edu/~call
http://www.tesol.edu (TESOL web site)

International Association for Language Learning Technology
Ed Dente, IALL Membership
    Coordinator
Language Media Center
Tufts University
Medford, MA 02155
Phone: (617) 627-3036
http://iall.net

International Society for Performance Improvement
1300 L Street NW, Suite 1250
Washington, DC 20005
(202) 408-7969; fax: (202) 408-7972
http://www.ispi.org

International Society for Technology in Education
480 Charnelton Street
Eugene, OR 97401-2626
(800) 336-5191; fax: (541) 302-3778
http://www.iste.org

International Technology Education Association
1914 Association Drive, Suite 201
Reston, VA 20191-1539
Phone (703) 860-2100;
    fax (703) 860-0353
http://www.iteawww.org

National Education Association
1201 16th Street NW
Washington, DC 20036
(202) 833-4000
http://www.nea.org

Rehabilitation Engineering and Assistive Technology of North America
1700 North Moore Street, Suite 1540
Arlington, VA 22209-1903
(703) 524-6686; TTY: (703) 524-6639;
    fax: (703) 524-6630
http://www.resna.org

Technology and Media
The Council for Exceptional Children
1920 Association Drive
Reston, VA 20191-1589
(888) 232-7733 or (703) 620-3660;
    TDD: (703) 264-9446;
    fax: (703) 264-9494
http://www.tamcec.org

CURRICULUM AND INSTRUCTION DEVELOPERS

American Association for Adult and Continuing Education
1200 19th Street NW, Suite 300
Washington, DC 20036
(202) 429-5131; fax: (202) 223-4579
http://www.albany.edu/aaace

American Association of School Administrators
1801 North Moore Street
Arlington, VA 22209-9988
(703) 875-0748
http://www.aasa.org

American Chemical Society
1155 16th Street, NW
Washington, DC 20036
(800) 227-5558 or (202) 872-4600
http://www.acs.org

American Society for Training and Development
1640 King Street, Box 1443
Alexandria, VA 22313-2043
(800) 628-2783 or (703) 683-8100;
    fax: (703) 683-1523
http://www.astd.org

Association for Computing Machinery
1515 Broadway
New York, NY 10036
(800) 342-6626 or (212) 626-0500
http://www.acm.org

Association for Educational Communications and Technology
1800 N. Stonelake Drive, Suite 2
Bloomington, IN 47404
(812) 335-7675; fax: (812) 335-7678
http://www.aect.org

Association for Supervision and Curriculum Development
1703 North Beauregard Street
Alexandria, VA 22311-1714
(800) 933-ASCD or (703) 578-9600;
    fax: (703) 575-5400
http://www.ascd.org

Association for the Advancement of Computing in Education
P.O. Box 2966
Charlottesville, VA 22902
(804) 973-3987; fax: (804) 978-7449
http://www.aace.org

Association of Internet Professionals
15 East 26th Street, Suite 1403
New York, NY 10010
(877) AIP-0800 or (212) 689-7047
http://www.association.org

Association of Shareware Professionals
ASP Executive Director
157-F Love Avenue
Greenwood, IN 46142
(317) 888-2194; fax: (317) 888-2195
http://www.asp-shareware.org

Council for Exceptional Children
1920 Association Drive
Reston, VA 20191-1589
(888) CEC-SPED or (703) 620-3660;
    TTY: (703) 264-9446;
    fax: (703) 264-9494
http://www.cec.sped.org

Editorial Freelancers Association
71 West 23rd Street, Suite 1910
New York, NY 10010
(212) 929-5400; fax: (212) 929-5439
http://www.the-efa.org

Educational Software Cooperative
11846 Balboa Boulevard, PMB 226
Granada Hills, CA 91344
http://www.edu-soft.org

IEEE Computer Society, a society of the Institute of Electrical and Electronics Engineers
1730 Massachusetts Avenue NW
Washington, DC 20036-1992
(202) 371-0101; fax: (202) 728-9614
http://computer.org

International Reading Association
800 Barksdale Road
P.O. Box 8139
Newark, DE 19714-8139
(302) 731-1600; fax: (302) 731-1057
http://www.reading.org

International Society for Performance Improvement
1300 L Street NW, Suite 1250
Washington, DC 20005
(202) 408-7969; fax: (202) 408-7972
http://www.ispi.org

MENC: The National Association for Music Education
1806 Robert Fulton Drive
Reston, VA 20191
(800) 336-3768 or (703) 860-4000;
    fax: (703) 860-9143
http://www.menc.org

National Association of Elementary School Principals
1615 Duke Street
Alexandria, VA 22314
(800) 38-NAESP; fax: (800) 39-NAESP
http://www.naesp.org

National Association of Secondary School Principals
1904 Association Drive
Reston, VA 20191-1537
(703) 860-0200; fax: (703) 476-5432
http://www.nassp.org

National Council for the Social Studies
3501 Newark Street NW
Washington, DC 20016
(202) 966-7840
http://www.ncss.org

National Council of Teachers of English
1111 W. Kenyon Road
Urbana, IL 61801-1096
(800) 369-6283
http://www.ncte.org

National Middle School Association
4151 Executive Parkway, Suite 300
Westerville, OH 43081
(800) 528-6672
http://www.nmsa.org

TESOL, Inc. (Teachers of English to Speakers of Other Languages, Inc.)
700 South Washington Street, Suite 200
Alexandria, VA 22314
(703) 836-0774; fax: (703) 836-7864
http://www.tesol.edu

EMPLOYEE TRAINING SPECIALISTS

American Society for Training and Development
1640 King Street, Box 1443
Alexandria, VA 22313-2043
(800) 628-2783 or (703) 683-8100; fax: (703) 683-1523
http://www.astd.org

Information Technology Training Association
1616 North Ft. Myer Drive, Suite 1300
Arlington, VA 22209
(703) 522-5055; fax: (703) 525-2279
http://www.itaa.org

International Society for Performance Improvement
1300 L Street NW, Suite 1250
Washington, DC 20005
(202) 408-7969; fax: (202) 408-7972
http://www.ispi.org

INDEPENDENT INSTRUCTORS

Aircraft Owners and Pilots Association
421 Aviation Way
Frederick, MD 21701
(301) 695-2000; fax: (301) 695-2375
http://www.aopa.org

American Association of Riding Schools
8375 Coldwater Road
Davison, MI 48423-8966
(810) 653-1440; fax: (810) 658-9733
http://www.ucanride.com

American Dance Guild
P.O. Box 2006, Lenox Hill Station
New York, NY 10021
(212) 932-2789
http://www.americandanceguild.org

American Horse Council
1700 K Street NW, Suite 300
Washington, DC 20006
Fax: (202) 296-1970
http://www.horsecouncil.org

American Riding Instructors Association
28801 Trenton Court
Bonita Springs, FL 34134
(941) 948-3232; fax: (941) 948-5053
http://www.win.net/~aria

Dance Educators of America
P.O. Box 607
Pelham, New York 10803
(800) 229-3868 or (914) 636-3200; fax: (914) 636-5895
http://www.deadance.com

Horse Industry Alliance
8314 White Settlement Road
Fort Worth, Texas 76108
(817) 246-7433; fax: (817) 246-4388
http://www.horseindustryalliance.com

Music Teachers National Association
The Carew Tower
441 Vine Street, Suite 505
Cincinnati, Ohio 45202
(513) 421-1420
http://www.mtna.org

National Association of Flight Instructors
EAA Aviation Center
P.O. Box 3086
Oshkosh, WI 54903-3086
(920) 426-6801; fax: (920) 426-6778
http://www.nafinet.org

National Dance Association
1900 Association Drive
Reston, VA 20191
(703) 476-3436; fax: (703) 476-9527
http://www.aahperd.org/nda/nda-main.html

RECREATION AND FITNESS PROFESSIONALS

Aerobics and Fitness Association of America
15250 Ventura Boulevard, Suite 200
Ventura, CA 91403-3297
(800) 446-2322; fax: (818) 788-6301
http://www.afaa.com

American College of Sports Medicine
401 W. Michigan Street
Indianapolis, IN 46202-3233
(317) 637-9200; fax: (317) 634-7817
http://www.acsm.org

American Council on Exercise
5820 Oberlin Drive, Suite 102
San Diego, CA 92121-3787
(800) 825-3636; fax: (858) 535-1778
http://www.acefitness.org

APPENDIX II   285

American Fitness Professionals and Associates
P.O. Box 214
Ship Bottom, NJ 08008
(609) 978-7583
http://www.afpafitness.com

Aquatic Exercise Association
P.O. Box 1609
Nokomis, FL 34274-1609
(888) AEA-WAVE or (941) 486-8600;
   fax: (941) 486-8820
http://www.aeawave.com

Ecotourism Society
P.O. Box 755
North Bennington, VT 05257
(802) 447-2121; fax: (802) 447-2122
http://www.ecotourism.org

IDEA
6190 Cornerstone Court East, Suite 204
San Diego, CA 92121-3773
(800) 999-4332 or (858) 535-8979;
   fax: (858) 535-8234
http://www.ideafit.com

International Association of Tour Managers, North America
9500 Rainier Avenue S, #603
Seattle, WA 98118
(206) 725-7108
http://members.aol.com/iatmone
http://www.iatm.co.uk (web site for world headquarters)

National Dance-Exercise Instructors Training Association
1503 S Washington Avenue, Suite 208
Minneapolis, MN 55454-1037
(800) AEROBIC (800-237-6242)
   or (612) 340-1306;
   fax: (612) 340-1619
http://www.NDEITA.com

National Strength and Conditioning Association
1955 N. Union Boulevard
Colorado Springs, CO 80909
(719) 632-6722; fax: (719) 632-6367
http://www.nsca-lift.org/menu.htm

National Tour Association
546 East Main Street
Lexington, KY 40508-2300
(800) 682-8886; fax: (606) 226-4414
http://www.ntaonline.com

Outdoor Guides Association
P.O. Box 12996
Tallahassee, Florida 32317
(850) 671-4409; fax: (850) 668-2340
http://wwwdi.com/oga

ENVIRONMENTAL EDUCATORS AND ANIMAL TRAINERS

American Horse Council
1700 K Street, Suite 300
Washington, DC 20006
http://www.horsecouncil.org

American Humane Association
63 Inverness Drive East
Englewood, CO 80112-5117
(800) 227-4645 or (303) 792-9900;
   fax: 303-792-5333
http://www.americanhumane.org

American Society for the Prevention of Cruelty to Animals (ASPCA)
National Shelter Outreach
201 East 86th Street
New York, NY 10028
(212) 876-7700; fax: (212) 860-3435
http://www.aspca.org/adopt/sa.html

Animal Behavior Society
Indiana University
2611 East 10th Street, #170
Bloomington, IN 47408-2603
Fax: (812) 856-5542
http://www.animalbehavior.org/ABS

Association of National Park Rangers
P.O. Box 108
Larned, KS 67550-0108
(316) 285-2107
http://www.anpr.org

Association of Pet Dog Trainers
66 Morris Avenue, Suite 2A
Springfield, NJ 07081
(800) PET-DOGS
http://www.apdt.com

Guide Dog Users Inc.
14311 Astrodome Drive
Silver Spring, Maryland 20906-2245
(301) 598-2131
http://www.infinet.com/~jeninems/gdui.html

Humane Society of the United States
2100 L Street NW
Washington, DC 20037
http://www.hsus.org

National Association for Humane and Environmental Education
P.O. Box 362
East Haddam, CT 06423-0362
(860) 434-8666
http://www.nahee.org

National Association for Interpretation
Mailing address:
P.O. Box 2246
Fort Collins, CO 80522
Street address:
528 South Howes
Fort Collins, CO 80521
(888) 900-8283 or (970) 484-8283;
   fax: (970) 484-8179
http://www.interpnet.com

National Association of Dog Obedience Instructors
Attn: Corresponding Secretary
729 Grapevine Highway, Suite 369
Hurst, TX 76054-2085
http://www.nadoi.org

National Association of Environmental Professionals
6524 Ramoth Drive
Jacksonville, FL 32226-3202
(888) 251-9902; fax: (904) 251-9901
http://naep.org

National Audubon Society
700 Broadway
New York, NY 10003
(212) 979-3000
http://www.audubon.org

National Society for Park Resources, a branch of the National Recreation and Park Association
22377 Belmont Ridge Road
Ashburn, VA 20148
(703) 858-2170; fax: (703) 858-0794
http://www.activeparks.org/npra/bsr/branches/nspr/index_n spr.htm

National Wildlife Federation
8925 Leesburg Pike
Vienna, VA 22184
(703) 790-4000
http://www.nwf.org

Nature Conservancy
4245 North Fairfax Drive, Suite 100
Arlington, VA 22203-1606
(800) 628-6860
http://www.tnc.org

North American Association for Environmental Education
1825 Connecticut Avenue NW, 8th Floor
Washington, DC 20009-5708
(202) 884-8912; fax: (202) 884-8455
http://www.naaee.org

North American Police Work Dog Association
4222 Manchester Avenue
Perry, Ohio 44081
(888) 4CANINE
http://www.napwda.com

Sierra Club
85 Second Street, Second Floor
San Francisco, CA 94105-3441
(415) 977-5500; fax: (415) 977-5799
http://www.sierraclub.org

United States Police Canine Association
http://www.uspcak9.com
Contact persons are:

- Ivan 'Skip' Brewster
  National Secretary, USPCA
  9600 Island Lake Road
  Dexter, MI 48130
  (888) 371-4014

- James Nichols, Jr.
  National President, USPCA
  P.O. Box 973
  Punta Gorda, FL 33951
  Fax: (941) 743-7497

- Kevin Conroy
  National Treasurer, USPCA
  4 Coed Lane
  Farmingville, NY 11738-2202
  (516) 732-4565

APPENDIX III
STATE EDUCATION LICENSURE AGENCIES

The following is a list of state education agencies that grant licensure for public school teachers, administrators, and other school professionals. Addresses and phone numbers are given so you can contact agencies for further information.

(Note: Street addresses, phone numbers, and web site addresses change from time to time. You may be able to find an agency's new web site by entering its name in a search engine. If a street address or phone number is no longer available, contact a local school district office.)

Alabama Department of Education
Teacher Certification Section
Gordon Persons Building
P.O. Box 302101
Montgomery, AL 36130-2101
(334) 242-9977
http://www.alsde.edu

Alaska Department of Education and Early Development
Teacher Certification Administrative Services
801 West 10th Street, Suite 100
Juneau, AK 99801-1894
(907) 465-2831; fax: (907) 465-2441
http://www.eed.state.ak.us

Arizona Department of Education
Teacher Certification Unit
1535 W. Jefferson Street, Bin 34
Phoenix, AZ 85007
(602) 542-4367; fax: (602) 542-1141
http://www.ade.state.az/us

Arkansas Department of Education
Office of Professional Licensure
4 Capitol Mall
Little Rock, AR 72201-1071
(501) 682-4344
http://arkedu.state.ar.us

California Commission on Teacher Credentialing
1900 Capitol Avenue
Sacramento, CA 95814-4213
(916) 445-0184
http://www.ctc.ca.gov

Colorado Department of Education
Educator Licensing Unit
201 E. Colfax Avenue
Denver, CO 80203
(303) 866-6628
http://www.cde.state.co.us/index_home.htm

Connecticut Department of Education
Bureau of Certification and Professional Development
P.O. Box 150471, Room 243
Hartford, CT 06115-0471
(860) 566-5201; fax: (860) 566-8289
http://www.state.ct.us/sdel

Delaware Department of Education
Professional Standards and Certification
The Townsend Building
P.O. Box 1402
Dover, DE 19903
(800) 433-5292 or (302) 736-4688
http://www.doe.state.de.us

District Of Columbia Department of Education
Teacher Education and Certification Branch
215 G Street NE, Room 101A
Washington, DC 20002
(202) 724-4246; fax: (202) 724-8784
http://www.k12.dc.us

Florida Department of Education
Bureau of Teacher Certification
325 West Gaines Street, Suite 201
Tallahassee, FL 32399-0400
(800) 445-6739, in-state number;
   (850) 448-2317, out-of-state number
http://www.firn.edu/doe

Georgia Professional Standards Commission
Certification Section
1452 Twin Towers East
Atlanta, GA 30334
(404) 657-9000; fax: (404) 651-9185
http://www.doe.k12.ga.us

Hawaii Department of Education
Personnel Certification and Development Unit
Queen Liliuokalani Building
Room 301
Honolulu, HI 96813
(808) 586-3276
http://www.k12.hi.us

Idaho State Department of Education
Teacher Education and Certification
P.O. Box 83720
Boise, ID 83720-0027
(208) 332-6800
http://www.sde.state.id.us/Dept

Illinois State Board of Education
State Board of Teacher Education and Certification
100 N. First Street
Springfield, IL 62777-0001
(217) 782-2805
http://www.isbe.state.il.us

Indiana Professional Standards Board
Teacher Certification Program
251 E. Ohio, Suite 201
Indianapolis, IN 46204-2133
(317) 232-9010; fax: (317) 232-9023
http://ideanet.doe.state.in.us

Iowa Board of Educational Examiners
Licensing Bureau
Grimes State Office Building
Des Moines, IA 50319
(515) 281-3245
http://www.state.ia.us/educatel

Kansas State Department of Education
Certification and Teacher Education
 Department
120 SE 10th Avenue
Topeka, KS 66612-1182
(785) 296-2288; fax: (785) 296-7933
http://www.ksbe.state.ks.us

Kentucky Department of Education
Office of Teacher Education and
 Certification
1024 Capital Center Drive, Suite 225
Frankfort, KY 40601
(502) 573-4606
http://www.kde.state.ky.us

Louisiana Department of Education
Division of Teacher Standards,
 Assessment and Certification
P.O. Box 94064
Baton Rouge, LA 70804-9064
(225) 342-3490; fax: (225) 342-3499
http://www.doe.state.la.us/DOE/asps/
 home.asp

Maine Department of Education
Division of Certification and Placement
23 State House Station
Augusta, ME 04333-0023
(207) 287-5944
http://janus.state.me.us/education/
 homepage.htm

**Maryland State Department of
 Education**
Division of Certification and Accreditation
200 W. Baltimore Street
Baltimore, MD 21201
(410) 767-0412
http://www.msde.state.md.us

**Massachusetts Department of
 Education**
Office of Certification
 and Credentialing
350 Main Street
Malden, MA 02148
(781) 338-6600; fax: (781) 338-3391
http://www.doe.mass.edu

Michigan Department of Education
Office of Professional Preparation and
 Certification
608 West Allegan Street
Hannah Building
Lansing, MI 48933
(517) 373-3310; fax: (517) 373-0542
http://www.mde.state.mi.us

**Minnesota Department of Children,
 Families and Learning**
Personnel Licensing
1500 Highway 36 West
Roseville, MN 55113-4266
(651) 582-8691
http://www.educ.state.mn.us

Mississippi Department of Education
Division of Teacher Certification
P.O. Box 771
Jackson, MS 39205-0771
(601) 359-3483
http://www.mde.k12.ms.us

**Missouri State Department of
 Elementary and Secondary
 Education**
Teacher Education and Certification
P.O. Box 480
Jefferson City, MO 65102-0480
(573) 751-3486
http://services.dese.state.mo.us

Montana Office of Public Instruction
Certification Division
P.O. Box 202501
Helena, MT 59620-2501
(406) 444-3150; fax: (406) 444-2893
http://www.metnet.mt.gov

Nebraska Department of Education
Teacher Education and Certification
301 Centennial Mail South
Lincoln, NE 68509
(402) 471-2496
http://www.edneb.org/IPS/mainNDE.html

Nevada Department of Education
Teacher Licensure
1850 East Sahara Avenue, Suite 205
Las Vegas, NV 89104
(702) 486-6458; fax: (702) 486-6450
http://www.nsn.k12.nv.us/nvdoe

**New Hampshire Department of
 Education**
Bureau of Credentialing
State Office Park South
101 Pleasant Street
Concord, NH 03301
(603) 271-2408; fax: (603) 271-1953
http://www.state.nh.us/doel

New Jersey Department of Education
Office of Licensing and Academic
 Credentials
CN 503
Trenton, NJ 08625-0503
(609) 292-2070
http://www.state.nj.us/education

New Mexico Department of Education
Professional Licensure Unit
300 Don Gaspar
Santa Fe, NM 87501-2786
(505) 827-6587
http://www.sde.state.nm.us

New York State Education Department
Office of Teaching
Cultural Ed. Center, Room 5-A-11
Albany, NY 12230
(518) 474-3901
http://www.nysed.gov

**North Carolina Department of Public
 Instruction**
Licensure Section
301 N. Wilmington Street
Raleigh, NC 27601-2825
(919) 733-4125;
http://www.dpi.state.nc.us

**North Dakota Department of Public
 Instruction**
Education Standards and Practices
 Board
600 East Boulevard Avenue
Bismarck, ND 58505-0440
(701) 328-2264
http://www.dpi.state.nd.us/dpi/index.htm

Ohio Department of Education
Division of Teacher Education and
 Certification
65 South Front Street, Room 412
Columbus, OH 43215-4183
(614) 466-3593; fax: (614) 466-1999
http://www.ode.ohio.gov/www/to/teacher.
 html

**Oklahoma State Department of
 Education**
Professional Standards Section
2500 N. Lincoln Boulevard, Room 211
Oklahoma City, OK 73105-4599
(405) 521-3337; fax: (405) 521-6205
http://sde.state.state.ok.us

Oregon Department of Education
Teacher Standards and Practices
 Commission
255 Capitol Street NE, Suite 105
Salem, OR 97310-1332
(503) 378-3586
http://www.ode.state.or.us

APPENDIX III

Pennsylvania Department of Education
Bureau of Teacher Certification and
 Preparation
333 Market Street
Harrisburg, PA 17126-0333
(717) 787-3356
http://www.pde.psu.edu

Rhode Island Department of Education
Teacher Education
255 Westminster Street
Providence, RI 02903
(401) 277-4600
http://instruct.ride.ri.net/RIDE1

**South Carolina Department
 of Education**
Office of Teacher Education,
 Certification, and Evaluation
1600 Gervais Street
Columbia, SC 2920-3414
(803) 734-8466; fax: (803) 734-2873
http://www.state.sc.us/sde/index.htm

**South Dakota State Department
 of Education and Cultural Affairs**
Teacher Education and Certification
700 Governors Drive
Pierre, SD 57501-2291
(605) 773-3553; fax: (605) 773-6139
http://www.state.sd.us/state/executive/deca

Tennessee Department of Education
Office of Teacher Licensing
Andrew Johnson Tower
710 James Robertson Parkway, 5th floor
Nashville, TN 37243-0377
(615) 532-4885; fax: (615) 741-6236
http://www.state.tn.us/education

Texas Education Agency
State Board for Educator Certification
1001 Trinity
Austin, TX 78701-2603
(512) 469-3000; fax: (512) 469-3018
http://www.tea.state.tx.us

Utah State Office of Education
250 East 500 South
Salt Lake City, UT 84111
(801) 538-7740
http://www.usoe.k12.ut.us

Vermont Department of Education
Licensing
120 State Street
Montpelier, VT 05620-2501
(802) 828-2445; fax: (802) 828-3140
http://www.state.vt.us/educ

Virginia Department of Education
Office for Teacher Education and
 Licensure
P.O. Box 2120
Richmond, VA 23818-2120
(804) 225-2022
http://www.pen.k12.va.us

**Washington Office of the Superintendent
 of Public Instruction**
Professional Education and Certification
Old Capitol Building
P.O. Box 47200
Olympia, WA 98504-7200
(360) 753-6773; fax: (360) 586-0145
http://www.k12.wa.us

**West Virginia Department
 of Education**
1900 Kanawha Boulevard East,
 Building 6
Charleston, WV 25305
(800) 982-2378 or (304) 558-7010
http://www.wvde.state.wv.us

**Wisconsin Department of Public
 Instruction**
Licensing Team
P.O. Box 7841
125 South Webster Street
Madison, WI 53707-7841
(608) 266-1028
http://www.dpi.state.wi.us

Wyoming Department of Education
Wyoming Professional Teaching
 Standards Board
2300 Capitol Avenue
Hathaway Building, 2nd Floor
Cheyenne, WY 82002-0050
(307) 777-6248; fax: (307) 777-6234
http://www.k12.wy.us/wdehome.html

APPENDIX IV
ADDITIONAL RESOURCES—ORGANIZATIONS AND INTERNET RESOURCES

Listed below are some organizations and web sites that can help you learn more about many of the different professions that are discussed in this book. You will also find some resources that offer general career information.

(Note: All web site addresses were current when this book was being written. If you come across an address that no longer works, you may be able find the new address by entering the name of the organization or the web page title in a search engine.)

GENERAL CAREER INFORMATION

U.S. Department of Education
400 Maryland Avenue SW
Washington, DC 20202
(800) USA-LEARN;
   TTY: (800) 437-0833;
   fax: (202) 401-0689
http://www.ed.gov

U.S. Office of Personnel Management
1900 E Street NW
Washington, DC 20415-0001
http://www.opm.gov

Web sites

Occupational Outlook Handbook 2000–2001
U.S. Bureau of Labor Statistics
http://stats.bls.gov/ocohome.htm

California Occupational Guides
California Employment Development Department
http://www.calmis.cahwnet.gov/htmlfile/subject/GUIDE.HTM

Michigan Occupational Information System
http://www.mois.org

The Educator's Network
(job postings for public and private positions)
http://www.school-jobs.com

K12jobs.com
(jobs postings for teaching and administrative positions)
http://www.k12jobs.com

America's Job Bank
http://www.ajb.dni.us

CareerMosaic
http://www.careermosaic.com

Monster.com
http://www.monster.com

USA Jobs
U.S. Office of Personnel Management
(for information about federal careers and job vacancies)
http://www.usajobs.opm.gov

ADULT EDUCATION AND CONTINUING EDUCATION INSTRUCTORS

ERIC Clearinghouse on Adult, Career, and Vocational Education
Center on Education and Training for Employment
College of Education
The Ohio State University
1900 Kenny Road
Columbus, OH 43210-1090
(800) 848-4815, extension 2-7069
   or (614) 292-7069; TTY/TDD:
   (614) 688-8734; fax: 614/292-1260
http://ericacve.org

National Institute for Literacy
1775 I Street NW, Suite 730
Washington, DC 20006
(202) 233-2025; fax: (202) 233-2050
http://novel.nifl.gov

Office of Vocational and Adult Education
U. S. Department of Education
4090 MES
400 Maryland Avenue SW
Washington, DC 20202
(202) 205-5451; fax: (202) 205-8748
http://www.ed.gov/offices/OVAE

Web sites

Division of Adult Education and Literacy Clearinghouse Bibliography of Resource Materials
http://www.ed.gov/offices/OVAE/bib98.html

Literacy Online
University of Pennsylvania
http://litserver.literacy.upenn.edu

Vocational Education Resources
by Steven E. Sorg, Ph.D.
http://pegasus.cc.ucf.edu/~sorg/vocation.html

COLLEGE/UNIVERSITY FACULTY AND ADMINISTRATORS

American Council on Education
1 Dupont Circle NW
Washington, DC 20036
(202) 939-9300; fax: (202) 833-4760
http://www.ACENET.edu

U.S. Department of Education
   Office of Postsecondary Education
Department of Education
Regional Office Building 3
7th and D Streets, SW
Washington, DC 20202
http://www.ed.gov/offices/OPE

Web sites

A Brief Summary of the Best Practices in College Teaching
compiled by Tom Drummand, North Seattle Community College
http://nsccux.sccd.ctc.edu/~eceprog/bstprac.html

HigherEdjobs.com
http://www.higheredjobs.com

About Student Affairs
by Jesuit Association of Student Personnel Administrators
http://jaspa.creighton.edu/about/student_affairs.htm

StudentAffairs.com
(internet resource for college student affairs)
http://studentaffairs.com

Campus Law Enforcement Web Sites
http://dpsw.usc.edu/UnivPDWeb.html

Campus Crime
http://www.bpinews.com/edu/pages/cc.htm

Campus Security
Office of Postsecondary Education, U.S. Department of Education
http://www.ed.gov/offices/OPE/PPI/security.html

Careers in Fundraising
http://www.charityvillage.com/charityvillage/research/rca r.html

Philanthropy News Network Online
http://www.pj.org

COOPERATIVE EXTENSION AGENTS

Cooperative State Research, Education and Extension Service
U.S. Department of Agriculture
Washington, DC 20250-0900
(202) 720-3029; fax: (202) 690-0289
http://www.reeusda.gov

Web sites

National Association of State Universities and Land-Grant Colleges
http://www.nasulgc.org

The National 4-H
http://www.4-h.org

United States Department of Agriculture
http://www.usda.gov

CORRECTIONAL INSTRUCTORS

International Association of Correctional Training Personnel
P.O. Box 471264
Lake Monroe, FL 32747-1264
(407) 321-4312
http://www.iactp.org

National Institute of Corrections
U.S. Department of Justice
Administrative Offices
320 First Street NW
Washington, DC 20534
(800) 995-6423 or (202) 307-3106
or
Information Center
1860 Industrial Circle, Suite A
Longmont, CO 80501
(800) 877-1461 or (303) 682-0213
http://www.nicic.org

Office of Correctional Education
U.S. Department of Education
400 Maryland Avenue SW
MES 4527
Washington, DC 20202-7242
(202) 205-5621; fax: (202) 401-2615 or (202) 205-8793
http://www.ed.gov/offices/OVAE/OCE

Web sites

Bureau of Prisons
http://www.bop.gov/recruit.html

Compass1
(resource page for correctional instructors)
http://www.voicenet.com/~compass1

The Corrections Connection
http://www.corrections.com

Correctional Education Connections
http://www.io.com/~ellie

Correctional Education Programs for Adults with Learning Disabilities
http://novel.nifl.gov/nalld/VOL3NO2.HTM

COUNSELING PROFESSIONS

The American Academy of Child and Adolescent Psychiatry
3615 Wisconsin Avenue NW
Washington, DC 20016-3007
(202) 966-7300; fax: (202) 966-2891
http://www.aacap.org

American Mental Health Counselors Association
801 N. Fairfax Street, Suite 304
Alexandria, VA 22314
(800) 326-2642 or (703) 548-6002;
  fax: (703) 548-4775
http://www.amhca.org

Art Therapy Credentials Board, Inc.
401 North Michigan Avenue
Chicago, IL 60611
(312) 527-6764; fax: (312) 527-6764
http://www.atcb.org

National Board for Certified Counselors, Inc.
3 Terrace Way, Suite D
Greensboro, NC 27403-3660
(336) 547-0607; fax: (336) 547-0017
http://www.nbcc.org

Web sites

Art Therapy
by Utahna Hancock
http://www.umsl.edu/~s1012824/utahna1.html

Art Therapy on the Web
http://www.sofer.com/art-therapy

Counseling Today Online
American Counseling Association
http://www.counseling.org/ctonline

The Counseling Web: Career Counseling Resources
http://seamonkey.ed.asu.edu/~gail/career.htm

The World Counseling Network for the Counseling Industry Professional
http://www.counselingnetwork.com/WCN asp/jobbank/main.asp

Guidance On Line
(precollege counseling resource)
http://www.magicnet.net/~nickw/guidance.html

Ohio Counseling Association Counselor Links
http://www.ohiocounselingassoc.com/counselorlinks.html

State Credentialing Boards
National Board for Certified Counselors, Inc.
http://www.nbcc.org/states/boards.htm

The School Psychologists' Home Page
http://www.bartow.k12.ga.us/psych/psych.html

School Psychology Resources Online
http://www.schoolpsychology.net

School Psychology Virtual Library
http://scott.lib.asu.edu/psych/Reflib_.htm

UC Berkeley School Psychology
http://www-gse.berkeley.edu/program/SP/sp.html

The WWW School Psychology Homepage
http://facpub.stjohns.edu/~ortizs/spwww.html

DOG TRAINERS

American Dog Trainers Network
http://www.inch.com/~dogs

Dr. P's Dog Training
http://www.uwsp.edu/acad/psych/dog/dog.htm

Leerburg Library: Articles on Dog Training
http://leerburg.com/articles.htm

rec.petes.dogs FAQ Homepage
http://www.k9web.com/dog-faqs

K9 Search—The Dog Directory
http://k9search.k9nation.net

Police K9 Resources on the Web
http://www.kasseburgcanine.com/k9webrng

Utah Police Academy Service Dog Program
http://www.sisna.com/wendellnope/post-psd.htm

EARLY CHILDHOOD EDUCATORS

Child Care Bureau
Administration for Children, Youth, and Families
U.S. Department of Health and Human Services
Switzer Building, Room 2046
330 C Street SW
Washington, DC 20447
(202) 690-6782
http://www.acf.dhhs.gov/programs/ccb

Web sites

Child Care Bulletin Online
National Child Care Information Center
http://ericps.crc.uiuc.edu/nccic/ccbullet.html

Circle of Inclusion
http://www.circleofinclusion.org/index.html

Early Childhood Educator Home Page
http://edpsych.com

Early Childhood Education On Line
(sponsored by University of Maine)
http://www.ume.maine.edu/~cofed/eceol/welcome.shtml

Inside the Kindergarten Survival Handbook
http://www.parent-education.com/h.html#1

Jill's Early Childhood Pages
by Jill M. Davis
http://www.galstar.com/~davii/jilllink.html

APPENDIX IV 293

National Child Care Information Center
http://ericps.crc.uiuc.edu/nccic/index.html

Welcome to Kinder Korner!
http://www.geocities.com/Heartland/Hollow/1213

EDUCATIONAL AND INSTRUCTIONAL TECHNOLOGY SPECIALISTS

ERIC Clearinghouse on Information & Technology
4-194 Center for Science and Technology
Syracuse University
Syracuse, NY 13244-4100
(315) 443-3640; fax: (315) 443-5448
http://ericir.syr.edu/ithome

Web sites

Assistive Technology Resources
University of Kentucky
Department of Special Education and Rehabilitation Counseling
http://serc.gws.uky.edu/www/resources/at.html

Educational and Instructional Technology Links
http://freenet.buffalo.edu/~ap381/educate.html

Education Technology News Online
(K–12 resources)
http://www.bpinews.com/edu/pages/etn.htm

From Now On
The Educational Technology Journal
http://www.fno.org

Electronic School On-line
(a school technology on-line publication)
http://www.electronic-school.com

Hanau Model Schools Partnership
http://modelschools.terc.edu

Hessen Model Schools Partnerships
http://www.hess-dso.odedodea.edu/HMSP/index.html

Higher Education Technology News Online
http://www.bpinews.com/edu/pages/hetn.htm

Journal of Technology Education
http://scholar.lib.vt.edu/ejournals/JTE

K-12 Technology Leaders' Forum
http://www.cccoe.k12.ca.us/snorkel/welcome.shtml or http://www.thesnorkel.org

NETS for Students: Connecting Curriculum and Technology
National Educational Technology Standards Project
http://cnets.iste.org

Nettech: Educational Technology for Education
Northeast Regional Technology in Education Consortium
http://www.nettech.org

SupportNet Online
Tech Support Resources and Links
Michigan Department of Education
http://supportnet.merit.edu

techlearning.com
online magazine produced by "Technology and Learning Magazine" and others
http://www.techlearning.com

The Technology Director
by Brian Hedney
http://www.hedney.com/it.htm

EMPLOYEE TRAINING SPECIALISTS

Learning and Training FAQs
http://www.learnativity.com/training_FAQs

The Masie Center
http://www.masie.com

Training and Development Resource Center
http://www.tcm.com/trdev

The Training Media Association
http://www.trainingmedia.org

ENVIRONMENTAL EDUCATORS

U.S. Environmental Protection Agency
401 M Street SW
Washington, DC 20460
http://www.epa.gov

National Park Service
U.S. Department of Interior
1849 C Street NW
Washington, DC 20250
http://www.nps.gov

Web sites

Animal Behavior Society Newsletter
http://www.animalbehavior.org/ABS/Newsletters/Directory/d ir.htm

Articles Listed by Subject
The Humane Educator Online
http://www.animalink.ab.ca/humaneeducator/noframes/hesubj ect.htm#People

ee link
(environmental education resources)
http://eelink.net

Green Teacher
http://www.web.net/~greentea

Humane Education Sources
by Elizabeth Gredley
http://www.animalink.ab.ca/humaneeducator/noframes/he98-2 p8.htm

Resources on the Web for the Ranger/Naturalist/Interpreter
Park Rangers on the Web
http://www.geocities.com/Yosemite/6081/interpretation.htm #Interpretation%20and%20Programming

Teacher's Lounge
U.S. EPA Region 7
http://www.epa.gov/rgytgrnj/kids/
  teach.htm

Ubiquity Environmental page
http://www.geocities.com/
  RainForest/8974/homepage.htm

**U.S. EPA Office of Environmental
  Education**
http://www.epa.gov/enviroed/
  eedefined.html

ESL AND EFL TEACHERS

**National Clearinghouse for ESL
  Literacy Education**
4646 40th Street NW
Washington, DC 20016-1859
(202) 362-0700, extension 200;
  fax: (202) 363-7204
http://www.cal.org/ncle

**ERIC Clearinghouse on Languages
  and Linguistics**
4646 40th Street NW
Washington, DC 20016-1859
(202) 362-0700
http://www.cal.org/ericcll

Web sites

**The Digital Education Network's ELT
  Job Center**
The TEFL Job Center
http://www.jobs.edunet.com/main.htm

eflweb
(resources for teaching and learning
  English)
http://www.eflweb.com

English as a Second Language
by Rong-chang Li
http://www.lang.uiuc.edu/r-li5/esl

Everything ESL.net
by Judie Haynes
http://www.everythingesl.net

The Internet TESL Journal
http://www.aitech.ac.jp/~iteslj

The TEFL Farm
http://www.teflfarm.com

Topic Areas K-12 ESL Education
by the Center for Applied Linguistics
http://www.cal.org/public/topics/k12ed.htm

FITNESS AND RECREATION PROFESSIONALS

FitnessLink
http://www.fitnesslink.com/index.html

NetSweat.com
(fitness resource)
http://www.netsweat.com

TourDirector.Com
(resources for tourist guides and tour
  managers)
http://www.tourdirector.com

FLIGHT INSTRUCTOR

U.S. Federal Aviation Administration
800 Independence Avenue SW
Washington, DC 20591
http://www.faa.gov

Web sites

FAA Aviation Education
http://www.faa.gov/education/index.htm

Greg Brown's Adventure of Flying!
http://www.ufly.com/gbrown/main.html

HEALTH EDUCATORS

**Coalition of National Health Education
  Organizations**
Towson University
Department of Health Science
146 Burdick Hall
Towson, Maryland 21252-0001
(410) 830-4217; fax: (410) 830-4670
http://www.med.usf.edu/~kmbrown/
  CNHEO.htm

Web sites

Becoming a Childbirth Educator FAQ
http://www.childbirth.org/articles/cbefaq.
  html

Brochure Resource Library
Fronske Health Center, Northern Arizona
  University
http://www.nau.edu/fronske/broch.html

**Certified Childbirth Educator
  Information Clearinghouse**
http://www.geocities.com/HotSprings/9947

**Emergency Cardiovascular Care
  Website**
American Heart Association
http://www.proed.net/ecc

Nutrition Entrepreneurs
http://www.nutritionentrepreneurs.org

HORSE INSTRUCTORS AND TRAINERS

Adair Horse Training Magazine
http://www.adairmag.com

Equerry.com—Information and Education for the Horse Enthusiast
http://www.equerry.com

Equine Info: Your Gateway to Horses and Everything Horse Related
http://www.equineinfo.com

EQUUSite.com The Ultimate Horse Resource
http://www.equusite.com

Gaited Horses: A Site for the Smooth Ride Enthusiast
http://www.gaitedhorses.net

Shadowood Horse Pages
http://www.geocities.com/Heartland/Valley/1633/horse.html

LIBRARIANS

Ex Libris, an e-zine for librarians
http://marylaine.com/exlibris

librarian.net
by Jessamyn West
http://www.librarian.net

Library Journal Digital
http://www.ljdigital.com

Peter Milbury's School Librarian Web Pages
http://wombat.cusd.chico.k12.ca.us/~pmilbury/lib.html

School Library Journal Online
http://slj.com

MUSIC TEACHERS (SCHOOL AND PRIVATE INSTRUCTION)

American Music Conference
5790 Armada Drive
Carlsbad, CA 92008
(619) 431-9124; fax: (619) 438-7327
http://www.amc-music.com

Web sites

Bulletin Boards for the Music Classroom
http://members.aol.com/jasontracy/bulletinboards.html

A Career Guide to Music Education
by Barbara Payne
http://www.menc.org/industry/job/caropen.html

Music Education Articles—Suite 101.com
http://www.suite101.com/articles.cfm/music_education

Music Education and Teaching Guide—The Search Beat
http://www.search-beat.com/learnmusic.htm

Music Education Online
http://www.geocities.com/Athens/2405

"Preparing to Teach Music in Today's Schools: The Best of *MEJ*"
MENC: The National Association for Music Education
http://www.menc.org/music_classes/college/bom.htm

Welcome to MusicStaff.com
http://www.musicstaff.com

OVERSEAS TEACHING PROFESSIONS

Peace Corps
1111 20th Street NW
Washington, DC 20526
(800) 424-8580
http://www.peacecorps.gov

Web sites

American International Schools
Office of Overseas Schools
U.S. State Department
http://www.state.gov/www/about_state/schools/index.html

American-Sponsored Overseas Schools links
http://www.state.gov/www/about_state/schools/olink.html

Bureau of Educational and Cultural Affairs
United States Information Agency
http://exchanges.state.gov/education/int-l

China Diary
by Lisa McLure
http://tussah.com/diary

Dave's ESL Cafe
by Dave Sperling
http://www.eslcafe.com

The Digital Education Network's ELT Job Center
(The TEFL Job Center)
http://www.jobs.edunet.com/main.htm

National Peace Corps Association
http://www.rpcv.org

One Small Planet
(general Information about working, studying, and traveling overseas)
http://www.onesmallplanet.com/geninfo.htm

The TEFL Farm
http://www.teflfarm.com

PRIVATE AND INDEPENDENT SCHOOL EDUCATORS

American Montessori Society
281 Park Avenue South, 6th floor
New York, NY 10010-6102
(212) 358-1250; fax: (212) 358-1256
http://www.amshq.org

National Association of Independent Schools
1620 L Street NW
Washington, DC 20036-5606
(202) 973-9700; fax: (202) 973-9790
http://www.nais.org

Web sites

The Anthroposophy Network
Waldorf Education
http://www.anthroposophy.net/waldorf/index.htm

Council for American Private Education
http://www.capenet.org

The Klingenstein Center
http://www.klingenstein.org

Schools Online
Association of Boarding Schools
http://www.schools.com

SCHOOL ADMINISTRATORS

Council of the Great City Schools
1301 Pennsylvania Avenue NW, Suite 702
Washington, DC 20004
(202) 393-2427; fax: (202) 393-2400
http://www.cgcs.org

ERIC Clearinghouse on Educational Management
5207 University of Oregon
Eugene, OR 97403-5207
(800) 438-8841 or (541) 346-5043;
 fax: (541) 346-2334
http://eric.uoregon.edu/directory/about.html

Substitute Teaching Institute
6516 Old Main Hill
Logan, UT 84322-6516
(800) 922-4693
http://subed.usu.edu

Web sites

Developing Educational Standards: Overview
compiled by Putnam Valley Central Schools, Putnam Valley, New York
http://putwest.boces.org/Standards.html

Instructional Supervision Network
Association for Supervision and Curriculum Development
http://turbo.kean.edu/~jglanz/network.html

SCHOOL BUS DRIVERS

Joe's School Bus World
http://hometown.aol.com/hamjoe/busmain.html

Ladydriver's Homepage
http://www.geocities.com/Heartland/Valley/2733

School Bus Fleet
(on-line magazine)
http://www.schoolbusfleet.com

The School Bus Yard
http://members.aol.com/njtbus/sbyard.htm

SCHOOL TEACHERS

American Association of Colleges for Teacher Education
1307 New York Avenue NW
Suite 300
Washington, DC 20005-4701
(202) 293-2450; fax: (202) 457-8095
http://www.aacte.org

ERIC Clearinghouse on Teaching and Teacher Education
1307 New York Avenue NW
Suite 300
Washington, DC 20005-4701
(800) 822-9229
http://www.ericsp.org/index.html

National Board for Professional Teaching Standards
26555 Evergreen Road, Suite 400
Southfield, MI 48076
(248) 351-4444; fax: 248-351-4170
http://www.nbpts.org

National Clearinghouse for Professions in Special Education
The Council for Exceptional Children
1920 Association Drive
Reston, VA 20191
(800) 641-7824 or (703) 264-9476;
 TTY: (703) 264-9480
http://www.cec.sped.org/ncpse.htm

National Dropout Prevention Center and Network
Clemson University
209 Martin Street
Clemson, SC 29631-1555
(864) 656-2599; fax: (864) 656-0136
http://www.dropoutprevention.org

Recruiting New Teachers, Inc.
385 Concord Avenue, Suite 103
Belmont, MA 02478
(800) 45-TEACH or (617) 489-6000
http://www.rnt.org

Web sites

AskERIC Lesson Plans
http://ericir.syr.edu/Virtual/Lessons

Awesome Library: K–12 Education Directory
http://www.awesomelibrary.org

Collaborative Teaching: Special Education for Inclusive Classrooms
by Barrie Jo Price
http://www.parrotpublishing.com/sped

Developing Educational Standards: Overview
compiled by Putnam Valley Central Schools, Putnam Valley, New York
http://putwest.boces.org/Standards.html

ednow.com
(resources for teachers, administrators, and librarians)
http://ednow.com

Education Week Online
http://www.edweek.org

Future Educators of America
http://www.aurora.edu/education/fea.htm

MiddleWeb: Exploring Middle School Reform
http://www.middleweb.com

Online Community for K–8 Educators
http://www.teachernet.com

PE Central
(resources for physical education teachers)
http://pe.central.vt.edu

PE Digest
http://www.pedigest.com

Physical Education Hotlinks
http://www.usoe.k12.ut.us/curr/pe/link_dir.html

The Praxis Series Online
Professional Assessments for Beginning Teachers, an Educational Testing Service program
http://www.teachingandlearning.org/licnsure/praxis

Schools on the Web: Sites of Interest to Bilingual/Multicultural Educators
http://www.ncbe.gwu.edu/classroom/bilschool.htm

Special Education Resources on the Internet
http://www.hood.edu/seri/serihome.htm

Sports Media: Physical Education Lesson Plans
http://www.sports-media.org

Substitute Teacher's Help Page
http://homepage.netspaceonline.com/~kristy/subpage/subpag e.htm

Substitute Teaching—Tricks of the Trade
by Mr. Sturgeon, Substitute Teacher
http://www.av.qnet.com/~rsturgn/index.htm

Syllabus Magazine Online
http://www.syllabus.com

United States Department of Defense Education Activity
http://www.odedodea.edu/pa/americas.html

APPENDIX V
BIBLIOGRAPHY

A. PERIODICALS

The following are some periodicals that different professionals read. You may be able to find copies at a school, academic, or public library. Many periodicals also have on-line versions.

Adult Education

Adult Basic Education:
  An Interdisciplinary Journal
  for Adult Literacy Educators
P.O. Box 592053
Orlando, FL 32859-2053
http://www.albany.edu/aaace/
  publications/abe

Adult Education Quarterly
1200 19th Street NW, Suite 300
Washington, DC 20036
(202) 429-5131
http://www.albany.edu/aaace/publications/
  aeq

Adult Learning
1200 19th Street NW, Suite 300
Washington, DC 20036
(202) 429-5131
http://www.albany.edu/aaace/
  publications/adlearn

Bilingual Education and Teaching ESL or EFL

(Note: Some publications provide general information or job listings for teaching overseas.)

Career Counsel
TESOL
700 South Washington Street, Suite 200
Alexandria, VA 22314
(703) 836-0774; fax: (703) 836-7864
http://www.tesol.edu
(Note: This is a free publication that contains general information about becoming ESL and TEFL instructors.)

The International Educator
P.O. Box 513
Cummaquid, MA 02637
(508) 362-1414; fax: (508) 362-1411
http://www.tieonline.com

Counseling and Other Mental Health Professions

Art Therapy: Journal of the American
  Art Therapy Association
American Art Therapy Association, Inc.
1202 Allanson Road
Mundelein, IL 60060-3808
(888) 290-0878 or (847) 949-6064; fax:
  (847) 566-4580
http://www.arttherapy.org

The Career Development Quarterly
American Counseling Association
P.O. Box 2513
Birmingham, AL 35201-2513
(800) 633-4931

Journal of College Counseling
American Counseling Association
P.O. Box 2513
Birmingham, AL 35201-2513
(800) 633-4931

Journal of Counseling and
  Development
American Counseling Association
P.O. Box 2513
Birmingham, AL 35201-2513
(800) 633-4931

Journal of Employment Counseling
American Counseling Association
P.O. Box 2513
Birmingham, AL 35201-2513
(800) 633-4931

Journal of Multicultural Counseling
  and Development
American Counseling Association
P.O. Box 2513
Birmingham, AL 35201-2513
(800) 633-4931

Journal of Technology Education
James E. LaPorte, JTE Editor
144 Smyth Hall
Virginia Tech
Blacksburg, VA 24061-0432
http://scholar.lib.vt.edu/ejournals/JTE

Journal of the American Academy
  of Child and Adolescent Psychiatry
Lippincott, Williams and Wilkins
12107 Insurance Way
Hagerstown, MD 21740
(800) 638-3030 or (301) 714-2300;
  fax: (301) 824-7390

Measurement and Evaluation
  in Counseling and Development
American Counseling Association
P.O. Box 2513
Birmingham, AL 35201-2513
(800) 633-4931

Early Childhood Education

Child Assessment News
Guilford Publications
72 Spring Street
New York, NY 10012
(800) 365-7006 or (212) 431-9800;
  fax: (212) 966-6708

Early Childhood News
330 Progress Road
Dayton, OH 45449
(800) 558-2292, extension 121
http://www.earlychildhoodnews.com

Educational Technology/Instructional Technology

CSS Journal: Computers in the Social
  Studies
P.O. Box 521127
Tulsa, OK 74152-1127
http://www.cssjournal.com

Technology & Learning
P.O. Box 5052
Vandalia, OH 45377
(800) 607-4410
http://www.Techlearning.com/content/
    magazine/sub.html

Higher Education

The Chronicle of Higher Education
1255 Twenty-Third Street NW
Washington, DC 20037
(800) 728-2803
http://chronicle.com

American School & University
Primedia Intertec
Subscriptions
P.O. Box 12983
Overland Park, KS 66282-2983
Fax: (913) 967-1903
http://www.asumag.com/home

University Business
22 West 38th Street
New York, NY 10018
http://www.universitybusiness.com

Elementary and Secondary Education

American School Board Journal
1680 Duke Street
Alexandria, VA 22314
http://www.asbj.com

Education Week
(800) 728-2790 or fax: (301) 280-3250
http://www.edweek.org

Journal of School Nursing
National Association of School Nurses
P.O. Box 1300
Scarborough, ME 04070
(207) 883-2117; fax: (207) 883-2683
http://www.nasn.org/Journal

Kappan
Phi Delta Kappa International
Subscription Department
P.O. Box 789
Bloomington, IN 47402-0789
(800) 766-1156; fax: (812) 339-0018
http://www.pdkintl.org/kappan/kappan.htm

Learners Online, Inc.
3131 Turtle Creek Boulevard, Suite 1250
Dallas, Texas 75219-5441
(800) 672-6988; fax: (214) 521-1021
http://www.learnersonline.com

Principal
National Association of Elementary
    School Principals
1615 Duke Street
Alexandria, VA 22314
(800) 38-NAESP; fax: (800) 39-NAESP
http://www.naesp.org

The School Administrator
American Association of School
    Administrators
1801 N. Moore Street
Arlington, VA 22209-1813
(703) 875-0772; fax: (703) 528-2146
http://www.aasa.org

School Planning and Management
330 Progress Road
Dayton, OH 45449
Fax: (800) 370-4450
http://www.spmmag.com

Teaching K-8 Magazine
40 Richards Avenue
Norwalk, CT 06854
(800) 249-9363
http://www.teachingk-8.com

Teacher Magazine
(800) 728-2753 or fax: (301) 280-3250
http://www.teachermagazine.org

Library Services

Library Journal
245 West 17th Street
New York, NY 10011
(212) 463-6819 or (212) 463-6734
http://www.ljdigital.com

School Library Journal
P.O. Box 16388
North Hollywood, CA
(800) 595-1066
http://slj.com

Software Development

Software Development
P.O. Box 1126
Skokie, IL 60076-8126
(847) 647-5972
http://www.sdmagazine.com

B. BOOKS

Listed below are some book titles about general career information and about some of the different professions that are discussed in this book. To find other books, ask your school or public librarian for help. Also talk with different professionals, and ask them to recommend titles for you to read.

Career Information

Bureau of Labor Statistics, U.S. Department of Labor. *Career Guide to Industries, 1998–99 edition* (Bulletin 2503). Washington, D.C.: Superintendent of Documents, US GPO, 1998.

Camenson, Blythe. *Great Jobs for Liberal Arts Majors.* Lincolnwood, Ill.: VGM Career Horizons, 1997.

Cosgrove, Holli R. (editorial director). *Encyclopedia of Careers and Vocational Guidance.* 10th ed. Chicago: J. G. Ferguson Publishing Co., 1997.

Editors. *The Top 100: The Fastest Growing Careers for the 21st Century.* Chicago: Ferguson Publishing Co., 1998.

Eikleberry, Carol. *The Career Guide for Creative and Unconventional People.* Berkeley, Calif.: Ten Speed Press, 1995.

Employment and Training Administration, U.S. Department of Labor. *Dictionary of Occupational Titles.* Washington, D.C.: Superintendent of Documents, US GPO, 1991.

Krannich, Ronald L. and Caryl Rae Krannich. *The Best Jobs for the 1990s and into the 21st Century.* Manassas Park, Va.: Impact Publications, 1993.

Krantz, Les. *Job Rated Almanac.* New York: St. Martin's Press, 1999.

Yate, Martin. *Career Smarts: Jobs With a Future.* New York: Ballantine Books, 1997.

ADULT-EDUCATION INSTRUCTORS

Merriam, Sharon B. and Rosemary S. Caffarella. *Learning in Adulthood: A Comprehensive Guide.* 2d ed. San Francisco: Jossey-Bass Publishers, 1999.

Rios, Lorna. *Me... Teach Criminals? The True Adventures of a Prison Teacher.* New York: Vantage Press, 1996.

Vella, Jane. *Learning to Listen, Learning to Teach: The Power of Dialogue in Educating Adults.* San Francisco: Jossey-Bass Publishers, 1997.

ANIMAL TRAINERS

Bryson, Sandy. *Police Dog Tactics.* New York: McGraw-Hill, 1996.

Eden, R. S. *K9 Officer's Manual.* Calgary: Detselig Enterprises, 1993.

Henderson, Kathy. *I Can Be a Horse Trainer.* Chicago: Childrens Press, Inc., 1990.

Lee, Price Mary and Richard Lee. *Opportunities in Animal and Pet Care Careers.* Lincolnwood, Ill.: VGM Career Horizons, 1984.

BILINGUAL AND ESL TEACHERS

Ashton-Warner, Sylvia. *Teacher.* New York: Simon and Schuster, 1986.

Bialystok, Ellen, ed. *Language Processing in Bilingual Children.* New York: Cambridge University Press, 1991.

Franklin, Elizabeth, ed. *Reading and Writing in More Than One Language: Lessons for Teachers.* Alexandria, Va.: Teachers of English to Speakers of Other Languages, 1998.

Gehbard, Jerry G. *Teaching English as a Foreign or Second Language.* Ann Arbor, Mich.: University of Michigan Press, 1996.

Genesee, Fred, ed. *Educating Second Language Children: The Whole Child, the Whole Curriculum, the Whole Community.* New York: Cambridge University Press, 1994.

Ovando, Carlos J., and Virginia P. Collier. *Bilingual and ESL Classrooms: Teaching in Multicultural Contexts.* 2d ed. Boston: McGraw-Hill, 1997.

COUNSELORS

Baxter, Neale, and Philip A. Perry. *Opportunities in Counseling and Development Careers.* Lincolnwood, Ill.: VGM Career Horizons, NTC Publishing Group, 1997.

Figler, Howard and Richard Nelson Bolles. *Career Counselor's Handbook.* Berkeley, Calif.: Ten Speed Press, 2000.

Kennedy, Eugene and Sara Charles. *On Becoming a Counselor: A Basic Guide for Non-Professional Counselors.* New York: Continuum, 1990.

Neukrug, Ed. *The World of the Counselor: An Introduction to the Counseling Profession.* Pacific Grove, Calif.: Brooks/Cole Publishing Co., 1998.

DANCE TEACHERS

Hanna, Judith Lynne. *Partnering Dance and Education: Intelligent Moves for Changing Times.* Champaign, Ill.: Human Kinetics, 1999.

H'Doubler, Margaret N. *Dance: A Creative Art Experience.* 3d ed. Madison, Wisc.: University of Wisconsin Press, 1998.

CHILDHOOD EDUCATORS

Dowd, Tom, et. al. *Effective Skills for Child-Care Workers: A Training Manual From Boys Town.* Boys Town, Nebr.: Boys Town Press, 1994.

Fujawa, Judy. *(Almost) Everything You Need to Know About Early Childhood Education: A Book of Lists for Teachers and Parents.* Beltsville, Md.: Gryphon House, 1998.

Paley, Vivian Gussin. *The Girl with the Brown Crayon.* Cambridge, Mass.: Harvard University Press, 1998.

Tertell, E. A., S. M. Klein, and J. L. Jewett eds. *When Teachers Reflect: Journeys Toward Effective, Inclusive Practice.* Washington, D.C.: National Association for the Education of Young Children, 1998.

EDUCATIONAL/INSTRUCTIONAL TECHNOLOGY SPECIALISTS

Connelly, Robert. *Opportunities in Technical Education Careers.* Lincolnwood, Ill.: VGM Career Horizons, NTC Publishing Group, 1997.

Druin, Allison and Cynthia Solomon. *Designing Multimedia Environments for Children.* New York: John Wiley and Sons, 1996.

Heinich, Robert, et. al. *Instructional Media and Technologies for Learning.* Upper Saddle River, N.J.: Merrill, 1999.

Liberty, Jesse. *The Complete Idiot's Guide to A Career in Computer Programming.* Indianapolis, Ind.: Que, 1999.

Seels, Barbara and Rita C. Richey. *Instructional Technology: The Definition and Domains of the Field.* Washington, D.C.: Association for Educational Communications and Technology, 1994.

Stair, Lila B. *Careers in Computers.* Lincolnwood, Ill.: VGM Career Horizons, 1996.

EMPLOYEE TRAINING SPECIALISTS

Driscoll, Margaret and Larry Alexander. *Web-Based Training: Using Technology to Design Adult Learning Experiences.* San Francisco: Jossey-Bass Publishers, 1998.

Gordon, Edward E., Catherine M. Petrini, and Ann P. Campagna. *Opportunities in Training and Development Careers.* Lincolnwood, Ill.: VGM Career Horizons, NTC/Contemporary Publishing Company, 1998.

Klatt, Bruce. *The Ultimate Training Workshop Handbook.* New York: McGraw-Hill, 1997.

Kruse, Kevin, Jason Keil, and Elliot Masie. *Technology-Based Training: The Art and Science of Design, Development, and Delivery.* San Francisco: Jossey-Bass Publishers, 1999.

Piskurich, George M., Peter Beckschi, and Brandon Hall, eds. *The ASTD Handbook of Training Design and Delivery.* New York: McGraw-Hill, 1999.

ENVIRONMENTAL EDUCATORS

Fasulo, Michael and Paul Walker. *Careers in the Environment.* Lincolnwood: VGM Career Horizons, NTC Publishing Group, 1995.

Ferguson Publishing Company. *What Can I Do Now? Preparing for a Career in the Environment.* Chicago: Ferguson Publishing Company, 1998.

Lingelbach, Jenepher, ed. *Hands-On Nature: Information and Activities for Exploring the Environment with Children.* Woodstock, Vt.: Vermont Institute of Natural Science, 1989.

Orr, David W. *Earth in Mind: On Education, Environment, and the Human Prospect.* Washington, D.C.: Island Press, 1994.

Shenk, Ellen. *Outdoor Careers: Exploring Occupations in Outdoor Fields.* Harrisburg, Pa.: Stackpole Books, 1992.

FITNESS AND RECREATION PROFESSIONALS

Aerobics and Fitness Association of America. *Exercise Standards and Guidelines: A Reference Manual for Fitness Professionals.* Sherman Oaks, Calif.: Aerobics and Fitness Association of America, 1995.

Camenson, Blythe. *Careers for Health Nuts and Others Who Like to Stay Fit.* Lincolnwood, Ill.: VGM Career Horizons, NTC Publishing Group, 1996.

Cotton, Richard T. *Personal Trainer Manual: The Resource for Fitness Professionals.* 2d ed. San Diego, Calif.: American Council on Exercise, 1996.

Gaut, Ed. *The Personal Trainer Business Handbook.* Gaithersburg, Md.: Willow Creek Publications, 1994.

Jordan, Peg, ed. *Fitness: Theory and Practice* 2d ed. Sherman Oaks, Calif.: Aerobics and Fitness Association of America, 1997.

Rosenbaum, Jean and Mary Miller. *Opportunities in Fitness Careers.* Lincolnwood: VGM Career Horizons, NTC Publishing Group, 1991.

Taylor, Bill and Christine Cochrane Yukevich. *Personal Training: Why Not You?* Allison Park, Pa.: Lion Press, 1996.

HEALTH EDUCATORS

American Heart Association. *Heartsaver Facts: First Aid, AED, CPR Training System.* Boston, Mass.: Jones and Bartlett Pub., 1998.

Korte, Diana and Roberta Scaer. *A Good Birth, A Safe Birth.* 3d ed. Boston, Mass.: Harvard Common Press, 1992.

National Safety Council. *CPR.* 2d ed. Boston, Mass.: Jones and Bartlett Pub., 1997.

National Safety Council. *Essentials of First Aid and CPR.* Boston, Mass.: Jones and Bartlett Pub., 1997.

Robotti, Suzanne B. and Margaret Ann Inman. *Childbirth Instructor Magazine's Guide to Careers in Birth.* New York: John Wiley and Sons, Inc., 1998.

LIBRARIANS

McCook, Kathleen de la Peña. *Opportunities in Library and Information Science Careers.* Lincolnwood, Ill.: VGM Career Horizons, NTC Publishing Group, 1997.

MUSIC TEACHERS

Bjorneberg, Paul (compiler). *Exploring Careers in Music.* Chicago, IL: American Music Conference; Reston, Va.: Music Educators National Conference, 1990.

Hamann, Donald L., ed. *Creativity in the Music Classroom.* Reston, Va.: Music Educators National Conference, 1991.

OVERSEAS TEACHING PROFESSIONS

Department of State's Bureau of Consular Affairs. *Tips for Americans Residing Abroad* (brochure, Publication 10391). U.S. Department of State, Revised September 1996. (This may be found at the web page *http://travel.state.gov/americansabroad.html*).

Griffin, Susan. *Teaching English Abroad: Talk Your Way Around the World!* 4th ed. Princeton, N.J.: Vacation-Work, 1999.

Francis, David, ed. *ELT Guide.* 9th ed. Waldorf, MD, TESOL Publications, 1999.

Krannich, Ronald L. and Caryl Rae Krannich. *Jobs for People Who Love Travel: Opportunities at Home and Abroad.* 2d ed. Manassas Park, Va.: Impact Publications, 1995.

SCHOOL ADMINISTRATORS

Ackerman, Richard H., et. al. *Making Sense as a School Leader: Persisting Questions, Creative Opportunities.* San Francisco: Jossey-Bass Publishers, 1996.

American Association of School Administrators. *Guidelines for the Preparation of School Administrators.* Arlington, Va.: American Association of School Administrators, 1982.

Carter, Gene R. and William G. Cunningham. *The American School Superintendent: Leading in an Age of Pressure.* San Francisco: Jossey-Bass Publishers, 1997.

Darling-Hammond, Linda. *The Right to Learn.* San Francisco: Jossey-Bass Publishers, 1997.

Monroe, Lorraine. *Nothing's Impossible: Leadership Lessons from Inside and Outside the classroom.* New York: Public Affairs, 1999.

Thorpe, Ronald, ed. *The First Year as Principal: Real World Stories form America's Principals.* Portsmouth, N.H.: Heinemann, 1995.

SCHOOL SUPPORT STAFF

Policy Studies Associates. *Roles for Education Paraprofessionals in Effective Schools: An Idea Book.* Washington, D.C.: U.S. Dept. of Education, 1997 (Note: This may be found on the Internet at *http://oeri.ed.gov/pubs/Paraprofessionals/title.html*).

SCHOOLTEACHERS

Bambino, Deborah. *Teaching Out Loud: A Middle Grades Diary.* Westerville, Ohio: National Middle School Association, 1999.

Codell, Esmé Raji. *Educating Esmé: Diary of a Teacher's First Year.* Chapel Hill, N.C.: Algonquin Books, 1999.

Connelly, F. Michael, and D. Jean Clandinin, eds. *Shaping a Professional Identify: Stories of Educational Practice.* New York: Teachers College Press, 1999.

Connelly, Robert. *Opportunities in Special Education Careers.* Lincolnwood, Ill.: VGM Career Horizons, NTC Publishing Group, 1994.

Cramer, Eugene H., and Marietta Castle, eds. *Fostering the Love of Reading: The Affective Domain in Reading Education.* Newark, Del.: International Reading Association, 1994.

Cunningham, Patricia Marr (preface) and Richard L. Allington (preface). *Classrooms That Work: They Can All Read and Write.* 2d ed. New York: Longman, 1998.

Culatta, Richard A. and James R. Tompkins. *Fundamentals of Special Education: What Every Teacher Needs to Know.* Upper Saddle River, N.J.: Merrill, 1999.

Cutlip, Glen W. and Robert J. Shockley. *Careers in Teaching.* New York: The Rosen Publishing Group, Inc., 1994.

Edelfelt, Roy A. *Careers in Education.* Lincolnwood: NTC/Contemporary Publishing Company, 1998.

Fine, Janet. *Opportunities in Teaching Careers.* Lincolnwood: VGM Career Horizons, 1995.

Gallas, Karen. *The Languages of Learning: How Children Talk, Write, Dance, Draw, and Sing Their Understanding of the World.* New York: Teachers College Press, 1994.

Glasser, William. *The Quality School Teacher.* 3d ed. New York: HarperPerennial, 1998.

Hancock, Joelie, ed. *The Explicit Teaching of Reading.* Newark, Del.: International Reading Association, 1999.

Haselkorn, David and Andrew Calkins. *Careers In Teaching Handbook.* Belmont, Mass.: Recruiting New Teachers, Inc., 1993.

Kane, Pearl Rock, ed. *Independent Schools, Independent Thinkers.* San Francisco: Jossey-Bass, 1992.

Kraut, Harvey. *Teaching and the Art of Successful Classroom Management: A How-to-Guidebook for Teachers in Secondary Schools.* 2d ed. Staten Island, N.Y.: Aysa Pub., 1996.

MacKenzie, Robert J. *Setting Limits in the Classroom: How to Move Beyond the Classroom Dance of Discipline.* Rocklin, Calif.: Prima Pub, 1996.

Palmer, Parker J. *The Courage to Teach: Exploring the Inner Landscape of a Teacher's Life.* San Francisco: Jossey-Bass Publishers, 1998.

Siegel, Lawrence M., and Marcia Stewart, ed. *The Complete IEP Guide: How to Advocate Your Special Ed Child.* Berkeley, Calif.: Nolo Press, 1999.

Sizer, Theodore R., and Nancy Faust Sizer. *The Students are Watching: Schools and the Moral Contract.* Boston: Beacon Press, 1999.

Wilhelm, Jeffrey D., and Michael W. Smith. *'You Gotta Be the Book': Teaching Engaged and Reflective Reading with Adolescents.* New York: Teachers College Press, 1996.

Winebrenner, Susan, and Pamela Espeland, ed. *Teaching Kids with Learning Disabilities in the Regular Classroom.* Minneapolis: Free Spirit Pub, 1996

INDEX

A

academic librarian 193–194
adult education instructor 95–97
Aerobics and Fitness Association of America 244, 247
aerobics instructor 242–244
Aircraft Owners and Pilots Association 240
Alliance for Technology Access 204
American Academy of Husband-Coached Childbirth 180
American Art Therapy Association 66
American Association for Adult and Continuing Education 84, 97, 99, 102, 105, 214
American Association for Health Education 174
American Association for Higher Education 84, 87, 89, 144, 152, 154, 157, 160
American Association of Collegiate Registrars and Admissions Officers 136, 138
American Association of Family and Consumer Sciences 102
American Association of Riding Schools 238
American Association of School Administrators 121, 124, 127, 129, 132, 198, 211
American Association of School Librarians 191
American Association of School Personnel Administrators 129
American Association of University Administrators 136, 138, 141, 154, 157, 160
American Association of University Professors 84, 87, 89
American Chemical Society 214
American College Health Association 174
American College of Sports Medicine 247
American College Personnel Association 141, 149

American Conference of Academic Deans 154
American Correctional Association 105
American Council on Exercise 244, 247
American Counseling Association 166
American Dairy Science Association 102
American Dance Guild 236
American Dietetic Association 177
American Farm Bureau 102
American Federation of School Administrators 118, 121, 129
American Federation of Teachers 6, 12, 16, 19, 22, 25, 32, 35, 37, 41, 44, 47, 51, 70, 72, 75, 77, 79, 84, 87, 94, 164, 192, 201
American Fitness Professionals and Associates 244
American Heart Association 182
American Horse Council 238, 268
American Humane Association 259
American Jail Association 105
American Library Association 186
American Nurses Association 51
American Occupational Therapy Association 64
American overseas school teacher 108–109
American Psychological Association 56
American Public Health Association 174, 177
American Red Cross 182
American Riding Instructors Association 238
American Safety and Health Institute 182
American School Counselor Association 164
American School Food Service Association 77, 130
American School Health Association 51, 174
American Society for Industrial Security 147
American Society for Information Science 186, 194

American Society for Nutritional Sciences 177
American Society for the Prevention of Cruelty of Animals 259, 261
American Society for Training and Development 94, 206, 216, 223, 227, 230
American Speech-Language-Hearing Association 61
American String Teachers Association 32
Animal Behavior Society 261
Aquatic Exercise Association 244
art therapist 65–66
assistant principal 119–121
assistant superintendent 125–127
Association for Career and Technical Education 94
Association for Computing Machinery 219
Association for Educational Communications and Technology 192, 197, 201, 206, 216
Association for Library Services to Children 189
Association for Supervision and Curriculum Development 118, 124, 127, 129, 132, 211
Association for the Advancement of Computing in Education 198, 201, 206, 216
Association for the Advancement of International Education 109
Association of College Administration Professionals 136, 138, 141, 144, 147, 149, 152, 154, 157, 160
Association of College and Research Libraries 194
Association of Internet Professionals 216
Association of Labor Assistants and Childbirth Educators 180
Association of National Park Rangers 257
Association of Pet Dog Trainers 261
Association of School Business Officials 129

Association of Shareware Professionals 219
athletic director 142–144

B

bilingual teacher 42–44
Birthworks, Inc. 180

C

cafeteria manager 76–77
campus monitor 78–79
career guidance technician 71–72
careers in community, nonprofit, and government settings
    adult education instructor 95–97
    childbirth educator 178–180
    child care aide 2–3
    children's librarian 187–189
    continuing education instructor 98–99
    cooperative extension agent 100–102
    correctional instructor 103–105
    CPR/first aid instructor 181–182
    early childhood program director 7–9
    early childhood teacher 4–6
    employment counselor 168–170
    environmental educator 252–254
    guide dog instructor 262–263
    health educator 172–174
    humane educator 258–259
    K-9 trainer (police dogs) 264–266
    nutritionist 175–177
    park naturalist 255–257
    public librarian 184–186
careers in business and corporate settings
    educational software developer 218–219
    instructional designer 215–217
    textbook editor 212–214
    trainer (in-house) 222–224
    training developer 225–227
    training manager 228–230
careers working with animals
    dog trainer 260–261
    guide dog instructor 262–263
    horse trainer 267–268
    humane educator 258–259
    K-9 trainer (police dogs) 264–266
    riding instructor 237–238
careers working with technology. *See* educational and instructional technology professions

child care aide 2–3
childbirth educator 178–180
children's librarian 187–189
college and university administrators
    athletic director 142–144
    dean (academic) 153–154
    dean of students 148–149
    director of admissions 134–136
    director of development 150–152
    director of public safety 145–147
    director of student activities 139–141
    president 158–160
    provost 155–157
    registrar 137–138
College and University Personnel Association 141, 149
college and university teaching professions
    community college instructor 82–84
    continuing education instructor 98–99
    lecturer 88–89
    professor 85–87
    vocational instructor 92–94
college career counselor 165–167
community college instructor 82–84
Computer Assisted Language Instruction Consortium 208
Computer-Assisted Language Learning Interest Section, TESOL, Inc. 208
continuing education instructor 98–99
cooperative extension agent 100–102
Correctional Education Association 105
correctional instructor 103–105
Council for Exceptional Children 6, 16, 27, 41, 53, 61, 64, 70, 105, 129, 132, 164, 211
counseling professions
    art therapist 65–66
    college career counselor 165–167
    employment counselor 168–170
    nutritionist 175–177
    school counselor 162–164
    school psychologist 54–56
    school social worker 57–58
CPR/first aid instructor 181–182
curriculum and instruction development professions
    curriculum specialist 210–211
    educational software developer 218–219
    instructional designer 215–217
    instructional supervisor 131–132

    instructional technology specialist (higher education) 205–206
    instructional technology specialist (K-12) 199–201
    program director 128–130
    reading specialist 36–38
    textbook editor 212–214
    training developer 225–227
curriculum specialist 210–211

D

Dance Educators of America 236
dance teacher 235–236
dean (academic) 153–154
dean of students 148–149
director of admissions 134–136
director of development 150–152
director of public safety 145–147
director of student activities 139–141
dog trainer 260–261

E

early childhood educators
    child care aide 2–3
    early childhood program director 7–9
    early childhood teacher 4–6
    kindergarten teacher 10–12
    special education teacher 39–41
early childhood program director 7–9
early childhood teacher 4–6
Ecotourism Society 250
Editorial Freelancers Association 214
educational diagnostician 52–53
Educational Software Cooperative 219
educational software developer 218–219
educational and instructional technology professions
    educational software developer 218–219
    instructional designer 215–217
    instructional technology specialist (higher education) 205–206
    instructional technology specialist (K-12) 199–201
    language technology specialist (higher education) 207–208
    library media specialist 190–192
    special education technology specialist 202–204
    technology director 196–198
    trainer (in-house) 222–224

INDEX 305

EFL (English as a foreign language) teacher 110–112
elementary school teacher 14–16
employment counselor 168–170
environmental educator 252–254
environmental educators
    environmental educator 252–254
    humane educator 258–259
    park naturalist 255–257
Epsilon Sigma Phi 102
ESL (English as a second language) teacher 45–47

F

flight instructor (freelance) 239–240

G

guide 248–250
guide dog instructor 262–263
Guide Dog Users Inc. 263

H

health educator 172–174
health educators
    childbirth educator 178–180
    CPR/first aid instructor 181–182
    health educator 172–174
    nutritionist 175–177
    physical education teacher 33–35
    school nurse 50–51
higher education administrators. *See* college and university administrators
higher education teaching professions. *See* college and university teaching professions
high school teacher 23–25
Horse Industry Alliance 238
horse trainer 267–268
humane educator 258–259
Humane Society of the United States 259

I

IDEA, The Health and Fitness Source 244, 247
IEEE Computer Society 219
independent instructors
    aerobics instructor 242–244
    childbirth educator 178–180
    CPR/first aid instructor 181–182
    dance teacher 235–236
    dog trainer 260–261
    flight instructor (freelance) 239–240
    horse trainer 267–268
    K-9 trainer (police dogs) 264–266
    music teacher (studio owner) 232–234
    personal trainer 245–247
    riding instructor 237–238
Information Technology Training Association 223
instructional designer 215–217
instructional supervisor 131–132
instructional technology specialist (higher education) 205–206
instructional technology specialist (K-12) 199–201
International and American Associations of Clinical Nutritionists 177
International Association for Language Learning Technology 208
International Association of Campus Law Enforcement Administrators 147
International Association of Chiefs of Police 147
International Association of Teachers of English as a Foreign Language 111
International Association of Tour Managers 249
International Childbirth Education Association, Inc. 180
International Reading Association 19, 27, 37, 105, 109, 132, 211
International Society for Performance Improvement 206, 216, 223, 227, 230
International Society for Technology in Education 197, 201
International Technology Education Association 201

J

junior high school teacher 20–22

K

K-9 trainer (police dogs) 264–266
kindergarten teacher 10–12

L

Lamaze International 180
language technology specialist (higher education) 207–208
Learning Disabilities Association of America 41, 53
lecturer 88–89
library media specialist 190–192
library professions
    academic librarian 193–194
    children's librarian 187–189
    library media specialist 190–192
    public librarian 184–186

M

Medic First Aid 182
MENC: The National Association for Music Education 32, 211
middle school teacher 17–19
music teacher 30–32
music teacher (studio owner) 232–234
Music Teachers National Association 234

N

National Art Education Association 25
National Association for Bilingual Education 44, 70
National Association for Humane and Environmental Education 254, 259
National Association for Interpretation 254, 257
National Association for Pupil Transportation 75, 130
National Association for Sport and Physical Education 35
National Association for the Education of Young Children 3, 6, 9, 12, 16, 70, 164
National Association for Women in Education 149, 154, 157
National Association of Collegiate Directors of Athletics 144
National Association of Collegiate Women Athletic Administrators 144
National Association of County Agricultural Agents 102
National Association of Dog Obedience Instructors 261
National Association of Elementary School Principals 118, 121, 124, 127, 211
National Association of Environmental Professionals 254
National Association of Extension 4-H Agents 102
National Association of Flight Instructors 240

National Association of Industrial and Technical Teacher Educators 94
National Association of Scholars 84, 87, 89, 154, 157, 160
National Association of School Nurses 51
National Association of School Psychologists 56
National Association of Secondary School Principals 118, 121, 124, 127, 211
National Association of Social Workers 58
National Association of Student Personnel Administrators 141, 149
National Audubon Society 257
National Business Education Association 132
National Career Development Association 72, 166
National Child Care Association 9
National Coalition of Arts Therapies Associations 66
National Council for the Social Studies 27, 132, 211
National Council of Teachers of English 22, 25, 214
National Council of Teachers of Mathematics 22, 109
National Dance Association 236
National Dance-Exercise Instructors Training Association 244
National Education Association 6, 12, 16, 19, 22, 25, 32, 35, 37, 41, 44, 47, 51, 70, 72, 75, 77, 79, 84, 87, 94, 164, 192, 201
National Employment Counseling Association 170
National Extension Association of Family and Consumer Sciences 102
National Head Start Association 6
National Middle School Association 19, 118, 124, 127, 129, 164, 211
National Safety Council 182
National Science Teachers Association 22, 25
National Sheriffs' Association 147
National Society for Park Resources 257
National Society of Fund Raising Executives 152
National Strength and Conditioning Association 247
National Tour Association 249
National Wildlife Federation 254, 257
Nature Conservancy 254, 257
North American Association for Environmental Education 254
North American Police Work Dog Association 266
nutritionist 175–177

O

Outdoor Guides Association 250
overseas teaching opportunities
    American overseas school teacher 108–109
    EFL (English as a foreign language) teacher 110–112
    Peace Corps volunteer 113–114

P

park naturalist 255–257
Peace Corps volunteer 113–114
personal trainer 245–247
Phi Delta Kappa 118
physical education teacher 33–35
physical fitness and recreation professions
    aerobics instructor 242–244
    dance teacher 235–236
    guide 248–250
    personal trainer 245–247
    physical education teacher 33–35
president 158–160
principal 116–118
professor 85–87
program director 128–130
provost 155–157
public librarian 184–186
Public Library Association 186

R

reading specialist 36–38
registrar 137–138
Rehabilitation Engineering and Assistive Technology of North America 204
riding instructor 237–238

S

school administrators
    assistant principal 119–121
    assistant superintendent 125–127
    curriculum specialist 210–211
    early childhood program director 7–9
    instructional supervisor 131–132
    principal 116–118
    program director 128–130
    superintendent 122–124
    technology director 196–198
school bus driver 73–75
school counselor 162–164
school nurse 50–51
school occupational therapist 62–64
school psychologist 54–56
School Social Work Association of America 58
school social worker 57–58
Service Employees International Union 70, 72, 75, 77, 79
Sierra Club 254
SkillsUSA-VICA 94
Society for Public Health Education 174
special education program specialists
    art therapist 65–66
    educational diagnostician 52–53
    school occupational therapist 62–64
    school psychologist 54–56
    school social worker 57–58
    special education teacher 39–41
    special education technology specialist 202–204
    speech-language pathologist 59–61
special education teacher 39–41
special education technology specialist 202–204
speech-language pathologist 59–61
student services professions (higher education)
    athletic director 142–144
    college career counselor 165–167
    dean of students 148–149
    director of admissions 134–136
    director of public safety 145–147
    director of student activities 139–141
    registrar 137–138
student services professions (K-12)
    cafeteria manager 76–77
    campus monitor 78–79
    career guidance technician 71–72
    educational diagnostician 52–53
    school bus driver 73–75
    school counselor 162–164
    school nurse 50–51
    school occupational therapist 62–64
    school psychologist 54–56
    school social worker 57–58
    speech-language pathologist 59–61
substitute teacher 26–27
superintendent 122–124
support professions in K-12 schools
    cafeteria manager 76–77
    campus monitor 78–79
    career guidance technician 71–72

INDEX 307

school bus driver 73–75
teacher aide (instructional) 68–70

T

teacher aide (instructional) 68–70
teaching careers in public, private, and independent schools
    American overseas school teacher 108–109
    bilingual teacher 42–44
    EFL (English as a foreign language) teacher 110–112
    elementary school teacher 14–16
    ESL (English as a second language) teacher 45–47
    high school teacher 23–25
    instructional technology specialist (K-12) 199–201
    junior high school teacher 20–22
    kindergarten teacher 10–12
    middle school teacher 17–19
    music teacher 30–32
    physical education teacher 33–35
    reading specialist 36–38
    special education teacher 39–41
    substitute teacher 26–27
teaching careers instructing adults
    adult education instructor 95–97
    aerobics instructor 242–244
    childbirth educator 178–180
    community college instructor 82–84
    continuing education instructor 98–99
    cooperative extension agent 100–102
    correctional instructor 103–105
    CPR/first aid instructor 181–182
    dance teacher 235–236
    dog trainer 260–261
    EFL (English as a foreign language) teacher 110–112
    flight instructor (freelance) 239–240
    guide dog instructor 262–263
    health educator 172–174
    K-9 trainer (police dogs) 264–266
    lecturer 88–89
    music teacher (studio owner) 232–234
    nutritionist 175–177
    personal trainer 245–247
    professor 85–87
    riding instructor 237–238
    trainer (in-house) 222–224
    vocational instructor 92–94
teaching specialists in K-12 schools
    bilingual teacher 42–44
    ESL (English as a second language) teacher 45–47
    instructional technology specialist (K-12) 199–201
    library media specialist 190–192
    music teacher 30–32
    physical education teacher 33–35
    reading specialist 36–38
    special education teacher 39–41
Technology and Media 204
technology director 196–198
TESOL Inc. (Teachers of English to Speakers of Other Languages, Inc.) 44, 46, 97, 111, 214
textbook editor 212–214
trainer (in-house) 222–224
training developer 225–227
training manager 228–230

U

United States Police Canine Association 266
Urban Superintendents Association of America 124

V

vocational instructor 92–94